A Roadmap for Enabling Industry 4.0 by Artificial Intelligence

Scrivener Publishing
100 Cummings Center, Suite 541J
Beverly, MA 01915-6106

Publishers at Scrivener
Martin Scrivener (martin@scrivenerpublishing.com)
Phillip Carmical (pcarmical@scrivenerpublishing.com)

A Roadmap for Enabling Industry 4.0 by Artificial Intelligence

Edited by
Jyotir Moy Chatterjee
Harish Garg
and
R. N. Thakur

Scrivener Publishing

WILEY

This edition first published 2023 by John Wiley & Sons, Inc., 111 River Street, Hoboken, NJ 07030, USA and Scrivener Publishing LLC, 100 Cummings Center, Suite 541J, Beverly, MA 01915, USA

For more information about Scrivener publications please visit www.scrivenerpublishing.com.

Wiley Global Headquarters
111 River Street, Hoboken, NJ 07030, USA

For details of our global editorial offices, customer services, and more information about Wiley products visit us at www.wiley.com.

Library of Congress Cataloging-in-Publication Data

ISBN 978-1-119-90485-4

Cover image: Pixabay.Com
Cover design by Russell Richardson

Set in size of 11pt and Minion Pro by Manila Typesetting Company, Makati, Philippines

Printed in the USA

10 9 8 7 6 5 4 3 2 1

Contents

Preface

The Industry 4.0 vision has been baking for quite a while, but the enabling technologies are now ripe enough to turn this vision into a grand reality sooner rather than later. Known by many as the fourth industrial revolution, it involves the infusion of deeper and more decisive technology-enabled automation into manufacturing processes and activities. Several illustrious information and communication technologies (ICT) are being used to attain the acceleration and augmentation of the manufacturing process, and this book explores and discloses the recent advancements in blockchain technology and artificial intelligence and their crucial impact on realizing the goals of Industry 4.0. In other words, it provides a conceptual framework and roadmap for decision makers to make this transformation.

In addition to undergraduate and postgraduate students with big data analytics as part of their curriculum, this book will be useful to students who want to develop and deploy their skills to achieve a thorough knowledge of analytics and have an in-depth education experience that pertains to their unique interests. Moreover, acknowledging the huge demands of industry professionals today, this book has also been designed to create trained computer science graduates to fulfill industry requirements. Furthermore, artificial intelligence applications in the industrial sector are explored, including IoT technology. Up-to-date technology and solutions in regard to the main aspects of applications of artificial intelligence techniques in Industry 4.0 are also presented, thereby covering the training needs of the scientific research community. Finally, for your convenience, the information presented in the book's well-conceived chapters is summarized below.

- Chapter 1 is a systematic literature review on how Industry 4.0 has been remarkably successful due to the multifaceted specialisms in digitalization and artificial intelligence (AI).
- Chapter 2 starts with an overview of the evolution of Industry 4.0 that enabled digital transformation in manufacturing

and other related industries. Next, the chapter dwells on how cloud computing can economically support IoT on a large scale.
- Chapter 3 discusses the high importance of the supply chain in manufacturing businesses, especially in fast-moving consumer goods (FMCG) industries, which are one of the most important industries in our daily lives. It provides a framework for using this technology in the supply chain in these industries.
- Chapter 4 provides a comprehensive framework for accelerating supply chain decisions with respect to Industry 4.0.
- Chapter 5 briefly introduces IoT and deep learning models. Subsequently, a detailed description of the deployment of deep learning methods in IoT networks for industrial application is presented.
- Chapter 6 attempts to show several ideas about the functionalities of blockchain technology that could be widely applied in a wide range of circumstances.
- Chapter 7 aims to identify the approaches that can be used to identify value depending on the factors in the datasets and correct the missing data value, which can be used later on to analyze the data better.
- Chapter 8 presents the novel privacy issues caused by the advent of AI techniques in a cyber-physical system ecosystem. It then moves on to discuss the measures used to mitigate such issues.
- Chapter 9 reviews most IoT-based environmental applications for a smart environment, agriculture, and smart environmental monitoring of air, soil, and water.
- Chapter 10 outlines many of the IoT protection threats or problems and countermeasures in a level-by-level manner.
- Chapter 11 reviews all the opportunities presented by Industry 4.0 and the challenges involved in implementing it.
- Chapter 12 discusses the manufacturing techniques of Industry 4.0 along with their various opportunities and challenges.
- Chapter 13 describes the essence of Industry 4.0 along with its primary objectives and basic features.

- Chapter 14 proposes methods for improving multimedia encryption standards in explainable artificial intelligence using residue number systems for security.
- Chapters 15 and 16 appropriately complete the book focusing on "Market Trends with Cryptocurrency Trading in Industry 4.0" and Blockchain and Its Applications in Industry 4.0.

Jyotir Moy Chatterjee
Kathmandu, Nepal
Harish Garg
Patiala, India
R.N. Thakur
Kathmandu, Nepal
October 2022

1

Artificial Intelligence—The Driving Force of Industry 4.0

Hesham Magd[1]*, Henry Jonathan[2], Shad Ahmad Khan[3] and Mohamed El Geddawy[4]

[1]*Quality Assurance & Accreditation, Faculty of Business and Economics, Muscat, Sultanate of Oman*
[2]*Department of Transportation, Logistics, and Safety Management, Faculty of Business and Economics, Muscat, Sultanate of Oman*
[3]*College of Business, University of Buraimi, Al-Buraimi, Sultanate of Oman*
[4]*Prince Mohammed University, Al Khobar, Kingdom of Saudi Arabia*

Abstract

The 21st century reminds the dawn of the 4th industrial revolution (IR), which has brought new frontiers of technology utilization to industries. Industry 4.0 chiefly relays from the 3rd revolution, taking further the application of computer and automation domain to the current century. Industry 4.0 already has shown remarkable success due to the multifaceted specialisms in digitalization and artificial intelligence (AI). However, in the face of rapidly changing technology, the growth of industrialization depends significantly on the progressive involvement of artificial intelligence applications in wide areas of industrial products and processes. AI technology potential contribution to the global economy is $15.7 trillion currently with 2% contribution from the middle east region. The manufacturing sector investment and funding on project gained in USA and China through AI-enabled technologies by automotive and IT sectors leading GDP by 115% accounting to $77.5 billion in 2021. The factors driving the industry 4.0 mainly are competitiveness and innovation, cost reduction, and performance improvement, which led to the use of AI technology applications to industrial sector. AI-enabled applications are explored in automotive, consumer products, industrial manufacturing, telecommunication sectors to enhance product quality,

**Corresponding author*: hesham.magd@mcbs.edu.om

Jyotir Moy Chatterjee, Harish Garg and R. N. Thakur (eds.) A Roadmap for Enabling Industry 4.0 by Artificial Intelligence, (1–16) © 2023 Scrivener Publishing LLC

design in the process. Despite the benefits offered by the AI applications to industries, the barriers for effective adoption of industry 4.0 ideology to all sectors is a time-taking process.

***Keywords*:** Technology, organization, manufacturing, industry, sector, application, tools

1.1 Introduction

The current century marks the renaissance of fourth industrial revolution the term that was first introduced by Klaus Schwab in 2016 to denote the future trend of industrial world [1]. The industry 4.0 principles are built upon the developments of third industrial revolution that already has introduced computerization technology to the world. This paved the way to the most prominent applications, such as automation and artificial intelligence, and in addition to digital transformation of process and business operations along the different industrial revolutions [2]. The first industrial revolution marks the advent of mechanization from steam and waterpower during 1750 and 1850, followed by second revolution bringing in electrical power and mass production systems during 1870 to 1914 and third revolution in the 20th century gave entry of computer and electronics into industrial process after 1970.

Currently, the industry 4.0 began during 2014, where it works on conceptualizing the use of innovative technology and advanced digital production together contributing to a sustainable industrial development [3, 4]. According to research studies by UNIDO, industry 4.0 scope has not made full advancement in all sectors as of yet, in Argentina and Brazil claims that 3% to 4% of firms have adopted few applications, while countries like Ghana, Vietnam and Thailand has very much behind in exploiting the benefits of the fourth revolution.

In this viewpoint, this chapter will deal in describing the role of artificial intelligence technology particularly in spearheading the industry 4.0 concept in the context of manufacturing sector globally. In combination, the chapter will likewise attempt to provide a comprehensive account on the factors that are considered contributing to the employment of industry 4.0 across different organizations.

1.2 Methodology

The purpose of the chapter is to provide an overview and in-depth understanding of the factors that are driving the industry 4.0 in the perspective of artificial intelligence technology. To elaborate the details, published literature and reports from previous studies are referred to meet the objectives of the study, and secondary sources of information by visiting different organizational websites were conducted to examine the factors contributing to the industry 4.0. Thorough searches from previously published work by various researchers was conducted to examine the different driving factors for industry 4.0 and were analyzed. Information related to the industry 4.0 technologies, their roles toward manufacturing sector, statistical information on status global economy with artificial intelligence technology were collected from secondary data published in government information portals and global private organizations like price Waterhouse coopers, McKinsey & Company, Deloitte etc. For presenting the findings from the analysis, the authors have maximized the available information published in researchers and details provide in various organizational websites.

1.3 Scope of AI in Global Economy and Industry 4.0

The fourth industrial revolution is fueled from its predecessor industrial phase essentially pushing the trend toward automation and fully integrating the digitalization process in industries, expanding the applicability through some of the significant applications like internet of things (IoT), cyber physical systems, smart factory, cloud computing, cognitive computing, artificial intelligence, etc. Theoretically, the fourth industrial revolution is driven by four key ideologies, enabling interconnection between different technological applications, transparency in information and procurement, technical assistance, and regionalized decisions enabling the industry 4.0 concept a distinctive approach from the third revolution [5].

Artificial intelligence (AI) can be explained as the use of computer programming to mimic human thought and actions to create human-like responses through machine learning, logic, perception, and reasoning. Legendary physicist Stephen Hawking quotes "Success in creating effective AI could be the biggest event in the history of our civilization. Or the worst. We just don't know. So, we cannot know if we will be infinitely helped by AI, or ignored by it and side-lined, or conceivably destroyed by it."

Artificial intelligence (AI) obviously is a significant technology among the other technological applications in the industry 4.0 as it principally works on the foundation of computer learning and augmentation pertinent to the entire industry ecosystem. Most importantly, AI technology has tremendous scope for its application in manufacturing industries in the production and design stages enabling reduction in human errors, production efficiency and reduction in losses. Moreover, the use of AI techniques, such as machine learning and deep learning, have substantial contribution toward advancement of global economy as the global race for embedding AI into businesses have already started reaching milestones in some countries, for example 82% of Spanish companies have explored AI technology in their industrial system.

Following the prospective growth in utilizing AI technology, global projection shows the technology has the potential to contribute $15.7 trillion to the economy by 2030 of which middle east expects to claim 2% of the benefits accounting to $320 billion. AI Technologies in the GCC four countries (Bahrain, Kuwait, Oman, and Qatar) is likely to contribute around 8.2% of GDP by 2030, while in comparison to no middle east economies, the share of AI to the GDP is large, 26.1% in China, and 14.5% in North America. Notwithstanding to say, the prospects of AI technology to industries especially in the developing nations is tremendous as the potential for embedding AI in manufacturing and allied sectors is increasing gradually. In addition, in the UAE, KSA, GCC, and Egypt, the annual growth of AI from 2018 to 2030 is expected to be 33.5%, 31.3% 28.8%, and 25.5%, respectively [6].

In developed nations, the importance of AI technology to business achievement shows more promising growth in the UK from 14 % to 45%, United States 11% to 42%, Germany 4% to 32%, Australia 12% to 29% in the next few years [7]. Regional analysis on the investment scenario on AI in Asian markets shows $0.69 billion in 2019 with the global market expected to reach $9.89 billion by 2027, in the UK, investment on AI stands at $1.3 billion; further, there are growth returns expected from the increasing investment on AI north and south America according to Market research report of Fortune Business Insights [8].

1.3.1 Artificial Intelligence—Evolution and Implications

The period from 1950 to 1960 marks the birth and evolution of AI to the world, later in the six decades of its journey, the technology has taken leaps and bounds along with the industrial revolutions [9]. Presently, in the 21st century, AI is certainly the prominent technology for the industry 4.0 and for the future. Global economists also estimate the wide applications AI will be very much instrumental for global expansion in the future, and quite obviously AI will be one of the most preferred technologies to be used by companies by the year 2025 according to the reports by world economic forum [10]. Added to this, COVID-19 pandemic has necessitated remote work and work for home policies, which has created potential demand for industries to rely upon some of the allied technology applications of AI to business operations. Symbiotically, AI technology came to the aid of many researchers, planners, and decision makers in tracking, predicting the movement and evolution of COVID pandemic from 2020 [9].

In the present industrial revolution, AI technology is making remarkable contribution in multiple sectors boosting production and enhancing business operations in healthcare, financial and banking, agriculture, transport, science, and research etc., [11]. AI in the next industrial revolutions prospectively will take a leap into many businesses and industries making better integration between humans and machines. In contrast to the diverse benefits AI would provide, the disadvantages from the use of AI in certain fields far outweigh the advantages, and employing AI in some sensitive fields certainly have considerable risks and implications that will pose to societies, and in general to low-economic countries particularly escalating unemployment further and other repercussions [12].

1.3.2 Artificial Intelligence and Industry 4.0—Investments and Returns on Economy

The global industrial sector is bound to get complete overhaul from the invasion of digitalization transformation and digitalization of operations in the industry 4.0 era where artificial intelligence is going to be the futuristic concept in the next decades. Global economic empires, the United States of America (USA) and China, are leading the way on total investments in different AI-enabled technologies across all industrial sectors. We can convincingly say that the global AI in terms of investment and funding on projects is at a remarkable position. The global investment and finance on AI were $40 billion in 2017, of which 70% were in China alone followed by the US, resulted in a projected increase of GDP in manufacturing and construction sector by 6.5% by 2030 [13].

Reports from anonymous studies show global investment on AI-enabled companies increased by 115% that accounts to $77.5 billion in 2021 over the previous years. The GDP growth from AI-enabled technologies would be 26.1% in China and 14.5% in North America together contributing $10.7 trillion of global economy by 2030. Leading business analysts predict that the global GDP will rise to 14% by 2030, the highest effect to USA and China in the forefront; however, all regions would obviously benefit [6] (Figure 1.1).

In the manufacturing sector, the AI investments mainly in software, hardware, and services were $2.9 billion in 2018 and expected at $13.2

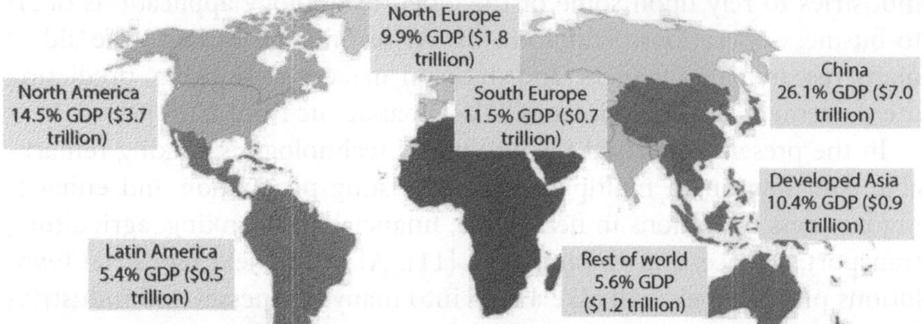

Figure 1.1 World regions gaining impact from artificial intelligence through GDP growth in percent and trillion US dollars.

billion by 2021 with a projected spending of $9.5 during the year 2021 in the sector standing second to banking and financial services [14]. The increasing funding and returns from investment on AI show an increasing curve during the current industry 4.0 because of increasing AI-enabled companies and business startups globally, which stand at 4925 enterprises and 3465 startups by 2018. USA and China are currently global leaders in having the highest number of AI enterprises and startups by 2018, and the overall funding on AI across all industries in the USA from 2012 to 2018

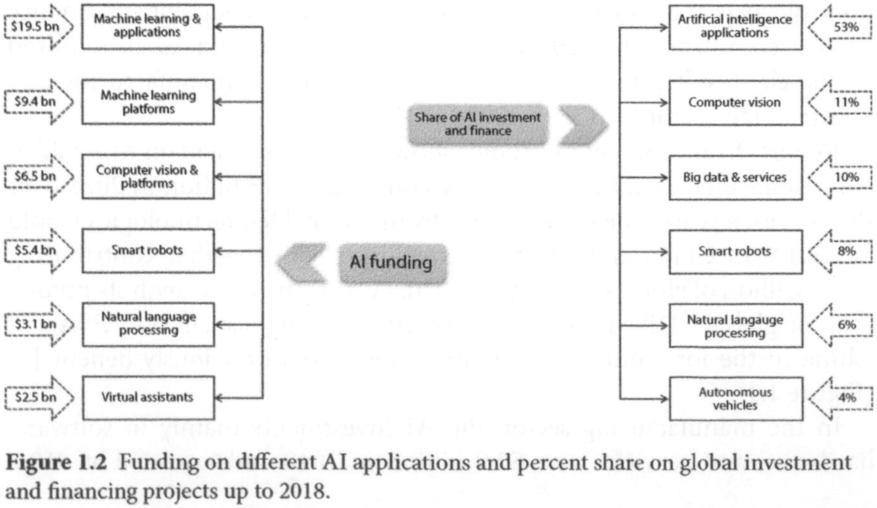

Figure 1.2 Funding on different AI applications and percent share on global investment and financing projects up to 2018.

rose from $595 million to $4218 million, while the funding on AI startups in the first half of 2021 was $38 million [13].

In China, the funding on AI-related projects by the end of 2018 was $428.9 million with the AI market size gaining an increase from $1.6 billion in 2015 to $14.3 billion in 2020. Leading the way are top global companies like Google, Amazon, Apple, Intel, IBM, Microsoft, Facebook, Twitter, etc. are in the forefront of investments and development in AI across all applications. The projected GDP increase from funding on AI in Chinese manufacturing and construction sector by 2030 would experience 12% in productivity and 11.5% in consumption. Such futuristic scenario is also going to boost employment opportunities for AI professionals in all sectors with estimates reporting around 1.9 million in 2017 with highest recorded in USA, followed by India and UK [13] (Figure 1.2).

1.3.3 The Driving Forces for Industry 4.0

Industry 4.0 synonymously known as fourth industrial revolution (4 IR) is tagged as the era of digital transformation and digitalization of industrial ecosystems globally. The present industrial revolution is grounded on the concept of automation, cyber physical systems, cloud computing, cognitive computing, and artificial intelligence with different components and systems employed to operate them. These concepts form the source for deploying different technological tools and applications across a wide range of sectors, for example, in manufacturing, production, transportation, healthcare, tourism, hospitality, etc.

Contrary to the concepts that is imminent in the fourth industrial revolution, examining the factors that are influencing the industrial ecosystem to implement industry 4.0 is more important to know the needs of the society and customers rather than the industry [15]. However, from the nature of business operation, there would be specific driving forces that can be cited from every industrial sector contributing to industry 4.0 apart from the general driving factors. The number of sources from literature review have also described the driving factors in specific industrial sectors (includes both large firms and small and medium enterprises SMEs) that are encouraging them toward industry 4.0 concept. Horvath and Szabo 2019 [16] point to several factors from his literature analysis that are promoting the four IR irrespective of the industrial sector. [15] also from his analysis describes five contributing factors that are generally influencing industry 4.0 implementation across different industrial sectors. Garcia (2021) from his review depicted eight factors that are driving the industry 4.0 landscape in organizations. While Camarinha-Matos *et al.* [17] indicate two major driving forces leading 4 IR.

Table 1.1 Contributing factors driving the 4 IR analyzed from literature.

Driving factors	Source
Competitive and business model innovation	Horvath and Szabo 2019; Herceg *et al.*, 2020; Garcia 2021; Ghadge *et al.*, 2020
Cost reduction and performance improvement	Herceg *et al.*, 2020; Garcia 2021; Ghadge *et al.*, 2020
Customer needs	Horvath and Szabo 2019; Herceg *et al.*, 2020
Market changes and demand	Herceg *et al.*, 2020; Matos *et al.*, 2017
Sustainability in energy	Horvath and Szabo 2019; Garcia 2021
Financial factors	Horvath and Szabo 2019; Ghadge *et al.*, 2020
Support to management functions	Horvath and Szabo 2019; Garcia 2021
Increased innovation capacity and productivity	Horvath and Szabo 2019; Garcia 2021
Supply chain	Garcia 2021
Efficiency, quality and flexibility	Garcia 2021; Ghadge *et al.*, 2020
Government policies	Garcia 2021
Optimized production practices and better working conditions	Garcia 2021
New technological possibilities	Matos *et al.*, 2017

Literature analysis by Ghadge *et al.* [18] reveals four main driving forces for implementation of industry 4.0. The comparation and coincidence of different driving forces to industry 4.0 described by various researcher from their literature analysis is presented in Table 1.1.

1.4 Artificial Intelligence—Manufacturing Sector

Manufacturing and service sectors are known as the largest sectors globally and by far also the leading sectors in terms of diversity of operations, workforce employed and output to the economy. Manufacturing and service sectors takes a critical position among other sectors in all types of economies and gains more prominence to the developing countries. Currently, in industry 4.0, the manufacturing sector takes a significant spot contributing 16% of global GDP and 14% toward employment, with share of 30% to 55% in service jobs [19]. Moreover, the prospects of manufacturing sector in the next few decades would continue to raise with the increase in global consumption and usage, probably leading to shift in demand on certain products and goods. At the same time, these sectors must move with the changing pace of technology and developments along with the industrial revolutions. Besides, the core area of industry 4.0 is to bring a shift toward digital transformation in the manufacturing, process and information sharing, value creation, the different technological tools and applications under each concept are best compatible to bring tremendous improvement and momentum to today's manufacturing sector.

Artificial intelligence is being the most advanced technological application in the 4 IR is claimed as the powerhouses influencing the manufacturing industry currently and extensively being used to deliver quality, efficiency, and consistent management in supply chain. Likewise global studies reveal that there are as many as 25 different applications that AI can render to manufacturing through operations and other services. Subsequent to the positive impact of AI had on manufacturing sector, market research reports claim that the global AI in manufacturing market was $1.82 billion in 2019, increased to $2.1 billion in 2020 and is expected to reach $11.5 billion by 2027 with huge investments planned on AI in Asia pacific region economies (Market research report 2020). Analyzing the application areas of AI in manufacturing sector globally, the market share contribution is highest in production planning followed by predictive maintenance and machinery inspection, logistics and inventory management and process control.

1.4.1 AI Diversity—Applications to Manufacturing Sector

Artificial intelligence is gaining extensive application in manufacturing sector right through the onset of four IR from the diversity, scope of application and technologies available that can be employed in different phases of production process. Machine learning (ML), a branch of AI, is the mostly wide used application in the manufacturing sector, enabling companies to modulate the production process and enhance quality. Research studies by Capgemini shows that there is increasing trend of AI uses in manufacturing sector globally, nearly 29% of use cases are observed in maintenance and 27% in quality [20].

Overall, global surveys indicate that 60% of manufacturing companies have embarked on using AI into their businesses to enhance product quality, faster production in addition to the significant benefits the technology offers regardless of the type and nature of business operation. To some extent, the COVID-19 pandemic situation has created a trend among manufacturers to employ AI applications more intensively, which caused shift toward AI-enabled operations across many companies. Fundamentally, AI technology, in the manufacturing sector, contributes to the growth of

Table 1.2 Companies showing areas AI uses for enhancement in their manufacturing process.

Company	Area for enhancement	Sector
BMW	Product quality	Automotive
Ford	Predictive quality & maintenance	
	Autonomous vehicles	
GM	Intelligent maintenance	
	Generative design	
Nissan	Product validation	
Carlberg	Product enhancement	Consumer products
Kellogg's	New product development	
Canon	Product quality inspection	Industrial manufacturing
Thales SA	Intelligent maintenance	Aerospace
Boeing	Product quality inspection	
Nokia	Realtime optimization of process parameters	Industrial manufacturing
Bombardier		
Verizon	Autonomous vehicles	Telecommunications
GE	Generative design	Industrial manufacturing

companies through predicting the quality and output, predicting maintenance requirements and schedules, human robot interface, generating custom made designs, market adaptation strategies and value addition in supply chain, all that can be achieved through applying various technologies driving the 4 IR (Table 1.2).

AI applications to the manufacturing sectors attract some strategic benefits as well, which are instrumental in reducing human errors, helping in taking faster decisions, facilitating workforce in repetitive jobs, quick assistance in trouble shooting problems, round-the-clock access, scope for new inventions and entries, ability to execute tasks in remote working conditions, digital assistance, and in certain fields, improving security. AI-enabled technologies use cases related to manufacturing sector include both direct and indirect applications covering upstream and downstream operations. Some of these applications of AI finds best fit are in logistics, robotics, supply chain management, autonomous vehicles, factory automation, IT, design and manufacturing, warehouse management, process automation, product development, visual inspection, quality control, cybersecurity, etc. In the upstream sector, AI provides assistance in supporting supply chain management operations by facilitating warehouse and logistics functions, maintaining seamless communications with suppliers, manufacturers and customers, procurement of raw materials (Table 1.3).

Apart from multiple use cases that AI can extend to different type of manufacturing industries, it also has the agility in performing quality checks, forecasting product demands based on the customer demands, product inventory through some of the systems like digital twins, virtual agents, biometrics, process automation, image recognition, machine learning etc. in the manufacturing companies. The success of AI tools in today's industrial sector is mainly from its ability to penetrate significantly in the manufacturing sector because of the compatibility to merge easily with some of its subset technologies, such as machine learning, deep learning, artificial neural networks, computer vision etc. enabling the technology for wider reach (Figure 1.3).

Lastly, while AI technology-specific applications in manufacturing sector are elaborately discussed, there are many more applications and use cases in other sectors as well, which are also being explored extensively in the current 4IR. In the end, with the diversity of applications and variability AI technology is going to provide to manufacturing sector, AI-enabled operations would take a significant position in future industrial revolutions.

Table 1.3 Information technology companies using AI-enabled technologies employed in product enhancement.

Company	Application
Apple	Optimal character recognition
	Speech recognition
IBM	Cognitive service technology
	Speech recognition
Microsoft	Deep learning
	Machine learning
Google	Deep learning
	Optimized hardware
AT & T	Image recognition
Dell	Generative design
	Predictive maintenance
Intel	Generative design
	Product quality and yield
Nvidia	Optimized hardware
	Deep learning

1.4.2 Future Roadmap of AI—Prospects to Manufacturing Sector in Industry 4.0

The future of artificial intelligence holds very bright for the industrial sectors notably with the introduction of automation and digital transformation to the business operations. Projections indicate by 2035, AI application technologies may accelerate production by 40% globally that is bound to bring more wider utilization in manufacturing more than any other sector. In this changeover, most large firms are going to gain significantly than smaller firms in terms of use cases and adoption rate, regardless of investment and funding on AI-enabled projects in future. With the progressing industry 4.0 era, AI will be able to explore its applicability to all nature of industries, including service and hospitality fields

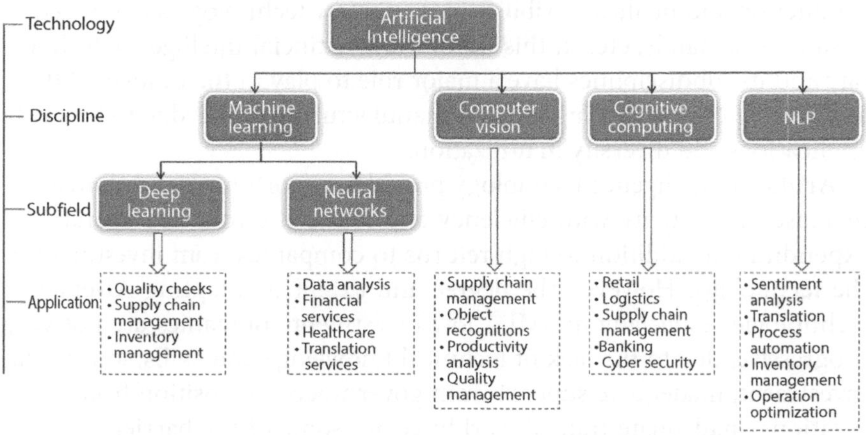

Figure 1.3 Classification of AI technology and its allied functions showing applications in manufacturing sector.

to substantial extent, which can bring new benefits and opportunities in employment generation in some fields. In the manufacturing sector, AI would take inroads into automotive industry in design and innovation toward autonomous vehicles, autopilot, smart cars in public and private transportation. AI technology among nonindustrial sectors, AI-enabled applications will gain a tremendous breakthrough into agriculture, better surveillance in natural calamities, in disaster management and mitigation, education, banking and finance operations, etc. From a futuristic standpoint, leading global economies should shed their focus on the adoption rates of AI technology applications by industries subject to the measures taken to overcome the different challenges industries face at organizational and individual level.

1.5 Conclusion

The fourth industrial revolution that has currently started and taken effect globally is a tremendous boost to industrial sector to modernize and improvise their production and operations to meet the global standards. Consequently, there is also substantial improvement in the global economy due to the various technological applications that has brought enhancement in the industrial sector. From the industrial perspective, many factors had led to the implementation of industry 4.0 in organizations, mainly due to the competitiveness in business operation, increasing efficiency in production and quality, flexibility in using new technologies and meeting customer demands, etc. In this framework, artificial intelligence technology and its subdisciplines have a major role to play in the industry 4.0 era and is a significant driving force to manufacturing sector due to the wide applications and diversity in utilization.

Artificial intelligence technology provides opportunity for automation, increase productivity with efficiency and reduced errors and operational expenditure in addition to high returns to companies from investment in the technology. However, the degree and extent of adopting AI-enabled technologies especially in SMEs, low investment companies are not very progressive, due to the lack of technical knowledge and skills, low capital investment, inadequate support from government, opposition from organizations, inadequate trained workforce are some of the barriers that are limiting the employability of AI in the industry 4.0 concept.

References

1. Lavopa, A. and Delera, M., What is fourth industrial revolution. *Ind. Analytics Platform*, 2021. https://iap.unido.org/articles/what-fourth-industrial-revolution.
2. Lasi, H., Fettke, P., Kemper, H.G., Feld, T., Hoffmann, M., Industry 4.0. *Bus. Inf. Syst. Eng.*, 6, 239–242, 2014. https://doi.org/10.1007/s12599-014-0334-4.
3. UNIDO 2021, Fourth industrial revolution. *UNIDO 19th General Conference*, https://www.unido.org/gc19-fourth-industrial-revolution.
4. Fonseca, L.M., Industry 4.0 and the digital society: Concepts, dimensions and envisioned benefits. *Proc. Int. Conf. Bus. Excell.*, 12, 1, 386–397, 2018.
5. Hermann, M., Pentek, T., Otto, B., Design principles for industrie 4.0 scenarios. *2016 49th Hawaii International Conference on System Sciences (HICSS)*, pp. 3928–3937, 2016.
6. PWC, The potential impact of AI in the middle east, 2018. https://www.pwc.com/m1/en/publications/potential-impact-artificial-intelligence-middle-east.html.
7. Loucks, J., Hupfer, S., Jarvis, D., Murphy, T., Future in the balance? How countries are pursuing an AI advantage. Insights from Deloitte's state of AI in the enterprise, 2nd edition survey, Deloitte, pp 1–20, 2021. https://www2.deloitte.com/us/en/insights/focus/cognitive-technologies/ai-investment-by-country.html.
8. Fortune Business Insights, AI in manufacturing market, global industry analysis, insights and forecast, 2020-2027. Fortune Business Insights, AI in manufacturing market to Hit USD 9.89 million by 2027, Market Research Report, p. 150, 2021. globenewswire.com.

9. Council of Europe, AI and control of COVID-19 corona virus, overview carried out by the Ad hoc committee on artificial intelligence secretariat, 2021. https://www.coe.int/en/web/artificial-intelligence/ai-and-control-of-covid-19-coronavirus.
10. World Economic Forum, 5 ways AI is doing good to the world right now. *World Economic Forum*, 2020, https://www.weforum.org/agenda/2021/07/ai-artificial-intelligence-doing-good-in-world/.
11. Chowdhury, M., The evolution of artificial intelligence: Past, present and future. *Analytics Insights*, 2021. https://www.analyticsinsight.net/the-evolution-of-artificial-intelligence-past-present-future/.
12. Tai, M.C., The impact of artificial intelligence on human society and bioethics. *Tzu Chi Med. J.*, 32, 4, 339–343, 2020. https://doi.org/10.4103/tcmj.tcmj_71_20.
13. Hoist. A., In depth report: Artificial intelligence. Statista Digital Market Outlook, p. 153, 2021. https://spaces.statista.com/study_id59297_artificial-intelligence-ai%20(1).pdf.
14. World Manufacturing Foundation, *The 2020 World Manufacturing Report Manufacturing in the Age of Artificial intelligence,* World manufacturing foundation, Italy, 2020.
15. Herceg, I.V., Kuc, V., Mijuskovic, V.M., Herceg, T., Challenges and driving forces for industry 4.0 implementation. *Sustainability*, 12, 4208, 2020.
16. Horvath, D. and Szabo, R., Zs., Driving forces and barriers for industry 4.0: Do multinational and small medium- sized companies have equal opportunities? *Technol. Forecast. Soc. Change*, 146, 119–132, 2019.
17. Camarinha-Matos, L.M., Fornasiero, R., Afsarmanesh, H., Collaborative networks as a core enabler of industry 4.0, in: *Collaboration in a Data-Rich World. PRO-VE 2017. IFIP Advances in Information and Communication Technology*, L. Camarinha-Matos, H. Afsarmanesh, R. Fornasiero, (Eds.), p. 506, Springer, Cham, 2017, https://doi.org/10.1007/978-3-319-65151-4_1.
18. Ghadge, A., Kara., M., Moradlou, H., Goswami, M., The impact of industry 4.0 implementation on supply chains. *J. Manuf. Technol. Manage.*, 31, 4, 669–686, 2020.
19. Manyika, J., Sinclair, J., Dobbs, R. *et al.*, *Manufacturing the Future: The Next Era of Global Growth and Innovation*, McKinsey Global Institute, United States of America, 2012.
20. Dilmegani, C., Top 12 uses cases/applications of AI in manufacturing. *AI Multiple*, 2020. aimultiple.com.

2

Industry 4.0, Intelligent Manufacturing, Internet of Things, Cloud Computing: An Overview

Sachi Pandey[1], Vijay Laxmi[2*] and Rajendra Prasad Mahapatra[1]

[1]SRM Institute of Science and Technology, Delhi - NCR Campus, Modinagar, India
[2]Information Technology, Boston, MA, United States

Abstract
This chapter starts with an overview of the evolution of Industry 4.0 that enabled digital transformation in manufacturing and other related industries. Provides concepts, definitions, and real-life examples in the intelligent manufacturing industry. Next, describes how the ecosystem of intelligent sensors, devices, and applications increase productivity and streamline business operations. Highlights the integration of manufacturing operational technology with information technology using data science, machine learning, and artificial intelligence. Next, the chapter dwells on how cloud computing can support IoT at a large scale and economically. Finally, it finishes with an overview of security controls and best practices in realizing smart manufacturing.

Keywords: Smart manufacturing, Internet of Things, connected world, cloud computing, data science, machine learning, artificial intelligence, predictive analytics

2.1 Introduction

Digitization, or digital transformation, has become necessary for any firm, industry, or country seeking relevance in the new digital economy [1].

**Corresponding author*: vijay.laxmi@gmail.com

Jyotir Moy Chatterjee, Harish Garg and R. N. Thakur (eds.) A Roadmap for Enabling Industry 4.0 by Artificial Intelligence, (17–30) © 2023 Scrivener Publishing LLC

Driven by changes in the digital economy and information technology, the industrial transformation is replacing the traditional nonflexible value chain with flexible, dynamic, and connected value networks [2]. Industrial IoT (IIoT), the industrial transformation, brings devices, cloud computing, data analysis, and human intelligence together to improve the performance and productivity of industrial operations [3]. This chapter summarizes all these concepts and terminologies in industrial automation.

This chapter has five sections. The first section discusses industrial transformation along with value and supply chains, including suppliers, producers or manufacturers, distributors, resellers, and consumers. The second section defines the Internet of Things and introduces the reference architecture (IoT). The third section defines technical terms, such as Internet of Things (IoT) devices, stream processing, big data, machine learning, and artificial intelligence. The fourth section examines associate with cloud computing. The fifth section discusses common security controls to handle data security in this scenario.

2.2 Industrial Transformation/Value Chain Transformation

The term "Industry 4.0" refers to a significant fourth industrial revolution in which current industrial processes are transformed through the use of digital technologies to boost productivity and efficiency. The first industrial revolution refers to the steam engine that changed the manufacturing process by introducing human-operated machines and transforming agrarian society into an industrial society. The second industrial revolution included mass production, assembly line, and electricity that benefited large-scale manufacturing, mechanical engineering, and automotive industries. The third industrial revolution, use of electronics and information technology to automate the manufacturing process further and led to the "Supply Chain Management" concept. The fourth industrial revolution refers to the end-to-end digital transformation of the industrial process and entire value creation process (Figure 2.1).

Value creation is a process that produces more valuable outputs than its inputs and creates efficiency and productivity [4]. One way to add value to an industry is to minimize waste, improve turnaround time, increase uptime and efficiency, and optimize productivity and production capacity in order to reduce input costs. The second option is to reinvent industrial

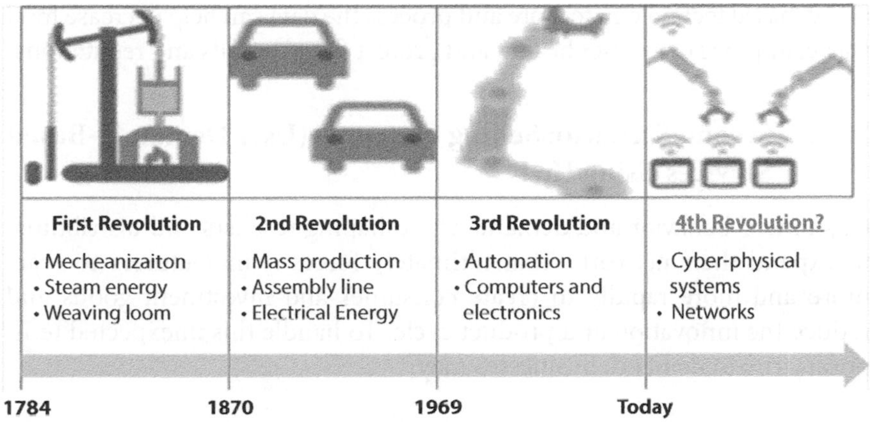

Figure 2.1 Industrial revolution adapted from the study of Horvath [5].

business models by shifting away from product-based to outcome-based (usage-based) [4].

2.2.1 First Scenario: Reducing Waste and Increasing Productivity Using IIoT

Let us use the Food and Logistics industries as an example to show how the Industrial Internet of Things contributes to waste reduction and productivity growth. This value chain process in the Food and Logistics Industry is an example of "Vertical IIoT Integration," in which each layer adds value to the preceding layer. The value chain begins with farmers and ends with distributors, resellers, and customers. To increase crop yields and reduce waste, producers use embedded software and IoT sensors to gather data about soil variability and adjust the fertilizer mix to produce better food. With mounted cameras, drones can help detect anomalies in fields, such as variations in moisture or color [6].

Once the food reaches the distribution stations, IoT sensors and data analytics help follow the journey of items to market and help in identifying the safest and quickest route to market. Consumers are interested in learning about the origins of food and its ingredients. They get this information through the use of food tags, IoT readers, and sensors in smart refrigerators.

A combination of IoT sensors in the manufacturing and transportation processes, barcode and smart label technologies for consumers, and cloud-based technology to store and process the data can help decrease food waste, improve consumer health, and protect firms' brands and reputations.

2.2.2 Second Scenario: Selling Outcome (User Demand)–Based Services Using IIoT

Customers' behavior and demand are reshaping resellers and distributors to expand their network. That ultimately forces manufacturers to react more and more rapidly to create consumer and investment goods and reduce the innovation and product cycle. To handle this unexpected temporary rise in demand, businesses may:

- Either leverages a flexible network of other manufacturers to help meet that demand surge where devices, systems, and processes are intelligent and can interoperate within the network requiring no additional investment. The flexible network of producers is like "horizontal IIoT Integration among suppliers" and requires three key assumptions–open ecosystem based on standards, interoperability among various systems and decentralization & focus on specialization. For example, with manufacturing covid vaccines, Pfizer and BioNTech collaborated to build a massive number of vaccines leveraging existing infrastructure [7].
- OR use adaptable manufacturing configuration within a factory to meet the fluctuation in demand. In adaptable manufacturing, the system is modular, and the machine provider focuses on enhancing machines/devices that can integrate and interoperate. Machines use standard internet protocol (TCP IP) to communicate with other machines, devices, processes, and exchange data in a standard way (interoperability).

In summary, the IIoT enables industrial organizations to leverage intelligent devices and connect device data with operational and supply chain data to get actionable insights.

2.3 IIoT Reference Architecture

Industry 4.0, in its simplest form, refers to the intelligent networking of the physical devices, machines, processes, and software systems that are interconnected and exchange data continuously to drive productivity and sustainability throughout the supply chain [8]. Both above-defined scenarios–whether reducing waste to add value or shifting to outcome-based selling—follow common theme across the different components of the IIoT reference architecture.

- **Open Ecosystem.** The IIoT architecture must accommodate heterogeneity in terms of hardware and software, while processing data patterns, devices, and standards.
- **Flexible.** The reference architecture must be modular to allow for the coexistence of diverse first-party and third-party technologies.
- **Scalable.** The reference architecture must support millions of linked devices, allowing initiatives to start small and scale up.
- **Secure.** To design secure systems, the reference model must consider data security into account across all IIoT components, including device identification, device configuration, data protection—data at rest and data in motion.

Figure 2.2 shows the IIoT reference architecture based on the above reference architecture principles.

The Internet of Things application/framework/architecture comprises the following subcomponents:

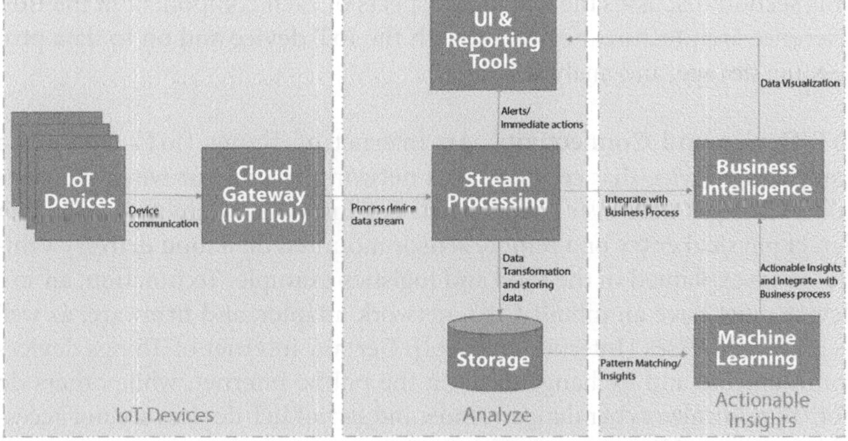

Figure 2.2 IIoT reference architecture adapted from Microsoft Azure [9].

1. **Internet of Things (IoT) devices** that communicate with an IoT Hub or Cloud gateway in order to exchange data with the Hub or Cloud.
2. **An IoT Hub or Cloud gateway** accepts data from IoT devices and integrates functions, such as device management, secure networking, and data ingestion.
3. **Stream processors** consume device data from the Hub and apply rules to the data stream to trigger immediate actions and alarms before storing the data.
4. **Data transformation** manipulates the data in the telemetry stream, such as converting from one format to another format or merging data points from many devices.
5. **Storage** stores telemetry data for the long term that is used for reporting and visualization when needed.
6. The **machine learning (ML)** method analyzes data and correlates it to previous outcomes in order to predict future outcomes.
7. **Business intelligence** makes use of machine learning predictions to guide decision making across the company.
8. A graphical **user interface** for visualizing device telemetry data and facilitating device maintenance or business intelligence reporting.

2.4 IIoT Technical Concepts

This section discusses the technical aspects of each component in the IIoT reference architecture, beginning with the IoT device and on to data processing, storage, and analytics.

IoT Device and Connectivity: An Internet of Things (IoT) device is a computing device that connects to a network by cable or wireless means and exchanges data over the internet. For instance, a remote camera can detect physical entry or a remote sensor mounted on a food delivery vehicle, as we explained in the food and logistics example. To function, an IoT device must have an inbuilt CPU, network adapter, and firmware, as well as an IP addresses (Internet Protocol). Certain Internet of Things devices communicate and exchange data via the public internet, while others do not. To minimize cyber dangers, most Industrial IoT devices are not accessible via the public internet.

IoT devices communicate with other devices, the IoT Hub, or the Cloud gateway via **transport communication protocols**. LoRa, NB-IoT, Zigbee, Wi-Fi, Thread, and Bluetooth Low Energy are all common protocols for IoT transport level communication. Depending on the frequency, data rate, bandwidth, power consumption, and cost, one can choose the communication protocol at the transport layer.

Once connected, IoT device is ready to publish or exchange the data, which entails transmitting messages to and from other apps or back-end services with low latency and high throughput. These devices communicate with one another via a variety of data communication protocols, including MQTT, AMQP, HTTP, CoAP, and DDS. Depending on the priority–low latency, message type support, lightweight, built-in security, and encryption–one can use the right data protocol for data transfer.

The entire IoT stack collapses if the communication or data protocol is incorrect. As a result, selection of the IoT transport and data communication protocols for various IoT scenarios is essential.

Data Processing, Storage and Analytics: The IoT device transmits data to gateway, which forward it to stream processors for additional processing. Three actions are available to the data stream processor:

- Either stream processor can send telemetry data for visualization and reporting component.
- And/or stream processor analyzes data, identifies anomalies, and triggers actions or alerts in response. A stream processor is a fast process that displays and analyzes incoming messages in order to generate essential information and actions, such as alarms.
- Or, in a more complex circumstance, a stream processor discovers patterns between various devices and processes. In this situation, stream processor is a slow process conducting complex analysis, such as aggregating various data points and over a longer period (e.g., hours or days), and generating new patterns and business insights [9].

Big Data: IoT systems can create large amounts of data (time series), depending on the number of devices in the solution, the frequency with which they communicate data, and the amount of the data records sent by devices. Big Data is a process of collecting, processing, and analyzing enormous amounts of structured (such as telemetry data) and unstructured data (such as IoT device metadata) in order to get insight into varying

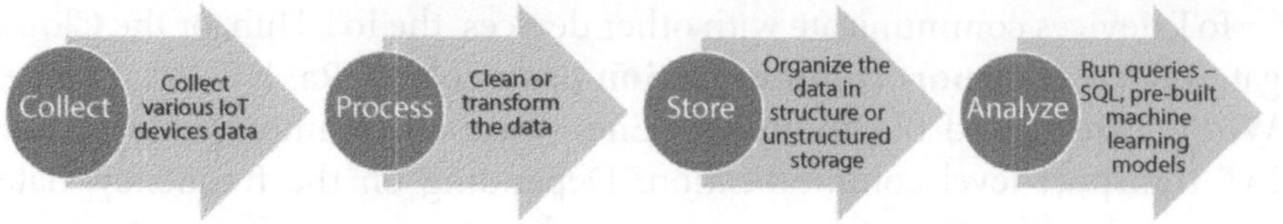

Figure 2.3 IoT data analytics. Adapted from AWS IoT [3].

business patterns. Stream processing works on a continuous stream of data, whereas Big Data works on both continuous and stored data. The following is the sequence for processing large amounts of data (Figure 2.3):

Collect data: Collect structured and unstructured data from a variety of sources, ranging from IoT sensors and devices to cloud storage and mobile applications and beyond;
Process data: All data, regardless of size, requires scrubbing to improve data quality, including removing duplicates and generating more robust results;
Store data: After cleaning of data, it must be filtered and organized in order to generate correct analytical queries for large and unstructured data;
Analyze data: Once clean data are available, complex analytics techniques can transform it into valuable insights. Several of these large data analysis techniques include:

- Data mining—A technique for filtering massive datasets and detecting patterns and correlations.
- Predictive analytics—Rather than grouping or clustering data, this strategy makes predictions and identifies trends based on an organization's past data.
- Deep learning—Method for simulating human pattern recognition through the use of artificial intelligence and machine learning.

Big Data and Machine Learning: Machine learning analyzes huge amounts of device telemetry data (Big Data) and uses sophisticated human-written algorithms to predict behavior or patterns. Following are three distinct machine learning methodologies or types:

- Supervised learning: A supervised learning model analyzes sampled (trained) data to provide an output that may generate comparable output to future data. The machine uses data labels or targets as inputs and identifies the correlation. The labels on the data assist the algorithm in correlating the data. As mentioned in the food and logistics example, producers collect data about soil variability and change the fertilizer mix to produce better food using embedded software and IoT sensors. The fertilizer adjustment is based on supervised learning in this case.

- Unsupervised learning: Unlike supervised learning, unsupervised learning makes use of unlabeled data to search for structure and pattern. The objective of unsupervised learning is to discover clusters, or groupings of linked observations, within the input data.
- Reinforcement learning: In reinforcement learning, algorithms predict the best or optimal combination/action in a context. Reinforcement learning does not require labeled data and operates in an interactive, changing environment that provides continuous feedback. The reinforcement learning technique combines the advantages of unsupervised and supervised learning.

  Today, supervised machine learning is more often employed in industrial settings to do predictive analytics and asset management.

Big Data, Machine Learning and Artificial Intelligence: Artificial intelligence (AI) is a computer program that simulates human thought and self-directed behavior using data. Machine learning is a subset of Artificial Intelligence (AI), in which machines learn from data inputs using human-created models. Machine learning helps make predictions based on previous patterns, whereas artificial intelligence generates behaviors devoid of human intervention in response to such predictions. Intelligent manufacturing integrates real-time data insights, machine learning models, and artificial intelligence into the manufacturing process to perform tasks like predictive maintenance and asset management. When used with the appropriate intelligent algorithms that are less error-prone than those operated by people, artificial intelligence provides various benefits to the manufacturing business, including error reduction, cost reduction, and revenue growth.

In recent years, manufacturing production lines have used artificial intelligence. For instance, in the food and logistics industries, there are prototypes of self-driving machines capable of harvesting without human involvement, as well as automated systems for diagnosing illnesses or pests in specific crops.

2.5 IIoT and Cloud Computing

To process data stream with varying business requirements, it is necessary to have infrastructure that can scale up and down in response to those requirements. Cloud Computing is an economical solution for consumers since it eliminates the need for customers to invest in on-premises computation, storage, network, and analytics infrastructure. As business needs grow, so do its requirements and Cloud Computing can provide a scalable solution. Cloud computing is a centralized system that enables the processing and delivery of data across the Internet and between data centers. There are three cloud computing service models and four deployment methods. The three service models are:

- SaaS (Software as a Service): In the SaaS service paradigm, a service provider delivers Cloud-based infrastructure and services for Internet of Things applications (i.e., cloud gateway, stream processors, storage, machine learning, and business intelligence). Consumer firms connect their devices to the service provider's network and administer the entire operation via a web browser.
- PaaS (Platform as a Service): In the PaaS service model, the service provider supplies the components necessary to construct and deploy cloud applications, and consumers do not need to purchase and maintain equipment, software, storage, and networking. PaaS offers greater flexibility than SaaS because it enables consumer businesses to create their own machine learning models and business intelligence reports. Microsoft Azure and Amazon Web Services, for example, both offer IoT PaaS services.
- IaaS (Infrastructure as a Service): The most versatile yet time-consuming of the three service models, IaaS provides businesses with storage, servers, networks, and gateways for each need. Under the IaaS model, consumers do not purchase physical hardware, storage, or network infrastructure, but subscribe to a service provider's basic infrastructure as a service. It is up to consumers to develop their own stream processors, data formats, and machine algorithms.

The four deployment methods or alternatives for utilizing any of these service models are:

- Public Cloud: Cloud Providers maintain data centers and provide instant access to customers (both service providers and consumers) via the public network. Amazon Web Services and Microsoft Azure are two examples.
- Private Cloud: Identical to a public cloud, except that single consumer can access, which can be an organization, or an individual firm. PTC and Hitachi are two such companies.
- Hybrid Cloud: Hybrid cloud is a combination of public and private cloud computing in which companies process some data or information on-premise or in a private cloud and some in a public cloud. It is the most frequently used deployment architecture in an industrial context, where collection and monitoring of operational data from devices are done on-premise, while data related to integrating other systems, such as predictive maintenance, is processed in the public Cloud.
- Community Cloud: A community cloud is a platform shared by a few consumers with comparable requirements. This is uncommon in the Internet of Things (IoT) domain.

Cloud computing enables the collecting, processing, and storage of IoT data over the internet and offers secure and efficient access when necessary.

2.6 IIoT and Security

As with any other digital solution, Internet of Things (IoT) solutions are vulnerable to hacking attempts, including unauthorized access, denial of service assaults, data tampering, and data exfiltration. As shown in the reference architecture, the IIoT components—IoT Device, IoT Hub, Stream Processor, Big Data Storage, and Machine Learning—are all connected and are formatting, processing, storing, or analyzing data. It is necessary to provide secure connectivity between these components, as well as data security throughout transit, use, and storage.

IoT solutions are vulnerable because they may transmit data over the internet and any tampering with the data may cause a security breach. There are well-established security frameworks, controls, and best practices accessible throughout the industry. Identification and authentication, configuration management, system and communication protection and information integrity are all examples of common security controls.

- Identification and authentication concerns with who can access what (person, system, or device) and how to authenticate that access. According to the National Institute of Technology and Standards (NIST), each Internet of Things (IoT) device must have a unique identification–both logical and physical. Unique identifiers will assist the company in managing assets, including vulnerabilities and patch management. Access to the IoT device interface must be limited to only specific people or systems, and provided to only when the device is in a specific state. In the food and logistics examples above, the farmer's equipment, distributor sensors, and reseller bar codes all have unique identification.
- Device configuration refers to who can configure or change the configuration of an IoT device. An unauthorized action may cause an insecure environment that hackers can exploit to steal data. For instance, with an IP-based camera security firm, hackers got important data from the devices because of insecure code on the camera security firm's website, allowing hackers to change client data. In the food and logistics examples above, specific system administrator configures the farmer's equipment, distributor sensors, and reseller bar codes.
- System and communication protection means connectivity means connectivity between IoT devices and other components must be secure at all times and protect from eavesdropping, data tempering, and spoofing.
- Information integrity refers to the fact that data are not tampered with or manipulated while it is in transit or at rest. Especially with Big Data, where long-term storage keeps telemetry data, data need to be encrypted to avoid a breach.

While IoT in Industrial transformation provides the transparent, scalable, agile solution to add value to the supply chain and enables industries to respond to changing requirements, it is also the most vulnerable to security issues.

References

1. Laxmi, V., Data security, in: *Building the Future of Food Safety Technology || Data security*, D. Detwiler (Ed.), pp. 207–216, Elsevier, Academic Press, Cambridge, Massachusetts, USA, 2020.
2. Federal Ministry for Economic Affairs and Climate Action, *2030 Vision for Industrie 4.0*, Federal Ministry for Economic Affairs and Energy (BMWi, Berlin, 2019.
3. Amazon Web Services, Inc., Industrial IOT, 2022. Retrieved Dec 26, 2021, from Digital Transformation: https://aws.amazon.com/iot/solutions/industrial-iot/.
4. Sjödin, D., Parida, V., Jovanovic, M., Visnjic, I., Value creation and value capture alignment in business model innovation: A process view on outcome-based business models. *J. Prod. Innov. Manage.*, 37, 158–183, 2020.
5. Horvath, B., The recognition of resource use through industrial development from a social perspective. *Studia Mundi-Economica*, 68–78, 2018. http://studia.mundi.gtk.szie.hu/en/recognition-resource-use-through-industrial-development-social-perspective.
6. Shacklett, M., IoT gains a foothold in food supply chains, March 19, 2018. Retrieved from Food Logistics: https://www.foodlogistics.com/software-technology/article/20993391/iot-gains-a-foothold-in-food-supply-chains.
7. Pfizer, Pfizer and BioNTech announce further details on collaboration to accelerate global COVID-19 vaccine development, April 09, 2020. Retrieved from Pfizer: https://www.pfizer.com/news/press-release/press-release-detail/pfizer-and-biontech-announce-further-details-collaboration.
8. Federal Ministry of Economic Affairs and Energy, *2030 Vision for Industrie 4.0*, Federal Ministry for Economic Affairs and Energy (BMWi, Berlin, 2019, Retrieved from Plattform Industrie 4.0: https://www.plattform-i40.de/IP/Redaktion/EN/Downloads/Publikation/Vision-2030-for-Industrie-4.0.html.
9. Microsoft. Azure IOT reference architecture, May 10, 2021. Retrieved from azure.microsoft.com: https://azure.microsoft.com/mediahandler/files/resourcefiles/microsoft-azure-iot-reference-architecture/Microsoft_Azure_IoT_Reference_Architecture_2_1_1_update.pdf.

3

Artificial Intelligence of Things (AIoT) and Industry 4.0-Based Supply Chain (FMCG Industry)

Seyyed Esmaeil Najafi[1], Hamed Nozari[2] and S. A. Edalatpanah[3*]

[1]Department of Industrial Engineering, Islamic Azad University, Science and Research Branch, Tehran, Iran
[2]Department of Industrial Engineering, Islamic Azad University, Central Tehran Branch, Tehran, Iran
[3]Department of Applied Mathematics, Ayandegan Institute of Higher Education, Tonekabon, Iran

Abstract
Today, the term "Internet of Things" pervades the world of information and communication technology. The Internet of Things (IoT) and artificial intelligence (AI) are each powerful technology. When you combine AI and IoT, you get the Artificial Intelligence of Things, or AIoT. "AIoT" simply means using the IoT to perform intelligent tasks with the help of artificial intelligence integration. AIoT helps connect IoT devices to sensors that have artificial intelligence capabilities, and all of this is done without human intervention. Therefore, the industrial impact of this technology is very high and can have a powerful transformation on different parts of the business. Given the high importance of supply chain in manufacturing businesses and especially in FMCG industries as one of the most important industries in the daily lives of humans, this chapter provides a framework for using this technology on the supply chain in these industries. This framework sets a clear path for the various communications of these evolving technologies on the supply chain.

Keywords: Internet of Things (IoT), artificial intelligence, Artificial Intelligence of Things (AIoT), supply chain, FMCG industries

**Corresponding author*: s.a.edalatpanah@aihe.ac.ir

Jyotir Moy Chatterjee, Harish Garg and R. N. Thakur (eds.) A Roadmap for Enabling Industry 4.0 by Artificial Intelligence, (31–42) © 2023 Scrivener Publishing LLC

3.1 Introduction

The Internet of Things, or IoT, is an interconnected system of computer equipment, mechanical and digital machines, objects, animals, or individuals identified by unique identifiers (UIDs) and the ability to transmit data over a network without the need for human-to-human or human interaction [1]. The IoT technology ecosystem is a collection of Internet-connected and intelligent devices that use tools such as processors, sensors, and communication systems to collect, store, and process data received from the environment. The collected data are connected to the IoT ports or edge device for analysis or sent to the cloud environment or analyzed locally. These devices communicate with other devices on the IoT network and act on the support of information received from each other [2]. These devices do most of the work without human intervention. Of course, people can interact with devices, for example, they can adjust them, instruct them, or access the data. In today's world, most organizations in different businesses are increasingly using various attractive IoT capabilities to improve the performance and efficiency of their internal and external processes. By leveraging IoT achievements, they are able to better understand and provide better services to their customers. IoT technology facilitates the decision-making process in the organization by producing large and valuable data and increasingly increases the business value due to quality growth, as well as increasing decision-making power. The next generation in business does not like to wait. They want devices to make decisions ahead of time, but the need to process data with minimal latency is not the only issue [3]. In the case of intelligent vehicles, as well as many medical and industrial applications, the need for IoT systems for automated decision making as quickly as possible is a necessity. Edge computing technology meets these expectations. This technology enables command-related analysis by collecting integrated data from IoT devices and storage. In addition, it supports real-time decision making locally [4]. Artificial intelligence also uses a compact architecture but provides a powerful computational method that is efficient for guiding local decision making with local information. The smarter an edge device is, the more expensive it is, but it can also process and store large amounts of data locally, reducing the need to do so elsewhere. The complete combination of IoT technologies with AI technology, called AIoT, allows organizations to take advantage of both technologies simultaneously, increasing the efficiency and accuracy of organizational performance and computing. "AIoT" simply means using the Internet of Things to perform intelligent tasks with the help of artificial intelligence integration [5]. Now that AI and the Internet of Things have a separate and effective presence in the digital world, many IoT application development companies are moving to using AIoT technology to better manage IoT-connected devices with AI techniques. In the remainder of this chapter, we will look at the benefits of converging artificial intelligence and the Internet of Things for businesses. We use the use of this tool in the supply chain of FMCG industries as one of the most important effective industries in human life. Finally, we provide a framework for the valuable and extensive communications and impacts of this technology in the supply chain.

3.2 Concepts

3.2.1 Internet of Things

The term IoT was first coined in 1999 by Kevin Ashton, who, according to Ashton, defines the IoT as any inanimate object of a digital nature that can be controlled by computer-based systems and its various dimensions. In fact, IoT refers to any physical phenomenon that has the ability to exchange incoming information without interacting with humans through a unique identifier (UIDs) in a network. The IoT ecosystem consists of devices that use processors, sensors, and communication hardware to collect, send, and analyze data. The IoT shares the data it collects from its environment by connecting to the Internet gateway and sometimes acts on the information it receives from each other. These devices often do things without human intervention. The Internet of Things has the potential to fundamentally change the way humans interact with their environment [6]. The ability to monitor and manage, optimize the performance of systems and processes, allows decisions based on data and information to enter a new phase [7]. The overall goal of the Internet of Things is to improve the quality of human life. Just as the traditional Internet has many components and is not a discrete product, the Internet of Things is made up of different components and must be put together at a basic level to create value-added services. Figure 3.1 presents the four broad categories of IoT technology that make up an ecosystem.

The Internet of Things has received considerable attention. Because it offers extensive communication and a variety of challenges and barriers, including scalability, security, big data, needs such as energy, and more [8]. Today, the limited Internet of Things has become so widespread that it encompasses a vast array of energy management infrastructures, health

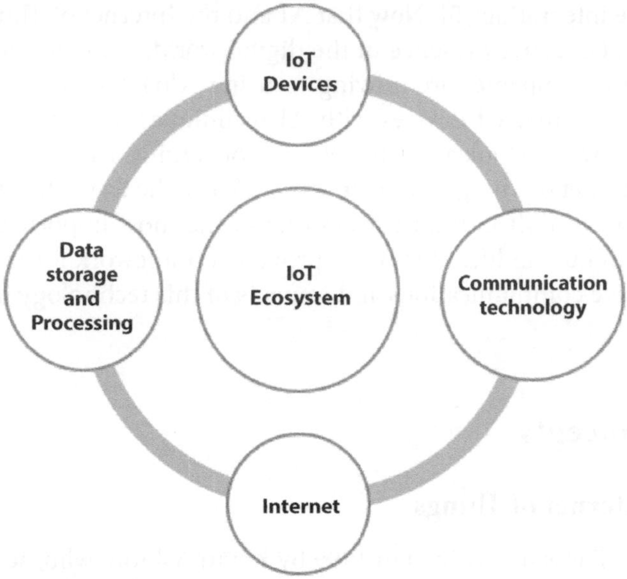

Figure 3.1 IoT ecosystem.

and care measures, home systems, urban affairs, and transportation systems. Undoubtedly, the revolution that the Internet of Things has launched in the world will have a profound effect on human life in a very short period of time. The growing use of smart devices and devices, the dramatic acceptance of smart cars and homes are just some of the rapid development of the Internet of Things and its role in human life today.

3.2.2 The Industrial Internet of Things (IIoT)

In general, the concept of IoT is the connection of different devices to each other via the Internet. With the help of the IoT, various applications and devices can interact with each other and with humans at the same time through an Internet connection. Smart refrigerators, for example, can notify you of the expiration of food in the refrigerator and even measure your interest in each food. The Internet of Things in the present age is a phenomenon that can take control of objects and processes and be a valuable facilitator. The IoT provides opportunities for the direct integration of the physical world and Internet-based systems and cyberspace, such as smart cities, smart cars and homes, tools and appliances used in smart everyday life that are growing these days. There are many types of digital developments and the effects of the digital economy, all of which fall into the category of IoT technology. The Internet of Things can collect and stream data. The collected data is sent to a cloud data center and then shared with other users. The Internet of Things will increase automation and automation in homes, schools, workplaces and industries. The use of the Internet of Things in the industry is called "Industrial IoT," which is referred to as IIoT or Industry 4.0. The Internet of Things will revolutionize manufacturing by providing the ability to access much larger amounts of data, much faster and more efficiently [9]. A number of innovative companies have begun to implement the IoT in their factories using interconnected smart devices. The Internet of Things is one of the most important factors in the prosperity and development of present and future industrial businesses. Today's industries are trying to modernize their equipment in order to quickly get used to the growing changes in the market and use existing technologies [10]. Businesses have used IoT in their infrastructure, growing dramatically in areas such as security, productivity, and profitability. As the use of the industrial IoT increases, so will the productivity mentioned. The use of the Internet of Things (IoT) will improve communication, productivity, scale development, and save time and money for industrial companies. This intelligent structure can cause people to interact with the equipment. The Internet of Things can also allow companies to get the most out of their systems and equipment without being hindered by technological and economic constraints. Given the benefits that the IoT can have for industry and companies, this structure can be highly regarded.

3.2.3 Artificial Intelligence of Things (AIoT)

The IoT and AI are powerful technologies. When you combine AI and the IoT, you get AI of Things, or AIoT. Imagine the Internet of Things is a digital nervous system, and artificial intelligence is the brain of that system. When AI is added to the IoT, it means that devices can analyze data, make decisions, and act on that data without human intervention. These devices are "smart" devices and thus contribute to power and effectiveness [11]. Intelligence in AIoT is data analytics that is used to optimize the system and create better performance in the business. This intelligence helps to create data for better decision making and system learning. The data that millions of IoT devices collect is so large that it is difficult to separate and extract useful information from it. In order to organize this unstructured data into meaningful datasets, artificial intelligence-based algorithms are used to remove useless data and maximize the use of any business model. Senior IT executives (CTOs) can now make decisive decisions based on the valuable information gained from this data, along with others responsible

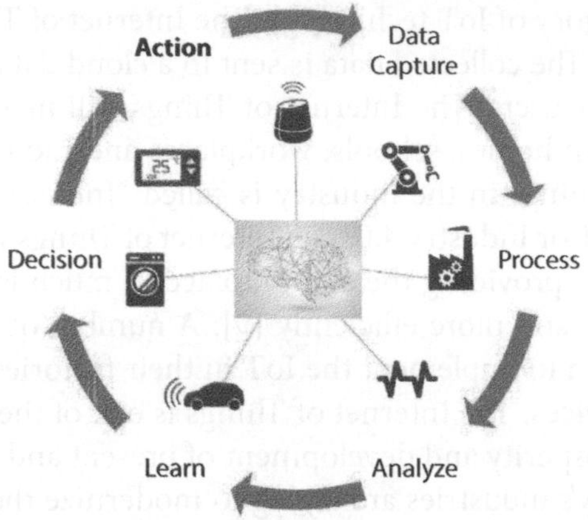

Figure 3.2 Elements of AIoT.

for an organization's important decisions. Figure 3.2 shows the key elements of artificial intelligence of things [12].

AIoT adds analytical calculations to big data from IoT. In this case, AIoT intelligent technologies embedded in all system processes can automatically analyze data extracted by sensors and other IoT tools. The technology can then use these analyses to provide solutions for decision making.

3.3 AIoT-Based Supply Chain

Supply chain management is a goal-based goal of linking business-institutional operations to provide a common view of market opportunity. On the other hand, the supply chain is the result of the integration of various operational loops, at the beginning of which are suppliers and at the end of which are customers. The existence of comprehensive and valid information platforms is one of the requirements of supply chain management. Therefore, benefiting from integrated information management systems based on IoT technology is very important in this part of organizational management. Accurate and simultaneous access to this information improves the activities in the organization and at the same time makes the processes very transparent [13]. One of the most distinctive benefits of IoT technology is that it can be used throughout supply chain management. The Internet of Things can affect the entire supply chain process. The main purpose of using IoT technology is to bridge the gap between real-world business processes and display them in information systems.

The Internet of Things and artificial intelligence, in addition to evolving technologies for most industries, are also growing. They have also demonstrated their growing impact on well-to-do processes in organizations such as supply chain management. Organizational management tools, forecasting procedures and comprehensive monitoring of supply, production and distribution processes help managers to improve the operational efficiency of their organization and increase their optimal and targeted decisions. So more than ever, the benefits of using the Internet of Things and AI are visible in the supply chain. Because IoT and AI programs are used in various parts of supply chain management. This improves the comprehensive tracking and monitoring of the behavior of the goods and makes the transparency and at the same time more accurate in the communication and planning process. All areas of the complex supply chain process can be improved with the Internet of Things and its combination with artificial intelligence. Logical, high-powered tracking, monitoring, and analysis are some of the main goals of deploying IoT and artificial intelligence in supply chain management. This technology allows warehouse and fleet managers to track their shipments and inventory and provide more accurate calculations in the analysis [14].

The logistic industry, or transportation, plays a very important role in the supply chain. Almost all goods depend on the transportation industry before production (raw materials) and after production. This dependence makes logistics a key issue in the supply chain for industry stakeholders. Today, with the decrease in the price of various sensors, we are witnessing the presence of the Internet of Things in all areas of logistics. The importance of the supply chain has led activists in this sector to seek to implement the latest methods to improve conditions and increase efficiency. Supply chain automation significantly speeds up processes. With the development of the Internet of Things and the formation of smart cities, the need to implement an intelligent supply chain in future cities is strongly felt. In a smart city, all procedures need to be done intelligently. The Internet of Things plays a very important role in the supply chain. With the advancement of the Internet of Things, supply chains are becoming more modern and powerful. Of course, the existence of various challenges in the supply of basic goods in a smart city shows that chain services still need further development and improvement. Anticipating needs in advance will improve municipal services. Information technology, IoT and data processing are among the topics that will further improve the supply and logistics processes. In addition, artificial intelligence has changed the supply chain process from a reactive state (reacting to the current needs of the customer) to a dynamic state (reacting based on creating a need).

This will lead to a greater change in the way supply chain data-driven processes work. The real role of artificial intelligence in the supply chain is to strengthen human intelligence and decision making. AI plays two roles in improving supply chain processes. The first role is to improve tasks and optimize iterative processes in all supply chain processes and the second role is to provide new and different solutions for strategic decisions and provide collaborative solutions [15].

The combined use of IoT technology and artificial intelligence has many benefits for supply chain management. For example, AIoT models specialize in predictive analytics to predict demand. These frameworks can reveal hidden paths in time-based supply and demand data. For example, they can relate customer buying behavior to navigation patterns, geographic location, and personal preferences. Also in terms of supply chain management, the high comprehension power of computer-based systems can lead to more accurate inventory management. At the same time, quality management of demand is always costly and time consuming, because manufacturers in industries that are heavily influenced by component management must control thousands or even millions of pieces from different suppliers to ensure that all standards are met correctly. Machine learning malgos can greatly facilitate auditing and compliance monitoring in these industries. Finally, the benefits of combining AIoT and IoT in supply chain management are such that these technologies highlight the role of hidden information and data in business processes and enable them to add more value to their organization. Therefore, data play an essential role in the use of these technologies. In this research, we provide a framework for the use and application of artificial intelligence technology in the industrial age in the FMCG industry. For this reason, Figure 3.3 shows the data generation pathways in the FMCG industry. The reason for choosing

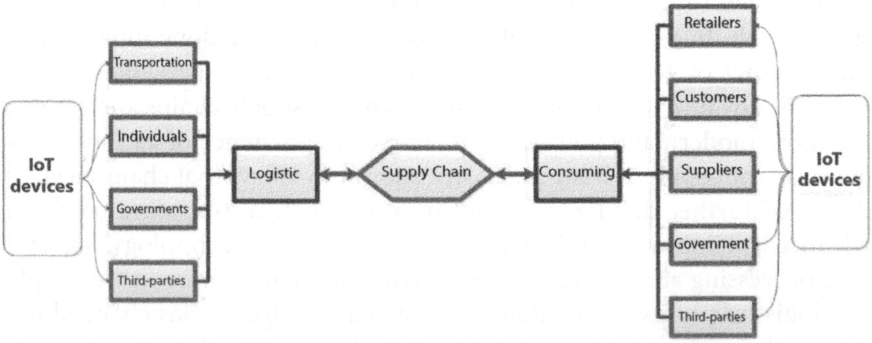

Figure 3.3 Big data generation sources in the FMCG industry.

these industries is their tremendous impact on people's lives, and secondly, researchers have had more access to experts working in FMCG companies to approve the framework.

As shown in Figure 3.3, most of the data can be retrieved from IoT tools. These data are Big Data type. Because they have a high diversity, and due to their presence in the FMCG industry, they have a high production speed and a very high volume. Using these data, the proposed IoT-based supply chain framework as well as artificial intelligence or AIoT can be presented in Figure 3.4.

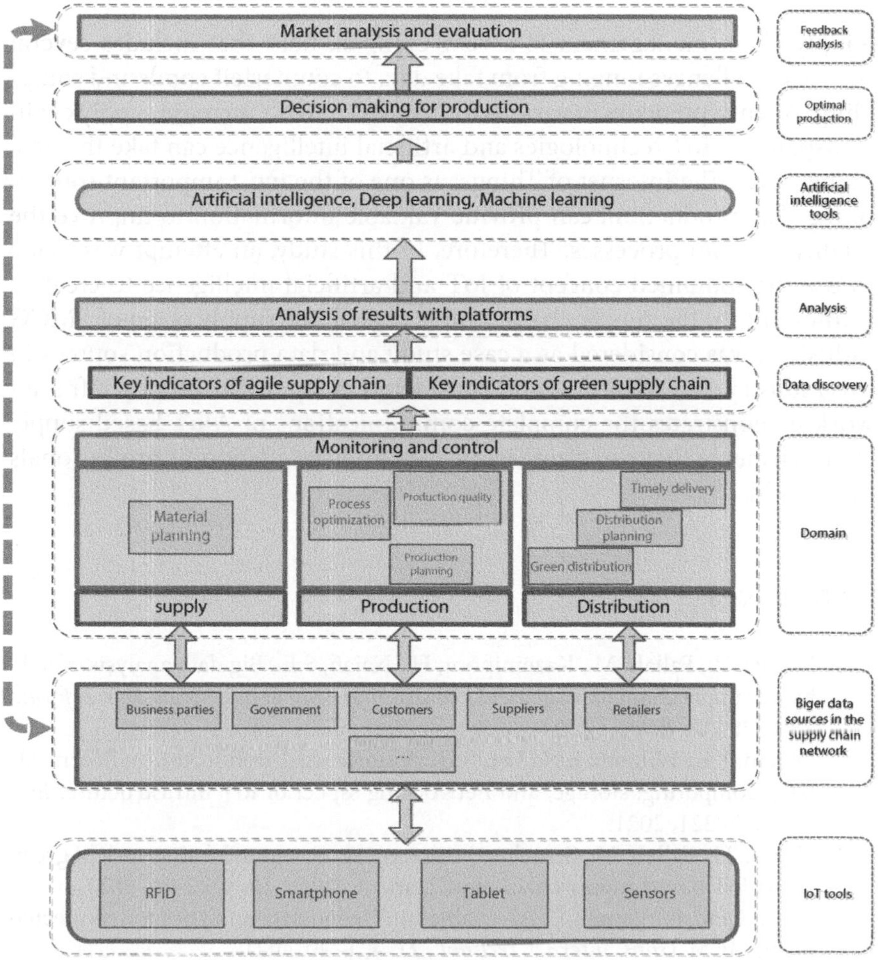

Figure 3.4 Communication framework for the AIoT supply chain.

The use of these two technologies is an investment that is done once, but has a long-term and permanent return. Using AIoT technology, data analysis, and production, as well as data processing can be done simultaneously, all with the goal of drawing better conclusions from larger and more fundamental data.

As Figure 3.4 shows, larger data are extracted through IoT tools and, after refinement, evaluated and analyzed by AI tools, which in turn will provide more powerful returns for supply chain operation.

3.4 Conclusion

Supply chain management is a very complex field that includes several business challenges ranging from fake data to counterfeit goods and smuggling. As entrepreneurs in various industries strive to increase supply chain transparency, IoT technologies and artificial intelligence can take this to a higher level. The Internet of Things, as one of the most important sources of big data production, can provide valuable information to improve the quality of chain processes. Therefore, in this study, an attempt was made to use the combined concept of IoT and artificial intelligence to create a framework for the supply chain. In this regard, the supply chain of FMCG industries was considered as a case study and data production sources in this industry were identified and considered as input. The proposed framework demonstrates the complete communications of AIoT-based supply chain elements that can guide its proper implementation to professionals in the field.

References

1. Nozari, H., Fallah, M., Kazemipoor, H., Najafi, S.E., Big data analysis of IoT-based supply chain management considering FMCG industries. *Bus. Inform.*, 15, 1, 78–96, 2021.
2. Oktian, Y.E., Witanto, E.N., Lee, S.G., A conceptual architecture in decentralizing computing, storage, and networking sspect of IoT infrastructure. *IoT*, 2, 2, 205–221, 2021.
3. Nozari, H., Fallah, M., Szmelter-Jarosz, A., A conceptual framework of green smart IoT-based supply chain management. *IJRIE*, 10, 1, 22–34, 2021.
4. Lv, Z., Qiao, L., Verma, S., AI-enabled IoT-edge data analytics for connected living. *ACM Trans. Internet Technol.*, 21, 4, 1–20, 2021.

5. Dong, B., Shi, Q., Yang, Y., Wen, F., Zhang, Z., Lee, C. Technology evolution from self-powered sensors to AIoT enabled smart homes. *Nano Energy*, 79, 105414, 2021.
6. Fallah, M. and Nozari, H., Quantitative analysis of cyber risks in IoT-based supply chain (FMCG industries). *J. Decis. Oper. Res.*, 5, 4, 510–521, 2021.
7. Aliahmadi, A., Jafari-Eskandari, M., Mozafari, A., Nozari, H., Comparing linear regression and artificial neural networks to forecast total productivity growth in Iran. *Int. J. Inf. Bus. Manage.*, 8, 1, 93, 2016.
8. Liu, L., Guo, X., Lee, C., Promoting smart cities into the 5G era with multi-field Internet of Things (IoT) applications powered with advanced mechanical energy harvesters. *Nano Energy*, 88, 106304, 2021.
9. Zhang, P., Wang, C., Jiang, C., Han, Z. Deep reinforcement learning assisted federated learning algorithm for data management of IIoT. *IEEE Trans. Industr. Inform.*, 17, 12, 8475–8484, 2021.
10. Chalapathi, G.S.S., Chamola, V., Vaish, A., Buyya, R., Industrial internet of things (iiot) applications of edge and fog computing: A review and future directions, in: *Fog/Edge Computing For Security, Privacy, and Applications*, pp. 293–325, 2021.
11. Sun, H., Chen, L., Hao, X., Liu, C., Ni, M., An energy-efficient and fast scheme for hybrid storage class memory in an AIoT terminal system. *Electronics*, 9, 6, 1013, 2020.
12. Normanno, N., Barberis, M., De Marinis, F., Gridelli, C., Molecular and genomic profiling of lung cancer in the era of precision medicine: A position paper from the Italian association of thoracic oncology (AIOT). *Cancers*, 12, 6, 1627, 2020.
13. Ghahremani-Nahr, J., Nozari, H., Bathaee, M., Robust box approach for blood supply chain network design under uncertainty: Hybrid moth-flame optimization and genetic algorithm. *IJIE*, 1, 2, 40–62, 2021.
14. Samadzad, S. and Hashemi, M., Concentration and its effect on advertising: Case study: Iranian food and beverage industries. *IJIMES*, 1, 1, 55–64, 2021. Retrieved from https://ijimes.ir/index.php/ijimes/article/view/9.
15. Nozari, H., Najafi, E., Fallah, M., Hosseinzadeh Lotfi, F., Quantitative analysis of key performance indicators of green supply chain in FMCG industries using non-linear fuzzy method. *Mathematics*, 7, 11, 1020, 2019.

4

Application of Artificial Intelligence in Forecasting the Demand for Supply Chains Considering Industry 4.0

Alireza Goli[1]*, Amir-Mohammad Golmohammadi[2] and S. A. Edalatpanah[3]

[1]*Department of Industrial Engineering and Future Studies, Faculty of Engineering, University of Isfahan, Isfahan, Iran*

[2]*Department of Industrial Engineering, Arak University, Arak, Iran*

[3]*Department of Applied Mathematics, Ayandegan Institute of Higher Education, Tonekabon, Iran*

Abstract

Nowadays, the speed of implementation of technological advances is increasing. Moreover, the economic challenges posed by technological and social developments have led industrial companies to increase their agility and responsiveness in order to be able to manage the entire value chain. On the other hand, one of the most interesting and at the same time one of the most important challenges facing supply chains is Industry 4.0, which is based on digital technology and varies greatly in scale and complexity. It is more than what humanity has experienced through previous industrial revolutions, and decisions need to be made faster and more accurately. Accordingly, in this paper, a comprehensive framework for accelerating supply chain decisions with respect to Industry 4.0 is provided. In this regard, first, Industry 4.0 is described in detail. Next, a framework for demand forecasting in the 4.0 industry-based supply chain is provided using artificial intelligence tools. In this context, the simultaneous use of time series methods and machine learning methods is emphasized. The analysis of the proposed framework demonstrates the suitable benefits of using it in different supply chains.

Keywords: Industry 4.0, supply chain, artificial intelligence, IoT, demand prediction

**Corresponding author*: Goli.A@eng.ui.ac.ir

Jyotir Moy Chatterjee, Harish Garg and R. N. Thakur (eds.) A Roadmap for Enabling Industry 4.0 by Artificial Intelligence, (43–56) © 2023 Scrivener Publishing LLC

4.1 Introduction

Countless eyes and corners around us share our activities with big data centers moment by moment, making our image clearer and clearer in the minds of production lines, and distinguishing us from others in order to make our future products more precise. Moreover, intelligent products that share our interactions with manufacturers via the Internet of Things, analyzing and predict our behavior by recording it across large amounts of big data and then using cloud computing. By monitoring the expiration dates and expiration dates of the devices around us, they send our needed and replacement equipment to the local vendors around us in advance and encourage us to buy replacement products by sending special offers. In this way, our needs will be met without spending money and fossil fuels, without polluting the air, and spending time [1].

Moving toward smarter supply chains and paying attention to the fact that reducing the cost of the product equals more profit is very important for manufacturers. Because in today's competitive markets, a product that is offered at a more reasonable price will always snatch the lead from competitors. In the meantime, manpower has always been considered as one of the costly pillars in the production line. Achieving technology that has all the characteristics of human resources and has eliminated its weaknesses has always been the dream of senior managers. The use of ligaments will significantly reduce these costs and eliminate the remaining manpower on production lines in the future [2].

The Fourth Industrial Revolution (FIR) transforms the world once again by establishing the connection between man and machine, which include: Mass production with flexibility, real-time coordination, value chain optimization, reduce complex costs, and completely new business models [3, 4].

The entry of the FIR into production has a great impact on the entire supply chain. Cooperation between suppliers, manufacturers, and customers is very important to increase the transparency of all stages (from the beginning of the order to the end of the product life). On the other hand, due to the digitalization and automation of processes in the entire supply chain management structure, in order to identify opportunities and potential threats arising from the introduction of new technologies, it is necessary to examine its impact on the supply chain [5]. But what is the fourth industry and what will we face in this industry?

4.2 Literature Review

4.2.1 Summary of the First Three Industrial Revolutions

The terms "industrial revolution" and "industrialization" have been used interchangeably and its development is illustrated in Figure 4.1 [6–9].

4.2.2 Emergence of Industry 4.0

The first industrial revolution took place after the period of early industrial production. It started in the late 18th and early 19th centuries [10]. At this time, mining was the reason for the creation of a new type of energy that later helped accelerate the construction and production of railways and accelerated economic growth [11]. Next, the second industrial revolution was emerged. This revolution resulted in the invention of the internal combustion engine, which began to reach its maximum power [12–14]. By utilizing new technologies, the Third Industrial Revolution opened the door to space exploration, research, and biotechnology [15].

In the industrial world, two great inventions, programmable logic controllers (PLCs) and robots have contributed to the age of high-level automation. The fourth-generation industry began at the dawn of the third millennium with something that humans use today at all times [16].

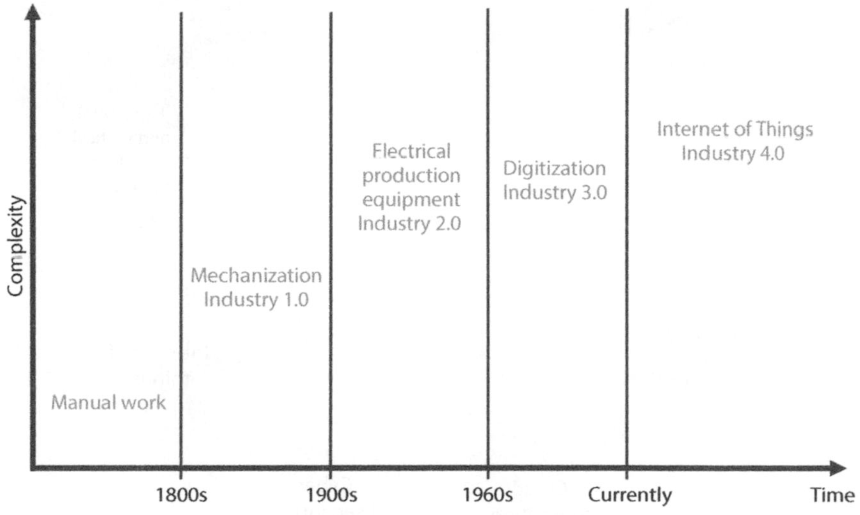

Figure 4.1 An overview of the four industrial revolutions.

The fourth industrial revolution is the age of intelligent devices, storage systems, and production equipment that can independently exchange information, perform operations, and control equipment without human intervention [17].

Less than ten years have passed since the discussion of the Fourth Industrial Revolution in industrial and production circles, but observers are now predicting a new revolution. If the current revolution focuses on turning factories into intelligent IoT-enabled facilities that utilize cognitive computing and connectivity via cloud servers, the Fifth Industrial Revolution will focus on the return of the human hand and mind to the industrial framework. This new revolution is called the advent of artificial intelligence [18]. The process of developing the technologies is illustrated in Figure 4.2.

Table 4.1 shows the core technology of Industry 4.0, which modernizes production.

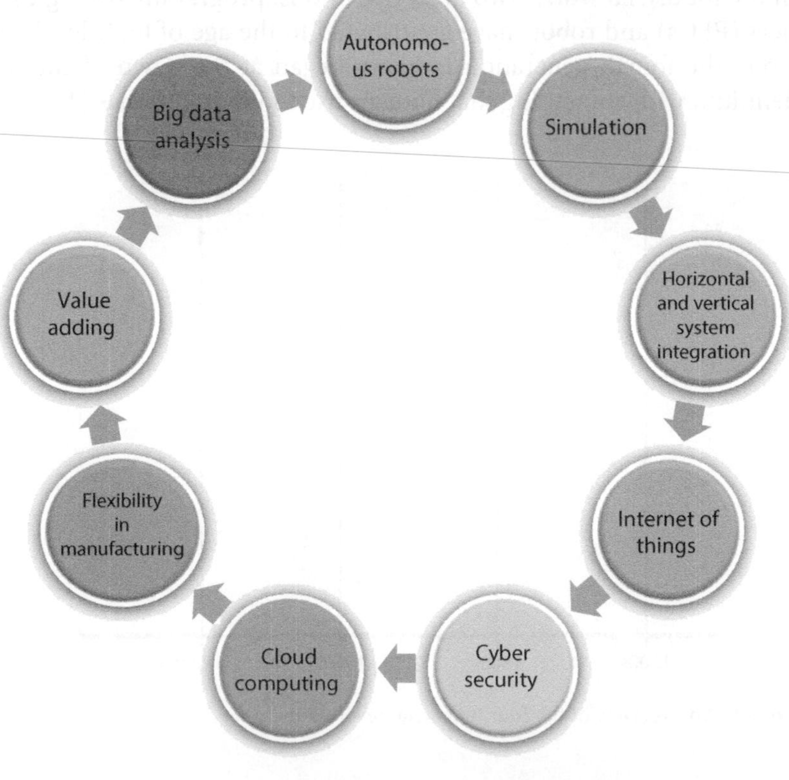

Figure 4.2 Nine technologies that are changing industrial production [18].

Table 4.1 Nine technologies that are used in Industry 4.0 [19, 20].

Technology	Effects
Advanced robots	• Independent and cooperative industrial robots, with integrated sensors and standard interfaces
Flexibility in manufacturing	• 3D printers, which are mainly used to make spare parts and prototypes. • Decentralized 3D printing facilities, which reduce inventory shipping distance.
Value adding	• Digital enhancement, which displays system performance equipment, logistics and display devices.
Simulation	• Network simulation and optimization, which uses real-time data from intelligent systems
Horizontal and vertical system integration	• Integration of data inside and outside companies using a standard data transfer protocol • An integrated value chain (from supplier to customer) and organizational structure (from management to store)
Internet of Things	• A network of machines and products • Multidimensional communication between network objects
Cloud computing	• Manage huge amounts of data in open systems • Real-time communication for production systems
Cyber security	• Manage increased security risks due to high levels of networking among smart machines, products and systems
Big data analysis	• A comprehensive evaluation of existing data (e.g. from CRM, ERP, and SCM systems as well as through MES and machinery • Support for optimal real-time decision making

4.2.3 Some of the Challenges of Industry 4.0

The technological aspects of the fourth industry have attracted the attention of all industries [21]. However, the profound impact of this industry at the managerial level has been underestimated [22]. According to the

World Economic Forum, the impact of automation is such that it is estimated that 57% of all businesses are at risk of automation over the next 5 years, which means little opportunity can be found to raise awareness and infrastructure are such as education and legal barriers.

Moreover, despite many anticipated problems, many solutions have not yet gone beyond pure theory [21, 22]. Rising unemployment and job losses are high prices we have to pay in the face of an unequal war on automation and traditional tasks. Creating security and protecting the privacy of individuals from cyberspace along with controlling cyber conflicts is one of the important issues that will affect all businesses, especially the government. Lack of internal digital culture and education and sufficient talent to implement new business models also exploit digital opportunities [23]. Digital technologies and global communications infrastructure are significantly changing the traditional concepts of work and pay [24]. Therefore, the challenge of changing the business model requires more flexibility in economics and commodity ownership (virtual and real). In general, these challenges can be summarized as follows:

- Unclear technological boundaries and a clear program framework.
- Poor IT infrastructure.
- Not spending financial resources and spending to analyze the market and improve the current situation.
- Uncertainty about financial benefits and lack of specialized knowledge [24].

In order to be successful and achieve their goals, organizations must identify the existing challenges and find solutions to address them. Failure to remove the barriers will certainly delay the continuation of the status quo and digital development and the promotion of the industry to a higher level.

4.3 Application of Artificial Intelligence in Supply Chain Demand Forecasting

The supply chain is a dynamic structure of the constant flow of information, product, and capital between different stages In this structure, demand forecasting plays the most important role. Demand forecasting is at the core of inventory management, which determines whether a business is profitable or not, as well as optimizing it. High accuracy in forecasting leads to increased profits, better product design, reduced losses, waste, etc. With the growth of different types of businesses and the variety of stores that affect demand, as well as increasing competition, the importance of forecasting demand has increased more than ever [25].

In recent years, we have seen great advances in machine learning methods. Technological advances and data enhancement have increased the popularity of using these methods. Speed in calculation, high accuracy, and online analysis are some of the features that increase the desire to use these methods. With previous demand data, we can easily use these methods. Since the factors affecting the demand are identifiable and there is a demand for different periods, with a mapping of these factors with the demand, we can make a good forecast with good accuracy [26].

This procedure helps to integrate and streamline all elements of the supply chain. Since information is an important flow between the pillars of the supply chain, more accurate forecasting leads to improved information quality and ultimately better supply chain performance as well as reducing the whipping effect [27].

The customer first places an order with the retailer and orders the retailer to the wholesaler and the wholesaler to the distributor as shown in the figure below. Eventually, the distributor orders the manufacturer and the chain is formed. Demand forecast analysis is very valuable for all stages of the chain because fluctuations in the difference between actual demand and projected demand will lead to a whipping effect [28, 29]. The more accurately forecasting customer demand, the more avoiding larger fluctuations in the future planning, and this shows the importance of more accurate forecasting of customer demand. An example of the supply chain structure studied is presented in Figure 4.3.

In the research that has been done so far on demand forecasting, no expert opinion has been applied and the research has relied only on data and forecasting methods. In the proposed process of this research, after predicting the demand, its value is entered into a mathematical model based on expert opinion. This model seeks to minimize the costs of forecasting error and can reduce the supply chain by reducing and counteracting

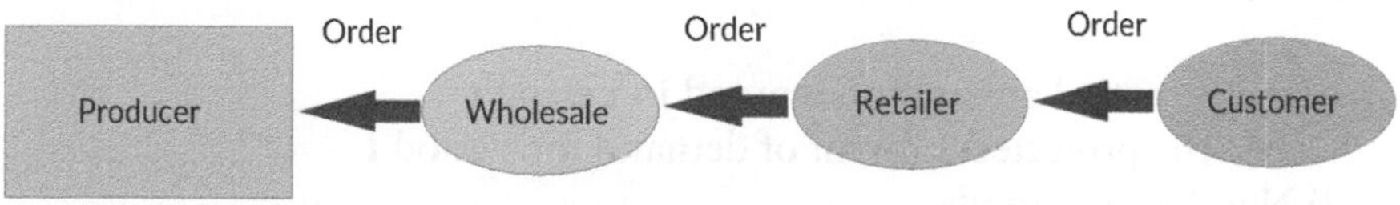

Figure 4.3 The general structure of the studded supply chain.

the error. To decide for this process, a cycle consisting of predicting method selection with the least squares of error and applying expert opinion is constantly repeated.

4.4 Proposed Approach

In this proposed approach, first, the demand data for previous periods are collected and set into the database and measure the relationship between each feature and the amount of demand. Next, the database is divided into two parts: training and test in a completely random way. The training section is used to map a predictor and the test section to calculate the accuracy of the forecast, which prevents the predictor from overfitting.

To apply this proposed approach, a continuous comparison of the machine learning method and traditional method is used. In this way, the regression method is more suitable than machine learning, which is more appropriate compared to other methods such as neural network, support vector regression, etc., and the time series method, which is average compared to other traditional methods such as fashion, and naive prediction has less error. The experimental data set is implemented, then the best method for prediction is selected using the mean squared error (MSE).

4.4.1 Mathematical Model

The expert or manager determines two fixed values to control demand based on knowledge of the situation, environmental feedback, and seasonal decrease and increase in demand. The first value is the constant value of *fce*. This value indicates how much it will cost the organization on average per unit difference between the actual value and the projected value. This means that if the projected amount is higher than the actual amount, we will have a cost for perishable materials and maintenance costs, and conversely, if the projected amount is less than the actual amount, the cost There will be unmet demand. Another constant value is $e(t)$, which means that in the t period, what is the maximum allowable difference between the actual value and the predicted value? This number indicates the measures taken in period t to maintain, store or cover excess demand.

$y(t)$: The actual amount of demand in period t
$yp(t)$: The projected amount of demand for period t
T: Number of periods

fce: The fixed cost amount that the expert determines for each unit of the difference between actual and projected demand (lost sales, warehousing, perishable materials, etc.).

e (t): The maximum amount of forecast and actual difference allowed for the period to be determined by the expert (or management). It refers to the projected capacity to control fluctuations and differences.

$$Min \sum_{t=1}^{T} | y(t) - yp(t) | * fce$$

$$st:$$

$$| y(t) - yp(t) | < e(t)$$

$$y(t), yp(t), e(t) > 0$$

If there is no limit in a period, two main cases will be considered:

- The first case is when the effect of one or more attributes on the target value is more or less.
- The second case is one in which there are attributes or attributes that are not considered in the database but affect the value of the target. Such as environmental or economic characteristics that may have affected the amount of the target.

Of course, these two cases are when the expert is well aware of the factors and parameters affecting the demand and also, has determined the fixed values well. The process is generally shown in Figure 4.4.

4.4.2 Advantages of the Proposed Model

One of the main advantages of this model is that it does not rely solely on data and demand forecasting methods, but also includes expert control and monitoring, which reduces forecasting error and thus reduces related costs. Supplied with an error along the chain. Moreover, considering that this model takes into account the control limits (*e (t)*) for the difference between the actual demand and the forecast, it reduces the costs related to the shortage or corruption of surplus materials.

In addition, the simultaneous use of time-series methods and artificial intelligence methods helps to make predictions in a short time when the

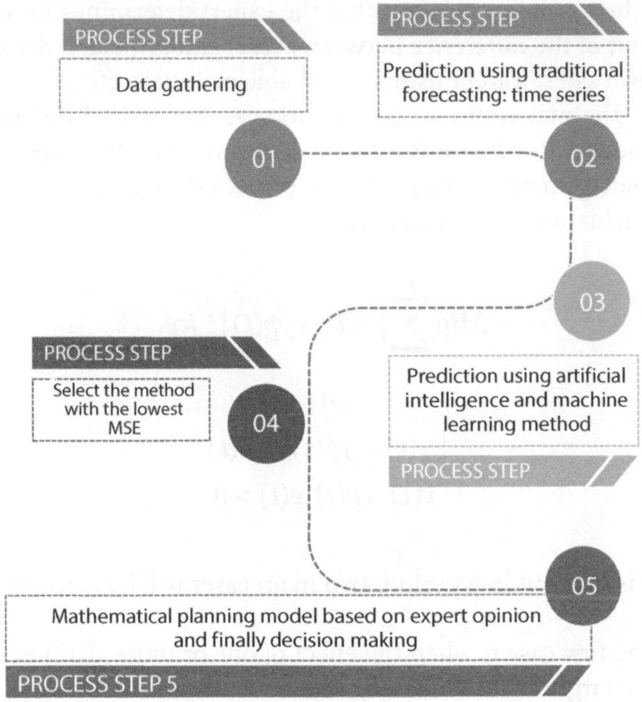

Figure 4.4 The proposed steps of forecasting supply chain demand.

data behavior is simple. In some cases, time-series methods with very little error may provide the desired prediction. In such cases, the problem is easily solved and the desired prediction can be provided in a short time.

4.5 Discussion and Conclusion

In this article, an attempt was made to review the fourth industry. Since entering the fourth industry, we are witnessing extensive changes. We should always pay special attention to it and make the most of the new opportunities that arise.

The FIR is an emerging reality that will lead to many changes in various economic, social, educational, etc. in the future. Digitization and Digitalization are essential and the future and the industry will inevitably lead to it. In such a revolution, the Internet, big data, in other words, information systems, play a key role in economic regeneration. The use of technologies based on the FIR helps us to improve performance in terms of financial, cost, and quality dimensions and achieve a competitive advantage.

In the FIR, we seek to digitize the entire supply chain. This is an opportunity for all walks of life and organizations in the sense that all elements of the business can interact in a digital context. Supply chains should take full advantage of the benefits of flexibility, raising quality standards, increasing efficiency, productivity, etc.

On the other hand, since fluctuations between projected demand and actual demand are the most important factor in creating a whipping effect, accurate demand forecasting is one of the most important factors in the supply chain. Moreover, high accuracy in forecasting leads to increased profits, better product design, reduced costs due to losses and waste, and so on. As a result, given the competitive environment in today's market, forecasting demand as accurately as possible is one of the main concerns of managers.

In this regard, this paper presented a process for better forecasting supply chain demand. This process leads to increased accuracy of prediction, because the use of expert opinion causes, in addition to the analysis of past information, a knowledge that is only by the expert and by experience and taking into account all environmental factors. It can also be applied in forecasting, and this significantly improves the accuracy of the forecast.

This model seeks to minimize the costs that are imposed on the organization due to low-accuracy forecasting. These costs include maintenance costs, corruption of perishable materials, shortage costs, lost demand, etc.

References

1. Salkin, C., Oner, M., Ustundag, A., Cevikcan, E., A conceptual framework for Industry 4.0, in: *Industry 4.0: Managing the Digital Transformation*, pp. 3–23, Springer, Cham, 2018.
2. Qin, J., Liu, Y., Grosvenor, R., A categorical framework of manufacturing for industry 4.0 and beyond. *Proc. CIRP*, 52, 173–178, 2016.
3. Alexopoulos, K., Makris, S., Xanthakis, V., Sipsas, K., Chryssolouris, G., A concept for context-aware computing in manufacturing: The white goods case. *Int. J. Comput. Integr. Manuf.*, 29, 8, 839–849, 2016.
4. Hofmann, E. and Rüsch, M., Industry 4.0 and the current status as well as future prospects on logistics. *Comput. Ind.*, 89, 23–34, 2017.
5. Tjahjono, B., Esplugues, C., Ares, E., Pelaez, G., What does industry 4.0 mean to supply chain? *Proc. Manuf.*, 13, 1175–1182, 2017.
6. Coleman, D.C., Industrial growth and industrial revolutions. *Economica*, 23, 89, 1–22, 1956.
7. Vries, P., The industrial revolution, in: *Encyclopaedia of the Modern World*, vol. 4, pp. 158–161, 2008.

8. Stearns, P.N., *The Industrial Revolution in World History*, Westview Press, 2012.
9. Jazdi, N., Cyber physical systems in the context of industry 4.0, in: *2014 IEEE International Conference on Automation, Quality and Testing, Robotics*, IEEE, pp. 1–4, May 2014.
10. Wu, Y., *Achieving Supply Chain Agility*, Springer International Publishing, Harrison, 2019.
11. Stock, T. and Seliger, G., Opportunities of sustainable manufacturing in industry 4.0. *Proc. CIRP*, 40, 536–541, 2016.
12. Lasi, H., Fettke, P., Kemper, H.G., Feld, T., Hoffmann, M., Industry 4.0. *Bus. Inf. Syst. Eng.*, 6, 4, 239–242, 2014.
13. Brettel, M., Friederichsen, N., Keller, M., Rosenberg, M., How virtualization, decentralization and network building change the manufacturing landscape: An industry 4.0 perspective. FormaMente, 12, Germany, 2017.
14. Alicke, K., Rexhausen, D., Seyfert, A., Supply chain 4.0 in consumer goods. Mckinsey & Company, 1–11, 2017.
15. Swafford, P.M., Ghosh, S., Murthy, N., Achieving supply chain agility through IT integration and flexibility. *Int. J. Prod. Econ.*, 116, 2, 288–297, 2008.
16. Chiang, C.Y., Kocabasoglu-Hillmer, C., Suresh, N., An empirical investigation of the impact of strategic sourcing and flexibility on firm's supply chain agility. *Int. J. Oper. Prod. Manage.*, 32, 1, 49–78, 2012.
17. Popkova, E.G., Ragulina, Y.V., Bogoviz, A.V., Fundamental differences of transition to industry 4.0 from previous industrial revolutions, in: *Industry 4.0: Industrial Revolution of the 21st Century*, pp. 21–29, Springer, Cham, 2019.
18. Rüßmann, M., Lorenz, M., Gerbert, P., Waldner, M., Justus, J., Engel, P., Harnisch, M., *Industry 4.0: The Future of Productivity and Growth in Manufacturing Industries*, vol. 9, pp. 54–89, Boston Consulting Group, 2015.
19. Brunelli, J., Lukic, V., Milon, T., Tantardini, M., *Five Lessons from the Frontlines of Industry 4.0*, The Boston Consulting Group, Boston, MA, USA, 2017.
20. Pfohl, H.C., Yahsi, B., Kurnaz, T., The impact of Industry 4.0 on the supply chain, in: *Innovations and Strategies for Logistics and Supply Chains: Technologies, Business Models and Risk Management. Proceedings of the Hamburg International Conference of Logistics (HICL)*, vol. 20, EPubli GmbH, Berlin, pp. 31–58, 2015.
21. Kang, H.S., Lee, J.Y., Choi, S., Kim, H., Park, J.H., Son, J.Y., Do Noh, S., Smart manufacturing: Past research, present findings, and future directions. *Int. J. Precis. Eng. Manuf. Green Technol.*, 3, 1, 111–128, 2016.
22. Hamzeh, R., Zhong, R., Xu, X.W., A survey study on industry 4.0 for New Zealand manufacturing. *Proc. Manuf.*, 26, 49–57, 2018.
23. Paschou, T., Adrodegari, F., Rapaccini, M., Saccani, N., Perona, M., Towards Service 4.0: A new framework and research priorities. *Proc. CIRP*, 73, 148–154, 2018.

24. Schwab, K., *The Fourth Industrial Revolution*, Currency, 2017.
25. Zhou, H. and Benton Jr., W.C., Supply chain practice and information sharing. *J. Oper. Manage.*, 25, 6, 1348–1365, 2007.
26. Goli, A. and Davoodi, S.M.R., Coordination policy for production and delivery scheduling in the closed loop supply chain. *Prod. Eng.*, 12, 5, 621–631, 2018.
27. Goli, A., Zare, H.K., Tavakkoli-Moghaddam, R., Sadegheih, A., Multiobjective fuzzy mathematical model for a financially constrained closed-loop supply chain with labor employment. *Comput. Intell.*, 36, 1, 4–34, 2020.
28. Dejonckheere, J., Disney, S.M., Lambrecht, M.R., Towill, D.R., Measuring and avoiding the bullwhip effect: A control theoretic approach. *Eur. J. Oper. Res.*, 147, 3, 567–590, 2003.
29. Kilimci, Z.H., Akyuz, A.O., Uysal, M., Akyokus, S., Uysal, M.O., Atak Bulbul, B., Ekmis, M.A., An improved demand forecasting model using deep learning approach and proposed decision integration strategy for supply chain. *Complexity*, 1–15, 2019, 2019.

5

Integrating IoT and Deep Learning—The Driving Force of Industry 4.0

Muhammad Farrukh Shahid[1]*, Tariq Jamil Saifullah Khanzada[2] and Muhammad Hassan Tanveer[3]

[1]FAST-NUCES Karachi Pakistan, Mehran University of, Engineering and Technology, Jamshoro, Pakistan
[2]King Abdul Aziz University, Jeddah, Mecca, Kingdom of Saudi Arabia
[3]Kennesaw State University, Keenesaw, Georgia, USA

Abstract
Information and communication technology (ICT) has evolved significantly due to the developments and advancements in network systems. These days, users can avail various services and approach numerous applications on their mobile phones, revealing the perk of growth in the ICT field. Internet of Things (IoT) has emerged as a potential technology that aims to connect all the applications and fields to a single device or a network. More specifically, it is a network comprising several objects to facilitate communication and exchange of information. Devices in a CR-IoT network is equipped with cognitive capabilities to execute intelligent decision and efficiently use spectrum and network resources and adding more comfort to the people life. CR-IoT has revolutionized many fields, such as transport, healthcare, education, tourism, and many more, and at the same time, it is contributing significantly to the growth of the country's economy. We can perceive IoT as a future technology due to its numerous advantages and benefits. IoT-oriented network has been implemented in various fields, such as healthcare, education, transportation, and many more.

Deep learning (DL) has been evolving as a potential candidate in artificial intelligence (AI) technology. DL methods are more robust and powerful in extracting hidden features from the given data. While using DL models, we do not need to capture an attribute from the data because DL models exploit the complex pattern from the data and train the model. Hence, it is a data-driven approach that is more suitable for AI-related applications, such as self-driving cars, UAVs, and cognitive radios for 6G mobile communications. As an IoT network comprises several

**Corresponding author*: mfarrukh.shahid@nu.edu.pk

Jyotir Moy Chatterjee, Harish Garg and R. N. Thakur (eds.) A Roadmap for Enabling Industry 4.0 by Artificial Intelligence, (57–78) © 2023 Scrivener Publishing LLC

devices that generate a vast amount of data, therefore, it is essential to deploy and integrate deep learning methods into the IoT networks that exploit features from the data in an unsupervised fashion and train the model.

In this book chapter, we will present a brief introduction to IoT and deep learning models. Followed by this, we will describe in detail the deployment of deep learning methods into the IoT networks for industrial application. We have considered agriculture industry and discussed how to develop A-enable smart irrigation system to automate and revolutionize agriculture field. The chapter will also present how IoT and deep learning together will be reshaping the industry in the future.

Keywords: IoT, agriculture, deep learning, LSTM, smart irrigation, CR-IoT, artificial intelligence, UAV

5.1 Motivation and Background

Recent evolution in information and communication technologies invoked an emerging method to connect diverse objects in a network smartly, known as the Internet of Things (IoT). Such a network contains various devices to furnish ubiquitous connectivity and grant access to end-users for multifold applications. In IoT, several things present around us, and such items include tablets, sensors, smart phones, laptops, wireless headphones, smart watches, and other intelligent devices. IoT objects are empowered with mighty data processing potency and use several communication protocols to avail any service by using ideally any available link [1]. IoT is a rising and emerging network that influences a plethora of domains, such as healthcare, smart cities, home automation, industrial process, intelligent transportation, and many more. From a fundamental point of view, IoT connects everything to the Internet in the world. Technically, the "Internet of Things" can be explained as things or object connected to the Internet in time than people [2]. More comprehensively, IoT can be perceived as a network connecting various Internet-enabled devices and non–Internet-enabled objects. IoT can connect heat monitors, air conditioner, remote control, streetlights, cars, motorbikes, cycles, kitchen appliances, and virtually anything to the network, as shown in Figure 5.1. IoT has been evolving, and more smart devices will become part of the IoT network forthwith. More formally, IoT can be defined as [3].

The blanket of connected items or objects operating in a smart environment using autonomous links to communicate intelligently within environmental, social, and user contexts.

IoT has been evolving and, more smart devices will become part of the IoT network soon. And in the future, IoT will facilitate every field of life. The proliferation of IoT technology in the market is summarized as follows,

Figure 5.1 IoT—A network that connects everything to a single device and facilitating industry.

a) The number of connected devices/objects will reach approximately 10×10^9 by 2020, whereas in 2018, 7×10^9 devices were connected to the Internet.
b) According to Gartner, 14×10^9 devices will be connected in 2019, and by 2021, this connection will reach up to 25×10^9.
c) The smartphones are the integral component in the IoT network, and according to Newzoo, 3×10^9 smartphones were connected to the network in 2018.
d) Most of the devices are being used in the IoT network at home, and such devices are connected to wireless personal area networks (WPAN), such as Bluetooth, Zigbee.

There are myriad enabling technologies that have greased the implementation of IoT network in numerous applications such as clouding computing, wireless sensor network (WSN), wireless sensor and actuator networks (WSAN), and machine to machine (M2M) networks. Primarily, cloud computing provides the user with on-demand services such as ubiquitous access, resource pooling, and service provision [4]. It is foreseen that IoT functionalities will be brought by cloud-based IoT into the cloud servers, whereas the IoT-centric cloud will import cloud functionalities into IoT. WSN has been identified as a potential candidate for IoT networks over the few decades; particularly, IEEE 802.15.4, which supports low power and less bit rate, is widely deployed in WSN networks to connect tiny sensors. M2M communication has recently gained the popularity

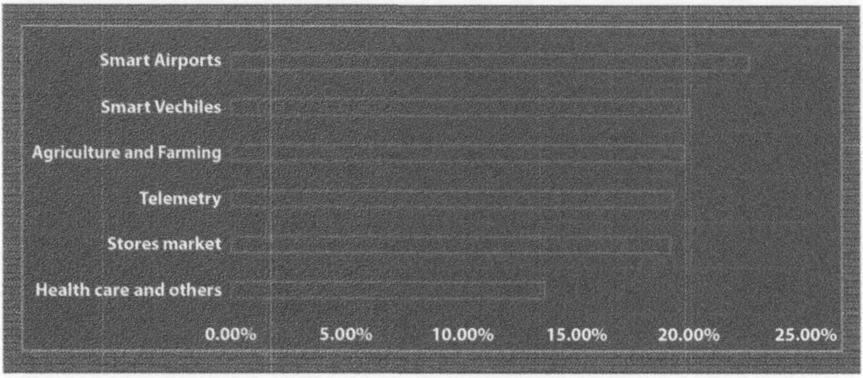

Figure 5.2 IoT growth in certain applications in certain applications [7].

that provides ubiquitous connections among devices and enables devices to interact without human interaction [5]. IoT network comprises several objects, which autonomously operate and adapt to changes according to the network requirements. Consequently, M2M technology has been the most relevant and vital option for IoT networks. IoT is supposed to be a single global network; nonetheless, IoT comprises multiple independent and complementary networks in various disciplines, such as home automation, transportation, industrial processes, and health care. IoT has penetrated many particle applications and has become an integral part of many technologies [6]. Such applications include smart cities, environment control, industrial process, home appliances, and healthcare. In smart cities, IoT potential use includes parking slot management, indoor localization, traffic light management, and crowd movement analysis. In contrast, IoT in environment control covers smart farming, air quality monitoring, and much more. Radiofrequency identification (RFID)-based object tagging is one of the main applications of IoT in the industry. Fitness tracking, health monitoring, and baby monitoring come under the IoT application for healthcare. The most exciting forms of IoT exist in a home for controlling temperature, open/close doors, etc. Figure 5.2 shows IoT growth in certain applications [7].

5.2 Bringing Intelligence Into IoT Devices

IoT network comprises various devices to furnish ubiquitous connectivity and grant access for the multifold applications to the end-users. IoT-oriented mesh expedites the substantial connectivity of billions of devices.

In this regard, connectivity among IoT devices in a network can be hastened through wired or wireless technologies, wherein the wireless method is a more befitting and feasible solution for the connections among devices due to the heterogeneous nature of the IoT network. However, furnishing wireless connection among devices in IoT is simply not adequate due to the following reasons [8, 9]:

a) Wireless connections endure from channel congestion sequel as there remains a chance of spectrum under-utilization by the devices. Studies have revealed that the spectrum is not exploited by the legitimate user most of the time and remains unoccupied. In a nutshell, the wireless network meets spectrum management issues.
b) IoT network is vulnerable to vicious attacks during the transmission that causes disruption to the communication and eventually deteriorates the overall network performance.

Thereupon, it is imperative to acquaint the capability to learn, think, and action into the IoT devices. Hence, unfolding a new paradigm, named CR-IoT network. CR-IoT empowers the existing IoT with a *brain* for high-state intelligence as shown in Figure 5.3. Invoking AI endowments into the CR-IoT system eventually settle the problem of spectrum underutilization wherein devices equipped with a level of intelligence can efficiently utilize the available channels and manage the spectrum.

Moreover, AI introduces a level of self-awareness (SA) into the CR-IoT network, which ensures devices are not only aware of their own state but their operating environment as well. Accordingly, when intimidating signals appear in a system, devices will automatically detect such abnormal

Figure 5.3 Introducing intelligence into IoT devices.

behavior, combat such attacks, and learn a new model to avoid such an experience. CR-IoT devices generate a large volume of data. AI methods act as a catalyst that extracts useful information from that raw data and executes the intelligent decision based on the information encoded in the data. We can formally defined CR-IoT network as,

CR-IoT comprises objects that are seamlessly connected and interlinked in a network with less or no external intervention. According to the CR cognitive cycle, such devices equipped with cognitive capabilities learn, interact, and perform several tasks.

Hence, CR-IoT networks are self-organized, self-configured, and self-adaptive due to the AI techniques that yield consciousness into the devices.

5.3 The Foundation of CR-IoT Network

CR-IoT has revamped the digital world by linking a plethora of technologies to bring comfort to life. Nowadays, people can access various applications on their smartphones and avail many services at any time, no matter where they are. Incontestably, cognitive radio has paved the way for robustness, cognition, and level of awareness to the IoT network. The significance of incorporating cognition capabilities into IoT devices is inevitable, as mentioned in the precedent section 2. The term Cognitive Radio was devised in 1991 by Miotal and Maguire [10] to sketch the concept of intelligent radios capable of learning, reasoning, and acclimating to the environment.

An essential feature of CR is the mastery of self-programming and autonomous learning. According to Haykin [11], CR radio meliorates spectrum utilization by using brain-empower devices to achieve fundamentally two objectives: 1) Efficient exploitation of spectrum. 2) Reliable communication. We can formally define CR as,

Intelligent radio that continuously learns the operating environment, tune parameters (modulation order, power level, coding schemes), and adapts the best transmission strategy to pursue smooth communication while effectively utilizing the radio spectrum

The preeminent driving force to bring the CR into existence comes from the escalated demand of data rates by the users to avail of different services such as Long-Term Evolution (LTE), 5G network, Wi-Fi, Bluetooth, Local Area Network (WLAN). Moreover, at the same time, new wireless technologies are being developed. As a result, the radio spectrum has become clogged and overcrowded.

However, the spectrum measurements have revealed that a major portion of the spectrum is not exploited most of the time and cannot be accessed by other unlicensed users. Spectrum allocated to the licensed user is never exploited by that user at its full extent. Therefore, one way to prevail over such a problem is to build the radio intelligent and awake enough to sense the spectrum proactively and access the vacant band when a licensed user is not conducting transmission in the frequency band inside a spectrum and grant empty channels to the secondary users. Cognitive radio (CR) is one of the emerging wireless communication technologies that intelligently boots the spectral efficiency by allocating vacant spaces (also called spectrum holes) in the spectrum to the secondary user when a legitimate user is not using the spectrum. Cognitive Radio (CR) is one of the emerging wireless communication technologies that intelligently boots the spectral efficiency by allocating vacant spaces (also called spectrum holes) in the spectrum to the secondary user when a legitimate user is not using the spectrum.

5.3.1 Various AI Technique in CR-IoT Network

Various AI techniques have been proposed and implemented to achieve awareness, learning, and CR's reasoning functionalities. These AI techniques can be divided in to following categories according to the specific application and objectives.

5.3.2 Artificial Neural Network (ANN)

ANN is a parallel computing-structure comprised of nonlinear functions with the tunable parameters to achieve a target output. ANN consists of several artificial neurons called $Perceptrons$, developed in the early 1950s by the scientist Frank Rosenblat, inspired by the work of neurophysiologist W.Mccollach in 1943. ANN consists of neurons interconnected and organized at different layers to perform specific tasks (such as prediction or classifications) in a network. The most popular ANN networks for CR IoT networks are nonlinear perceptron networks (NPN) [12], radial basis functions network (RBFN) [13], and multilayer perceptron networks (MLP) [14].

ANNs are robust models that learn network dynamics and extract patterns, features, and configurations from the objects. ANNs are highly adaptive and can be trained at any time. Due to such flexible nature of ANN, they have been deployed into various CR-IoT applications. For instance, ANN model is used to hand off scheme in CR networks [15]. ANN has been deployed to accomplish spectrum sensing tasks for CR-IoT network [16]. Multidimensional spectrum sensing is presented for CR network using AI technique in Sriharipriya and Sanju [17]. Data-driven for quality improvements for spectrum sharing in CR-IoT network [18].

5.3.3 Metaheuristic Technique

A highly impenetrable and heterogeneous CR network contains search and optimization problems that involve complexities, such as large dimensionality, nonlinearity, group of mixed variables, and nonconvexity. Therefore, classical algorithms based on a mathematical formulation can either become ineffective or inapplicable. To endure such problems, optimization algorithms have been proposed that can find an approximate solution while learning and establishing the relationship between various components in a CR network. Such algorithms are called metaheuristics [19] introduced for the first time in 1986 [20]. Metaheuristics techniques (MT) do not explicitly provide the exact optimal solution of a problem; instead, it gives the near-optimal solution in a computationally efficient manner.

MT methods are implemented in the CR network, where finding an optimal solution with objective function aim to identify a set of rules that follow the training examples during learning. The overall objective is to find a hypothesis that maximizes the training example of the target concepts. MT methods, such as genetic algorithm (GA), tabu searching and ant colony optimization (ACO) have been very famous in CR-IoT network to achieve several tasks. Morabit *et al.* [21] describe spectrum allocation technique in CR network using genetic algorithm. ACO algorithm is implemented to achieve spectrum utilization and fairness in CR network [22], whereas in Zhao *et al.* [23], ACO is used to perform energy optimization in mobile IoT network [24] discuss task allocation strategies in CR-IoT network using ACO algorithm.

5.3.4 Rule-Based System

For a specific domain, rule-based systems (RBS) are implemented, which extract rules according to the applications and apply such rules to the decision-making process inside a system. RBS was introduced in early 1980 and comprised essentially two components, a rule base, an inference engine. The deployment of RBS in CR is quite tempting and obvious. Using RBS, a radio can instantly learn or deduce actions for a given input. The rule-based reasoning (RBR) system is designed and analyzed based on cognitive engine (CE) for wireless rural area network applications. RBR CE has been implemented and evaluated for cognitive radio networks [11].

5.3.5 Ontology-Based System

In the AI field, OBS has been used since the 1980s. OBS system provides "format" and "explicit" depiction of a set of conceptions in a domain [11]. It is used to reason about the attributes of the domain of interest. Following essential components constitute an OBS system 1) classes 2) instances 3) attribute 4) relations. To facilitate machine processing, ontology language has developed. In CR, a radio based on OBS can logically deduce facts to understand the characteristics of itself and other radios in a network [25].

5.3.6 Probabilistic Models

Probabilistic models comprise statistical networks and have been implemented to analyse the complex dynamic behavior of random processes [26]. PM contains observable and hidden states of an inevitable process to characterize the occurrence of the observable states. Such a model can be deployed to recognized observation with similar attributes by selecting a model that will likely produce the observed sequence. Hence, PM can be implemented as an observation model in the CR network to achieve awareness and recognized received sequences. Wu *et al.* [27] describe variational Bayesian inference method to achieve spectrum sensing in a cooperative manner for cognitive radio networks. Bayesian estimator is deployed to perform sensing operation in CR network [28]. Spectrum sensing in CR is accomplished using HMM model is presented in [29].

5.4 The Principles of Deep Learning and Its Implementation in CR-IoT Network

The advancements in Machine Learning (ML) and Deep Learning (DL) have revolutionized the human lifestyle, including health care, transportation, education, and many more. The field of image processing, video processing, text and audio signal processing have been facilitated by the power of deep and machine learning models. There is a substitute difference between ML and DL models for a given application. ML techniques rely on feature extraction and selection before the model training phase.

Hence, we need to perform data pre-processing when dealing with the ML model to perform classification or prediction tasks. Whereas, in DL, prior feature extraction is not required as the model learns the complex pattern of the data and extracts the feature automatically during the training phase. DL model can learn end-to-end communication systems and perform excellent optimization tasks of the entire network. Convolutional Neural Network (CNN), Recurrent Neural Networks (RNNs), and Boltzmann are the popular DL models implemented in various applications and achieve remarkable performance. DL are complex convolutional neural networks (CNN). CNN is derived from single neural network that consists of several layers such convolutional, pooling and fully connected layers. A simple CNN architecture is shown in Figure 5.4. There has been a lot of work proposed and developed to perform radio signal classification by the researcher community. Kulin *et al.* [30] present end-to-end learning model for radio signal recognition. Signal identification for intelligent radios is demonstrated and discussed in the work of Dobre [31].

Zheng *et al.* [32] describes signal classification method for cooperative radio classification. According to the recent advancements and developments in the signal classification domain, classification techniques are categorized into the following categories as follows:

1) Maximum likelihood estimation (MLE): MLE techniques exploit statistical knowledge and properties of the received signal to perform estimation based on maximum-likelihood (ML) [33]. ML methods are quite complicated, but their

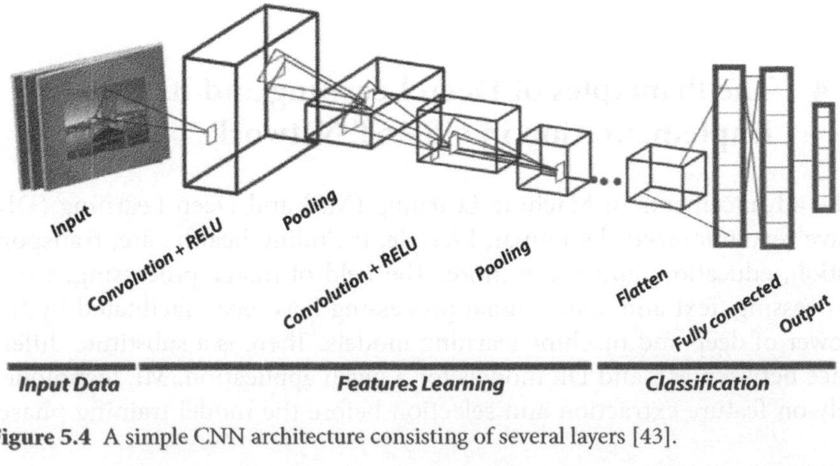

Figure 5.4 A simple CNN architecture consisting of several layers [43].

performance deteriorates in the dynamic radio environment [34].

2) Feature extraction-based techniques: Feature extraction methods capture relevant and noteworthy features from the signals of the radio spectrum. Such attributes of the signal include are as follows amplitude, phase, frequency, cyclo-stationary, and correlation coefficients. Such features are used to train the ML model for classification. Havryliuk *et al.* [35] presented a work that deploys wavelet transform and ANN classifier to track audio frequency in a network. In [36], cyclostationary features are used for Detection and classification of Quadrature Amplitude Modulation (QAM)/Orthogonal Frequency Division Multiplexing (OFDM) and OFDM/Off-set (OQAM) signals. In Satija *et al.* [34] modulation techniques have been classified using S-transform based features. Also, the comparison between different classifiers is presented under different range of signal-to-noise ratio (SNR).
3) Deep learning models: The DL model's capability has also mesmerized the performance of signal classification output, and a lot of researchers have developed revolutionary methods that demonstrate promising results. The inherent delicacy of the DL method is its ability to learn automatically features from the data. Li *et al.* [37] demonstrated deep learning model for modulations (FSK, PSK, ASK, MSK, QAM) identification. In Xie *et al.* [38], high-order cumulants are used to learn deep learning model to perform modulation recognition. Tang *et al.* [39] describes the method, which uses DL model Generative Adversarial Network (GAN) to automatically recognize modulation in cognitive radio network [40]. LSTM network is deployed as a deep learning model to perform wireless signals classification. Wang *et al.* [41] present data-driven approach which deploys CNN model for automatic modulation recognition in a CR. In [42] modulation classification is achieved using DL and signal constellation diagrams.

Deep learning methods can be deployed to classify legitimate and jammer signals in the CR-IoT network spectrum.

CR-IoT network deploying data-driven self-aware (SA) capabilities based on AI techniques will achieve next-generation wireless networks requirements and eradicate prevailing issues of the current wireless network (such as spectrum access and utilization challenges). These wireless networks generate, exchange, and communicate diverse data (text, images, and videos) in a massive quantity; therefore, it is essential to learn and discover the data transmission pattern to develop autonomous and intelligent systems. In this context, discriminative models have been very famous and made remarkable developments in computer vision and smart systems domains. Discriminative models (DM) facilitate to capture and discover hidden structure from the trove of data in an unsupervised fashion. However, DM becomes limited in a machine learning problem where direct learning a target is intractable. Moreover, DM models are not efficient in predicting out-of-samples.

For data-driven AI models with such an enormous amount of data in a network, the objective is to develop algorithms and build models to investigate and infer data in an unsupervised manner, this brings the need to implement a new class of models known as Generative Models (GM) [44]. GM models have been around for a long time and recently gained attention in data-driven SA based on AI applications. GM apprehends probability distribution from the input data samples and then samples from that probability distribution to generate output or target samples [45]. Such a generated output samples follow the input data samples closely.

DGM models have been implemented into robotics, speech recognition, and computer vision. GMs are good at exhibiting the following functionalities [44]:

1) Producing artificial yet realistic images.
2) Generating contents with predefined sentences and words.
3) Predicting and completing the missing or incomplete segments of data.
4) Capable of working with multimodal targets or outputs.
5) GMs can manipulate original images based on specific features. They can change the image events (image-to-image translation).

GMs have been classified into two classes:

A) **Energy-based models:** In an energy-based model, the energy function is deployed to define the joint probability functions. Boltzmann machines and deep belief networks are examples of energy-based models.

B) **Cost function model:** In this model, the cost function is used to define loss between input and generated samples. It includes models such as GANs and AE.

5.5 Realization of CR-IoT Network in Daily Life Examples

CR-IoT has been incorporated into a variety of applications.

In-Home

CR-IoT will be incorporated into home appliances to improve quality of life. Sensors will be deployed inside homes to perform home automation functions and home energy management. Smart fridge, smart meters, and smart lights are an example of intelligent home automation. For these examples, Wireless Fidelity (Wi-Fi) access points are usually installed, but this can cause severe Industrial Scientific and Medical (ISM) band interference. It is suggested to provide sensors with intelligent capabilities to alleviated deterrent in the ISM band.

Smart Cities

In cognitive cities, information, communication (ICT), and IoT are integrated to provide development in the cities. In smart cities, e-services to users are provided to enhance their lifestyle. To provide e-services, continuous connectivity is required. Moreover, data gathering, and user interaction are also important. Such data acquisition and gathering requirements can be facilitated by deploying cognitive capability in IoT.

In IoV technology, vehicle access control is obtained via power, communication, and embedded systems with less or no human intervention. The mobile vehicles use spectrum to support and facilitate IoV. Therefore, deploying CR functionalities into IoV will be an excellent solution to provide services on time.

Environmental Application

The temperature measurement, waste management, pollution monitoring, weather forecasting has been facilitated by deploying IoT network, and developments are being reported in this field. A heterogeneous network with several miniature devices is required to acquire such functionalities for environmental applications, and for such devices, static spectrum allocation is not viable. Therefore, IoT with cognitive capabilities is a plausible solution for environmental applications.

Health Care

In health care, temperature monitoring, fitness monitoring, heart rate status has been around, and people are using such application to keep themselves streamline with their health conditions. However, spectrum allocation for such applications is static and may become a challenge if a patient demands continuous monitoring of his/her health condition. Therefore, in health-care IoT, it is essential to deploy devices with cognitive capabilities and functionalities to access the spectrum whenever it is required.

Social activities

CR-IoT is quite famous in social activities such as autonomous transportation systems (ITS), which use multiple cognitive devices as a sensors on the road and in vehicles to monitor traffic and congestion on roads. In case of emergencies, Dedicated Short Range Communication (DSRC) with a channel bandwidth of 10 MHz is allocated, which can deliver small data over a short distance. Communication over longer distances requires the exchange of huge data, and DSRC won't be feasible. CR-IoT can eliminate this problem in a more efficient way. The traffic light management system is also supposed to incorporate cognitive capabilities in objects to perform a certain task related to traffic on the road.

5.6 AI-Enabled Agriculture and Smart Irrigation System—Case Study

IoT has also made a subtle impact on the agriculture and irrigation industry. Due to its potential, it has been possible to realize a fully automatic AI-enabled irrigation system. In an AI-enabled irrigation system, several tiny sensors, robots, UAVs, cloud servers, and databases form an adaptive and self-configure network to monitor and control the entire farming system from ploughing the seed till the crop gets ready and reaches to the market for sale. In this scenario, a farmer can get updates about soil quality, moisture level, humidity, and weather information on his ingenious devices. Moreover, in a fully automatic irrigation system, sensors sense the soil moisture, and if the moisture level is low, the system switches on water supply. In this perspective, many researchers and scientists are proposing methods to develop a sensor-based intelligent irrigation system using AI and deep learning models.

Figure 5.5 describes the considered scenario for developing an AI-enabled irrigation system. The network consists of several sensor nodes, a small base station (BS), cloud server, UAV (aerial monitoring),

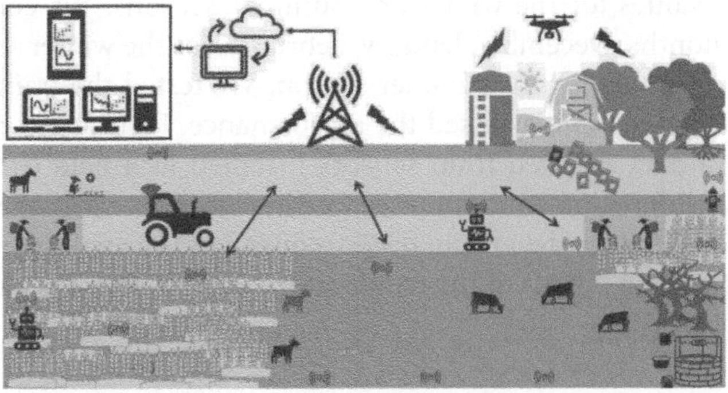

Figure 5.5 AI-enabled smart irrigation system.

sensor-equipped tractor, and mobile/PC. The sensors are buried in soil, installed in a tractor, and robots continuously sense the soil attributes such as moisture, humidity, and temperature. Both UAVs and robots continuously sense the weather and communicate weather information to the BS. BS, sensors, UAVs, and robots communicate and send information using long range wide area network (LORAWAN) communication technology. LORAWAN is a long-range and low-power system and is highly suitable for the IoT network due to its mobility, localization, and duplex communication mode. LORA also facilitates in providing contact RF coverage in suburban and rural areas.

We deploy LSTM deep learning model to perform prediction tasks. DL and ML have been popular in sequential data applications such as video data, text, written text, etc. To handle sequential data, Recurrent Neural Networks (RNN) is quite famous and produces promising results. However, RNN suffers from the vanishing gradient problem. LSTM has been introduced for sequential data to perform prediction tasks to resolve such issues. LSTM mitigates the issue of vanishing gradient. For a given input sequence x_t at time t, LSTM produces the output y_t using activation function f as [45],

$$u = f(W. [x_t; y_t] + b) \tag{5.1}$$

$$g^i = \sigma f(W_{gi} [x_t; y_t] + b_{gi}) \tag{5.2}$$

$$y_t = g^o \otimes f(c_t) \tag{5.3}$$

Hence, LSTM is trained on a data set containing temperature data obtained from sensors deployed in a farm field. To simplify the problem, we sensors values for the winter and summer seasons. We consider the following months, December, January, February, for the winter season, and May, June, and July for the summer season. We tested the trained model on the test data set and assessed the performance. Figures 5.6–5.11 show temperature data received from sensors installed in a field (refer Figure 5.5). We consider winter and summer weathers for this work. We have also analysed temperature data using time-frequency (TF) analysis and Figure 5.12 is depicting TF plots of the temperature data of both seasons (winter and summer).

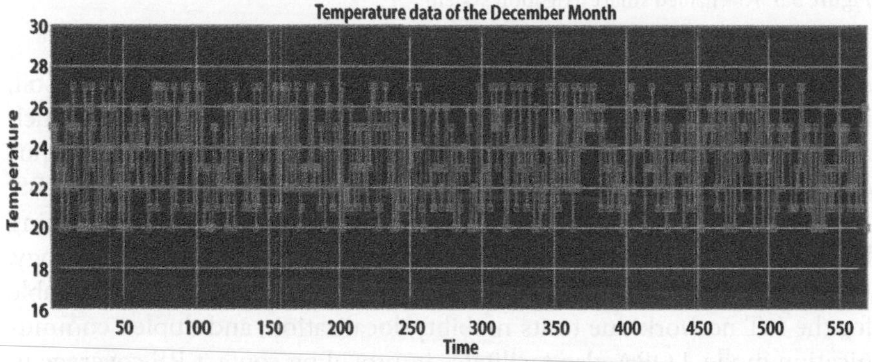

Figure 5.6 Temperature data of the December month received from sensors installed in a farm field.

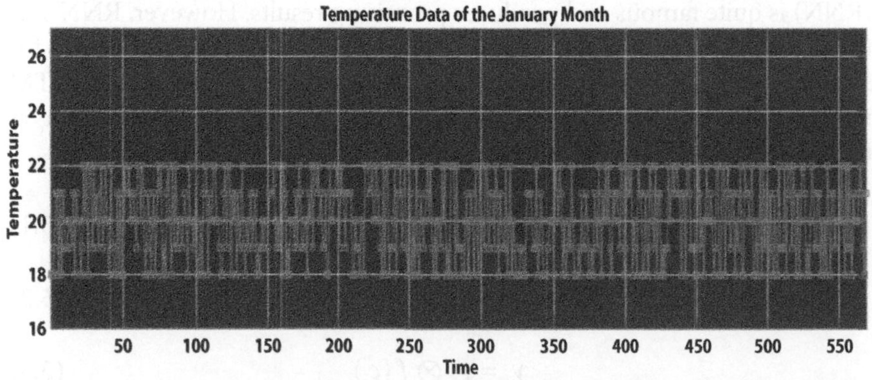

Figure 5.7 Temperature data of the January month received from sensors installed in a farm field.

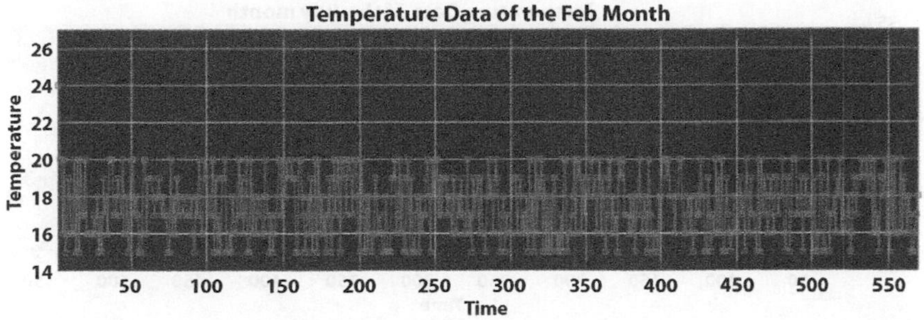

Figure 5.8 Temperature data of the February month received from sensors installed in a farm field.

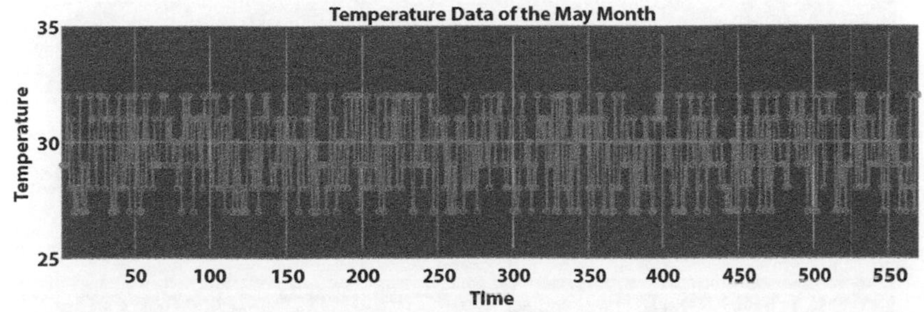

Figure 5.9 Temperature data of the May month received from sensors installed in a farm field.

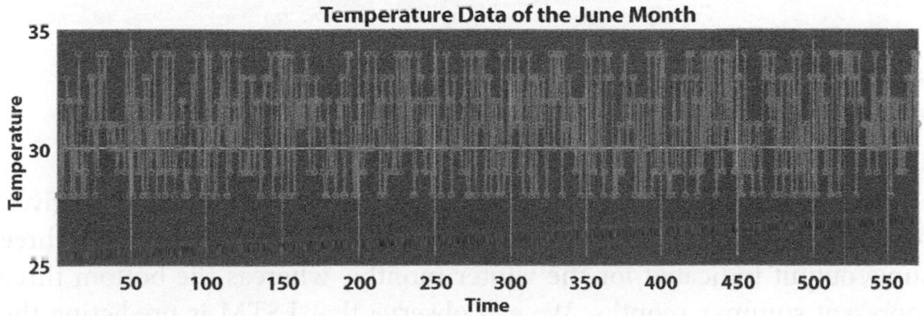

Figure 5.10 Temperature data of the June month received from sensors installed in a farm field.

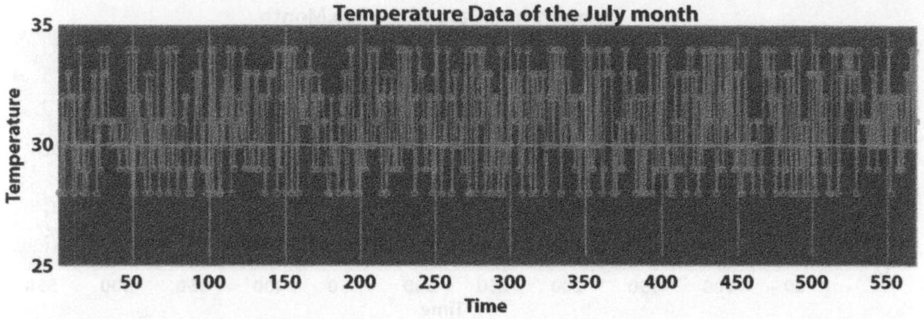

Figure 5.11 Temperature data of the July month received from sensors installed in a farm field.

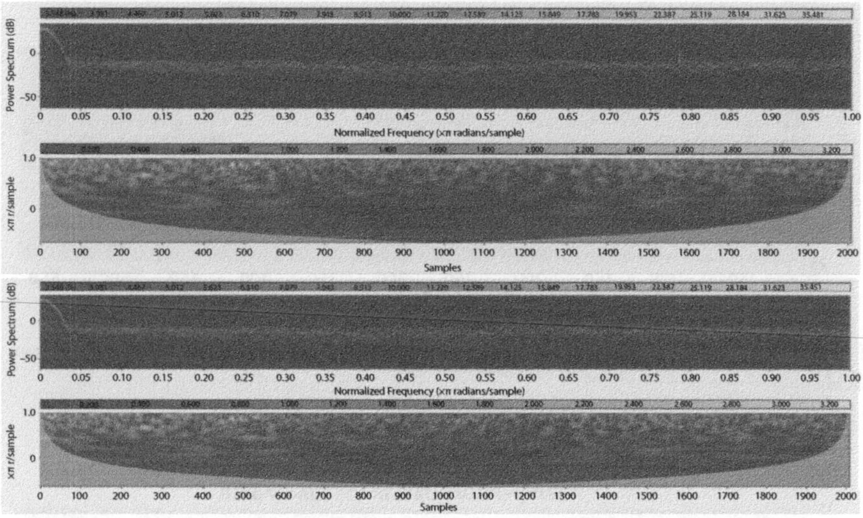

Figure 5.12 Time-Frequency analysis of the temperature data received from sensors installed in a farm field.

Figure 1.13 presents the predicted output by the trained LSTM on given temperature data for the months (December to July). The above top three show output indicated for the winter months, whereas the bottom three represent summer months. We can observe that LSTM is predicting the temperature data very well. Hence, the processing BS tower equipped with such an AI-driven model can perform temperature prediction based on the observed current temperature. Accordingly, high farming activities can be planned and executed. This approach is an intuition to realize AI-enabled intelligent irrigation systems.

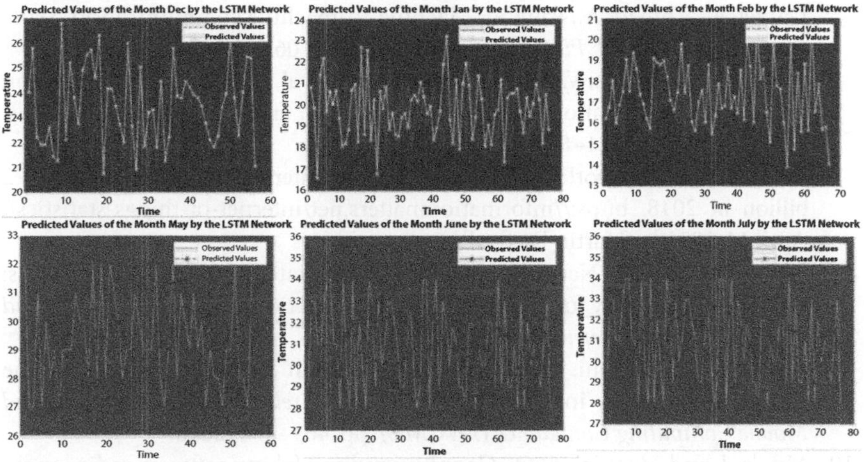

Figure 5.13 Predicted output by the LSTM network.

5.7 Conclusion

This chapter gives an overview of the CR-IoT network and the motivation for introducing cognitive capabilities into IoT objects. It provides deep learning and machine learning models details and discusses the famous generative models. This chapter provides a case study of the agriculture and irrigation industry and shows how the AI-enabled network can revolutionize agriculture. The chapter presents the integration of AI-enabled deep learning models in the industry to develop autonomous systems.

References

1. Ding, J., Nemati, M., Ranaweera, C., Choi, J., IoT connectivity technologies and applications: A survey. *IEEE Access*, 8, 67646–67673, 2020.
2. Saleem, Y., Crespi, N., Rehmani, M.H., Copeland, R., Internet of things aided smart grid: Technologies, architectures, applications, prototypes, and future research directions. *IEEE Access*, 7, 62962–63003, 2019.
3. Aijaz, A. and Aghvami, A.H., Cognitive machine-to-machine communications for internet-of-things: A protocol stack perspective. *IEEE Internet Things J.*, 2, 2, 103–112, 2015.
4. Biswas, A.R. and Giaffreda, R., Iot and cloud convergence: Opportunities and challenges, in: *2014 IEEE World Forum on Internet of Things (WF-IoT)*, pp. 375–376, 2014.

5. Daniel, A., Ahmad, A., Paul, A., Machine-to-machine communication-a survey and taxonomy. *J. Platform Technol.*, 2, 3–15, 06 2014.
6. Hassija, V., Chamola, V., Saxena, V., Jain, D., Goyal, P., Sikdar, B., A survey on iot security: Application areas, security threats, and solution architectures. *IEEE Access*, 7, 82721–82743, 2019.
7. IDC, Idc forecasts worldwide spending on the internet of things to reach 772 billion in 2018. https://informationmatters.net/internet-of-things-statistics/, April 14, 2021 by Martin De Saulles.
8. Saponara, S. and Neri, B., Mm-wave integrated wireless transceivers: Enabling technology for high bandwidth connections in IoT. *2015 IEEE 2nd World Forum on Internet of Things (WF-IoT)*, pp. 149–153, 2015.
9. Khan, A.A., Rehmani, M.H., Rachedi, A., When cognitive radio meets the internet of things?, in: *2016 International Wireless Communications and Mobile Computing Conference (IWCMC)*, pp. 469–474, 2016.
10. Mitola, J. and Maguire, G.Q., Cognitive radio: Making software radios more personal. *IEEE Pers. Commun.*, 6, 4, 13–18, 1999.
11. He, A., Bae, K.K., Newman, T.R., Gaeddert, J., Kim, K., Menon, R., Morales-Tirado, L., Neel, J., Zhao, Y., Reed, J.H., Tranter, W.H., A survey of artificial intelligence for cognitive radios. *IEEE Trans. Veh. Technol.*, 59, 4, 1578–1592, 2010.
12. Hu, H., Wang, Y., Song, J., Signal classification based on spectral correlation analysis and svm in cognitive radio, in: *22nd International Conference on Advanced Information Networking and Applications (AINA 2008)*, pp. 883–887, 2008.
13. Zhang, S., Hu, J., Bao, Z., Wu, J., Prediction of spectrum based on improved rbf neural network in cognitive radio, in: *2013 International Conference on Wireless Information Networks and Systems (WINSYS)*, pp. 1–5, 2013.
14. Xue, M., Wu, H., Zeng, Y., Multilayer perceptron for modulation recognition cognitive radio system, in: *2016 International Conference on Computer, Information and Telecommunication Systems (CITS)*, pp. 1–5, 2016.
15. Agarwal, V., Kumar, A., Kumar, D., Tripathi, P., Rajpoot, V., Tripathi, V.S., A novel ann based efficient proactive handoff scheme for cognitive radio network, in: *2019 International Conference on Computing, Power and Communication Technologies (GUCON)*, pp. 400–404, 2019.
16. Wu, Z., Luo, M., Yin, Z., Zhao, Y., Research of spectrum sensing based on ann algorithm, in: *2014 Fourth International Conference on Instrumentation and Measurement, Computer, Communication and Control*, pp. 493–496, 2014.
17. Sriharipriya, K.C. and Sanju, R., Artifical neural network based multi dimensional spectrum sensing in full duplex cognitive radio networks, in: *2017 International Conference on Computing Methodologies and Communication (ICCMC)*, pp. 307–312, 2017.
18. Li, X., Ding, H., Pan, M., Wang, J., Zhang, H., Fang, Y., Statistical qos provisioning over uncertain shared spectrums in cognitive iot networks: A

distributionally robust data-driven approach. *IEEE Trans. Veh. Technol.*, 68, 12, 12286–12300, 2019.

19. Blum, C. and Roli, A., Metaheuristics in combinatorial optimization: Overview and conceptual comparison. *ACM Comput. Surv.*, 35, 268–308, 01 2001.
20. Glover, F.W., Future paths for integer programming and links to artificial intelligence. *Comput. Oper. Res.*, 13, 533–549, 1986.
21. El Morabit, Y., Mrabti, F., Abarkan, E.H., Spectrum allocation using genetic algorithm in cognitive radio networks, in: *2015 Third International Workshop on RFID And Adaptive Wireless Sensor Networks (RAWSN)*, pp. 90–93, 2015.
22. Song, H., Bai, J., Yi, Y., Wu, J., Liu, L., Artificial intelligence enabled internet of things: Network architecture and spectrum access. *IEEE Comput. Intell. Mag.*, 15, 1, 44–51, 2020.
23. Zhao, H., Wang, J., Guan, X., Wang, Z., He, Y., Xie, H., Ant colony-based energy consumption optimization for mobile iot networks, in: *2019 International Conference on Internet of Things (iThings) and IEEE Green Computing and Communications (GreenCom) and IEEE Cyber, Physical and Social Computing (CPSCom) and IEEE Smart Data (SmartData)*, pp. 118–122, 2019.
24. Zannou, A., Boulaaam, A., Nfaoui, E.H., A task allocation in IoT using ant-colony optimization, in: *2019 International Conference on Intelligent Systems and Advanced Computing Sciences (ISACS)*, pp. 1–6, 2019.
25. Kokar, M.M. and Lechowicz, L., Language issues for cognitive radio. *Proc. IEEE*, 97, 4, 689–707, 2009.
26. Rabiner, L.R., A tutorial on hidden Markov models and selected applications in speech recognition. *Proc. IEEE*, 77, 2, 257–286, 1989.
27. Wu, M., Song, T., Shen, L., Jia, Z., Variational Bayesian inference based cooperative spectrum sensing in cognitive radio networks, in: *2014 IEEE 3rd Global Conference on Consumer Electronics (GCCE)*, pp. 108–109, 2014.
28. Tavares, C.H.A. and Abrao, T., Bayesian estimators for cooperative spectrum sensing in cognitive radio networks, in: *2017 IEEE URUCON*, pp. 1–4, 2017.
29. El Din, M.S., El-Tarhuni, M., Assaleh, K., Kiranyaz, S., An hmm-based spectrum access algorithm for cognitive radio systems, in: *2015 International Conference on Information and Communication Technology Research (ICTRC)*, pp. 116–119, 2015.
30. Kulin, M., Kazaz, T., Moerman, I., De Poorter, E., End-to-end learning from spectrum data: A deep learning approach for wireless signal identification in spectrum monitoring applications. *IEEE Access*, 6, 18484–18501, 2018.
31. Dobre, O.A., Signal identification for emerging intelligent radios: Classical problems and new challenges. *IEEE Instrum. Meas. Mag.*, 18, 2, 11–18, 2015.
32. Zheng, S., Chen, S., Yang, X., Deep learning for cooperative radio signal classification, arXiv: Signal Processing, 2019.
33. Boiteau, D. and Le Martret, C., A general maximum likelihood framework for modulation classification, in: *Proceedings of the 1998 IEEE International*

Conference on Acoustics, Speech and Signal Processing, ICASSP '98 (Cat. No.98CH36181), vol. 4, pp. 2165–2168, 1998.

34. Satija, U., Mohanty, M., Ramkumar, B., Automatic modulation classification using s-transform based features, in: *2015 2nd International Conference on Signal Processing and Integrated Networks (SPIN)*, pp. 708–712, 2015.
35. Havryliuk, V., Audio frequency track circuits monitoring based on wavelet transform and artificial neural network classifier, in: *2019 IEEE 2nd Ukraine Conference on Electrical and Computer Engineering (UKRCON)*, pp. 491–496, 2019.
36. Vukotic, S. and Vucic, D., Detection and clasiffication of ofdm/qam and ofdm/oqamnn signals based on cyclostationary features, in: *2015 23rd Telecommunications Forum Telfor (TELFOR)*, pp. 232–235, 2015.
37. Li, J., Qi, L., Lin, Y., Research on modulation identification of digital signals based on deep learning, in: *2016 IEEE International Conference on Electronic Information and Communication Technology (ICEICT)*, pp. 402–405, 2016.
38. Xie, W., Hu, S., Yu, C., Zhu, P., Peng, X., Ouyang, J., Deep learning in digital modulation recognition using high order cumulants. *IEEE Access*, 7, 63760–63766, 2019.
39. Tang, B., Tu, Y., Zhang, Z., Lin, Y., Digital signal modulation classification with data augmentation using generative adversarial nets in cognitive radio networks. *IEEE Access*, 6, 15713–15722, 2018.
40. Rajendran, S., Meert, W., Giustiniano, D., Lenders, V., Pollin, S., Deep learning models for wireless signal classification with distributed low-cost spectrum sensors. *IEEE Trans. Cogn. Commun. Netw.*, 4, 3, 433–445, 2018.
41. Wang, Y., Liu, M., Yang, J., Gui, G., Data-driven deep learning for automatic modulation recognition in cognitive radios. *IEEE Trans. Veh. Technol.*, 68, 4, 4074–4077, 2019.
42. Peng, W.P. and Ye, Z.H., Ofdm blending modulation systems in practical cognitive radio application, in: *2011 4th International Congress on Image and Signal Processing*, vol. 4, pp. 2237–2240, 2011.
43. Amiruddin, B.P. and Abdul Kadir, R.E., Cnn architectures performance evaluation for image classification of mosquito in Indonesia, in: *2020 International Seminar on Intelligent Technology and Its Applications (ISITIA)*, pp. 223–227, 2020.
44. Oussidi, A. and Elhassouny, A., Deep generative models: Survey, in: *2018 International Conference on Intelligent Systems and Computer Vision (ISCV)*, pp. 1–8, 2018.
45. Pulver, A. and Lyu, S., Lstm with working memory, in: *2017 International Joint Conference on Neural Networks (IJCNN)*, pp. 845–851, 2017.

6

A Systematic Review on Blockchain Security Technology and Big Data Employed in Cloud Environment

Mahendra Prasad Nath[1*], Sushree Bibhuprada B. Priyadarshini[1†], Debahuti Mishra[1‡] and Brojo Kishore Mishra[2§]

[1]Siksha 'O' Anusandhan Deemed to be University, Bhubaneswar, India
[2]GIET University, Gunupur, India

Abstract

Blockchain is fundamentally a dispersed database or collective archive of all transactions or digital events performed and shared between stakeholders. A number of service members in the centralized archive agree that each transaction can never be removed until the information has been reached. A sufficiently clear record of the trade has ever been established in the blockchain. The most widely recognized case of utilizing blockchain innovation is Bitcoin, the decentralized shared computerized cash. The computerized money bitcoin itself is profoundly dubious yet the hidden blockchain innovation gets performed perfectly and found a wide assortment of utilizations in both the budgetary and nonmonetary universes. The key hypothesis is that in the new online world, the blockchain gives an instrument to deliver a worldwide agreement. This causes taking part associations to know for making sure that through the advancement of an evident record in an open record, a computerized occasion has happened.

***Keywords*:** Authentication, bitcoin, blockchain, cloud computing, computer security

**Corresponding author*: mahendranath272@gmail.com
†*Corresponding author*: bimalabibhuprada@gmail.com
‡*Corresponding author*: debahutimishra@soa.ac.in
§*Corresponding author*: brojokishoremishra@gmail.com

Jyotir Moy Chatterjee, Harish Garg and R. N. Thakur (eds.) A Roadmap for Enabling Industry 4.0 by Artificial Intelligence, (79–110) © 2023 Scrivener Publishing LLC

6.1 Introduction

Blockchain is a completely new technology, and successful blockchain studies have been undertaken to ensure the safe and sound utilization of electronic money through conveying just among peers and without outsider intercession while getting a gander at those cloud computing specialized advances. A blockchain is the public transaction database, which prevents fraud during electronic cash transactions. As a kind of repository being transmitted and as a persistently expanding information file show, it is intended to deactivate abstract control by the dispersed friend administrator. Exchange records are encoded and controlled in computers running the blockchain program according to a statute. Bitcoin is a blockchain-based electronic currency as well as a network enhancement and encryption technology. The use of blockchain has better security compared with all data contained in a single database. The utilization of these advancements in Bitcoin's "mining" has been innovative data storage and management aspects can prevent harm from attacks on a database. In addition, because the blockchain has an attribute of openness, when applied to an environment that requires data disclosure, it can give straightforwardness in information. In view of these qualities, it can very well be used in a variety of fields, such as the budgetary segment and IoT applications to be developed [1–3].

By the definition of job validation practice, the blockchain finalizes an exchange record at a point where a person who gets Ecash produces a square by combining exchanges over the system. The hashing value made by checking it at that point and interacting with the past node. This block is revised regularly and dependent on the Ecash exchange points of interest to share the latest exchange block of information. This approach offers protection for Ecash transactions and enables the need for a secure network. What is more, cloud security and protection concerns that were tended to regarding center security components: secrecy, genuineness, and verification, get to control, and so forth [1].

Late years have seen the blast of enthusiasm for blockchain, and over a wide range of utilizations from digital currencies to ventures [3, 7]. The quick advancement in the selection of blockchain is troublesome innovation that is making ready for the up and coming age of monetary and modern assistance divisions. Undoubtedly, new research exercises on blockchain and its applications occur each day, affecting numerous parts of our lives, for example, land [3], fund [5], vitality [7], and taxpayer supported organizations [8, 9]. From the specialized point of view, blockchain is a disseminated record innovation that was right off the bat used to fill in as the open computerized record of digital currency.

Bitcoin [10–20] is normally used for financial exchanges. The blockchain is essentially a decentralized, unchanging and open database. The idea of blockchain depends on a distributed system engineering in which data exchange is not constrained by any single brought together substance. Both blockchain-organized entities are able to exchange in a chain of blocks efficiently. Blockchain utilizes accord systems and cryptography to approve the authenticity of information exchanges, which ensures opposition of connected squares against adjustments and changes [11]. Specifically, the blockchain innovation likewise brags the attractive attributes decentralization, responsibility, and security, which improve administration effectiveness and spare altogether operational expenses. Such remarkable properties advance the utilization of uses based on blockchain engineering lately.

On the opposite side, the unrest in the field of data and correspondence has made abundant chances for trend setting innovations, particularly IoT and Cloud computing. With various modern mechanical, shopping and business software and apps, IoT has transformed and changed our lives. The IoT is a standard arrangement of physical articles that can, by all-present electronic gadgets, be observed, managed or transmitted to improve overarching computing. IoT is commonly implemented in various mechanical systems, such as bright urban spaces, high-profile projects, medical facilities and agri-business.

Sadly, they typically delegate IoT application companies to the Cloud, which offers a world view on the cloud of things, because of a lack of memory, power and computing properties of IoT gadgets. The Information Cloud model provides infinite capability and manageability to IoT apps across cloud administrators. Besides, it gives an adaptable, hearty distributed computing condition, which permits dynamic information incorporation from a gigantic system of IoT gadgets, while demonstrating incredible possibilities to improve nature of client experience, framework execution and effectiveness of administrative conveyance [21–30].

In any case, the customary cloud computing frameworks will in general be incapable because of the accompanying difficulties. Ordinary cloud computing structures have relied, in general, on focused mail models where target cloud servers associate, identify and supervise IoT computers. With IoT networks becoming more common, so this model is unlikely to scale. Critically, this totally unified engineering likewise brings about bottleneck issues and solitary purposes of disappointments, which can prompt disturbances of the whole Cloud processing system [2]. Second, the majority of incorporated Cloud computing frameworks order confiding in an outsider, for example a cloud specialist co-op, for IoT information preparing, which raises information protection concerns.

In reality, the cloud cutoff will sincerely play out the IoT calculation, yet in the interim may get individual data without assent of clients, which prompts genuine data spillage and framework security issues, as needs to be done. Second, unlike conventional Cloud computing platforms, IoT users ignore data control. With recent Cloud computing plans, IoT proprietors have insignificant command over their own information and think that it is hard to monitor the trading of their information over the cloud IoT situations. Last, the brought together system foundation brings about higher correspondence inactivity and force utilization for IoT gadgets because of long information transmission, which ruins the enormous scope arrangements of cloud computing in commonsense situations.

With such basic difficulties, a brought together engineering is certifiably not a practical answer for a decentralized and dispersed cloud computing biological system with countless conveyed IoT sensors and gadgets. So as to accomplish a reasonable turn of events and long haul appropriation of cloud computing in different applications, fabricating a progressively decentralized biological system is viewed as a future bearing. The incorporated programming schemes with shut-in knowledge have been stepped up to perfect versions, which are typically found in existing implementations, and have half-unified cloud structures.

In any case, it is expected, with innovative block chain arrangements, that the community of people yet to come with IT creativity and the autonomous cloud IoT ideal models will be opened up. In these days, a transparent, stable and clear architecture has been developed to resolve fundamental problems of the ordinary frameworks and to accelerate up and future development in cloud computing. Cloud computing has been a promising breakthrough.

In this context, huge information is a term used to represent the extensive amount of ordered and unorganized information, which is too huge to handle using common database and timetable tactics. In current time of quick development of data advances, Big Data has become an advantage for some associations. Presently a-days, the fast development of industry impacts number of machines, procedures, and administrations for which a huge amount of information is required in the following future. In this association, Supply Chain plays a significant benefactor to Big Data. Due to its growing multifaceted nature, the flexible chain of the board needs additional arrangements. This problem cannot be addressed by existing arrangements and IT technologies. As the usage cases appear, structures that do not just give the enormous amount of data a unique treatment are now being created, but show how large-scale data insights can affect action plans. SC joins producing, coordination's, retail information, and so forth. In this association, to create dynamic for foreseeing the hazard in SC, the utilization of Big Data Analytics and met heuristic methodologies in gracefully chain is vital [25–28].

6.2 Overview of Blockchain

A blockchain is a framework that requires all participants to hold a record that holds all trade data and renew their records in order to secure straightforwardness when another exchange is occurring. Since advances in the Internet and cryptography have made it possible for all participants to track the genuineness of an exchange, the sole aim of departure is to rely on an approved outsider [1]. The blockchain is open to dealer Peer to peer utility and evacuates via p2p transactions without outside permission over the top compensation. Such an enormous number of individuals having the substitute data make it hard to hack, security costs are spared, exchanges are naturally acknowledged and enlisted through mass cooperation, and immediacy is guaranteed. In comparison, the programmer, using an open-source and open access to trade reports, will be conveniently executed, linked and expanded to allow companies clearly informed and expensive management. Blockchain basically involves the following:

a. The blockchain represents a normalized list that stores information in a way like an appropriated database, and is intended to make it difficult to self-assertively control as the blockchain is put away and checked by the system members.
b. Each square is a header and a body made out of a structure. The header contains going before and present square and nonce hash esteems. In the database, the square information is looked through utilizing the record technique. While the square does not contain the following square's hash esteem, it is additional as a norm.
c. As the hash esteems put away in each companion in the blocks are affected by past square qualities, distortion and change of enrolled information is troublesome.
d. While information change is conceivable if simultaneously 51% of companions are undermined, the situation of the assault is hypothetically very troublesome.

e. Fast, key-based authentication, and a decryptable hash function are also used in blockchain security.
f. The "Elliptic Curve Electronic Signature Algorithm" (ECDSA) [4], electronic marking calculation checks the computerized fingerprint provided throughout an individual transaction.
g. It is utilized to demonstrate that the exchange information has not been changed [7]. It is very odd to open access code, as record technology enables somebody to acknowledge who sent the amount to another partner. It also guarantees protection, given that it is completely difficult to find information related to the owner.
h. Hash work is used to see that exchange data is not modified and that the nonce possibility to find another position is identified, just as the validity of trading data is secured in the course of a bitcoin. Portion information can be checked in their authenticity through the open key-based encryption of the portion that the data's hash regards.
i. The hash estimate of each trade number can be accumulated by using the source key look. If the bitcoin data has been altered it makes it easier to pick [20].

Figure 6.1 represents the blockchain connection framework. There are many ongoing studies that use these features of blockchain to improve safety. The blockchain's most important area is security pertaining to the individual token used for encoding. An intruder attempts a "reuse attack" to hack the bitcoin and multiple assaults to put away the individual keys in the machine of a friend. The assailant will hack the bitcoin, in such a case that the aggressor can get the individual key, and the information will be spilled. Studies on the utilization of both equipment and programming protections are to approve exchanges that are in progress to illuminate this issue.

Bitcoin is entirely helpless against malware assault since it is frequently exchanged on gadgets that are generally utilized, viz., peers PCs or cell phones. Malware that enters through different manners, for instance, USB, poor security applications, or email must be recognized and managed considering the way that it can deteriorate a partner's PC. There is a developing requirement for security, especially with regards to exchange of the products utilized in games and the same number of them uses bitcoins. Work was also carried out into the detection and treatment of malware in the gaming ambience [30–36].

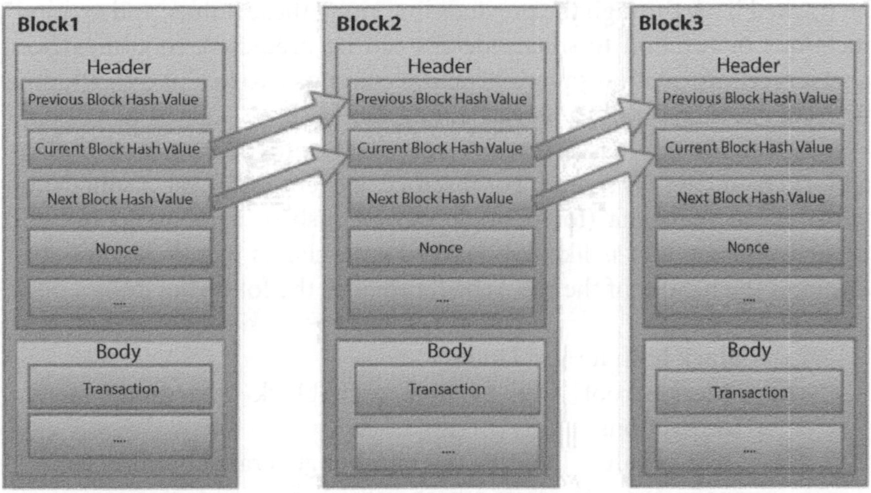

Figure 6.1 Blockchain connection framework.

One of the upsides of Bitcoin is that it is hectic to adulterate and change the record, since the transaction ledger is owned by so many peers. Since it takes the information reported in many records, hacking is for all intents and purposes unimaginable except if the gatecrasher expels and misrepresents 51% of the records in all things considered, despite the fact that specific records information is changed. In any case, there are questions about 51% of documents being corrupted and altered simultaneously while taking into account developing registering limit, and studies showing the middle confirmation strategy or plan of the check procedure to tackle the issue.

6.3 Components of Blockchain

Blockchain comprises several main components that are described as follows.

6.3.1 Data Block

Blockchain is a chain of squares, a direct structure that starts from a supposed beginning square and is linked to each new square. The block comprises multiple transactions and is connected to its immediately corresponding block by means of a hash mark. All of the blocks in the chain can be tracked back through the previous line along these points, and no modifications or rotation to square details can be predicted. In comparison, an average information square structure contains two key parts, including interchange records and a blockchain header [17].

In a "Merkle tree-based system" [12], a leaf centre is here sorted, where a blockchain client is shared. For instance, a client can make a solicitation with related metadata (for example moved cash or agreement) to build up an exchange that is likewise marked with clients private key for trust ensures. The header of the blockchain provides the following info:

(a) Block hash for validation
(b) "Merkle root" [19] to store each block of a group of transactions
(c) "Nonce value" [33] that is a number generated by consensus in order to create a hash value below the target complexity level.
(d) Timestamp that refers to the time of formation of the block.

An average blockchain structure can be viewed as Figure 6.2 of database which is shared and duplicated among the elements of a distributed system.

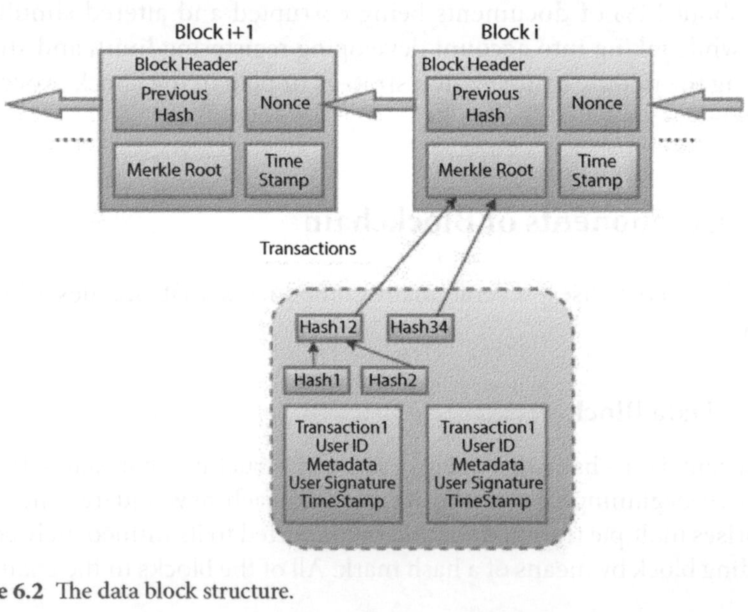

Figure 6.2 The data block structure.

The mutual database is accessible for all system members inside the blockchain environment. Disseminated record exchanges like the procedure of information trade among the individuals from the system. Members of the system can accomplish on the understanding by an accord instrument in a conveyed situation where no outsider is required to play out the exchange [16].

For instance, in the event that an individual joins the Bitcoin application, at that point he needs to comply with all standards and rules which are set up in the programming code of the Bitcoin application. It would directly share money or information with someone without a third party such as a financial institution. Each record has a consistent, time stamp-related cryptographically label, which makes the record permanent and auditable. In addition it also guarantees high decency amongst blockchain participants and enhances device stability through expelling the critical problem of power [20].

6.3.2 Smart Contracts

A shrewd agreement is a programmable application that sudden spikes in demand for a blockchain arrange. Since the principal shrewd agreement stage known as Ethereum [6] was discharged in 2015, and keen agreements have progressively gotten one of the most creative points in the blockchain region.

(a) When we speak about intelligent contracts, the obvious question is: What makes intelligent contracts so smart? This is due to their self-existence, which ensures that the code immediately applies the statutory rules set down in the arrangement until the conditions have been fulfilled [19, 20]. For instance, when an individual signs a shrewd agreement to move his assets, the assets will move naturally by themselves over the blockchain organized.

(b) At that point, data is registered as an interchange that is held as an unchanging record in the blockchain.

(c) Such an interpretation of oneself according to the code renders informed contracts unchangeable and unprotective of foreign assaults [10].

6.3.3 Consensus Algorithms

At the point when hubs begin to share or trade information on a blockchain stage, there is no unified gatherings to direct exchange rules and protect information against security dangers. In this respect, it is important to verify the trustworthiness of the block, keeping track of the data flow and ensure secure exchange of information to avoid fraud issues, such as double-spending attacks [8, 18]. The consent conventions referred to as an arrangement measurement will satisfy these necessities.

In the blockchain setting, an accord calculation is a procedure used to agree on solitary information obstruct among various temperamental hubs. A case of accord applications is in "Bitcoin blockchain" [11]. Bitcoin receives a "Proof of Work (PoW)" [10] calculation as an empowering agreement component run by diggers to guarantee security in an untrusted organize.

Programming on the excavator system uses its calculating assets to light up complicated numerical riddles. The principal digger illuminating the riddle is to make another square that will get an award as a consolation for future mining commitments. Notwithstanding, a basic downside of PoW is its high asset utilization which would be impractical later on. Accordingly, other effective agreement calculations show up as solid other options, for example, "Proof-of-stake (PoS)" [12], "Byzantine Faulty Tolerant (BFT)" [19]. Fantastic overviews may be cited by subtleties of applied highlights and the relevant special issues of such agreement measurements [20].

Bitcoin

The following are the features of bitcoin:

(i) Exchanges of money between peers with no focal power or a server are made using bitcoin as advanced currency.
(ii) Bitcoins are exchanged with distributed networks based on Peer to Peer, focusing on cryptology in the public key.
(iii) Bitcoin has been among the first cryptocurrencies implementations since 1998.
(iv) The information about the bitcoin trade is transmitted over the framework so it will, in general, be checked by all allies and along these lines is confined.
(v) There are the same blockchain for co-workers in the scheme.
(vi) The information on the exchange is put in hurdles close to the dissemination of the stockpile [12].

6.4 Safety Issues in Blockchain Technology

Blockchain innovation is realized or accepted as digital cash. Notice that separate security concerns in blockchain knowledge, trade, wallet and programming have been taken into account. The improvements made in security problems so far and the security standards of the current blockchain are discussed in this section. This endeavor is significant in the light of the fact that the outcomes will fill in as the reason for the formation of future blockchain innovation and the expansion of security [30–40].

a. Safety of Folder

The bitcoin tackle is a mysterious key hash gauge encoded with certain private and individual keys. The convincing material of a bitcoin trade can be opened thusly, with a limited time dress as yield. With the underlying substance making the worth set apart with the locale open access token and the individual access token. Bitcoin archive is used to process information on the individual key of the location to be used for the time of content launch. This means that data loss in the folder causes the loss of bitcoin as the data is central to the use of bitcoin. In this manner, the bitcoin wallet got the key target of bitcoin attack by hacking. This is done by following steps:

(i) Administrations have provided multi-signature for various marks to guarantee the security of the bitcoin wallet.
(ii) Since multi-signature can allow an exchange when there is more than one mark, it tends to be used as the wallet's excess security feature depending on the environment. For example, if the various marks are embedded in an online bitcoin wallet that the owner requires to be graved, considering the function of the online wallet website.
(iii) Subsequently, if the wallet performs a transaction, pernicious withdrawal of bitcoin may be avoided. In addition, multi-signature uses a two-factor authentication to proceed into organizations to separate equipments [15].
(iv) As the main response to hacking the attacks of a bitcoin wallet, wallets of form stockpiling are opened disengaged. For example, a physical bitcoin coin or a web-based paper bitcoin wallet.
(v) Practically identical approaches incorporate the Bitcoin wallets style gear to lessen the danger related to online trades. For instance, the hardware wallet, Trezor, stores the key in a deliberately fabricated PC-related limit

unit by means of USB, for example just when utilized and the stamped trade is moved to utilize the expelled inside the key and just when the client is confirmed.

In this connection, the force unit is related to the day's end just when there is a need to set up a bitcoin trade, most of the time staying in cool amassing like status [17].

b. Safety of Transaction

Because the material used in information sources and yields is a programming language with adaptability, use of this can be made with different exchange structures. A Bitcoin deal is an approach for applying bitcoin to the current affirmation and provide help related to money. A widely used scenario includes requiring the contract to use content that uses a particular collection of marks called multi-signatures. As the multifaceted complexity of the information increases, the likelihood of an incorrectly organized exchange has further increased. A bitcoin which uses an incorrectly arranged bolting data is depleted because no one can use it as the opening content cannot be produced. It is considered that models of contract-type Bitcoin exchanges are proposed to validate the accuracy of a material used in an exchange [13].

c. Blockchain Agreement

Since there can be just one blockchain, as it is the following connection of obstacles. A blockchain could be separated in two in terms of the unexpected formation of the two last squares where two incredible collaborators are able to simultaneously burrow up the sewer to supply it. For such a scenario, the square that most of the friends in the bitcoin network do not pick as the most recent square for holding extraction also get good for nothing. Finally, the bitcoin will follow most of friends who have half or additionally working capacity. In such a way, if an aggressor has 51% mining capacity, a "51% Attack," in which the attacker has blockchain control and people can intertwine traded off exchanges that be an issue [14].

As suggested by an inspection, an assailant with only 25% working ability will understand illicit addition through a malevolent mining method rather than 51%. Since the current working proficiency of the whole bitcoin framework is presently viewed as risky to be amazingly raising considerable capacity to work. However, mining pools have fairly been mining to increase the likelihood of mining, the relation of the mining peer. That hazard has become a concern, accordingly. Starting late, G. Hash, a primary mining pool, by chance outperformed the half edge, driving the bitcoin system to encounter inside and outside changes as per adjust to the liability. Specifically, the chance of controlling the blockchain is connected to the Bitcoin's incredible assurance and these security dangers have immediately influenced the monetary segments because of the qualities of the Cryptocurrency, which is firmly identified with the market cost for every circumstance [20].

d. Computer Security

The item bug utilized in bitcoin can be a straightforward one. Regardless of how all bitcoin systems are explicitly described by the authority "Bitcoin Developer Documentation" platform. The bit-coin based composing PC programs is so far persuading as the guide since the early bitcoin framework's point by point systems.

In any case, bit coin's center programming, which must be steadier than everything else, is as yet not liberated from breaking down programming like a bug. The most eminent security bug in August 2010 is the helplessness CVE-2010-5139. A wrong exchange whereby "0.5 bitcoin" was conveyed as "184 trillion bitcoin" was remembered for an ordinary square because of the bug brought about by number flood, and the issue was not fixed until "8 hour" later [9, 11].

Likewise, there has been where a square handled in adaptation 0.8 has not been prepared in rendition 0.7 in light of the fact that the database has been refreshed from BerkeleyDB to LevelDB as the bitcoin center variant has been overhauled from 0.7 up to 0.8. It enabled its Form "0.7" friends and "0.8" companion variant to have 6 h diverse blockchains. Both of these issues show that the general trust of a square in the security of bitcoin exchanges is basic over some stretch of time and can be undercut by a thing bug [20].

6.5 Usage of Big Data Framework in Dynamic Supply Chain System

As per "IEEE Standard 1471-2000" Architecture is the crucial association of a framework exemplified in its segments, their connections to one another and to the earth and the standards directing its structure and development [21, 22]. This section describes briefly a generalized large-scale architecture suggested by "Chan" in 2013 [21–35]. This architecture illustrates simply but extensively how many sections and their co-operations are viewed in a standard big data system. At this point, we are recommending an SCM knowledge analysis Big Data system and executives that can cope with the length, unpredictability and persistent need of a real SCM worldwide systems service as follows:

(i) In the customer side, the creator proposes a design that comprises of NoSQL databases, circulated document frameworks and a dispersed preparing structure.
(ii) In general, a NoSQL database is a nonsocial, non-SQL database. In any event, it maintains documents and deals productively for obsolete details in main estimation sessions, equivalent to a traditional social archive.
(iii) NoSQL databases are scalable and adaptable to shared systems, making them suitable for large database applications.
(iv) On the part of the company, underneath the NoSQL layer, "Chan [75]" suggests an adaptable disseminated record framework that is fit for dealing with an enormous volume of information, and an appropriated handling system that is liable for conveyance of calculations over huge server bunches.
(v) Hadoop is a database system that is incredibly common and can be placed in this framework. The two key components that allow the storing of enormous information indexes in the correct style across groups of PCs are (a) "Hadoop Distributed File System (HDFS)" and (b) "MapReduce" [35–40].

Although HDFS is a technology system that disseminates data records through a big bunch of servers, MapReduce is a suitable preparatory mechanism that logs the procedures under equivalent conditions of handling.

As suggested by "Chan [75]," server architecture requires equivalent registration stages that can handle a massive amount of information processing at a remarkably fast speed. Hadoop infrastructure involves consumer equipment and a software kit that is inaccurately linked to fill out the HDFS information processing center and MapReduce. Once preparation is complete, the customer loads input information in the group, submits MapReduce preparation of jobs and recovers the handled return from the server's group.

The HDFS hubs are fitted with the Name Nodes to manage the list of all records within the HDFS archive system. Therefore, again the MapReduce hubs consist of work trackers preparing tasks for slave hubs. In order to

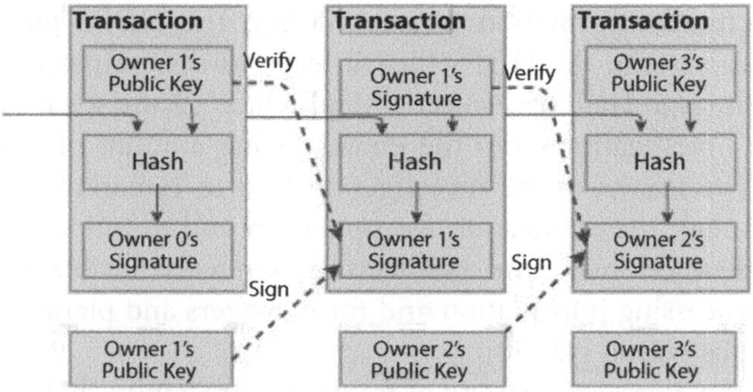

Figure 6.3 Represents the transaction in bitcoin.

decide the region of the data node containing the content, the "Job Tracker module identifies" the Name Node and re-legates the assignment to the "Job Tracker Module" residing to a specific hub at last performing the operation. Based on the HDFS guide, the "HBase" module facilitates fast record inquiries and upgrades [33–44]. Figure 6.3 displays transaction in case of bit coin.

"Chan [75]" addresses the Big Data system's client and server architecture. Applications architecture is suggested. This architecture complies with "BI&A Standard 3.0 (Business Intelligence and Analytics 3.0)." The features of big data investigation network are as follows:

- The Big Data investigation framework has the capacity to catch organized information through different information sources including OLTP frameworks, inheritance frameworks and outside frameworks.
- The crude information at that point goes through the "Extract Transform and Load (ETL)" process from the source frameworks to the information warehouse.
- The data dwelling on the information distribution center is utilized with "Business Intelligence (BI)" investigation apparatuses, for example, OLAP for upgrading business activities and choice procedures.
- Unstructured and semi-organized info information sources in Big Data frameworks can be of various sorts, for example, click streams, internet-based life, satellites, web logs, sensors, cell phones, machine-to-machine, geo spatial gadgets and so forth.

Unstructured information is stacked into the HDFS group. In the MapReduce system, the HDFS Bunch leads to disseminated knowledge planning through Hadoop Project. “MapReduce” is also ideal for carrying out major investigations into the embarrassing amount of unstructured material. The results of the investigation lead to remarkable knowledge gained through the application for operation and examination. “HDFS” and “MapReduce” make the architecture extremely flexible and efficient both for processing information and for managers and planning perspectives for information [43–50].

Due to the increasing variety of facets, the gracefully chained management demands new structures. This problem cannot be resolved by current structures and IT processes. In recent years there have been new developments in this direction. When the user cases emerge, frameworks have been developed which not only require a superior processing of enormous data steps, but also demonstrate how Big Data Analytics could influence action plans. This might also cause the Amazon Patent to implement new courses of action [35–49].

In this article, we proposed innovative work to provide answers to the versatility of interpretation of chain based on the order and intended benefits of the information source. The aim is to create Big Data environment for new action plans and new types of client support by different organizations from different companies. This will lead to an improvement in the multifaceted complexity of the SCM much more rapidly.

6.6 Machine Learning and Big Data

Machine learning is a technology that relies on extensive quantities of data for model building and accurate prediction. Two major forms of machine learning are: supervised machine learning and unsupervised machine learning. The tracked learning is focused on helpful information. “Classification” is the frequently used “supervised machine learning” feature but time consuming and costly manually labeling the data. It also used in IDS. Thus, the lack of adequate marked information is the primary bottleneck for regulated learning. Conversely, soloing separates important component data from unmarked information, making it much easier to obtain information on preparation. In any case, the location of the implementation of solo learning strategies is typically less than that of directed learning techniques.

6.6.1 Overview of Shallow Models

Essentially, the traditional AI models for IDS ("shallow models") are the "Artificial Neural Network (ANN)," "Support Vector Machine (SVM)," "K- Nearest Neighbor (KNN)," Native Bayes, "Logistic Regression (LR)," "Decision Tree," grouping, and joined and crossover strategies. A portion of these techniques have been read for a very long while, and their approach is full grown. They center around the location impact as well as on down to earth issues, e.g., identification productivity and information the executives [49–56].

6.6.1.1 Support Vector Machine (SVM)

The objective of the technology is to discover a maximum hyperplane of edge detachment in the n measurement region. Be that as it may, SVMs are delicate to clamor close the hyper plane. SVMs can take care of straight issues well. For nonlinear information, portion capacities are typically utilized. A workpiece maps the first space to another space in order to isolate the first nonlinear details. The part stunts between SVMs and other AI calculations are limitless. SVMs can satisfy outcomes even with little scope preparing sets on the grounds that the division hyperplane is resolved distinctly by few help vectors [50–55].

6.6.1.2 Artificial Neural Network (ANN)

The ANN is employed to explain how people's minds function. An ANN has a data layer, various covered layers, and a layer of output. The modulcs are completely connected in adjacent layers. An ANN consists of several units and may assume a theory of subjective force. It thus has a good fitting potential for nonlinear configurations, in particular. The planning of ANNs is boring because of the mind-boggling layout structure. The "Back Propagation Algorithms" [34], which cannot be used to construct deep-rooted systems, should be built in ANN models.

6.6.1.3 K-Nearest Neighbor (KNN)

It depends on abstract intuition. On the opposite, most of the neighbors of an example have a place in a related class; the example is more likely to have a place in the classroom. In this manner, the characterization result is just identified with the "top-k closest neighbors" [50–55]. In this connection, the limit k has an incredible effect on KNN models presentation. More puzzling is the littler k and greater is the risk that it will be fitted. At the other hand, the bigger k, the simpler the model is and the more fragile the suit.

6.6.1.4 *Clustering*

Such standards depend on bunching, i.e. gathering of exceptionally comparable information in similar bunches and gathering of less comparative information in various groups. Clustering is, unlike grouping, a form of unattended schooling. No earlier information or information are required for the grouping of calculations; along these lines, the prerequisites for informational indexes are relatively little.

6.6.1.5 *Decision Tree*

Data are classified using a number of rules in the decision tree algorithm. The prototype is like a plausible tree. The "Decision Tree Algorithm" will rule out unnecessary and redundant features automatically. Moreover, the cycle of learning involves the collection of roles, the generation of trees and tree cutting. The calculation autonomously chooses the most appropriate highlights, and when preparing a choice tree model, it make kids hubs from the root hub. Further, the tree of decision is a fundamental classification. There are several advanced algorithms, like the "random forest" and the "Extreme Gradient Increase (XGBoosts)" [48–55].

6.7 Advantages of Using Big Data for Supply Chain and Blockchain Systems

Large information is more helpful than numerous individuals completely figure it out. There are many aspects in which tremendous knowledge can be used to gracefully advance chains across other organizations. This is claimed to be true. Such seven agreements will allow any organization to see how tremendous knowledge will help make its chains more competitive and innovative, so that its primary concern can be created.

6.7.1 Replenishment Planning

We will find more goods, see stock prices, search the network and our inventory of your trading partners, among many others. We may longer allow and then see if any thing needs to be replenished and not reliant on automated refills that might not be required on the calendar. Alternatively, we should build a refill schedule that works for you and can do everything you like.

6.7.2 Optimizing Orders

Streamline the things we are requesting and the requesting procedure by and large. We can enhance the quantity of requests that are on schedule, limit the expense of getting things, and truly ensure that we have what you requested when we request it. This implies you can genuinely have the most ideal experience without stressing over it something will be on schedule or late.

6.7.3 Arranging and Organizing

The most critical aspect of any supply chain can be the structure and the preparation. We can lose or spend so much money on planning and planning and can really optimize this process with Big Data. Using big data to provide end-to-end insight and know where our things are at all times, also provides us a high degree of support for decisions which can be vital if a split-second decision is incorrect.

6.7.4 Enhanced Demand Structuring

Another plus is that we can forecast and really meet demand. We can forecast and decide with big data which products are needed for demand. We can perceive what things are selling admirably, what things did not sell well, thus substantially more creation it conceivable to renounce getting things that we may not wind up having the option to utilize or sell.

6.7.5 Real-Time Management of the Supply Chain

In real time, we will see our shipments and supply chain to ensure it everything goes according to plan. We do not need to stress over where things are, what they are doing or in the event that we have to make changes. Having the option to utilize huge information can have a tremendous effect and can assist you with keeping our things coming in when they should be instead of think about where things are and surmise in the event that they will show up on schedule. Today we are able to see where the goods are and verify the shipping status, making that a valuable resource for those who want to see the production process.

6.7.6 Enhanced Reaction

This ensures that you can foresee what is happening and decide more what things and purchase, what things to skip and what items to purchase. It is really useful and will also allow us to recognize the products to be used in the distribution network.

6.7.7 Planning and Growth of Inventories

This offers consumers a lot of leeway in terms of preparation, tracking and just optimizing their supplies so that they do not waste space or waste money on stuff they may need to operate. We are able to look at consumption rates and inventory levels throughout the networks and take account of other aspects of our supply chain, so you can ensure that we always have whatever we need. This is incredible for organizations that work with bigger measures of freight and have issue with accepting nearly nothing or to an extreme.

6.8 IoT-Enabled Blockchains

In order to create tamperproof archives of everyday transactions, IoT permits devices across the Internet to transfer data through private blockchain networks. In this case IBM Blockchain helps your business partners, but without the need for central control or supervision, to exchange and view IoT data with you. In order to avoid conflict and create trust among all authorized network partners, any transaction should be checked. Analysis of IoT security is done through five layers of security threats:

(i) Sensing layer security threats
(ii) Network layer safety issues
(iii) Middleware layer safety issues
(iv) Application layer gateways safety issues, and
(v) Application layer safety

Using IoT, the data gathered by once isolated and obscure sensors outside of the gadget is presently open for access and audit by others. Regarding computerization and logical information this opens up a few prospects. IoT's highlights can be reached out to family units, stores, distribution centers or entire urban communities. In a house, it can help control temperature, mugginess, and utilization of power, utilization of gas, amount of nourishment in the cooler, gatecrashers and so forth. In a shop, it can help to monitor the amount of customers in the store, what items they concentrate on and how much time they spend, the usual sum per customer, etc. It can help oversee creation and efficiency in an industrial facility. Figure 6.4 shows the big data frameworks analysis.

6.8.1 Securing IoT Applications by Utilizing Blockchain

IoT and Blockchain are revolutionary developments that would ultimately impact IT companies and correspondences businesses. Such two developments depend on upgrading the clients' general availability, permeability, comfort level, and certainty level. The IoT gadgets give sensor information progressively and blockchain gives the way to information insurance through a circulated, open, and shared record. The hidden idea of driving the blockchain is straightforward. It is a conveyed record (likewise alluded to as shared log documents). The blockchain passages are sequentially

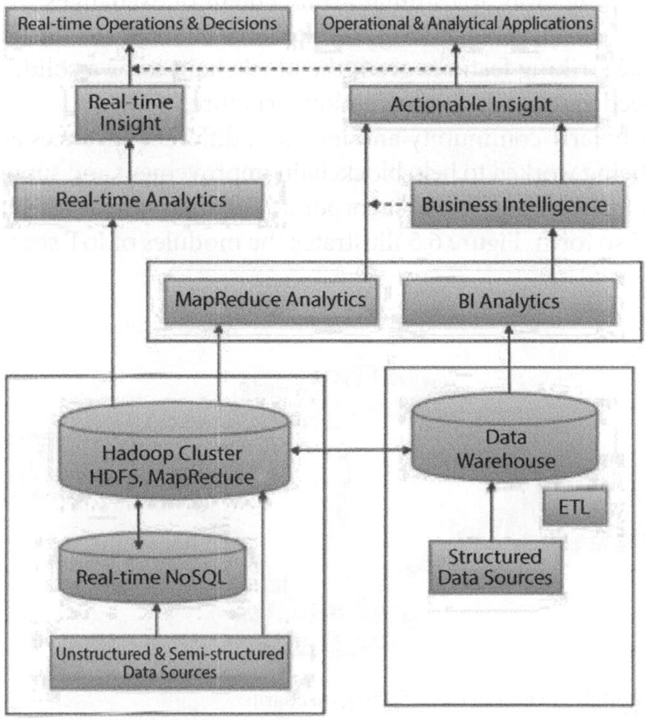

Figure 6.4 Chan's big data framework analysis.

stepped and time stamped. Utilizing cryptographic hash keys, each contribution to the record is firmly combined with the past section.

The individual exchanges are prepared with a Merkle tree, and the tree's root hash is handled in the blockchain. In the figure, speak to the individual exchanges in T1, T2, and T3 ... Tn. The exchanges are hashed and put away cryptographically on tree leaf hubs like Ha, Hb, Hc, etc. Kid hub hash is linked, and another root hash is framed. The last hash root "(e.g., H1 and H2)" is put away in the blockchain. It is possible to test the root hash simply to ensure that the exchanges associated with that root hash are steady and have not been monitored. The record supplier or the digger checks the documents or exchanges and provides a token to enable the new exchange to translate into a piece of the complete record. This procedure makes all hubs in the system accessible through the most recent sections. Since cryptographic hash keys are available in each square, messing with the blocks is too tedious and hard for the adversaries.

The excavators have no personal stake in the exchanges, and they are mining only to pick up motivating forces. The excavators do not know about the character of the exchange holder. Additionally, there are a few diggers chipping away at a similar arrangement of exchanges, and there is a substantial competition among them to add the trades to the blockchain. These whole striking features grant the blockchain to be a solid, controller check, flowed an open IoT information structure.

In the scholarly community and industry, different advances and frameworks are being worked to help blockchain improvement and support. A few instances of these frameworks incorporate Ethereum, texture Hyperledger, Ripple, and so forth. Figure 6.5 illustrates the modules of IoT scenario.

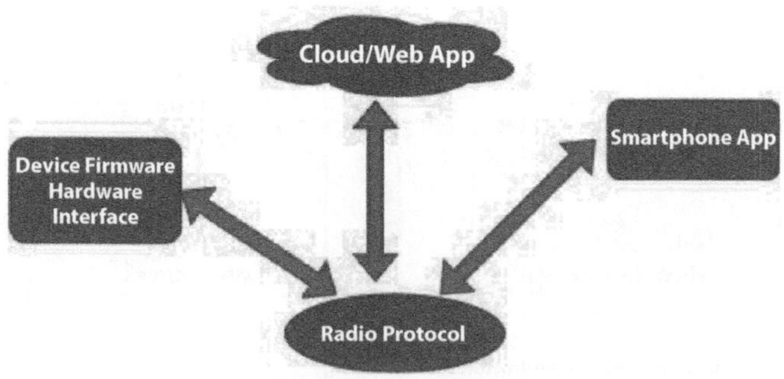

Figure 6.5 Modules in an Internet of Things scenario.

6.8.2 Blockchain Based on Permission

There have been two kinds of blockchain systems that rely on the type of information becoming implemented and the use of the application's blockchain utility. There is no unique consent essential in authorization less blockchain for a client to turn into an individual from the blockchain arrange or to turn into a digger. Anybody can enter or stop the blockchain-less consent organizes. Bitcoin is the most recent case to permit fewer blockchains. While exchange throughput is not extremely high, countless hubs inside the system can be empowered by the consent of fewer blockchains. Then again, the blockchains permitted to partake in the blockchain organize to have a predetermined arrangement of rules. The diggers are additionally the allowed people and it is simply after their endorsement that the squares might be appended to the connection. The blockchain "Ripple" and "Hyper ledger" are two prime examples of endorsed blockchain. The supported blockchain program constructs as contrasted the all-out exchange productivity and the award less blockchains [57–64].

6.8.3 Blockchain Improvements in IoT

There are several points of concern about the use of blockchain in IoT applications. The key focal points of utilizing blockchain in IoT applications are talked about beneath [58–63].

6.8.3.1 Blockchain Can Store Information Coming from IoT Devices

The IoT applications give a wide assortment of gadgets that are associated with one another. These gadgets are associated with different gadgets and controlled further. Furthermore, this device is connected to the cloud so IoT apps can be accessed from any situation. Given this expansive region of knowledge growth, blockchain is an innovative response to preserve the information and prevent its violence. Blockchain can fill in in a layer of IoT application as a piece of viable storage and moving arrangement for information.

6.8.3.2 Secure Data Storage with Blockchain Distribution

Even though blockchain development is distributed in scope, the probability of being a sole object of frustration can be restricted as it is faced by numerous cloud-based IoT applications. Despite the separation between the gadgets, the information made by them can undoubtedly be put away safely on the blockchain.

6.8.3.3 *Data Encryption via Hash Key and Tested by the Miners*

In the blockchain, following things happen for data encryption:

- It is conceivable to store just the "256-bit hash key" for the information instead of genuine data.
- Present information on the server can be stored, and guide the hash key with the first information.
- In the event that the information changes, the information hash will change. This guarantees information is sheltered and secret.
- The size of the blockchain will not be influenced by the size of the information in light of the fact that lone the hash esteems are put away in the chain.
- Just the proposed parties, permitted to utilize the information, may utilize the hash of the information to get to information from the cloud.
- Any assortment of information that is put away on the blockchain is appropriately checked by different diggers in the system, therefore decreasing the danger of putting away deceitful framework information by utilizing blockchain as an answer [57–62].

6.8.3.4 *Spoofing Attacks and Data Loss Prevention*

In spoofing attacks against IoT applications, another rival hub joins the IoT system and begins to mirror being the individual from the first system. The rival can without much of a stretch catch, watch or infuse information into the system through parodying. Blockchain goes about as a potential method to forestall these assaults [63–65].

Any substantial client or PC is enrolled on a blockchain, and clients can undoubtedly perceive and validate each other without the requirement for focal intermediaries or confirmation specialists. IoT gadgets are low fueled by plan and bear the chance of information misfortune. There may be circumstances in which both the sender and the receiver lose the data due to any external environmental issues. Use of blockchain will avoid these losses because there is no way to delete the block once it is attached to the chain.

6.8.3.5 Unauthorized Access Prevention Using Blockchain

Numerous IoT applications require ordinary contact between various hubs. Public and private keys are utilized to impart in blockchain, and just the proposed party or hub may get to the information. Regardless of whether the unintended party may get to the information, the information substances are immense as the information is ensured with keys. Along these lines, the information structure of the blockchain endeavors to handle different security issues that IoT applications face [66–73].

6.8.3.6 Exclusion of Centralized Cloud Servers

Blockchain will support IoT frameworks' security as it basically evacuates the brought together cloud servers and renders the system distributed. Brought together cloud servers are the information invaders [74] ideal objective. The information will indeed be scattered across all the hubs of the blockchain system and scrambled using the encryption algorithm.

6.9 Conclusions

This chapter has attempted to show the several ideas and functionalities of blockchain technology that could be widely applied to a wide range of circumstances. A blockchain removed the server to remove the central authority's interference and enabled transactions by participants who collectively maintained transaction records and eventually accepted communication using P2P set of connections expertise. The blockchain has a distributed architecture and uses apps for the identification of peers and companions. Specialized advances, for example, work verification and stack evidence, have been acquainted with progress of blockchain security.

The future research must also be associated with structuring structures and IT systems, from numerous external outlets. Thus, the order of sources of information is required to organize a regular information cleaning list that involves an assessment of information content and a document, as well as information purification and analysis. This is the following step, in order to gracefully recognize potential hazards and bottlenecks along chains of market processes and external details comparable to climate data.

References

1. Gilad, Y., Hemo, R., Micali, S., Vlachos, G., Zeldovich, N., *Algorand: Scaling Byzantine Agreements for Cryptocurrencies.*
2. Nath, M.P. and Sagnika, S., Capabilities of chatbots and its performance enhancements in machine learning, in: *International Conference on Machine Learning and Information Processing (ICMLIP)*, Pune, India, Springer, pp. 183–192, 27th-28th December 2019.
3. Priyadarshini, S.B.B. and Panigrahi, S., A distributed scalar controller selection scheme for redundant data elimination in sensor networks. *Int. J. Knowl. Discov. Bioinformatics (IJKDB)*, 7, 1, 91–104, 2017.
4. Petersen, K., Feldt, R., Mujtaba, S., Mattsson, M., Systematic mapping studies in software engineering, in: *12th International Conference on Evaluation and Assessment in Software Engineering (EASE)*, Proceedings of 12th International Conference on Evaluation and Assessment in Software Engineering (EASE), Bari, Italy, 26th–27th June 2008.
5. Nath, M.P., Sagnika, S., Das, M., Pandey, M., Object recognition using cat swarm optimization. *Int. J. Res. Sci. Innov.*, 4, 47–52, 2017.
6. Wressnegger, C., Freeman, K., Yamaguchi, F., Rieck, K., Automatically inferring malware signatures for anti-virus assisted attacks, in: *Asia Conference on Computer and Communications Security*, Abu Dhabi, UAE, 02nd–06th April 2017.
7. Priyadarshini, S.B.B., Panigrahi, S., Bagjadab, A.B., A distributed triangular scalar cluster premier selection scheme for enhanced event coverage and redundant data minimization in wireless multimedia sensor networks. *Indian J. Sci. Res.*, 14, 2, 96–102, 2017.
8. Nath, M.P., Goyal, K., Prasad, J., Kallur, B., Chat bot–An edge to customer insight. *Int. J. Res. Sci. Innov.*, 5, V, 29–32, 2018.
9. Singh, S., Jeong, Y.S., Park, J.H., A survey on cloud computing security: Issues, threats, and solutions. *J. Netw. Comput.*, 75, 200–222, 2016.
10. Priyadarshini, S.B.B., Panigrahi, S., Bagjadab, A.B., A distributed approach based on maximal far-flung scalar premier selection for camera actuation, in: *12th International Conference on Distributed Computing and Internet Technology (ICDCIT 2016)*, Lecture Notes in Computer Science (LNCS), Springer, Bhubaneswar, Odisha, 15th–18th January 2016.
11. Nath, M., Muralikrishnan, J., Sundarrajan, K., Varadarajanna, M., Continuous integration, delivery, and deployment: A revolutionary approach in software development. *Int. J. Res. Sci. Innov.*, 5, VII, 185–190, 2018.
12. Priyadarshini, S.B.B., Panigrahi, S., Bagjadab, A.B., Mishra, B.K., An investigative prolegomenon on various clustering strategies, their resolution and future direction towards wireless sensor systems, in: *International Conference on Emerging Technologies in Data Mining and Information Security (IEMIS)*, Kolkata, vol. 2, 23-25 February, Springer, 2018.

13. Aitzhan, N.Z. and Davor, S., Security and privacy in decentralized energy trading through multi-signatures, blockchain and anonymous messaging streams. *IEEE Trans. Dependable Secure Comput.*, 15, 840–852, 2016.
14. Nath, M.P., Pandey, P., Somu, K., Amalraj, P., Artificial intelligence & machine learning: The emerging milestones in software development. *Int. J. Res. Sci. Innov.*, 5, IX, 36–44, 2018.
15. Ziegeldorf, J.H., Matzutt, R., Henze, M., Grossmann, F., Wehrle, K., Secure and anonymous decentralized bitcoin mixing. *Future Gener. Comput. Syst.*, 80, 448–466, 2016.
16. Nath, M.P., Sridharan, R., Bhargava, A., Mohammed, T., Cloud computing: An overview, benefits, issues & research challenges. *Int. J. Res. Sci. Innov.*, 6, II, 25–35, 2019.
17. Bonneau, J., Miller, A., Clark, J., Narayanan, A., Kroll, J.A., Felten, E.W., Sok: Research perspectives and challenges for bitcoin and cryptocurrencies, in: *Proceedings of IEEE Symposium on Security and Privacy (SP)*, San Jose, CA, USA, 17th–21st May 2015.
18. Huang, H., Chen, X., Wu, Q., Huang, X., Shen, J., Bitcoin-based fair payments for outsourcing computations of fog devices. *Future Gener. Comput. Syst.*, 78, 850–858, 2016.
19. Kroll, J.A., Davey, I.C., Felten, E.W., The economics of bitcoin mining, or bitcoin in the presence of adversaries. *Proc. WEIS*, 2013.
20. Bradbury, D., The problem with bitcoin. *Comput. Fraud Secur.*, 11, 5–8, 2013.
21. Sooriaarachchi, C., Gunawardena, T., Kulasuriya, B., Dayaratne, T., A study into the capabilities of NoSQL databases in handling a highly heterogeneous tree. *IEEE 6th International Conference on Information and Automation for Sustainability (ICIAfS)*, pp. 106-111, 2012.
22. Chae, B., Yang, C., Olson, D., Sheu, C., The impact of advanced analytics and data accuracy on operational performance: A contingent resource based theory (RBT) perspective. *Decis. Support Syst.*, 59, 119–126, 2014.
23. Nath, M.P., Sagnika, S., Das, M., Pandey, M., Object recognition using cat swarm optimization. *Int. J. Res. Sci. Innov.*, 4, VIIS, 47–52, 2017.
24. Rajapaksha, S.K. *et al.*, Internal structure and semantic web link structure based ontology ranking. *4th International Conference on Information and Automation for Sustainability, ICIAFS 2008*, pp. 86–90, 2008.
25. Bandal, A. and Thirugnanam, M., Quality measurements of fruits and vegetables using sensor network, in: *Proceedings of the 3rd International Symposium on Big Data and Cloud Computing Challenges (ISBCC–16S)*, Springer, pp. 121–130, 2016.
26. Grosicki, E., Abed-Meraim, K., Hua, Y., A weighted linear prediction method for near-field source localization. *IEEE Trans. Signal Process.*, 53, 10, 3651–3660, 2005.
27. Zhu, H., Bayley, I., Younas, M., Lightfoot, D., Yousef, B., Liu, D., Big saas: The next step beyond big data, in: *2015 IEEE International Congress on Big Data (BigData Congress)*, IEEE, pp. 775–784, 2015.

28. Zhao, Q., Liu, Y., Yu, Y., Song, J., Zhou, G., Intelligent system for monitoring and controlling of the grain condition based on arm9, in: *The 26th Chinese Control and Decision Conference (2014 CCDC)*, IEEE, pp. 4117–4121, 2014.
29. Yu, Z., Zhang, Y., Lian, F., Fu, M., A research of stored grain moisture detection based on ris-k2 radar electromagnetic wave technology, in: *2010 International Conference on Educational and Information Technology (ICEIT)*, vol. 3, p. V3–265, IEEE, Chongqing, 2010.
30. Thessler, S., Kooistra, L., Teye, F., Huitu, H., Bregt, A.K., Geosensors to support crop production: Current applications and user requirements. *Sensors*, 11, 7, 6656–6684, 2011.
31. Parvin, S., Venkatraman, S., de Souza-Daw, T., Fahd, K., Jackson, J., Kaspi, S., Cooley, N., Saleemx, K., Gawanmeh, A., Smart food security system using iot and big data analytics, in: *15th International Conference on Information Technology: New Generations*, IEEE, Las Vegas, NV, USA, 2019.
32. Parvin, S., Gawanmeh, A., Venkatraman, S., Optimised sensor based smart system for efficient monitoring of grain storage, in: *2018 IEEE International Conference on Communications Workshops (ICC Workshops)*, IEEE, pp. 1–6, 2018.
33. Mabrouk, S., Abdelmonsef, A., Toman, A., Smart grain storage monitor and control. *Am. Sci. Res. J. Engineering, Technology, Sci.*, 31, 1, 156–162, 2017.
34. Liu, J., Lundqvist, J., Weinberg, J., Gustafsson, J., Food losses and waste in china and their implication for water and land. *Environ. Sci. Technol.*, 47, 18, 10137–10144, 2013.
35. Lehmann, M., Biørn-Hansen, A., Ghinea, G., Gronli, T.-M., Younas, M., Data analysis as a service: An infrastructure for storing and analyzing the internet of things, in: *International Conference on Mobile Web and Information Systems*, Springer, pp. 161–169, 2015.
36. Kaewmard, N. and Saiyod, S., Sensor data collection and irrigation control on vegetable crop using smart phone and wireless sensor networks for smart farm, in: *2014 IEEE Conference on Wireless Sensors (ICWiSE)*, IEEE, pp. 106–112, 2014.
37. Priyadarshini, S.B.B. and Panigrahi, S., A distributed scheme based on minimum camera actuation employing concentric hexagonal scalar premier selection for data redundancy minimization, in: *15th International Conference on Information Technology*, IEEE, Bhubaneswar, December 22-24, 2016.
38. Priyadarshini, S.B.B., Singh, D., Panda, M., A comparative study of redundant data minimization and event coverage in wireless multimedia sensor networks (WMSNs), in: *International Conference on Applied Machine Learning (ICAML)*, IEEE, Bhubaneswar, 27-28 September 2019.
39. Hamouda, Y. and Msallam, M., Variable sampling interval for energy efficient heterogeneous precision agriculture using wireless sensor networks. *J. King Saud Univ. Comput. Inf. Sci.*, 32, 88–98, 2018.
40. Priyadarshini, S.B.B., A hybrid approach based on scalar cluster leader selection for camera activation (HASL-CA) in wireless multimedia

sensor networks (WMSNs), in: *International Conference on Applied Machine Learning (ICAML)*, IEEE, Bhubaneswar, 27-28 September 2019.
41. Gustavsson, J., Cederberg, C., Sonesson, U., van Otterdijk, R., Meybeck, A., *Global Food Losses and Food Waste*, Food and Agriculture Organization of the United Nations Website, Global Coverage, 2015.
42. Spiegel, J.R., McKenna, M.T., Lakshman, G.S., Nordstrom, P.G., Amazon US patent anticipatory shipping, Amazon Technologies Inc., p. 12, 2013.
43. Griffiths, J.L., Phelan, A., Osman, K.A., Furness, A., Using item attendant information and communications technologies to improve supply chain visibility. *ICAM 2007 Agile Manufacturing*, pp. 172–180, 2007.
44. Barratt, M. and Oke, A., Antecedents of supply chain visibility in retail supply chains: A resource-based theory perspective. *J. Oper. Manage.*, 25, 1217–1233, 2007.
45. Siow Mong, R., Wang, Z. *et al.*, RiskVis: Supply chain visualization with risk management and real-time monitoring. *IEEE International Conference on Automation Science (CASE)*, pp. 207–212, 2013.
46. Garcia-Reyes, H. and Giachetti, R., Using experts to develop a supply chain maturity model in Mexico. *Supply Chain Manage.*, 15, 6, 415–424, 2010.
47. Han, S.-H. and Chu, C.-H., Developing a collaborative supply chain reference model for a regional manufacturing industry in China. *Int. J. Electron. Cust. Relationsh. Manage.*, 3, 1, 52–70, 2009.
48. Irfan, D., Xiaofei, X., Deng, S., A scor reference model of the supply chain management system in an enterprise. *Int. Arab J. Inf. Technol.*, 5, 3, 288–295, 2008.
49. Han, D., Kwon, I.G., Bae, M., Sung, H., Supply chain integration in developing countries for foreign retailers in Korea: Wal-mart experience. *Comput. Ind. Eng.*, 43, 111–121, 2002.
50. Bozcan, I., Oymak, Y., Alemdar, I.Z., Kalkan, S., What is (missing or wrong) in the scene? A hybrid deep Boltzmann machine for contextualized scene modeling, in: *2018 IEEE International Conference on Robotics and Automation (ICRA)*, pp. 1–6, 2018.
51. Seo, S., Park, S., Kim, J., Improvement of network intrusion detection accuracy by using restricted Boltzmann machine, in: *2016 8th International Conference on Computational Intelligence and Communication Networks (CICN)*, pp. 413–417, 2016.
52. Kim, J., Kim, J., Thu, H.L.T., Kim, H., Long short term memory recurrent neural network classifier for intrusion detection, in: *2016 International Conference on Platform Technology and Service (PlatCon)*, pp. 1–5, 2016.
53. Khan, A. and Zhang, F., Using recurrent neural networks (RNNs) as planners for bio-inspired robotic motion, in: *2017 IEEE Conference on Control Technology and Applications (CCTA)*, pp. 1025–1030, 2017.
54. Yin, C., Zhu, Y., Fei, J., He, X., A deep learning approach for intrusion detection using recurrent neural networks. *IEEE Access*, 5, 21954–21961, 2017.

55. Imamverdiyev, Y. and Abdullayeva, F., Deep learning method for denial of service attack detection based on restricted Boltzmann machine. *Big Data*, 6, 2, 159–169, 2018.
56. Hidaka, A. and Kurita, T., Consecutive dimensionality reduction by canonical correlation analysis for visualization of convolutional neural networks, in: *Proceedings of the ISCIE International Symposium on Stochastic Systems Theory and its Applications*, vol. 2017, pp. 160–167, 2017.
57. Mosenia, A. and Jha, N.K., A comprehensive study of security of internet-of-things. *IEEE Trans. Emerg. Topics Comput.*, 5, 4, 586–602, Dec. 2017.
58. Nath, M.P., Sridharan, R., Bhargava, A., Mohammed, T., Cloud computing: An overview, benefits, issues & research challenges. *Int. J. Res. Sci. Innov.*, 6, II, 25–35, 2019.
59. Li, C. and Chen, C., A multi-stage control method application in the -ght against phishing attacks, in: *Proc. 26th Comput. Secur. Acad. Commun. Across Country*, p. 145, 2011.
60. Dlamini, N.N. and Johnston, K., The use, benefits and challenges of using the Internet of Things (IoT) in retail businesses: A literature review, in: *Proc. Int. Conf. Adv. Comput. Commun. Eng. (ICACCE)*, pp. 430–436, Nov. 2016.
61. Stanciu, A., Balan, T.-C., Gerigan, C., Zam-r, S., Securing the IoT gateway based on the hardware implementation of a multi pattern search algorithm, in: *Proc. Int. Conf. Optim. Elect. Electron. Equip. (OPTIM) Int. Aegean Conf. Elect. Mach. Power Electron. (ACEMP)*, pp. 1001–1006, May 2017.
62. Huh, S., Cho, S., Kim, S., Managing IoT devices using blockchain platform, in: *Proc. 19th Int. Conf. Adv. Commun. Technol. (ICACT)*, pp. 464–467, Feb. 2017.
63. Basudan, S., Lin, X., Sankaranarayanan, K., A privacy-preserving vehicular crowdsensing-based road surface condition monitoring system using fog computing. *IEEE Internet Things J.*, 4, 3, 772–782, Jun. 2017.
64. Priyadarshini, S.B.B., Bagjadab, A.B., Mishra, B.K., The role of IoT and Big data in modern technological arena: A comprehensive study, in: *Internet of Things and Big Data Analytics for Smart Generation*, pp. 13–25, 2019.
65. Nath, M.P., Priyadarshini, S.B.B., Mishra, D., A comprehensive study on security in IoT and resolving security threats using machine learning (ML), in: *Advances in Intelligent Computing and Communication*, pp. 545–553, 2021.
66. Yu, Y., Li, Y., Tian, J., Liu, J., Blockchain-based solutions to security and privacy issues in the Internet of Things. *IEEE Wirel. Commun.*, 25, 6, 12–18, Dec. 2018.
67. Priyadarshini, S.B.B. and Panigrahi, S., A quadrigeminal scheme based on event reporting scalar premier selection for camera actuation in wireless multimedia sensor networks. *J. King Saud Univ. Eng. Sci.*, Elsevier, 31, 1, 52–60, 2019.
68. Priyadarshini, S.B.B. and Panigrahi, S., Redundant data minimization using minimal mean distant scalar leader selection for event driven camera

actuation, in: *International Conference on Information Technology (ICIT)*, IEEE, pp. 142–147, 2016.

69. Priyadarshini, S.B.B. and Panigrahi, S., A non-heuristic approach for minimizing the number of cameras actuated in wireless multimedia sensor networks, in: *Proceedings of 2nd ITR International Conference*, Bhubaneswar, India, pp. 12–16, 2014.
70. Sahani, A., Priyadarshini, S.B.B., Chinara, S., The role of blockchain technology and its usage in various sectors in the modern age: Various roles of blockchain and use cases in different sectors, in: *Blockchain and AI Technology in the Industrial Internet of Things*, pp. 221–245, IGI Global, 2021.
71. Priyadarshini, S.B.B., Bagjadab, A.B., Mishra, B.K., Digital signature and its pivotal role in affording security services, in: *Handbook of E-Business Security*, pp. 365–384, 2018.
72. Priyadarshini, S.B.B., Bagjadab, A.B., Mishra, B.K., Security in distributed operating system: A comprehensive study, in: *Cyber Security in Parallel and Distributed Computing: Concepts, Techniques, Applications and Case Studies*, pp. 221–230, 2019.
73. Priyadarshini, S.B.B., Concentric quadrivial scalar premier selection scheme based on sensing region segregation (CQSPS-SRS): An innovative marching towards optimum camera actuation and enhanced event coverage, in: *International Conference on Intelligent Computing and Communication Technologies*, pp. 494–501, Springer, Singapore, 2019.
74. Priyadarshini, S.B.B., Bagjadab, A.B., Sahu, S.K., Mishra, B.K., A Comprehensive review on soft computing framework. *Int. J. Adv. Mech. Eng.*, 8, 1, 221–228, 2018.
75. Chan, J.O., An architecture for big data analytics. *Commun. IIMA*, 13, 2, 2013.

7

Deep Learning Approach to Industrial Energy Sector and Energy Forecasting with Prophet

Yash Gupta[1]*, Shilpi Sharma[1], Naveen Rajan P.[1] and Nadia Mohamed Kunhi[2]

[1]*Department of Computer Science and Engineering, Amity School of Engineering & Technology, Noida, Uttar Pradesh, India*
[2]*Design Engineer, Binghalib Engineering, Sharjah, United Arab Emirates*

Abstract

Deep learning is a subset of the Machine learning method, which is a vital factor in the Energy Industrial sector, which helps optimize the contracting methods and minimize the overall cost in the expenses to produce energy. This research paper aims to identify the approaches that can be used to identify the valuable depending factors in the data sets and correct the missing datavalue, which can be later on used to analyze the data better. The data set, which we worked on within this research, is a data set of power plant productions of a decade in the US. Then deep learning will help us to be able to visualize the shortcoming in the approach and come up with an appropriate solution. Inspiration for this research was an old project, which included a smart power control system and a solar-wind hybrid power source, so by this research, we can identify the areas where better and smarter systems can be implemented replacing conventional methods and how to tackle the old data sets.

Keywords: Deep learning, data-handling, prophet, EDA

**Corresponding author*: yashbits73@gmail.com

Jyotir Moy Chatterjee, Harish Garg and R. N. Thakur (eds.) A Roadmap for Enabling Industry 4.0 by Artificial Intelligence, (111–126) © 2023 Scrivener Publishing LLC

7.1 Introduction

Deep Learning Algorithms use a model consisting of a neural network used to find associations between a set of data variables for inputs and outputs, this allows to form a relationship between the data sets and form an equation which isto predict the output or future possible outcomes.

Generally, the approach is it that takes in data variables which are treated as the input and later uses these variables for the prediction of the output, for example, the stock prices of the past week from the trading can be used as an input, the deep learning model here will be used for the prediction of the stock price for the coming day, week, or so. Figure 7.1 shows the data set used which is hourly power consumption data from PJM taken from Kaggle.com [16], which contains the regional power transmission organization (RTO) for the United States. It transmits power for a part of the Interconnection grid operating in the eastern area for an electric transmission system responsible for Illinois, Michigan, Indiana, Delaware, Pennsylvania, Kentucky, Virginia, Maryland, Ohio, North Carolina, West Virginia, District of Columbia, New Jersey, and Tennessee. Energy consumption has some unique characteristics. This data set contains the hourly power consumption which is shown in megawatts (MW).

The regions have been changing for power transmission from the time of the data collection so for some areas, the data is only appearing on certain dates for some regions. To overcome the 3 constraints which are faced in analyzing such large data, EDA (Exploratory Data Analysis) is used. Since energy production is an expensive endeavor so being able to identify the shortcoming and need for energy helps in tackling the economics for the same. It will be interesting to see how the prophet picks them up, it is a procedure is for forecasting in which it is used for the

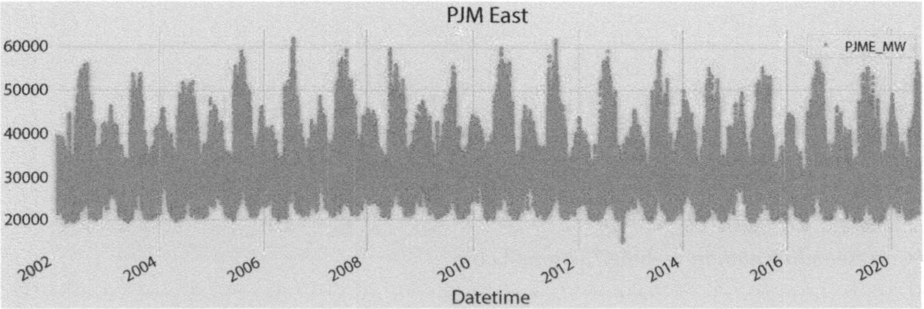

Figure 7.1 PJM data set.

data which is based on a times series here model in which the trends are nonlinear is fitted and it is an additive in nature with yearly, weekly, plus holiday effects and daily seasonality.

7.2 Related Work

The presented work by the author is for the investigation for a way for the most efficient and effective method for using the LSTM model for residential, commercial establishments using a neural network model for the load requirement and to perform forecasting on their future demand. This system consisted of two neural network models and the architecture is deployed for future forecasting of the load requirement. The model has been trained, made work, and also tested for the period of an hour using a one-minute step interval. Although effective the model architecture was unable to accurately forecast the load requirements [1]. In this implementation, a model was built based upon deep networks for the purpose to analyze and predict the wind power dataset and which can help to make wind farms and plan them out in the most efficient way. The research presented here compares the accuracy of wind power by applying various methods and how successful they are, based on these observations, the model will learn the various variationpatterns which are to be found in the wind power and also the hidden pattern or observations in historical data which are detected by a strong nonlinear mapping ability.

Since the author is only comparing wind power accuracy using different methods, the only gap identified would more approaches can be applied to improve the output [2].

The author here proposed a model based upon a deep belief method to help and formulate a methodto predict the wind power paper, this model is used as a comparison for the accuracy of the predictionof wind power by other methods. Based on the finding and the prediction from the model, it is evidentit can learn the various pattern and variations in the data set [3]. Manufacturing requires various parameters to ensure the smooth running of the process, one such parameter is the inspection system for the industry and as industrialization is moving in the smart era it is essential to have a smart inspection platform. The model represented in the paper is made in keeping in that mind only by employing state of art deep models to analyze the incoming images for identification of the defective products and also to ensure that only up to a certain degree of defect is allowed to pass on. For the implementation of such a system real-time data handling capability is implemented thus the author designed the system accordingly which is based upon fog computing [4]. Research done in this paper presents a formulated way towards a data mining approach that is 5 implemented in solving the energyprediction demand which is inside a steel plant. The data collected and which is used is directly froma working steel plant which consists of already the processed data and also that the feature selection on the data set already being performed on it [5]. The potential of deep learning to be applied to the air conditioning system for a big residential or commercial complex is being investigated and the following model was developed to read the data collected and the feature selection and identification of meaningful features to be able to perform a prediction on the load requirement for the cooling requirement to ensure the efficiency and unnecessary power [6]. The author aimed to formulate a model for the evaluation of the possible and unpredicted, unexpected events which can occur during the operation of the industrial machining processes by applying deep neural networks to identify the hidden patterns from the raw data and to be able to make it workable [7]. the author explored and established a model between the connection of the demand and supply and to be able to performa short-term supply forecast, later they discussed the various methods and models for the load forecasting. The results obtained at the end of forecasting showed that the proposed model can and can perform the forecast accurately for the daily needs [8].

7.3 Methodology

After going through various researches, the proposed energy forecasting and analysis of the data set are done firstly by creating some time-series features to see how the trends are impacted by day of the week, hour, time of year, etc. By this method, a way to visualize, summarize, and interpret the information that is hidden in rows and column format and allowing greater accuracy and data reading is created.

Table 7.1 represents the output of the sample data which divided the data into various columns and which will help us to work with it. Figure 7.2 represents the various trends identified, since energy consumption and demand depend strongly on daily and seasonal properties also different weeks of week sow significant changes, therefore plotting the features to see trends.

Table 7.1 Exploratory data analysis output.

Date time	Hour	Day of week	Quarter	Month	Year	Day of year	Day of month	Week of year	PJMMW
2002-12-31 01:00:00	1	1	4	12	2002	365	31	1	26498.0
2002-12-31 02:00:00	2	1	4	12	2002	365	31	1	25147.0
2002-12-31 03:00:00	3	1	4	12	2002	365	31	1	24574.0
2002-12-31 04:00:00	4	1	4	12	2002	365	31	1	24393.0
2002-12-31 05:00:00	5	1	4	12	2002	365	31	1	24860.0

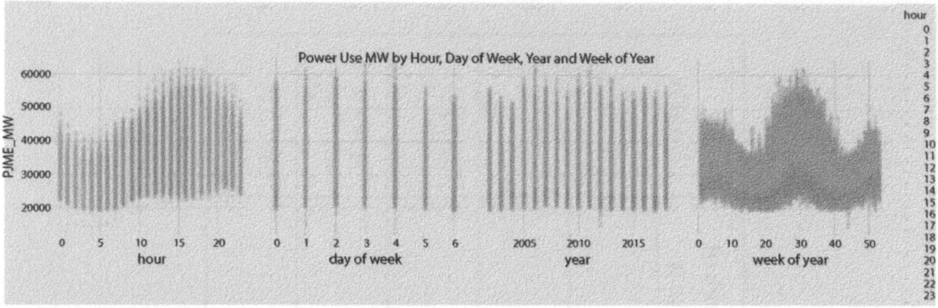

Figure 7.2 Plotting of trends and features.

7.3.1 Splitting of Data (Test/Train)

Figure 7.3 shows the train/test split of the data set to be able to train our model perfectly and to validate the outputs the data is divided into two categories which are Test data and Training data. In this data set, we cut off the data after 2015 to use as our validation set.

7.3.2 Prophet Model

The Prophet Model is an open-source software made by the Facebook data science team famously known as Facebook Prophet. It works best with data that have fixed names and has time-based properties such as holidays, days, months, and years. The best thing about this is that it gives output on messy data with minimal physical work. In the PJM data set, after reprocessing the data set it is represented as the output in Table 7.2 where "ds" represents the date and time and "y" represents consumption in MW.

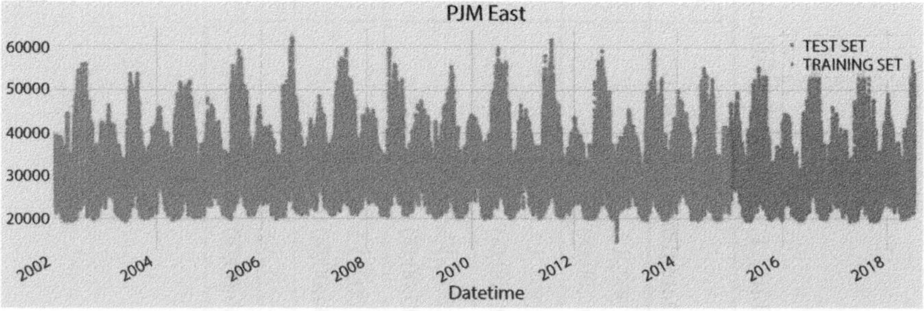

Figure 7.3 Train/test split.

Table 7.2 The output of the Prophet Model.

	The output of the Prophet Model	
	Date time	**y**
0	2002-12-31 01:00:00	26498.0
1	2002-12-31 02:00:00	25147.0
2	2002-12-31 03:00:00	24574.0
3	2002-12-31 04:00:00	24393.0
4	2002-12-31 05:00:00	24860.0

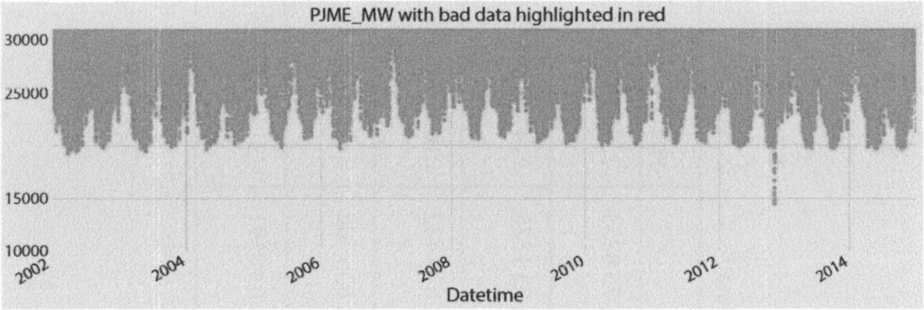

Figure 7.4 PJM data set with bad data.

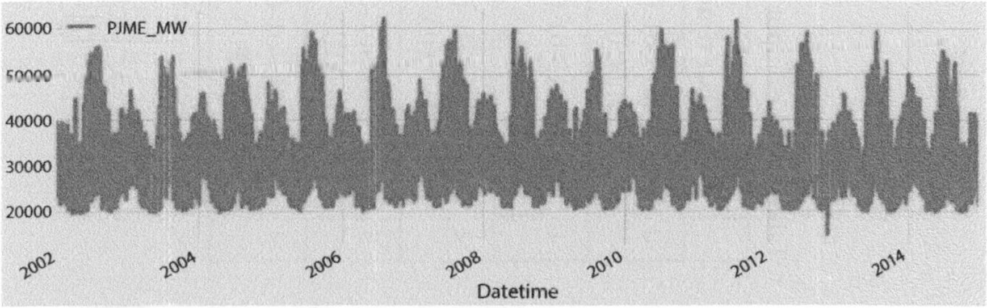

Figure 7.5 PJM data set with bad data removed.

Table 7.3 The output of training data.

	Date time	trend	yhat_lower	yhat_upper	trend_lower	trend_upper
0	2015-01-01 01:00:00	31214.76 8254	23934.308965	32672.170741	31214.768254	31214.768254
1	2015-01-01 02:00:00	31214.73 1338	22477.139233	31298.071321	31214.731338	31214.731338
2	2015-01-01 03:00:00	31214.69 4422	21636.265058	30412.770964	31214.694422	31214.694422
3	2015-01-01 04:00:00	31214.65 7506	21553.148239	30558.983054	31214.657506	31214.657506
4	2015-01-01 05:00:00	31214.62 0591	22190.940775	31021.538704	31214.620591	31214.620591

7.3.3 Data Cleaning

Data cleaning is an essential part of the forecasting process. If the training data or the input data contains useless or garbage values, the forecast will use these values when making predictions and this will raise serious issues. While working with this data set some empty data sets were being treated like garbage data. Figure 7.4 shows the bad data marked as red, which upon research it was found during the timeline of October 29–30, the Hurricane Sandy hit the US continent which brought high winds and coastal flooding to a very large portion of the eastern United States where main data set is focused upon, on further research it was found an estimated of around 8 million customers went without power. This is what caused a huge gap in the data and that part is being labeled as bad data.

Figure 7.5 shows the following outlier data removed to ensure the smooth running of our model as such events come under natural disasters which cannot be accounted for.

7.3.4 Model Implementation

The model is now set up after formatting and giving data appropriate heading and divided into the training data and testing data. The model is now fitted with the training data and output is obtained which is shown in Table 7.3. The trend shows the average unit consumption on that particular time frame and the tables next to it are the lowest and highest unit count in that hour.

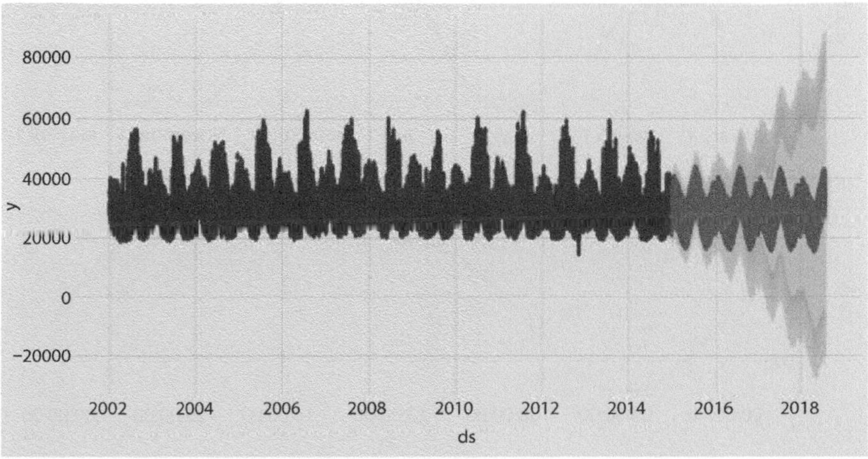

Figure 7.6 Forecast of energy consumption.

7.4 Results

Figure 7.6 shows the plot obtained after training the model the forecasting part comes up and we plot theforecasting graph in which the Y-axis represents the consumption and the X-axis represents the year.

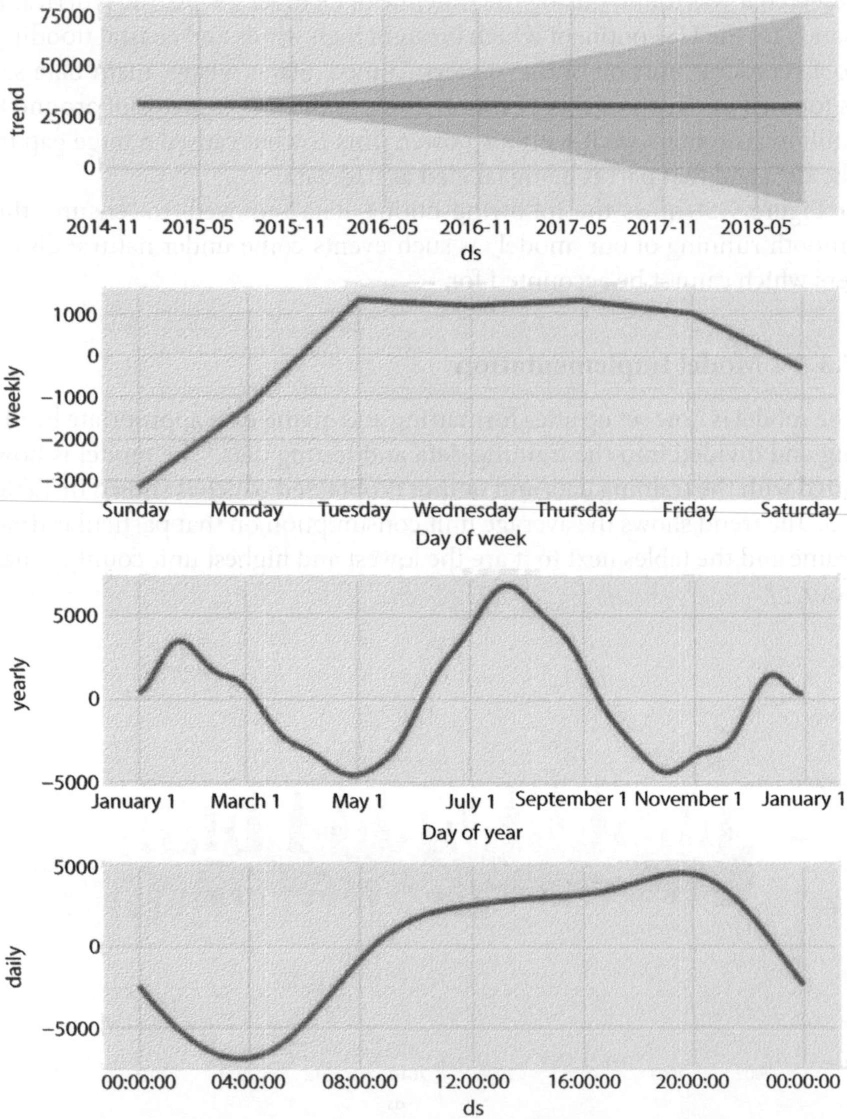

Figure 7.7 Forecast for weekly, yearly, daily, and trends energy consumption.

Figure 7.7 displays the forecast of the energy consumption on a weekly yearly, daily basis, and trends that are dependent on the increase or decrease with the population which can be used to compensate and provide greater accuracy in reading the data.

7.4.1 Comparing Forecast to Actuals

To validate the model a plot between the forecast of the energy consumption with the Actual reading. In Figures 7.8, 7.9, and 7.10, the predicted output of the prophet model is plotted on different time scales, yearly, monthly, and weekly, respectively.

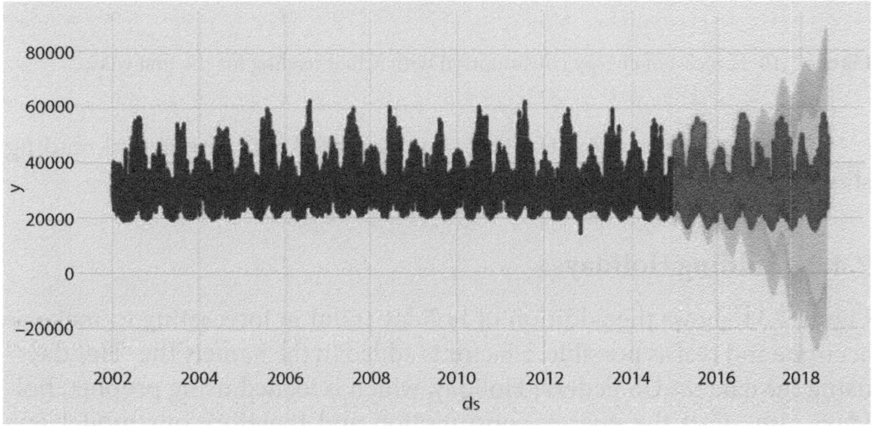

Figure 7.8 Forecast of energy consumption with actual reading.

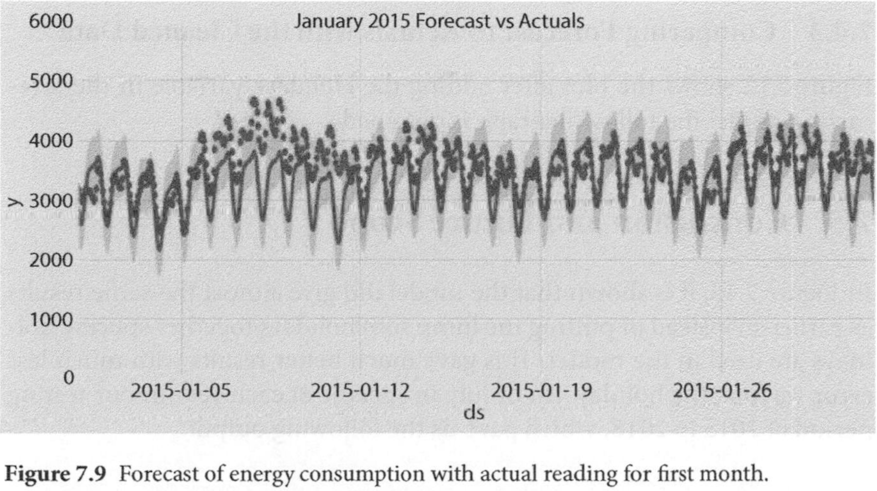

Figure 7.9 Forecast of energy consumption with actual reading for first month.

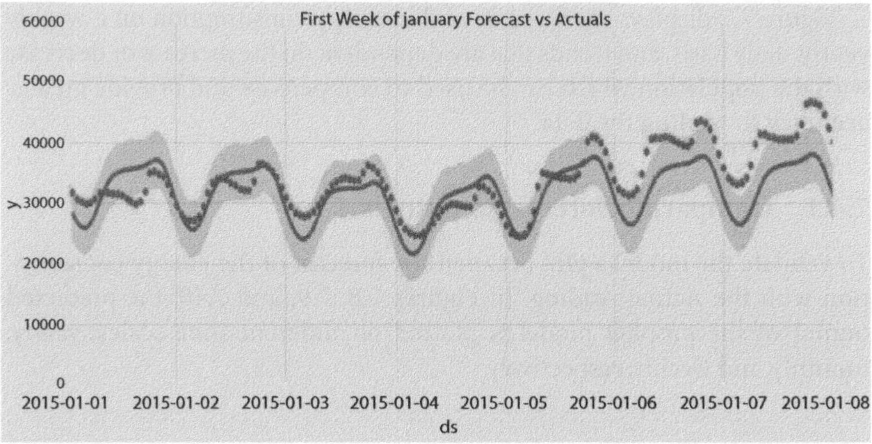

Figure 7.10 Forecast of energy consumption with actual reading for the first week.

The above figures show the forecast compared with the actual reading shown in "red" and forecast in"blue".

7.4.2 Adding Holidays

Figure 7.11 shows the addition of holiday trend in forecasting to make as accurate and real as possible, a factor is added in the namely the "Holidays" using the data set US Federal Holiday, which is loaded using prophet, holidays also affect the energy consumption and therefore our model was made forecasting with the following results.

7.4.3 Comparing Forecast to Actuals with the Cleaned Data

Figure 7.12 shows the plot after adding the Holidays variable in the forecasting model the followinggraph is obtained.

7.5 Conclusion and Future Scope

In Figure 7.13, it is shown that the model did give almost the same results as earlier so instead of putting the lump sum holidays together specific holidays are used in the model. This gave much better results with much less error we took the holiday 4th of July in specific of each year in our testing period of 2015 to 2018, which gave us the following output.

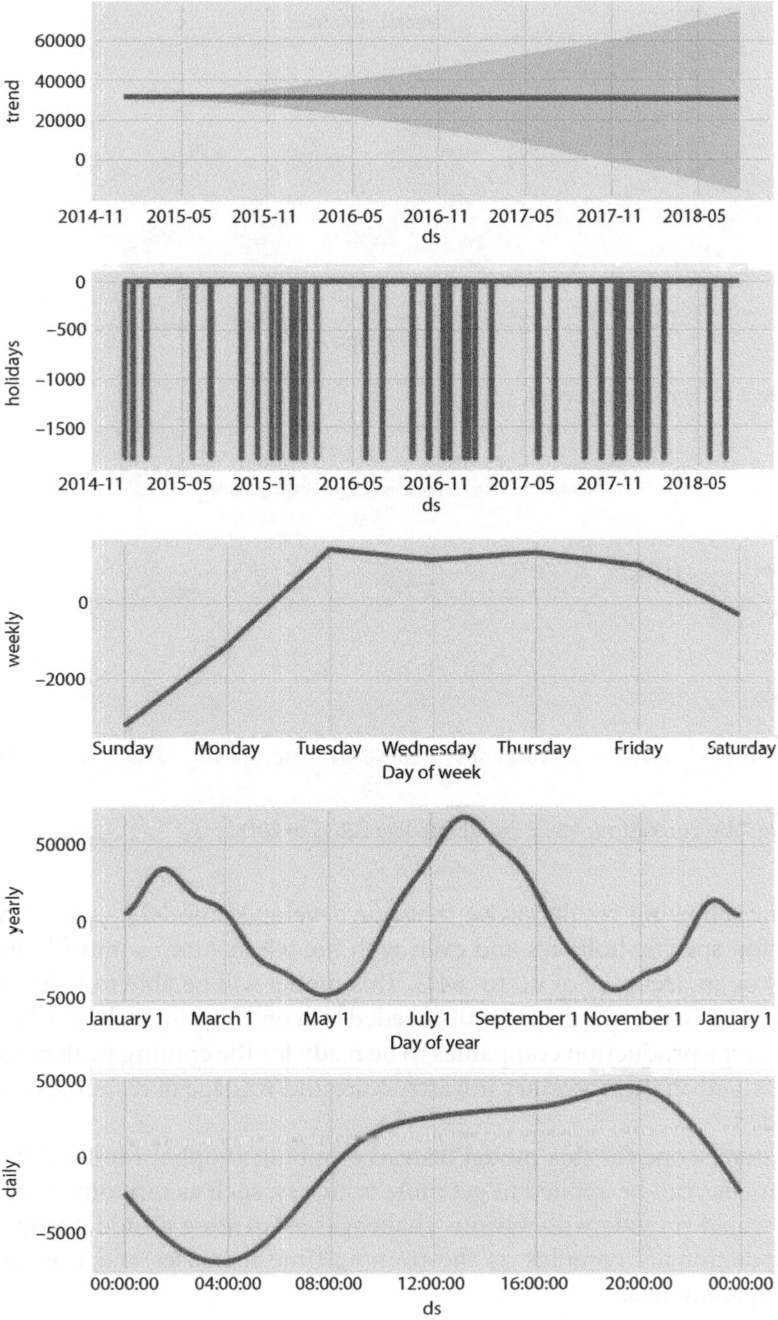

Figure 7.11 Forecast for weekly, yearly, daily, trends along with holidays energy consumption.

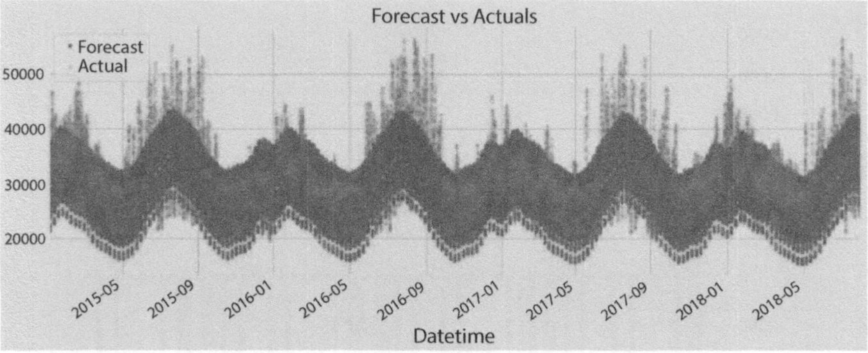

Figure 7.12 Forecast vs. actual.

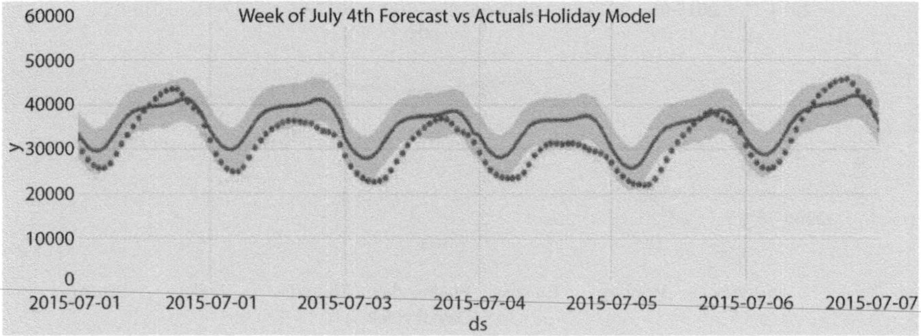

Figure 7.13 Forecast vs. actual for 4th of July of 2015 to 2018.

The following results prove that our developed model can work very well for specific holidays and even with the whole lump sum of holidays gives us an accuracy of up to 84%. This model will be able to help in the prediction of the number of units needed for consumption, which will help the energy production companies to be ready for the coming peak requirements, and all the necessary infrastructure and wastage of resources can be avoided.

Future scope for this model instead of inbuilt Prophet Model different techniques can be applied to get more accuracy, such as random forest but that would provide with various challenges as creating a model would be computationally complex as the training time increases and the tuning hyperparameters.

References

1. Marino, D.L., Amarasinghe, K., Manic, M., Building energy load forecasting using deep neural networks, in: *IECON 2016-42nd Annual Conference of the IEEE Industrial Electronics Society*, IEEE, pp. 7046–7051, October 2016.
2. Tao, Y., Chen, H., Qiu, C., Wind power prediction and pattern feature based on deep learning method, in: *2014 IEEE PES Asia-Pacific Power and Energy Engineering Conference (APPEEC)*, IEEE, pp. 1–4, December 2014.
3. Li, L., Ota, K., Dong, M., Deep learning for smart industry: Efficient manufacture inspection system with fog computing. *IEEE Trans. Industr. Inform.*, 14, 10, 4665–4673, 2018.
4. Chen, C., Liu, Y., Kumar, M., Qin, J., Energy consumption modeling using deep learning technique—A case study of EAF. *Proc. CIRP*, 72, 1063–1068, 2018.
5. Fan, C., Xiao, F., Zhao, Y., A short-term building cooling load prediction method using deep learning algorithms. *Appl. Energy*, 195, 222–233, 2017.
6. Vargas, R., Mosavi, A., Ruiz, L., Deep learning: A review, in: *Advances in Intelligent Systems and Computing*, 2017.
7. Sanchez, J.A., Conde, A., Arriandiaga, A., Wang, J., Plaza, S., Unexpected event prediction in wire electrical discharge machining using deep learning techniques. *Materials*, 11, 7, 1100, 2018.
8. Zhang, Q., Lu, J., Yang, Z., Tu, M., A deep learning-based real-time load forecasting method in electricity spot market, in: *Journal of Physics: Conference Series*, vol. 1176, p. 062068, IOP Publishing, March 2019.
9. Lv, Y., Duan, Y., Kang, W., Li, Z., Wang, F.Y., Traffic flow prediction with big data: A deep learning approach. *IEEE Trans. Intell. Transp. Syst.*, 16, 2, 865–873, 2014.
10. González Ordiano, J. Á., Waczowicz, S., Hagenmeyer, V., Mikut, R., Energy forecasting tools and services. *Wiley Interdiscip. Rev. Data Min. Knowl. Discovery*, 8, 2, e1235, 2018.
11. Navratil, M. and Kolkova, A., Decomposition and forecasting time series in the business economy using prophet forecasting model. *Cent. Eur. Bus. Rev.*, 8, 4, 26, 2019.
12. Hrnjica, B. and Mehr, A.D., Energy demand forecasting using deep learning, in: *Smart Cities Performability, Cognition, & Security*, pp. 71–104, Springer, Cham, 2020.
13. West, J.A., Techniques used in developing the US Department of the Interior Energy Forecast, United States Energy through the year 2000, in: *Energy Modeling: Art Science Practice*, p. 294, 2016.
14. Blázquez-García, A., Conde, A., Milo, A., Sánchez, R., Barrio, I., Short-term office building elevator energy consumption forecast using SARIMA. *J. Build. Perform. Simul.*, 13, 1, 69–78, 2020.

15. Mi, C., Xu, R., Lin, C.T., Real-time recognition of smartphone user behavior based on prophetalgorithms, 2019, arXiv preprint arXiv:1909.08997.
16. https://www.kaggle.com/robikscube/hourly-energy-consumption.

8

Application of Novel AI Mechanism for Minimizing Private Data Release in Cyber-Physical Systems

Manas Kumar Yogi[1]* and A.S.N. Chakravarthy[2]

[1]*Computer Science and Engineering Department Pragati Engineering College (Autonomous) Surampalem, A.P., India*
[2]*Department of Computer Science & Engineering, JNTUK-University College of Engineering, Kakinada, A.P., India*

Abstract
Cyber-physical systems are becoming indispensible part of human life day by day. With each passing year, as technological innovations are emerging, the application of artificial intelligence to leverage the functionality and usability of cyber-physical systems is also increasing. In this chapter, we present the novel privacy issues caused by advent of AI techniques in a cyberphysical system ecosystem and then we proceed to discuss the measures to mitigate such issues. We will also bring forth the state-of-the-art in privacy techniques, which are currently employed in cyber-physical systems. We propose an approach were formal methods of reasoning, learning, planning, and processing will be used in conjunction with privacy aspects so as to develop a trustable framework. This robust framework can be deployed for enhancing the degree of privacy preservation without affecting the data utility of any cyber-physical entity. The chapter concludes by highlighting the experimental results, which are quite worthy to note that AI-driven privacy mechanisms are equipped with much robustness to counter adversial attacks of any nature.

Keywords: Cyberphysical systems, AI, privacy, model, learning

**Corresponding author*: manas.yogi@gmail.com

Jyotir Moy Chatterjee, Harish Garg and R. N. Thakur (eds.) A Roadmap for Enabling Industry 4.0 by Artificial Intelligence, (127–140) © 2023 Scrivener Publishing LLC

8.1 Introduction

AI frameworks for the most part require a lot of information. Be that as it may, associations should follow the minimization rule under information insurance law if utilizing individual information. This implies guaranteeing that any private information is sufficient, applicable, and restricted to what exactly is vital for the reasons for which it is handled. What is satisfactory, important, and vital corresponding to AI frameworks will be use-case explicit [1]. Nonetheless, there are various procedures that associations can embrace to foster AI frameworks, which process as minimal individual information as could be expected, while as yet remaining utilitarian. In this blog, we investigate probably the most important strategies for directed machine learning (ML) frameworks, which are, at present, the most widely recognized sort of AI being used [2]. Inside associations, the people responsible for the risk the executives and consistence of AI frameworks should know that such strategies exist and have the option to examine various methodologies with their specialized staff. The default approach of information researchers in planning and building AI frameworks will not really consider any information minimization constraints [3]. Associations should, hence, have set up risk the executives practices to guarantee that information minimization necessities, and all significant minimization methods, are completely considered from the plan stage, or on the other hand, assuming AI frameworks are purchased or worked by outsiders, as a component of the obtainment interaction due perseverance. Nonetheless, information minimization strategies do not totally dispense with risk [4]. Likewise, while a few strategies will not need any trade off to convey information minimization benefits, some will expect associations to offset information minimization with other consistence or utility targets, e.g., making more exact and nonbiased ML models [5, 6].

A portion of the interesting attributes of AI mean consistence with information insurance law's security prerequisites can be more difficult than with other, more settled advancements, both from an innovative and human point of view.

According to a mechanical viewpoint, AI frameworks present new sorts of intricacy not found in more conventional IT frameworks that you might be accustomed to utilizing. Contingent upon the conditions, your utilization of AI frameworks is additionally prone to depend intensely on outsider code associations with providers, or both [7]. Additionally, your current frameworks should be incorporated with a few other new and existing IT parts, which are likewise unpredictably associated. Since AI frameworks work as a feature of a bigger chain of programming parts, information streams, hierarchical work processes and business processes, you should adopt a comprehensive strategy to security. This intricacy might make it harder to recognize and deal with some security risks, and may expand others, like the risk of blackouts [8].

According to a human viewpoint, individuals engaged with building and conveying AI frameworks are probably going to have a more extensive scope of foundations than expected, including customary computer programming, frameworks organization, information researchers, and analysts, just as domain specialists. Security practices and assumptions might shift fundamentally, and for some there might be less comprehension of more extensive security consistence prerequisites, just as those of information insurance law all the more explicitly [9, 10]. Security of individual information may not dependably have been a key need, particularly in the event that somebody was formerly assembling AI applications with nonindividual information or in an exploration limit. Further complexities emerge on the grounds that normal practices regarding how to deal with individual information safely in information science and AI designing are as yet being worked on. As a feature of your consistence with the security standard, you ought to guarantee that you effectively screen and consider the best in class security rehearses when involving individual information in an AI setting [11]. It is preposterous to expect to list all realized security risks that may be exacerbated when you use AI to deal with individual information. The effect of AI on security relies upon:

(1) the manner in which the innovation is assembled and sent;
(2) the intricacy of the association conveying it;
(3) the strength and development of the current risk the executive's capacities; and the nature, extension, setting and motivations behind the handling of individual information by the AI framework, and the risks acted to people like an outcome.

The accompanying speculative situations are expected to raise attention to a portion of the realized security risks and difficulties that AI can fuel [12]. The accompanying substance contains a few specialized details, so seeing how it might apply to your association might require consideration of staff in both consistence and specialized jobs.

Our key message is that you should survey your risk the board works on guaranteeing individual information is secure in an AI setting.

The individual information of individuals, who an AI framework, was trained on may be unintentionally uncovered by the results of the actual framework.

It is typically accepted that the individual information of the people whose information was utilized to train an AI framework cannot be induced by basically noticing the expectations the framework returns in light of new data sources [13]. Notwithstanding, new sorts of privacy attacks on ML models propose that this is here and there conceivable.

Specialists have zeroed in additional on two sorts of these privacy attacks—"model inversion" and "membership inference" [14].

What are model inversion attacks?

In a model inversion attack, in the event that attackers as of now approach a few individual information having a place with explicit people remembered for the training information, they can construe further private data about those equivalent people by noticing the sources of info and results of the ML model [15, 16]. The data attackers can find out about what goes past conventional inferences about people with comparable attributes.

What are membership inference attacks?

Membership inference attacks permit malevolent entertainers to conclude whether a given individual was available in the training information of a ML model. In any case, not at all like in model inversion, they do not really gain proficiency with any extra private information about the person.

For instance, assuming clinic records are utilized to train a model, which predicts when a patient will be released, attackers could involve that model in mix with different information about a specific person (that they as of now need) to work out in the event that they were essential for the training information. This would not uncover any singular's information from the training informational index itself; however, by and by, it would uncover that they had visited one of the medical clinics that created the training information during the period the information was gathered.

Membership inference attacks can take advantage of certainty scores gave close by a model's forecast. Assuming an individual was in the training information, then, at that point, the model will be lopsidedly sure about a forecast with regard to that individual since it has seen them previously. This permits the attacker to surmise that the individual was in the training information [17]. The gravity of the outcomes of models' weakness to membership inference will rely upon how touchy or uncovering membership may be. On the off chance that a model is trained on countless individuals drawn from everybody, then, at that point, membership inference attacks present less risk. However, assuming the model is trained on a powerless or delicate populace (e.g. persons having dementia, or infected with HIV), then, at that point, simply uncovering that somebody is important for that populace might be a not kidding privacy risk.

8.2 Related Work

The information minimization rule expects you to recognize the base measure of individual information you really want to satisfy your motivation, and to just handle that data, and no more. Be that as it may, AI frameworks for the most part require a lot of information. From the beginning it might accordingly be hard to perceive how AI frameworks can follow the information minimization standard, yet in the event that you are involving AI as a feature of your handling, you are as yet needed to do as such [16, 17]. While it might seem testing, by and by this may not be the situation. The information minimization standard does not mean either "process no private information" or on the other hand "assuming we process more, we will violate the law." The key is that you just cycle the individual information you want for your motivation. How you approach figuring out what is "sufficient, important and restricted" is subsequently going to be explicit to your conditions, and our current direction on information minimization details the means you should take. With regard to AI frameworks, what is "sufficient, important and restricted" is subsequently additionally case explicit. In any case, there are various methods that you can embrace to foster AI frameworks that interaction just the information you really want, while as yet remaining practical. Inside your associations, the people responsible for the risk the board and consistence of AI frameworks should know that such strategies exist and have the option to talk about and survey various methodologies with your specialized staff. For instance, the default approach of information researchers in planning and building AI frameworks may include gathering and utilizing however much information as could reasonably be expected, without pondering ways they could accomplish similar purposes with less information. You should in this manner carry out risk the board rehearses intended to guarantee that information minimization, and all pertinent minimization strategies, are completely considered from the plan stage. Additionally, assuming you purchase in AI frameworks or carry out frameworks worked by outsiders (or both), these contemplations should shape some portion of the obtainment interaction due persistence. You ought to likewise know that, while they might assist you with following the standard of information minimization, the procedures portrayed here do not wipe out different sorts of risk. Additionally, while a few strategies will not need any trade off to follow information minimization necessities, others might require you to offset information minimization with other consistence or utility targets. For instance, making all the more statistically precise and non-prejudicial ML models [13].

When planning and building ML applications, information researchers will by and large accept that all information utilized in training, testing and working the framework will be collected in a unified manner, and held in its full and unique structure by a solitary element in various spots all through the AI framework's lifecycle [14, 15]. In any case, where this is private information, you really want to consider whether it is important to deal with it for your purpose(s). Assuming you can accomplish similar result by handling less private information then by definition, the information minimization guideline expects you to do as such. Various methods exist which can assist you with limiting how much private information you want to process.

As we have explained, the training stage includes applying a learning calculation to a dataset containing a bunch of elements for every person who is utilized to produce the prediction or arrangement. In any case, not all elements remembered for a dataset will essentially be applicable to your motivation. For instance, not all monetary and segment highlights will be helpful to predict credit risk [11]. Thusly, you want to evaluate which highlights – and along these lines what information – are applicable for your motivation, and just cycle that information. There are assortments of standard component determination strategies utilized by information researchers to choose highlights, which will be helpful for consideration in a model. These strategies are great practice in information science; however they additionally go a few ways toward meeting the information minimization guideline. The way that a few information may later in the process be viewed as helpful for making predictions is not to the point of building up why you really want to save it for this reason, nor does it retroactively legitimize its assortment, use, or maintenance. You should not gather individual information in case it very well may be valuable later on, in spite of the fact that you might have the option to hold data for a predictable occasion that may not happen, however provided that you can legitimize it [10].

As a rule, when an AI framework gains from information (just like the case with ML models), the more information it is trained on, the more statistically exact it will be. That is, the more probable it will catch any fundamental, statistically valuable connections between the elements in the datasets. As explained in the segment on "What do we really want to do about measurable precision?" The fairness rule implies that your AI framework should be adequately statistically exact for your motivations. For instance, a model for predicting future buys dependent on clients' buy history would will more often than not be all the more statistically precise the more clients are remembered for the training information. Also, any new highlights added to a current dataset might be applicable to what the model is attempting to predict. For instance, buy chronicles increased with extra segment information may additionally work on the factual exactness of the model.

In any case, as a rule, the more information focuses gathered with regards to every individual, and the more individuals whose information is remembered for the informational index, the more noteworthy the risks to those people, regardless of whether the information is gathered for a particular reason. The guideline of information minimization requires you not to utilize a larger number of information than is needed for your motivations [17]. So on the off chance that you can accomplish adequate exactness with fewer elements or less people being incorporated (or both), you ought to do as such.

A portion of these procedures include changing the training information to decrease the degree to which it tends to be followed back to explicit people, while retaining its utilization for the motivations behind training great performing models. You can apply these sorts of privacy-upgrading strategies to the training information after you have effectively gathered it. Where conceivable, in any case, you ought to apply them prior to gathering any private information, as a piece of alleviating the risks to people that enormous datasets can present. You can numerically gauge the adequacy of these privacy-improving strategies in adjusting the privacy of people and the utility of a ML framework, utilizing techniques like differential privacy. Differential privacy is a method for estimating whether a model made by a ML calculation altogether relies upon the information of a specific individual used to train it [18]. While numerically thorough in principle, seriously carrying out differential privacy by and by is as yet testing. You should screen advancements in these strategies and evaluate whether they can give significant information minimization prior to endeavoring to carry out them. They may not be proper or adequately mature to convey in your specific setting.

8.3 Proposed Mechanism

In the past RAPPOR algorithm with basic modifications using Bloom's filter have been used by researchers to provide privacy preservation. In our novel mechanism we use one-time basic RAPPOR algorithm with ribbon filter to minimize the release of sensitive data. In various situations, ribbon filter provides 10% faster processing time than other filters like blooms filter and XOR filter. For large datasets, space overhead is also reduced by 1% by using the ribbon filter. The definition intends to guarantee that the result of the calculation does not altogether rely upon a specific person's information. The measurement of the expanded danger that investment in a help postures to an individual can, thusly, engage customers to make a better educated choice with regards to whether they need their information to be important for the assortment.

As a rule, the objective of information assortment utilizing RAPPOR is to realize which strings are available in the examined populace and what their comparing frequencies are. Since we utilize the Bloom channel (loss of data) and intentionally add noise for privacy protection, disentangling requires refined measurable methods. To work with learning, before any information assortment starts every customer is haphazardly allotted and turns into a long-lasting individual from one of m cohorts. Cohorts execute various arrangements of h hash capacities for their Bloom channels, subsequently lessening the shot at incidental crashes of two strings across every one of them. Overt repetitiveness presented by running m cohorts at the same time extraordinarily works on the bogus positive rate. The decision of m ought to be thought about cautiously, nonetheless. At the point when m is too little, then, at that point, impacts are still very logical, while when m is too huge, then, at that point, every individual companion gives lacking sign because of its little example size (around N=m, where N is the quantity of reports). Every customer should report its partner number with each submitted report, i.e., it is not private however made private.

Algorithm

Step 1: Initially when the Rappor Service is started, a client will produce a random 128-byte secret key which will be saved, which will not change and the server can never access it. It will also assign itself to a random cohort.
Step 2: For a given metric considered in collection, we store a ribbon filter, denoted as a vector of m bits. Each cohort employs a different set of hash functions for the ribbon filter. When a sample for recording is passed through the filter, it outputs bits in the ribbon filter for that concerned metric.
Step 3: After sample collection is completed, report is generated. We consider the vector of bits we have acquired for the metric and assign two levels of noise by taking the following steps.
Step 4: Include noise in deterministic degree:

Design a deterministic pseudo-random function by passing the client's secret key, the metric name, and the ribbon filter value into a privacy generator function.

Step 5: The server obtains results from the cohort that the client is assigned to.

8.4 Experimental Results

The huge measure of randomness implies that we cannot reach significant determinations from few reports. Regardless of whether we total many reports from a similar client, they incorporate similar pseudo-random noise in every one of their reports of a similar worth, so we are successfully restricted to one report for each particular worth. Without a doubt, even with limitless measures of information on a RAPPOR measurement, there are severe limits on how much data can be learned. Specifically, the information gathered from some random client or customer contains such critical vulnerability, and ensures such solid deniability, as to keep onlookers from making determinations without any hesitation.

We can observe from Figure 8.1 that the count of cohorts significantly impacts the percentage of privacy leak in a CPS ecosystem. For acceptable levels of privacy leaks of up to 2% to 3%, we must use at least a minimum of 40 cohorts. It may be difficult to manage the number of cohorts but it is the price of privacy we have to pay. We can also observe that by applying

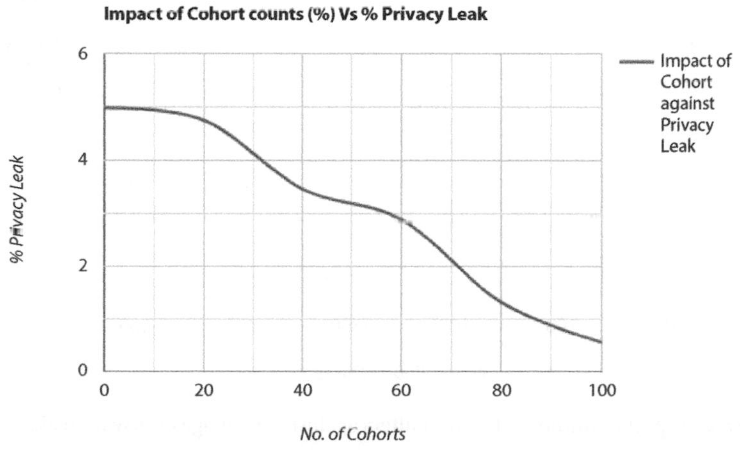

Figure 8.1 Impact of number of cohorts against percentage of privacy leak.

100 or more number of cohorts, the privacy leak can be maintained at a remarkable rate of below 0.5% but in practical implementations it is nearly impossible due to the fact that our AI algorithms need minimum about of data to learn about the privacy features in a CPS ecosystem. In case we do not provide more number of privacy features to the learning algorithm, then learning rate will reduce and this will ultimately impact the performance of our proposed novel mechanism. This trade-off has to be balanced but it is not quite easy.

From Figure 8.2, we can infer that the count of ribbon filters increases to bring down the percentage of privacy leak appreciably when we apply more than 300 ribbon filters to add noise to the Cohort of records. With less than 100 ribbon filters we are at a considerable risk of leaking the private data of nearly more than 3%. So, it becomes imperative to apply more than 200 ribbon filters to handle a strong adversary attack to reveal the identity of clients who participate in a CPS ecosystem.

In Figure 8.3, which represents the comparative performances of the current popular strategies for privacy preservation in a CPS we can easily infer that our proposed novel mechanism outperforms the rest of the techniques appreciably. Personalized privacy and Differential privacy are quite robust but without application of ribbon filters their performance is questionable. Our proposed mechanism uses the RAPPOR mechanism along with application of ribbon filters to add deterministic degree of

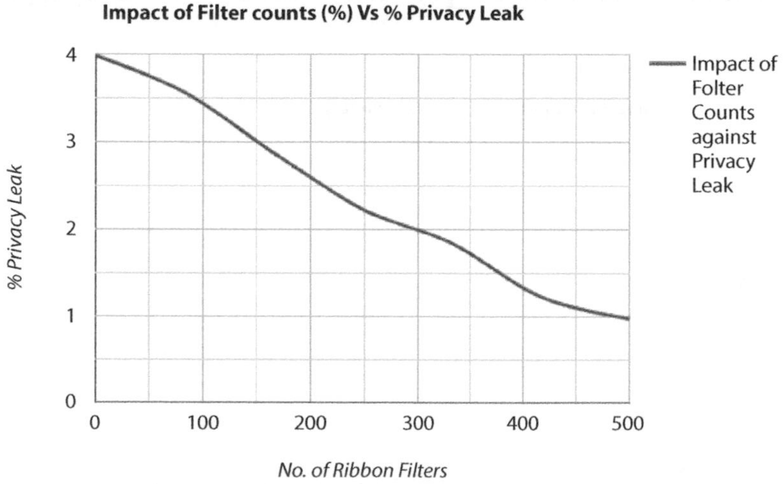

Figure 8.2 Impact of number of ribbon filters against percentage of privacy leak.

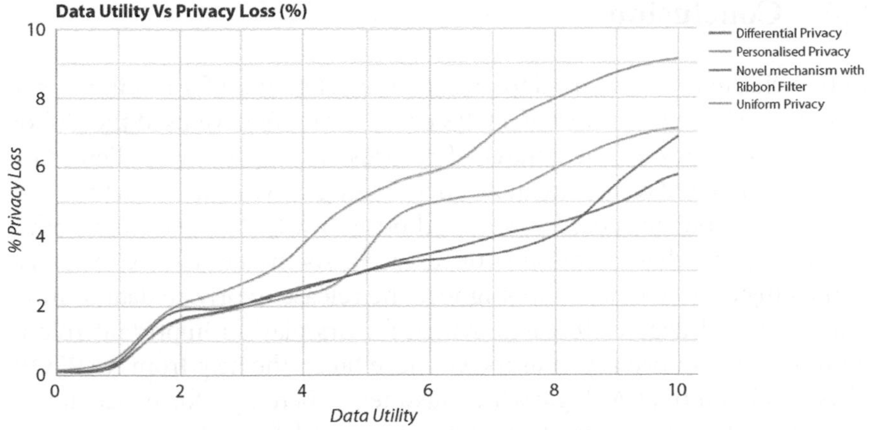

Figure 8.3 Comparative performance of popular approaches for privacy preservation.

noise, which can be fine-tuned by application of an AI learning algorithm. We can also observe that uniform privacy gives a high degree of data utility at the cost of more than 8% release of private data which is unacceptable in modern day applications.

8.5 Future Directions

On the basis of our novel understanding, we indicate few future directions for AI-enabled privacy preservation in an ecosystem where CPS entities are more than ever data driven in nature. Our paper calls for more dominant benchmarks to evaluate the robustness of our proposed approach. Empirical studies have to be extensively carried out to observe the change in data utility when the count of cohorts gets increased. Yet another research direction propels us to observe keenly the application of ribbon filters in adding a certain degree of deterministic noise so that the performance of our proposed system does not degrade. For this, fine-tuning of features has to be done by AI experts. More said than done, it will be imperative to watch how the learning rate improves by application of variants of RAPPOR with respect to the release of private data of clients. In our future work, we intend to apply our model to work with standard CPS datasets in terms of security features, as well as privacy features.

8.6 Conclusion

In this chapter, we have tried to present a novel method for minimum private data release in entities of a CPS ecosystem. We have used the ribbon filter to add noise to the dataset of records storing sensitive client data. Our experimental results are quite encouraging as we observe that the performance of our proposed novel method is nearly 2% better than other popular approaches in this area of research. As the utility of CPS is also enhancing every day we cannot ignore the release of private data to more than a limited degree. To gauge which factors play an important role in quantification of privacy of users will have taken the help from RAPPOR. This tool has inbuilt AI logic which justifies its better performance in hiding the identity of a legitimate users from a large dataset of users. In most of the CPS entities, the functionality is data-driven, so minimization of data for learning and feature selection is quite a challenge in hand. Our paper is a sincere contribution toward the same direction advocating the CPS designers to equip themselves with the characteristics of AI to minimize release of private data without affecting the data utility in an adverse way.

References

1. Hsu, J., Gaboardi, M., Haeberlen, A., Khanna, S., Narayan, A., Pierce, B.C., Roth, A., Differential privacy: An economic method for choosing epsilon, in: *Proceedings of 27th IEEE Computer Security Foundations Symposium (CSF)*, 2014.
2. Hsu, J., Khanna, S., Roth, A., Distributed private heavy hitters, in: *Proceedings of the 39th International Colloquium Conference on Automata, Languages, and Programming (ICALP) -Volume Part I*, pp. 461–472, 2012.
3. Kenthapadi, K., Korolova, A., Mironov, I., Mishra, N., Privacy via the Johnson-Linden Strauss transform. *J. Priv. Confid.*, 5, 1, 39–71, 2013.
4. Keren, D., Sagy, G., Abboud, A., Ben-David, D., Schuster, A., Sharfman, I., Deligiannakis, A., Monitoring distributed, heterogeneous data streams: The emergence of safe zones, in: *Proceedings of the 1st International Conference on Applied Algorithms (ICAA)*, pp. 17–28, 2014.
5. Kifer, D. and Machanavajjhala, A., No free lunch in data privacy, in: *Proceedings of the ACM SIGMOD International Conference on Management of Data (SIGMOD)*, pp. 193–204, 2011.
6. Liu, B., Jiang, Y., Sha, F., Govindan, R., Cloud-enabled privacy-preserving collaborative learning for mobile sensing, in: *Proceedings of the 10th ACM Conference on Embedded Network Sensor Systems (SenSys)*, pp. 57–70, 2012.

7. Graf, T.M. and Lemire, D., Xor filters: Faster and smaller than bloom and cuckoo filters. *ACM J. Exp. Algorithmics*, 25, 1–16, 2020, 2020. https://doi.org/10.1145/3376122.
8. Kirsch, A. and Mitzenmacher, M., Less hashing, same performance: Building a better bloom filter. *Random Struct. Algorithms*, 33, 2, 187–218, 2008, 2008.
9. Kirsch, A. and Mitzenmacher, M., The power of one move: Hashing schemes for hardware. *IEEE/ACM Trans. Netw.*, 18, 1752–1765, 2010.
10. Knuth, D.E., *Sorting and Searching, 2nd ed,* Addison-Wesley, Boston, Massachusetts, United States, 1998, http://dl.acm.org/citation.cfm?id=280635.
11. Kumar, S., Turner, J.S., Crowley, P., Peacock hashing: Deterministic and updatable hashing for high performance networking, in: *INFOCOM 2008. 27th IEEE International Conference on Computer Communications, Joint Conference of the IEEE Computer and Communications Societies*, Phoenix, AZ, USA, 13-18 April 2008, IEEE, pp. 101–105, 2008, https://doi.org/10.1109/INFOCOM.2008.29.
12. Lang, H., Neumann, T., Kemper, A., Boncz, P.A., Performance-optimal filtering: Bloom overtakes cuckoo at high-throughput. *Proc. VLDB Endow.*, 12, 5, 502–515, 2019. https://doi.org/10.14778/3303753.
13. Lemire, D., Fast random integer generation in an interval. *ACM Trans. Model. Comput. Simul.*, 29, 1, 1–12, 2019. https://doi.org/10.1145/3230636.
14. Keshk, M., Turnbull, B., Moustafa, N., Vatsalan, D., Choo, K.K.R., A privacy-preserving-framework-based blockchain and deep learning for protecting smart power networks. *IEEE Trans. Industr. Inform.*, 16, 8, 5110–5118, 2019.
15. Hassan, M.U., Rehmani, M.H., Chen, J., Differential privacy techniques for cyber physical systems: A survey. *IEEE Commun. Surv. Tut.*, 22, 1, 746–789, 2020.
16. Hossain, M.T., Islam, S., Badsha, S., Shen, H., Desmp: Differential privacy-exploited stealthy model poisoning attacks in federated learning, University of Exeter, UK, 2021, arXiv preprint arXiv:2109.09955.
17. Gong, X., Chen, X., Xing, K., Shin, D.-H., Zhang, M., Zhang, J., Personalized location privacy in mobile networks: A social group utility approach, in: *2015 IEEE Conference on Computer Communications (INFOCOM)*, IEEE, pp. 1008–1016, 2015.
18. Wen, R., Cheng, W., Huang, H., Miao, W., Wang, C., Privacy preserving trajectory data publishing with personalized differential privacy, in: *2020 IEEE Intl. Conf. on Parallel Distributed Processing with Applications, Big Data Cloud Computing, Sustainable Computing Communications, Social Computing Networking (ISPA/BDCloud/SocialCom/SustainCom)*, pp. 313–320, 2020.

9

Environmental and Industrial Applications Using Internet of Things (IoT)

Manal Fawzy[1,2,3], Alaa El Din Mahmoud[1,2,3] and Ahmed M. Abdelfatah[1,2]

[1]*Environmental Sciences Department, Faculty of Science, Alexandria University, Alexandria, Egypt*

[2]*Green Technology Group, Faculty of Science, Alexandria University, Alexandria, Egypt*

[3]*National Biotechnology Network of Expertise (NBNE), Academy of Scientific Research and Technology (ASRT), Cairo, Egypt*

Abstract

This chapter aims to depict the need to turn our daily life practices into smart ones to improve the quality of life. Internet technologies and data processing have advanced to allow access to and interaction with different equipments all around the world. Therefore, the role of the Internet of Things (IoT) and sensors in this respect was discussed. IoT as a physical system that is connected over the networks plays a critical role in intelligent decision making, system performance enhancement, and service management. IoT helps in the development of the most powerful industrial systems as well as a variety of applications in industry and environment. This chapter gives a review of most IoT applications in a smart environment, agriculture, and smart environmental monitoring, such as air, soil, and water monitoring. Also, the environmental health-related to COVID-19 monitoring is highlighted. The key challenges in IoT applications in industry and environment were also highlighted.

Keywords: IoT, smart environment, ecosystem, water, air, soil, quality, industry, COVID-19

**Corresponding author*: alaa-mahmoud@alexu.edu.eg

Jyotir Moy Chatterjee, Harish Garg and R. N. Thakur (eds.) A Roadmap for Enabling Industry 4.0 by Artificial Intelligence, (141–168) © 2023 Scrivener Publishing LLC

9.1 Introduction

The Internet of Things (IoT) is a manifestation of today's exponential progress in information and communication technologies [1]. According to Union [2] and Evans [3], IoT is "a dynamic worldwide network infrastructure that can identify, control, and monitor each object via the internet using a specific agreement protocol, via the interconnection of physical and virtual things." IoT is currently described as "the interconnection of identifiable embedded computing devices within the existing internet infrastructure." [4]. Figure 9.1 explains its concept through autonomous networked actors as mentioned in Yang, Yang [5]. It is worth mentioning that IoT is bringing many benefits to extend our perception and our ability to monitor and control the environment around us. With the integration of the Internet with several technologies, solving our day-to-day difficulties becomes extremely simple. The technology of IoT allows for fresh innovative ideas and progress to improve people's living standards. With the use of IoT in the workplace and the development of wireless technologies, it is now possible to monitor and manage devices remotely. As a result, new concepts that use IoT to benefit various areas of society and industry have emerged. For instance: ambient assisted living [6], smart cities [7], or smart logistics.

Additionally, the IoT applications enhance our lives to be valuable at the social, economic, and environmental levels [8, 9]. At the environmental level, IoT can be used for monitoring air and water pollution, noise level, temperature, and hazardous radiation [10, 11]. Furthermore, gathering and storing environmental records, as well as trigger warnings to the

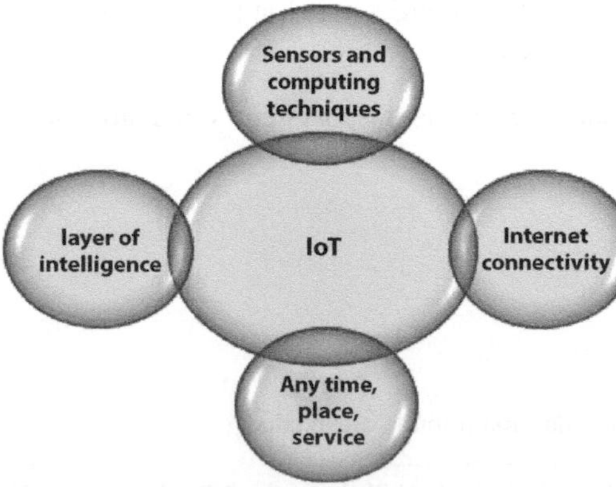

Figure 9.1 Internet of Things (IoT) concept.

public and authorities if the detected variables exceed the compliance [12]. Models can be estimated for environmental variables, explore and track pollution sources over time and space to ensure a suitable environment for all inhabitants.

It is observed that the number of publications on IoT is increasing substantially and reaches the maximum number in 2020, which is 1246 and it is expected that the number of publications will increase in 2021 as it is now 614 as shown in Figure 9.2a. The number of publications related to the environmental applications of IoT increased substantially especially in 2020 as the number reached almost 30 (Figure 9.2b). Additionally, the number of publications of IoT in the industry also increased to 1102 in 2020.

IoT has recently been used in smart environmental applications, allowing users to recognize and regulate environmental behavior via network of

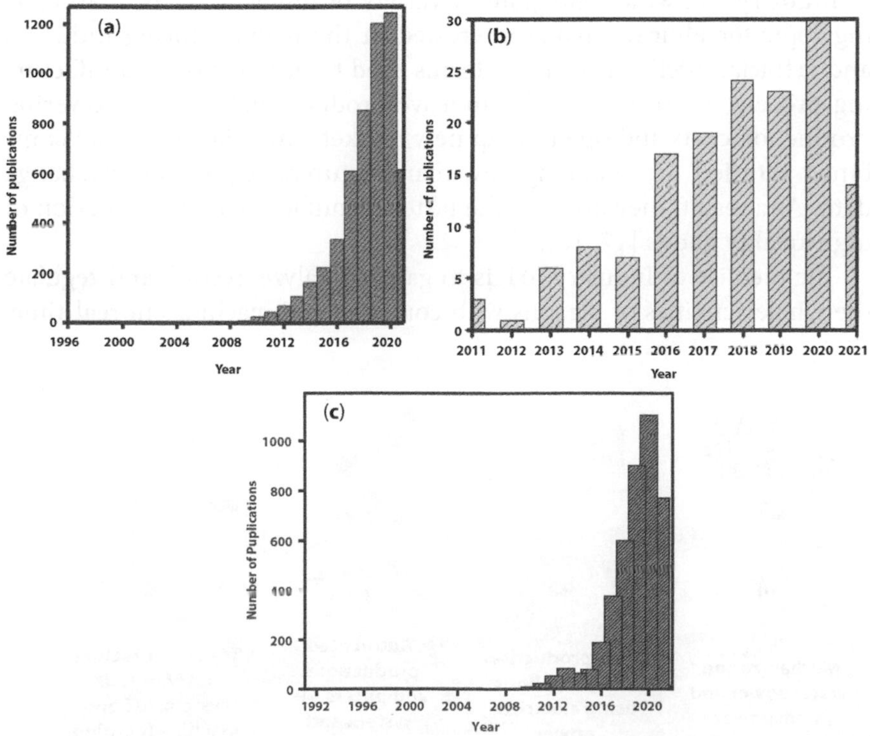

Figure 9.2 Number of publications concerning (a) IoT different applications, (b) environmental applications of IoT, and (c) IoT applications in Industry (Data obtained from Scopus; 6.2021).

connected devices [13]. Capella, Bonastre [14] stated that IoT-based environmental applications are currently in more progress and IoT presents a number of intriguing issues as well as enticing prospects. For instance, it is being integrated into existing applications as well as providing new insights for future applications [15].

In the late 18th century, mechanical industrial facilities were developed, resulting in Industry 1.0. At the beginning of the twentieth century, a new industry called Industry 2.0 formed, which produced electrically powered machinery. The industry developed a mass manufacturing technique and employed electrical energy as the primary energy source. Industry 3 began with the invention and manufacture of a wide range of electronic gadgets (Figure 9.3). The Internet and telecommunications industries have exploded as a result of Industry 4, which is still happening today. Manufacturing paradigms have shifted as a result as well as the application of sophisticated information and manufacturing technology (Figure 9.3) [16].

Industry 4.0, which integrates a variety of innovations, is a fascinating topic for almost anyone interested in the manufacturing industry, and artificial intelligence are all terms used to describe the manufacturing process. Sensors can help improve product quality while lowering production costs and opening up new markets. Intelligent sensors combined with IoT are changing how manufacturers acquire and exchange data. As a result, they assist in the faster manufacture and production of high-quality goods [17, 18].

The premise of Industry IoT is to gather, analyze, record, and regulate the whole activities of persons with computerized machines in real-time,

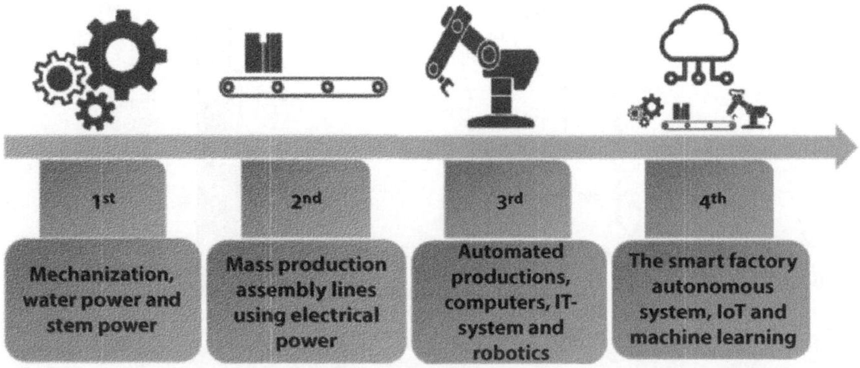

Figure 9.3 An overview of the industrial revolutions.

resulting in lower production costs and higher quality. It is inextricably linked to the growth of smart sensors, which are persuaded to allocate their resources efficiently. Additionally, they may monitor the entire control system (e.g., product selling/consumption expenses, product manufacturing rate, worker location, malicious activity, and so on) without the need for human interaction [19]. The use of IoT in the workplace, as well as emerging wireless technologies, allows for remote monitoring and control of devices [20].

Sensors are employed in a variety of industries for a variety of purposes, both routine and commercial. Sensor systems have recently become more popular in industrial sectors, showcasing their impressive capabilities. Sensors connect different devices and systems, allowing them to communicate with one another and track systems and equipment across the facility. As sensor capacities have increased, they have become exceedingly small and portable, allowing them to be connected to difficult-to-reach and potentially dangerous objects, transforming them into high-tech intellectuals. Sensors have long been a vital component of production, but there are issues have endured largely unsolved until recently. For instance, signal diminution and machine noise [21, 22].

The Industrial Internet of Things (IIoT) explains the IoT as it applies to numerous manufacturing organizations, such as logistic services, shipping, electricity and chemical usage. Industry 4.0 is concerned with the most recent industrial revolution, emphasizing mechanization, modernization, information, cyber-physical systems, procedures, and human interaction [23]. The emergence of the IIoT and Industry 4.0 opens up the possibility of linking computer-controlled control schemes for remote monitoring and rapid response to events that require concurrent processing. Furthermore, sensor deployment may provide several benefits over a variety of industrial systems [24].

The aim of this chapter is to highlight various environmental and industrial IoT-based applications, which have been recently presented. The main commitments of this account are:

- Screening the IoT applications in the environment and industry.
- Presenting the encounters for the environmental applications approaches in IoT.
- highlighting the future aspects and concerns in environmental IoT-based applications.

9.2 IoT-Based Environmental Applications

According to Ericsson and Cisco, "by 2021, roughly 50 billion small embedded sensors and actuators are connected to the internet, and the IoTs will generate 14.4 trillion dollars in value for industries." [25]. As a result, we may conclude that the IoT environment will be made up of an extremely high number of linked heterogeneous devices [26].

The data generated by heterogeneous smart IoT settings is enormous. This data is originally unprocessed and must be treated before it can be used. This raw data is either infrastructure-related or not to the environmental features of the IoT-built environment. It contains sensor data, such as recorded outputs and actuator operations [27]. Both types of data are by their very nature diverse. It may be mined for useful information if properly processed using the right data mining algorithm [28].

The main features and services of IoT in smart environments are summarized in this section (home, environment, health, cities, and factories). We will focus on the environmental applications of IoT. Figure 9.4 depicts several IoT applications in smart environments. Each application performs a certain task such as Ambient Assistant Living (AAL) in health care [29, 30]. AAL uses smart sensors, cameras, and communication devices. They are connected via Bluetooth, Wi-Fi, etc.

Many countries and organizations are vigorously pursuing research and contributing sensor-enabled connected devices to enhance their

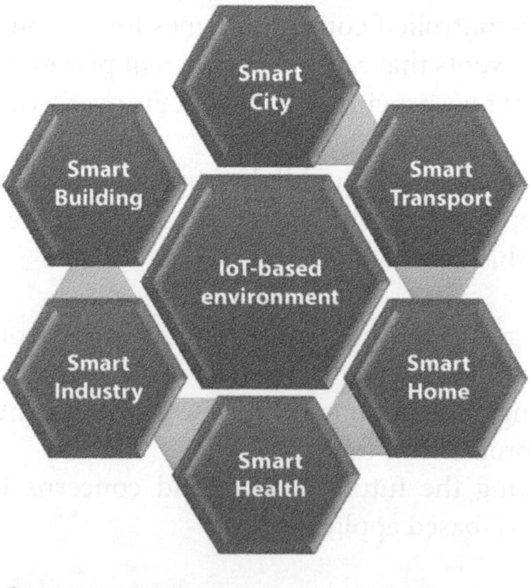

Figure 9.4 IoT-based smart environment.

performance with more quality and productivity in a shorter time. The global giant companies including Apple, Microsoft, Google, etc., are working on new concepts to create a Smart environment [26, 31].

In the 20th century, Industry 3.0 involved industrial automation. Industry 4.0 exists with the 4th-Generation Industrial Revolution that can connect to a network. Global economic powers, such as Germany, the USA, Korea, and China, have already developed a roadmap for smart manufacturing (SM) [32].

Lee *et al.* [33] reviewed the latest sustainable innovative services in smart remote machinery maintenance systems (SRMMS) with Komatsu. Further information on the above-mentioned points is addressed with good insight in Thibaud *et al.* [34]. For instance, sensors are connected in factories, as well as other branches of these factories to minimize human intervention.

Another issue is noise pollution in factories. Hachem, Mallet [35] presented a method for creating more precise noise maps by combining generated and measured noise levels. They demonstrated the improvements in quality enabled by the data assimilation method. Temperature, humidity, air pollution, and water pollution may all be sensed with a variety of sensors. Temperature is measured using sensors, such as RTDs and thermometers. Dust sensors and gas sensors can be used to assess air pollution [36]. Pattern recognition software is used in these technologies, these are used to measure pollution levels in cities.

9.3 Smart Environmental Monitoring

9.3.1 Air Quality Assessment

The increasingly degraded air quality in many regions of the world can be a consequence of increasing globalization, urbanization, and forest fires [37]. Hence, the detection of the harmful gases presents in the atmosphere, that is responsible for the poor quality of air, is a task that can be easily accomplished by the technology of "IoT-Internet of Things."

Environmental behavior analysis relies heavily on continuous monitoring. Kim *et al.* [38] developed chemically fluorinated graphene oxide (FGRO) sensors. When subjected to NH_3, the sensors improve their sensitivity, selectivity, and reversibility, with a theoretical detection limit of only 6 μg L^{-1}. This sensor has exceptional NH_3-sensing capabilities that can expand the integration of functionalized 2D materials in gas sensors. Spark plasma sintering was used to make superhydrophobic reduced graphene oxide for extremely selective NO_2 detection by Wu *et al.* [39]. It proved the ability to detect 50 μg L^{-1} NO_2, with a limit of detection of 9.1 μg L^{-1}. For this purpose, various nanomaterials including graphene oxide [40, 41], reduced graphene oxide [42], and metallic nanoparticles [43–45] that were synthesized in a sustainable way to be applicable in future sensor applications [46].

Duvall, Long [47] applied CairclipO_3/NO_2 sensors to measure and provide Ozone (O_3) and Nitrogen Dioxide (NO_2) concentrations in total. To get the concentration value of NO_2, the cairclipNO_2 sensor is used [48]. The NO_2 data had a low agreement with reference data ($r = 0.08$); however, the separate O_3 data had a high level of agreement ($r = 0.82$).

In order to control temperature, humidity, CO_2, and NH_3 parameters, an IoT monitoring system based on a wireless sensor network was proposed for henhouses [49]. Its key benefit is that it improves the data collection accuracy and decreasing maintenance cost despite the consumption of energy is not evaluated.

Gas sensors are used to detect the existence of various gases and monitor changes in air quality. They are also used in a variety of industries. Sensors of this sort can be found in a variety of shapes. These sensors are almost probably employed by collaborative robots because they are designed to create a constant working environment for employees. Tactile recognition devices, for example, send a signal to the robot ordering it to slow down or halt if it feels resistance on a soft surface [50].

9.3.2 Water Quality Assessment

Water scarcity is a major issue in many countries, so wastewater treatment is necessary to provide clean water [51–54]. This critical aspect of many living forms' existence has been overlooked for decades due to various human concerns about mankind's unrestrained progress [55]. Water quality analysis requires the measurement of numerous parameters [56, 57]. However, the water quality management (WQM) system proposed the measurement of the key water parameters: water's pH value, turbidity, water level present in the tank, and temperature [58]. Total suspended solids (TSS) in water, for example, increases as turbidity rises (nephelometric turbidity units [NTU]). Furthermore, the hydrogen ion is sensitive to electrode measurements with a potential that is proportional to the concentration of the solution [59, 60].

Various hazardous pollutants are reaching and contaminating the water bodies [61, 62]. The widely utilized Internet of Things (IoT) technology provides a good range of options for maintaining control over the situation. There is an increasing demand for autonomous sensors to detect contaminants in water on a continual basis. The literature on the deployable sensors for PO_4^{3-} and NO_3^- has been reviewed by Duffy and Regan [63], with an emphasis on analytical performance and cost. In addition, an overview of techniques for the monitoring of both anions is presented.

Capella *et al.* [64] have presented a novel method based on Cloud services and IoT for the creation of improved sensors. Their suggestion was used in the creation of a potentiometric sensor for determining bicarbonate in water. This sensor's data are posted to the cloud, where it may be accessed by anybody. Furthermore, by utilizing the sensor's network connection, this device makes use of data accessible in the Cloud (mostly pH readings), resulting in improved performance with lower cost and energy consumption. The results were with a high level of precision and accuracy.

The details and deployment of a portable, transportable, cost-effective, and water level control system were described by Lambrou, Anastasiou [65]. For wireless communication with the Internet server, radiofrequency transceivers (RF transceivers) are used. The system is totally manipulated by the user with a microcontroller unless the water in the bottle is drained or overflows. Dissolved oxygen, tumbling, pH, temperature, and other factors are detected using the sensor array. A collection of sensors' installation costs is reduced because of wireless technology.

Water quality must be monitored on a regular basis in institutions and industry. However, the techniques are usually expensive and time-consuming. Hence, low-cost sensors are required to apply their concept in field applications. The water level can be measured by the ultrasonic sensor, which offers a 2- to 4-m measurement [66]. The sensor of DHT11 that with negative temperature coefficient (NTC) measures the temperature and humidity. The merit of this sensor is its calibration by the factory so it is easy to interface [66].

Postolache, Pereira [67] proposed an IoT solution for the measurement of temperature, conductivity, and turbidity based on a WSN architecture that monitoring water quality parameters from urban lakes, estuaries, and rivers. Kassal *et al.* [68] have developed a wireless sensor for usage along with pH and ISEs (ion-selective electrodes). Furthermore, the detection of residual chlorine in the form of the hypochlorite ion [$HClO^-$] has been established using interdigitized microelectrode array (IDA) electrodes [69]. IDA sensors have a better sensitivity of 600 mV with HClO than traditional sensing methods, as well as a small size, quick response, low cost, and low power consumption, making them ideal for IoT applications. Capella *et al.* [64] have recently proposed the development of a potentiometric sensor for bicarbonate determination and can be accessed by users through a cloud. For instance, refer to Lambrou, Anastasiou [65].

9.3.3 Soil Quality Assessment

Conservation of soil layers in different ecosystems reflects the health of the plants, trees, and microorganisms so soil quality should be always monitored [70, 71]. Watt, Phillips [72] presented a wireless sensor for monitoring sediment transport and movement. However, the limitations of this coastal monitoring technique are requiring largely manual operation and limited to the visible beach, which is considered as an incomplete representation. Due to these current difficulties, WSN technology can overcome these limitations.

Devapal [73] develops a solar-powered soil monitoring system to detect moisture, temperature, and humidity in farmland. This system comprises three modules; IoT, data mining, and mobile application modules. The data mining module is in charge of extracting data. Farmers are then provided with necessary information and guidance for the cultivation of crops via the mobile application module. Such measurements can be an indicator to know water demand around crop roots accurately.

9.3.4 Environmental Health-Related to COVID-19 Monitoring

Due to the outbreak of COVID-19, Khan, Abutaleb [74] summarized impacts of the virus on the environment based on literature. There are two types of prediction models of COVID-19 epidemiology are statistical and mechanistic that consider future transmission scenarios whereas the former model was short-term forecasting. Further details can be found in Khan *et al.* [75] and Gwenzi, Selvasembian [76]. Machine learning is used to help social networks that can predict pandemic models by the calculations of people likelihood networking [77, 78]. However, these rates are challenging to expect especially in a complex geopolitical landscape such as the USA and India.

With convolutional neural network (CNN) of chest X-rays and MRI lung pictures, artificial intelligence (AI) is applied in COVID-19 radiologic imaging [79, 80]. Synthetic data generated by generative adversarial networks (GANs) could be also used [81]. Furthermore, utilizing AI to anticipate protein folding allows scientists to discover drugs neutralizing the viral proteins and forecast the structure of protein without relying on previous templates [82].

9.4 Applications of Sensors Network in Agro-Industrial System

Smart agriculture is the most recent IoT development. Farmers will be able to manage their land more efficiently, make operations faster and more agile, and achieve maximum yields thanks to smart agriculture [83]. Sensors in precision agriculture provide farmers with a variety of data, which is then processed to maximize crop production, as shown in Table 9.1. Mobile applications are used to control these sensors.

IoT can help to control environmental variables during the product transport and evaluate field variables (atmospheric conditions, soil state, etc.) [88]. Mafuta, Zennaro [89] demonstrated the use of a wireless sensor network (WSN) in a Malawi irrigation management system (IMS). All electrical devices in this study were powered by solar photovoltaic panels and rechargeable batteries. Irrigation valves were also turned on to irrigate the field. The findings revealed a weakness in deploying such a system.

A precision irrigation resolution grounded on a wireless sensor network was indorsed by Khriji, El Houssaini [74]. This scheme was structured using three nodules: the first focused on soil edaphic factors as moisture and temperature; the second related to climatic ones as air temperature, humidity, wind speed, whereas the third attached to a valve to regulate irrigation. The main challenge was to create an automated irrigation system that saves the resources and efforts.

Pang, Chen [88] developed an online microclimate monitoring and control system for greenhouses. Lee, Hwang [90] developed a crop growth and yield prediction system based on IoT for balancing agricultural supply/demand. In a different application, Saville, Hatanaka [91] demonstrated a system based on a real-time estimation using ultrasonic sensors.

A dynamic analysis of farmlands was presented in Lee, Kang [92]. The system was created with the goal of creating grape growth-control plans and viticulture activities. Devapal [73] created a low-cost soil and weather monitoring sensor that analyses several soil parameters and meteorological conditions, as shown in Figure 9.5. The soil moisture sensor, gas sensor, and temperature sensor are all connected by an ATMEGA 328 microcontroller. It has a 1KB programmable read-only memory that is electrically erasable (EEPROM).

Table 9.1 Commercially available sensors for smart agricultural use.

Sensor type	Name	Manufacture	Features	References
Electromagnetic sensors	Crop Canopy Sensor	Top Con Agriculture	• Measuring chlorophyll and nitrogen contents. • Data is collected using the reflectance principle and pulsating laser diodes.	[83]
	Clorofilog	Falker	• Measuring chlorophyll in leaves. • Determining the plant's nutritional status during its growing stage. • It must be physically connected to the leaf.	
	Crop Cycle Phenom	Holland Scientific	• Collecting air temperature, vegetation indices, humidity, etc.	
	Soil Doctor Systems	Crop Technology		
Available location sensors	Sequoia	Parrot	• Capturing light absorbed and reflected by plants, which monitor crop health.	[84]
Air-flow sensors	Amplified Airflow Sensors	Honeywell	• Boosting the output signal. • Low power consumption.	[85]
Optical sensors	Optical sensors	-	• Using light to determine properties of soil. • determining organic matter content, moisture content, and clay in the soil.	[86]
Acoustic sensors	Acoustic sensors	-	• It detects sound and is commonly used in the field to detect pests.	[87]

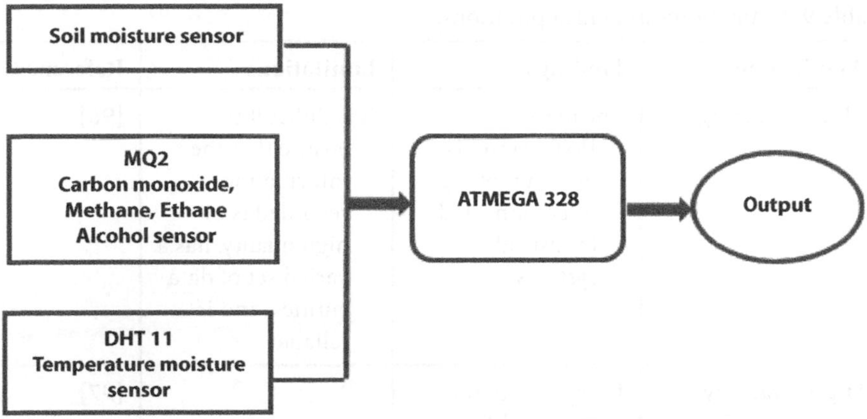

Figure 9.5 Connection of sensor with microcontroller.

9.5 Applications of IoT in Industry

The Internet of Things framework establishes a network connecting diverse systems (such as human beings, locomotive robots, wireless sensors, and so on) using a unique but realistic communication protocol to create a progressive multimodal network. The framework is made up of systems known as "things," and it has the competence to discover and investigate problems in systems, as well as design and equip systems to transmit data to IoT. People, machines, and information are the three categories of "things."

9.5.1 Application of IoT in the Autonomous Field

The majority of fields in autonomous applications are produced, autonomous robots, automotive factories, smart factories, remanufacturing, and process-related remanufacturing. These applications are shown in Table 9.2 below.

As stated by Sharma, Burman [20], there is wide applicability of IoT in manufacturing because there is a requirement for connectivity and information sharing among the various components. The Internet of Things (IoT) can be used to optimize many stages of product development. The method of self-optimization relies heavily on automation. At the center of these automated production systems are sensors [93]. Sensors in robotic automation enable robot manual labor safer [94]. Due to the obvious potential benefits for manufacturers, as greater operating performance, and lower operating costs, the market is already reshaping the manufacturing business. Sensors are used in a variety of applications, including automated production systems [95].

Table 9.2 Autonomous field applications.

Applications	Findings	Limitations	References
Manufacturing	The massive IIoT market is made up of big, interconnected industrial systems.	It is difficult to ensure that the information recorded is of high quality, has a varied set of data entities, and is reliable.	**[96]**
Digital factory	Every part of the product life cycle should be optimized.		**[97]**
Autonomous robot	Produce autonomously while maintaining security, elasticity, adaptability, and collaboration.		**[98]**
Smart factory	Data analytics are real-time dynamics applied to the industry.	The IWN signals do not have enough capacity to support a high-speed connection and a large volume of data, but they are superior to a wired network in the industry.	**[99]**
Re-manufacturing	Renovation and replacement using additive manufacturing.		**[100]**

9.5.2 Applications of IoT in Software Industries

In the disciplines of fundamental software domains, IoT has a wide range of applications. These enable better security standards, as well as remote data monitoring and analysis of predefined data values. Table 9.3 depicts this information.

Table 9.3 Software field applications.

Applications	Findings	Limitations	References
Data carrying devices (DCD)	Sustainable monitoring and allocation of resources	-	[100]
Software distinct cloud development	cloud industrialized designs software different systems software representation	-	[101]
Data mining	Early prediction of Bayesian reliability	-	[102]
Cyber physical system (CPS)	Integrated communication with a set of connections	Cybersafety dangers have increased dramatically as a result of greater connectivity.	[103]
Big data analytics	Integrating big data with 4.0, as well as the quantity and variety of data	Big data is not suitable for resolving offline processes.	[104]
Fog-enabled industrial IoT	Mining, transportation, waste management, the food sector, and agriculture are all examples of industries.		

9.5.3 Sensors in Industry

In Industry 4.0, an integrated and smart network is required to develop intelligent production. Sensors can gather and evaluate data to help with decision making, and production line automation can benefit from self-optimization. Factory automation allows for the optimization of all personalized product solutions and assembly lines. Asset management technologies are projected to be implemented in the coming years. This technology would soon be widely used in a variety of industries for process management [105]. Sensors will be essential for automated industrial activities in the Industrial Internet of Things (IIoT).

The varied capacities of sensors for the Industry 4.0 are depicted in Figure 9.6. It looks at the common aspects of sensors for the Industry 4.0 environment, such as predictive maintenance, building automation, asset monitoring or conditioning, and overall process automation [106].

Firmware operations for the sensor applications are included in the introduction of a new class of sensors. Wireless sensor networking is now a reality, and the potential for growth in this discipline will continue to expand. To make use of the IIoT, device networks must share and coordinate enormous amounts of data collected by various system sensors. It can readily monitor, calibrate, and regulate automatic control functions, as well as equipment like engines, allowing for forward-looking planning and maintenance [107].

All of these processes are starting to work properly for all of the wireless sensors. The entire network crumbles with all of its difficulties and dependencies until the stability and consistency are complete. The entire network

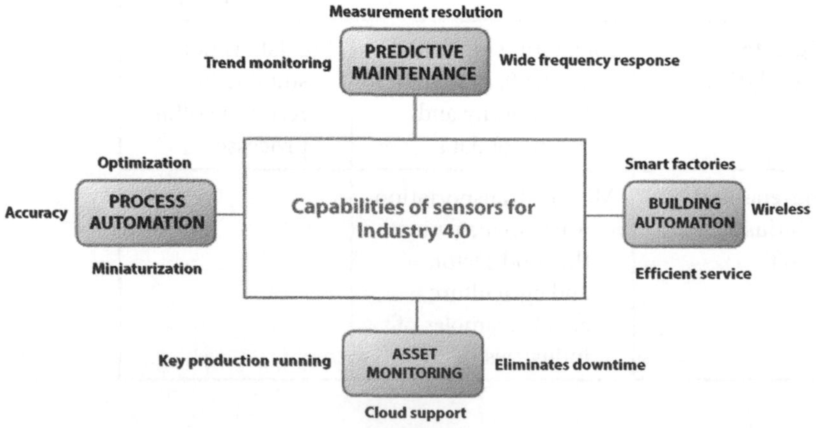

Figure 9.6 Capabilities of sensors in Industry 4.0.

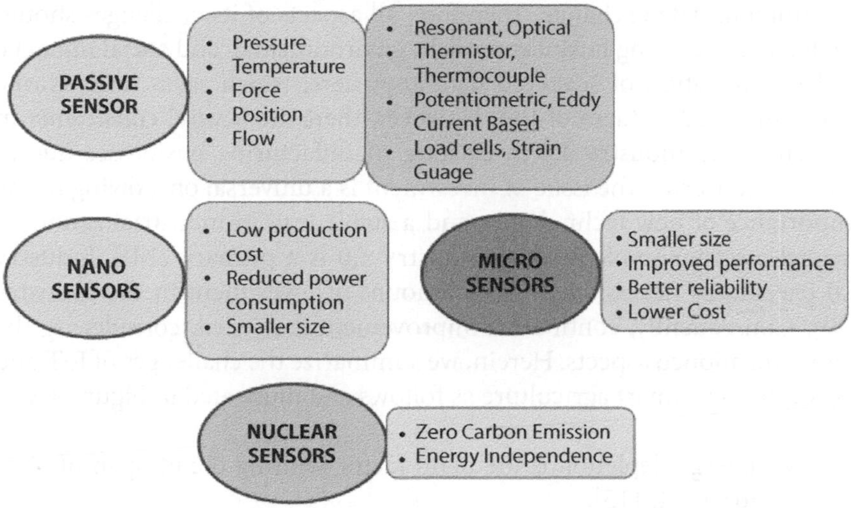

Figure 9.7 Various sensor types for Industry 4.0.

crumbles with all of its difficulties and dependencies until the stability and consistency are complete [107, 108].

Figure 9.7 shows the various sensors that can be used to implement the Industry 4.0 in the basic industrial background for social services [109].

The sensor is usually able to communicate and has some form of onboard diagnostics. Intelligent sensors can perform a wide range of functions and provide a wide range of options. Self-assays and auto-calibration are feasible with smart sensors [110]. Sensors will help us prevent athlete injuries and alleviate pain without the use of drugs in the future.

Millions of machines, including cellphones, now have access to sensors. Vibration sensing, tilt, and general acceleration are some of their applications. If an object is moved and must remain fixed, the sensor will convey an alarm through the device, which is utilized as an anti-theft defense. During the COVID-19 epidemic, this technology was also employed [111, 112].

9.6 Challenges of IoT Applications in Environmental and Industrial Applications

Čolaković and Hadžialić [113] stated that IoT based systems are typically complex due to the implementation of numerous technologies to enable autonomous data exchange. Therefore, all aspects of its challenges should be deemed including business models, environmental, and social impacts.

The integration of scattered data anywhere, which saves time, is one of the many advantages of IoT. However, there are several constraints in implementing Industry 4.0 in existing manufacturing businesses due to investor concerns. The issue of investment is a universal one, owing to the importance of new technologies and a stable lead in industrialization. A crucial asset for implementing Industry 4.0 is a primary SME. Industry 4.0 executions necessitate a large amount of investment in the industry [99]. Consequently, continuous improvement is needed, considering the above-mentioned aspects. Herein, we summarize the challenges of IoT and its solutions in smart agriculture as follows and illustrated in Figure 9.8.

- Energy depletion is the main factor limiting the lifespan of IoT [114, 115].
- Even the cost of computing platforms has been decreasing, it is not the same case for high-quality sensors. The costs have to be reduced even further [88].
- Know-how of IoT improvement and adaptation for large field applications beyond simple prototypes [116].

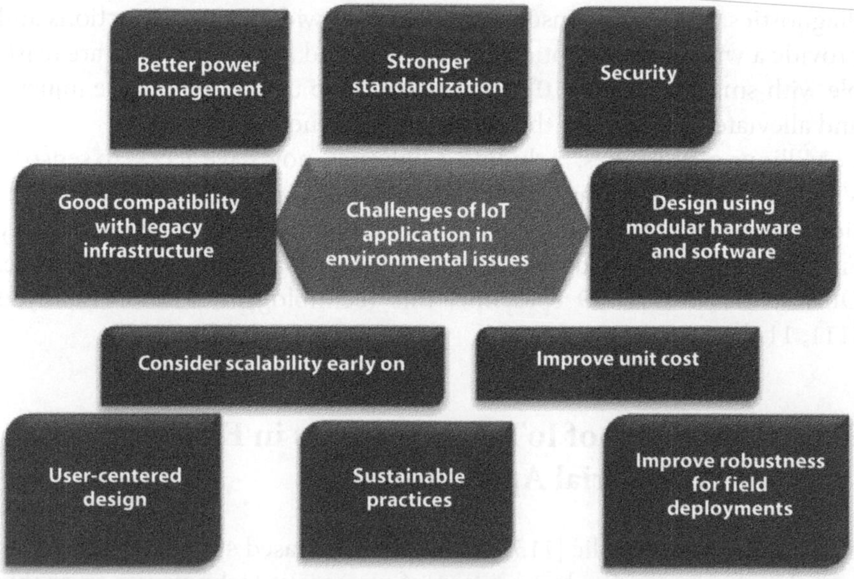

Figure 9.8 Challenges of IoT application in environmental issues.

9.7 Conclusions and Recommendations

In this chapter, we have outlined current applications of IoT in smart environments, which include smart homes, smart health, smart cities, and smart factories with more emphasis on the different uses of IoT sensors in smart factories and industries. We have also inferred further application of IoT in monitoring and analysis of air, water, and soil quality and highlighted the massive use of sensors in detecting different air pollutants such as NO_2, O_3, $PM_{2.5}$, CO_2, and NH_3 as well as atmospheric temperature and humidity detection. Likewise, application of sensors in detecting water quality such as pH, turbidity, water level besides, continuous monitoring of nutrient water content such as PO_4^{3-} and NO_3^-. This chapter also clarifies the various types of agricultural sensors, which were used in smart farming and to collect data. Finally, the use of artificial intelligence in environmental health related to COVID-19 for the epidemiology, diagnoses, and therapy during the pandemic was also discussed. We finally concluded that the Internet of Things (IoT) is a smart route to deal with different situations in our daily life.

Acknowledgments

M. Fawzy and A.E.D Mahmoud acknowledge the support from from Egypt's Academy of Scientific Research and Technology (ASRT) for SA-Egypt Joint Project and SMARTWATIR, ERANETMED-3-227 project.

References

1. Ashton, K., That 'internet of things' thing. *RFID J.*, 22, 7, 97–114, 2009.
2. Union, I.T., *The Internet of Things—Executive Summary*, ITU Internet Reports, Geneva, 2005.
3. Evans, D., The internet of things: How the next evolution of the internet is changing everything. *CISCO White Paper*, 1, 2011, 1–11, 2011.
4. Kotha, H.D. and Gupta, V.M., IoT application: A survey. *Int. J. Eng. Technol.*, 7, 2.7, 891–896, 2018.
5. Yang, L., Yang, S.-H., Plotnick, L., How the internet of things technology enhances emergency response operations. *Technol. Forecast. Soc. Change*, 80, 9, 1854–1867, 2013.
6. Calvaresi, D. *et al.*, Exploring the ambient assisted living domain: A systematic review. *J. Ambient Intell. Humaniz. Comput.*, 8, 2, 239–257, 2017.

7. Mora, H. *et al.*, A comprehensive system for monitoring urban accessibility in smart cities. *Sensors*, 17, 8, 1834, 2017.
8. Muralidharan, S., Roy, A., Saxena, N., MDP-IoT: MDP based interest forwarding for heterogeneous traffic in IoT-NDN environment. *Future Gener. Comp. Sy.*, 79, 892–908, 2018.
9. Terroso-Saenz, F. *et al.*, An open IoT platform for the management and analysis of energy data. *Future Gener. Comp. Sy.*, 92, 1066–1079, 2019.
10. Torres-Ruiz, M. *et al.*, Environmental noise sensing approach based on volunteered geographic information and spatio-temporal analysis with machine learning, in: *International Conference on Computational Science and Its Applications*, Springer, 2016.
11. Hachem, S. *et al.*, Monitoring noise pollution using the urban civics middleware, in: *2015 IEEE First International Conference on Big Data Computing Service and Applications*, IEEE, 2015.
12. Liu, Z. *et al.*, Real-time barrier lakes monitoring and warning system based on wireless sensor network, in: *2013 Fourth International Conference on Intelligent Control and Information Processing (ICICIP)*, IEEE, 2013.
13. Cicirelli, F. *et al.*, *The Internet of Things for Smart Urban Ecosystems*, Springer, Berlin, Germany, 2019.
14. Capella, J.V. *et al.*, IoT & environmental analytical chemistry: Towards a profitable symbiosis. *Trends Environ. Anal. Chem.*, 27, e00095, 2020.
15. Li, S., Xu, L.D., Zhao, S., The internet of things: A survey. *Inf. Syst. Front.*, 17, 2, 243–259, 2015.
16. Haleem, A. and Javaid, M., Additive manufacturing applications in industry 4.0: A review. *J. Ind. Integration Manage.*, 4, 04, 1930001, 2019.
17. Javaid, M. *et al.*, Significance of sensors for industry 4.0: Roles, capabilities, and applications. *Sensors Int.*, 2, 100110, 2021.
18. Wang, S. *et al.*, Wearable stretchable dry and self-adhesive strain sensors with conformal contact to skin for high-quality motion monitoring. *Adv. Funct. Mater.*, 31, 5, 2007495, 2021.
19. Rathee, G. *et al.*, A secure IoT sensors communication in Industry 4.0 using blockchain technology. *J. Ambient Intell. Humaniz. Comput.*, 12, 1, 533–545, 2021.
20. Sharma, A., Burman, V., Aggarwal, S., Role of IoT in industry 4.0, in: *Advances in Energy Technology*, Springer Singapore, Singapore, 2022.
21. Schütze, A., Helwig, N., Schneider, T., Sensors 4.0–smart sensors and measurement technology enable Industry 4.0. *J. Sensors Sensor Syst.*, 7, 1, 359–371, 2018.
22. Ali, F. *et al.*, An intelligent healthcare monitoring framework using wearable sensors and social networking data. *Future Gener. Comp. Syst.*, 114, 23–43, 2021.
23. Pavithra, D. and Balakrishnan, R., IoT based monitoring and control system for home automation. in: *2015 Global Conference on Communication Technologies (GCCT)*, IEEE, 2015.

24. Rathee, G. *et al.*, A trust computed framework for IoT devices and fog computing environment. *Wirel. Netw.*, 26, 4, 2339–2351, 2020.
25. Sunhare, P., Chowdhary, R.R., Chattopadhyay, M.K., Internet of things and data mining: An applications oriented survey. *J. King Saud Univ. Comput. Inf. Sci.*, 2020.
26. Kravchenko, Y. *et al.*, Technology analysis for smart home implementation, in: *2017 4th International Scientific-Practical Conference Problems of Infocommunications. Science and Technology (PIC S&T)*, IEEE, 2017.
27. Tsai, C.-W. *et al.*, Metaheuristic algorithms for healthcare: Open issues and challenges. *Comput. Electr. Eng.*, 53, 421–434, 2016.
28. Chen, Q. *et al.*, A survey on an emerging area: Deep learning for smart city data. *IEEE Trans. Emerg. Top. Comput. Intell.*, 3, 5, 392–410, 2019.
29. Samarah, S. *et al.*, An efficient activity recognition framework: Toward privacy-sensitive health data sensing. *IEEE Access*, 5, 3848–3859, 2017.
30. Youngblood, G.M. and Cook, D.J., Data mining for hierarchical model creation. *IEEE Trans. Syst. Man Cybern. C Appl. Rev.*, 37, 4, 561–572, 2007.
31. Stankovic, J.A., Research directions for the internet of things. *IEEE Internet Things J.*, 1, 1, 3–9, 2014.
32. Europe, E., A strategy for smart, sustainable and inclusive growth. *COM*, 2010, 2020.
33. Lee, J., Kao, H.-A., Yang, S., Service innovation and smart analytics for Industry 4.0 and big data environment. *Proc. CIRP*, 16, 3–8, 2014.
34. Thibaud, M. *et al.*, Internet of Things (IoT) in high-risk environment, health and safety (EHS) industries: A comprehensive review. *Decis. Support Syst.*, 108, 79–95, 2018.
35. Hachem, S. *et al.*, Monitoring noise pollution using the urban civics middleware, in: *2015 IEEE First International Conference on Big Data Computing Service and Applications*, 2015.
36. Bhattacharyya, N. and Bandhopadhyay, R., Electronic nose and electronic tongue, in: *Nondestructive Evaluation of Food Quality*, pp. 73–100, Springer, Berlin, Heidelberg, 2010.
37. Mansoor, S. *et al.*, Elevation in wildfire frequencies with respect to the climate change. *J. Environ. Manage.*, 301, 113769, 2022.
38. Kim, Y.H. *et al.*, Chemically fluorinated graphene oxide for room temperature ammonia detection at ppb levels. *J. Mater. Chem. A*, 5, 36, 19116–19125, 2017.
39. Wu, J. *et al.*, 3D superhydrophobic reduced graphene oxide for activated NO 2 sensing with enhanced immunity to humidity. *J. Mater. Chem. A*, 6, 2, 478–488, 2018.
40. Mahmoud, A.E.D., Stolle, A., Stelter, M., Sustainable synthesis of high-surface-area graphite oxide via dry ball milling. *ACS Sustain. Chem. Eng.*, 6, 5, 6358–6369, 2018.

41. Mahmoud, A. *et al.*, Adsorption technique for organic pollutants using different carbon mterials, in: *Abstracts of Papers of the American Chemical Society*, Amer Chemical Soc NW, Washington, DC USA, 2018.
42. Mahmoud, A.E.D., Eco-friendly reduction of graphene oxide via agricultural byproducts or aquatic macrophytes. *Mater. Chem. Phys.*, 253, 123336, 2020.
43. Badr, N.B.E., Al-Qahtani, K.M., Mahmoud, A.E.D., Factorial experimental design for optimizing selenium sorption on Cyperus laevigatus biomass and green-synthesized nano-silver. *Alex. Eng. J.*, 253, 123336, 2020.
44. Abdel Hamid, A.A. *et al.*, Phytosynthesis of Au, Ag, and Au–Ag bimetallic nanoparticles using aqueous extract of sago pondweed (potamogeton pectinatus L.). *ACS Sustain. Chem. Eng.*, 1, 12, 1520–1529, 2013.
45. Mahmoud, A.E.D., Nanomaterials: Green synthesis for water applications, in: *Handbook of Nanomaterials and Nanocomposites for Energy and Environmental Applications*, O.V. Kharissova, L.M.T. Martínez, B.I. Kharisov (Eds.), pp. 1–21, Springer International Publishing, Cham, 2020.
46. Mahmoud, A.E.D. and Fawzy, M., Nanosensors and nanobiosensors for monitoring the environmental pollutants, in: *Waste Recycling Technologies for Nanomaterials Manufacturing*, pp. 229–246, Springer, Cham, 2021.
47. Duvall, R.M. *et al.*, Performance evaluation and community application of low-cost sensors for ozone and nitrogen dioxide. *Sensors (Basel)*, 16, 10, 1698, 2016.
48. Okafor, N.U., Alghorani, Y., Delaney, D.T., Improving data quality of low-cost IoT sensors in environmental monitoring networks using data fusion and machine learning approach. *ICT Express*, 6, 3, 220–228, 2020.
49. Li, H. *et al.*, Development of a remote monitoring system for henhouse environment based on IoT technology. *Future Internet*, 7, 3, 329–341, 2015.
50. Ma, Z. *et al.*, Lightweight, flexible and highly sensitive segregated microcellular nanocomposite piezoresistive sensors for human motion detection. *Compos. Sci.Technol.*, 203, 108571, 2021.
51. Mahmoud, A.E.D., Graphene-based nanomaterials for the removal of organic pollutants: Insights into linear versus nonlinear mathematical models. *J. Environ. Manage.*, 270, 110911, 2020.
52. Mahmoud, A.E.D. *et al.*, Mechanochemical versus chemical routes for graphitic precursors and their performance in micropollutants removal in water. *Powder Technol.*, 366, 629–640, 2020.
53. Mahmoud, A.E.D. *et al.*, Equilibrium, kinetic, and diffusion models of chromium(VI) removal using Phragmites australis and Ziziphus spina-christi biomass. *Int. J. Environ. Sci. Technol.*, 18, 2125–2136, 2020.
54. Mahmoud, A.E.D. *et al.*, 26-Water resources security and management for sustainable communities, in: *Phytochemistry, the Military and Health*, A.G. Mtewa and C. Egbuna (Eds.), pp. 509–522, Elsevier, 2021.
55. Hosny, M. *et al.*, Comparative study between Phragmites australis root and rhizome extracts for mediating gold nanoparticles synthesis and their

medical and environmental applications. *Adv. Powder Technol.*, 32, 7, 2268–2279, 2021.
56. Vambol, S. *et al.*, Comprehensive insights into sources of pharmaceutical wastewater in the biotic systems, in: *Pharmaceutical Wastewater Treatment Technologies: Concepts and Implementation Strategies*, N.A. Khan (Ed.), IWA Publishing, UK, 2021.
57. Huang, L. *et al.*, Enhanced water purification via redox interfaces created by an atomic layer deposition strategy. *Environ. Sci. Nano*, 8, 4, 950–959, 2021.
58. Pasika, S. and Gandla, S.T., Smart water quality monitoring system with cost-effective using IoT. *Heliyon*, 6, 7, e04096, 2020.
59. El Din Mahmoud, A. and Fawzy, M., Bio-based methods for wastewater treatment: Green sorbents, in: *Phytoremediation: Management of Environmental Contaminants, Volume 3*, A.A. Ansari (Ed.), pp. 209–238, Springer International Publishing, Cham, 2016.
60. Mishra, B., Tiwari, A., Mahmoud, A.E.D., Microalgal potential for sustainable aquaculture applications: Bioremediation, biocontrol, aquafeed. *Clean Technol. Environ. Policy*, 1–13, 2022.
61. Mahmoud, A.E.D. *et al.*, Green copper oxide nanoparticles for lead, nickel, and cadmium removal from contaminated water. *Sci. Rep.*, 11, 1, 12547, 2021.
62. Mahmoud, A.E.D., Fawzy, M., Abdel-Fatah, M.M.A., Technical aspects of nanofiltration for dyes wastewater treatment, in: *Membrane Based Methods for Dye Containing Wastewater: Recent Advances*, S.S. Muthu and A. Khadir (Eds.), pp. 23–35, Springer Singapore, Singapore, 2022.
63. Duffy, G. and Regan, F., Recent developments in sensing methods for eutrophying nutrients with a focus on automation for environmental applications. *Analyst*, 142, 23, 4355–4372, 2017.
64. Capella, J.V. *et al.*, A new application of internet of things and cloud services in analytical chemistry: Determination of bicarbonate in water. *Sensors*, 19, 24, 5528, 2019.
65. Lambrou, T.P. *et al.*, A low-cost sensor network for real-time monitoring and contamination detection in drinking water distribution systems. *IEEE Sens. J.*, 14, 8, 2765–2772, 2014.
66. Myint, C.Z., Gopal, L., Aung, Y.L., Reconfigurable smart water quality monitoring system in IoT environment, in: *2017 IEEE/ACIS 16th International Conference on Computer and Information Science (ICIS)*, IEEE, 2017.
67. Postolache, O., Pereira, J.D., Girão, P.S., Wireless sensor network-based solution for environmental monitoring: Water quality assessment case study. *IET Sci. Meas. Technol.*, 8, 6, 610–616, 2014.
68. Kassal, P., Steinberg, I.M., Steinberg, M.D., Wireless smart tag with potentiometric input for ultra low-power chemical sensing. *Sens. Actuators B Chem.*, 184, 254–259, 2013.

69. Liu, Y. *et al.*, Polystyrene-coated interdigitated microelectrode array to detect free chlorine towards IoT applications. *Anal. Sci.*, 18, 460, 2018.
70. Ziarati, P. *et al.*, Investigation of prospects for phytoremediation treatment of soils contaminated with heavy metals. *J. Med. Discovery*, 4, 2, 1–16, 2019.
71. Sawicka, B. *et al.*, 27-Impacts of inorganic/organic pollutants on agroecosystems and eco-friendly solutions, in: *Phytochemistry, the Military and Health*, A.G. Mtewa and C. Egbuna (Eds.), pp. 523–552, Elsevier, 2021.
72. Watt, A.J. *et al.*, Wireless sensor networks for monitoring underwater sediment transport. *Sci. Total Environ.*, 667, 160–165, 2019.
73. Devapal, D., Smart agro farm solar powered soil and weather monitoring system for farmers. *Mater. Today Proc.*, 24, 1843–1854, 2020.
74. Khan, A.H. *et al.*, Co-occurring indicator pathogens for SARS-CoV-2: A review with emphasis on exposure rates and treatment technologies. *Case Stud. Chem. Environ. Eng.*, 4, 100113, 2021.
75. Khan, A.H. *et al.*, COVID-19 transmission, vulnerability, persistence and nanotherapy: A review. *Environ. Chem. Lett.*, 19, 4, 2773–2787, 2021.
76. Gwenzi, W. *et al.*, COVID-19 drugs in aquatic systems: A review. *Environ. Chem. Lett.*, 1–20, 2022.
77. Mousazadeh, M. *et al.*, Chapter 10-A review of deciphering the successes and learning from the failures in preventive and health policies to stop the COVID-19 pandemic, in: *Environmental and Health Management of Novel Coronavirus Disease (COVID-19)*, M.H. Dehghani, R.R. Karri, S. Roy (Eds.), pp. 269–303, Academic Press, 2021.
78. Mousazadeh, M. *et al.*, Chapter 9-Management of environmental health to prevent an outbreak of COVID-19: A review, in: *Environmental and Health Management of Novel Coronavirus Disease (COVID-19)*, M.H. Dehghani, R.R. Karri, S. Roy (Eds.), pp. 235–267, Academic Press, 2021.
79. Albahri, O. *et al.*, Systematic review of artificial intelligence techniques in the detection and classification of COVID-19 medical images in terms of evaluation and benchmarking: Taxonomy analysis, challenges, future solutions and methodological aspects. *J. Infect. Public Health*, 13, 10, 1381–1396, 2020.
80. Salehi, A.W., Baglat, P., Gupta, G., Review on machine and deep learning models for the detection and prediction of coronavirus. *Mater. Today Proc.*, 33, 3896–3901, 2020.
81. Albahli, S., Efficient GAN-based Chest Radiographs (CXR) augmentation to diagnose coronavirus disease pneumonia. *Int. J. Med. Sci.*, 17, 10, 1439, 2020.
82. Senior, A.W. *et al.*, Improved protein structure prediction using potentials from deep learning. *Nature*, 577, 7792, 706–710, 2020.
83. Ratnaparkhi, S. *et al.*, Smart agriculture sensors in IoT: A review. *Mater. Today Proc.*, 2020.
84. Ambrose, A.R. *et al.*, Leaf-and crown-level adjustments help giant sequoias maintain favorable water status during severe drought. *For. Ecol. Manage.*, 419-420, 257–267, 2018.

85. Hu, J. *et al.*, An airflow sensor array based on polyvinylidene fluoride cantilevers for synchronously measuring airflow direction and velocity. *Flow Meas. Instrum.*, 67, 166–175, 2019.
86. Meier, J. *et al.*, Assessments on the impact of high-resolution-sensor pixel sizes for common agricultural policy and smart farming services in European regions. *Comput. Electron. Agric.*, 169, 105205, 2020.
87. Eliopoulos, P.A., Potamitis, I., Kontodimas, D.C., Estimation of population density of stored grain pests via bioacoustic detection. *Crop Prot.*, 85, 71–78, 2016.
88. Pang, Z. *et al.*, Value-centric design of the internet-of-things solution for food supply chain: Value creation, sensor portfolio and information fusion. *Inf. Syst. Front.*, 17, 2, 289–319, 2015.
89. Mafuta, M. *et al.*, Successful deployment of a wireless sensor network for precision agriculture in Malawi. *Int. J. Distrib. Sens. Netw.*, 9, 5, 150703, 2013.
90. Lee, M., Hwang, J., Yoe, H., Agricultural production system based on IoT, in: *2013 IEEE 16Th International Conference on Computational Science and Engineering*, 2013IEEE.
91. Saville, R., Hatanaka, K., Wada, M., ICT application of real-time monitoring and estimation system for set-net fishery, in: *OCEANS 2015-MTS/IEEE Washington*, IEEE, 2015.
92. Lee, J. *et al.*, Dynamic crop field analysis using mobile sensor node, in: *2012 International Conference on ICT Convergence (ICTC)*, 2012.
93. Mahato, K. *et al.*, Clinically comparable impedimetric immunosensor for serum alkaline phosphatase detection based on electrochemically engineered Au-nano-Dendroids and graphene oxide nanocomposite. *Biosens. Bioelectron.*, 148, 111815, 2020.
94. Dutta, G., Regoutz, A., Moschou, D., Enzyme-assisted glucose quantification for a painless Lab-on-PCB patch implementation. *Biosens. Bioelectron.*, 167, 112484, 2020.
95. Chandra, P., *Nanobiosensors for Personalized and Onsite Biomedical Diagnosis*, The Institution of Engineering and Technology, 2016.
96. Sadiku, M.N. *et al.*, Industrial internet of things. *Int. J. Adv. Sci. Res. Eng.*, 3, 11, 1–4, 2017.
97. Stăncioiu, A., The fourth industrial revolution "industry 4.0". *Fiabil. Durab.*, 1, 74–78, 2017.
98. Vaidya, S., Ambad, P., Bhosle, S., Industry 4.0 a glimpse. *Proc. Manuf.*, 20, 233–238, 2018.
99. Rholam, O. and Tabaa, M., Smart device for multi-band industrial IoT communications. *Proc. Comput. Sci.*, 155, 660–665, 2019.
100. Kerin, M. and Pham, D.T., A review of emerging Industry 4.0 technologies in remanufacturing. *J. Clean. Prod.*, 237, 117805, 2019.
101. Thames, L. and Schaefer, D., Software-defined cloud manufacturing for industry 4.0. *Proc. CIRP*, 52, 12–17, 2016.

102. Tang, T.J. *et al.*, An IoT inspired semiconductor reliability test system integrated with data-mining applications, in: *2016 2nd International Conference on Cloud Computing and Internet of Things (CCIOT)*, IEEE, 2016.
103. Kim, J.H., A review of cyber-physical system research relevant to the emerging IT trends: Industry 4.0, IoT, big data, and cloud computing. *J. Ind. Integration Manage.*, 2, 03, 1750011, 2017.
104. Aazam, M., Zeadally, S., Harras, K.A., Deploying fog computing in industrial internet of things and industry 4.0. *IEEE Trans. Industr. Inform.*, 14, 10, 4674–4682, 2018.
105. Sun, M. *et al.*, Inside back cover: Aptamer blocking strategy inhibits SARS-CoV-2 virus infection (Angew. Chem. Int. Ed. 18/2021). *Angew. Chem. Int. Ed.*, 60, 18, 10431–10431, 2021.
106. Ghosh, A. *et al.*, Real-time structural health monitoring for concrete beams: A cost-effective 'Industry 4.0' solution using piezo sensors. *Int. J. Build. Pathol. Adapt.*, 39, 283–311, 2020.
107. Rodriguez-Manfredi, J. *et al.*, The mars environmental dynamics analyzer, MEDA. A suite of environmental sensors for the mars 2020 mission. *Space Sci. Rev.*, 217, 3, 1–86, 2021.
108. Elashery, S.E., Frag, E.Y., Sleim, A.A., Novel and selective potentiometric sensors for Cinchocaine HCl determination in its pure and co-formulated dosage form: A comparative study of *in situ* carbon sensors based on different ion pairing agents. *Measurement*, 173, 108549, 2021.
109. Bahl, S. *et al.*, Advancements in biosensor technologies for medical field and COVID-19 pandemic. *J. Ind. Integration Manage.*, 6, 2, 175–191, 2021.
110. Pinto, V.C. *et al.*, Antibiofouling strategy for optical sensors by chlorine generation using low-cost, transparent and highly efficient electrodes based on platinum nanoparticles coated oxide. *Chem. Eng. J.*, 404, 126479, 2021.
111. Dutta, N. *et al.*, Electrochemical biosensors for cytokine profiling: Recent advancements and possibilities in the near future. *Biosensors*, 11, 3, 94, 2021.
112. Mahapatra, S. and Chandra, P., Clinically practiced and commercially viable nanobio engineered analytical methods for COVID-19 diagnosis. *Biosens. Bioelectron.*, 165, 112361, 2020.
113. Colakovic, A. and Hadziali, M., Internet of Things (IoT): A review of enabling technologies, challenges, and open research issues. *Comput. Netw.*, 144, 17–39, c2018.
114. Bo, Z. *et al.*, Green preparation of reduced graphene oxide for sensing and energy storage applications. *Sci. Rep.*, 4, 4684, 2014.
115. Diedrichs, A.L. *et al.*, Low-power wireless sensor network for frost monitoring in agriculture research, in: *2014 IEEE Biennial Congress of Argentina (ARGENCON)*, IEEE, 2014.

116. Chen, Y. *et al.*, A scalable context-aware objective function (SCAOF) of routing protocol for agricultural low-power and lossy networks (RPAL). *Sensors*, 15, 8, 19507–19540, 2015.

10

An Introduction to Security in Internet of Things (IoT) and Big Data

Sushree Bibhuprada B. Priyadarshini[1]*, Suraj Kumar Dash[1], Amrit Sahani[1], Brojo Kishore Mishra[2] and Mahendra Prasad Nath[1]

[1]*Department of Computer Science & Information Technology, Siksha 'O' Anusandhan (Deemed to be University), Bubaneswar, India*
[2]*Department of Computer Science & Engineering, GIET University, Gunupur, India*

Abstract
The basics of Internet of Things (IoT) is the attribute of Internet of Objects, expected as a flexible strategy for giving several facilities. Condensed clever units create a critical phase of IoT. They vary extensively in practice, volume, service facility, and calculation strength. However, the incorporation of these clever matters in the widespread internetworking proposed IoT of safety threat due to the act the most internetwork technologies along with verbal exchange manners that had not been now designed to guide IoT. Furthermore, the trade of IoT has produced public safety matter, such as nonpublic secrecy issues, risk of cyber threats, and trained crime. Have guidelines or suggestions on the analysis of IoT security and contribute to improvement. This control offers full information of the open penetration and retrieval as opposed to the IoT edge side layer, which are done in three phases: edge nodes, transmission, and edge computing. The method to reach this target, first, we quickly define those popular IoT recommendation models and outline protection in the IoT's framework. We also talk about the feasible purposes of IoT and the inspiration of the intruder and set new goals in this new model. With such rise in IoT and with the advent of ongoing digital applications, huge amount of data is produced each and every day, leading to the emergence of the term big data. In this chapter, we will be collaborating the detailed security study in case of IoT and big data.

Keywords: Internet of Things (IoT), Wireless Sensor Network (WSN), fog computing

**Corresponding author*: bimalabibhuprada@gmail.com

Jyotir Moy Chatterjee, Harish Garg and R. N. Thakur (eds.) A Roadmap for Enabling Industry 4.0 by Artificial Intelligence, (169–200) © 2023 Scrivener Publishing LLC

10.1 Introduction

Until now, IoT has no particular description. No matter how, a large performance of IoT offers any facility to the common internetwork with the aid of allowing human communications with thing, thing communications with thing, or thing communications with things. IoT symbolize the interconnection networks of mixed objects. The period objects specified to human beings, sensor, or possibly any of the things that may lead to give a chance of carrier [1, 2]. Then, coming into view of the IoT model is among the most amazing marvels of the ultimate 10 years.

The evolution in quite several conversation protocols, alongside miniaturization in the transceivers present a probability of converting a remote system to a speaking tool. Also, calculating ability, strength, and storing capacities of the sensible machines have very much enhanced whilst volume have reduced extremely and these helps in advancing in devices and field of computer science technically and have provoked an exponential increase in the measure of internetwork related distinguishing and figuring tools (furthermore recognized as smart devices) that can grant offerings solely confined by way of visualization [3, 4]. With the rise in IoT and with the advent of ongoing digital applications, huge amount of data are generated each and every day, leading to the emergence of the term big data.

Due to various symptoms, the feasible dangers and the feasible assaults are the varieties in opposition to the protection or secrecy of an aspect that has been developed highly. Shockingly, this protection needs are not all around perceived yet. In this manner, the safety issues and normal protection concerns should be examined and tended to deepest. Simplifying the improvement in impenetrable smart gadgets that empowers plenty of administrations for people that could be done enormously, building mechanization to well-being observing, where altogether different objects, e.g., temperature sensing devices, light sensing devices, also the clinical sensing devices, would possibly connect with one another or then again with a human conveying a brilliant computing gadget, e.g., a laptop, smart cell phone, or advanced tablet [1–5].

IoT protection is a continuous topic of study that draws improved sustainability in scholarly, industrial and government science. The structure and progress of IoT-driven systems was active in many collaborations in the world and internationally. To give a huge number of solid administrations, architects experience a few challenges, specifically, in security-concerned research territories. Many analysis efforts endeavours are currently endeavouring to search the possible threats and giving recovery solution counter to them [5, 6]. This study abridges the safety of IoT dangers and countermeasures with level wise design. More over all those explicitly:

- Portray an extensive allusion diagram of Internet of Things,
- Give the meaning to the data per user, affirmation, and safety and the necessities of IoT,
- Outline dangers in the side layer of the edge of the design model,
- Survey the recovery solution to point the conceivable dangers,
- And present rising two safety test which are not yet being clarified in past composition.

This paper has the essential goal is to supply the chance to discover the readers about the assaults which are introduced, which are addressed, and the threats which will remain. Figure 10.1 illustrates a scenario of internet of things.

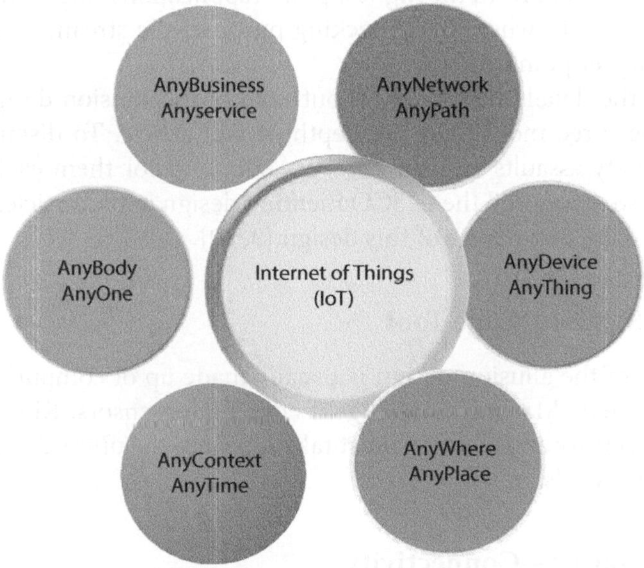

Figure 10.1 A scenario of Internet of Things (IoT).

10.2 Allusion Design of IoT

There are three allusion designs of IoT which are extensively considered in tutorial and technical productions. First three-level model indicates such models and their special levels [4–8]. It is the main allusion designs introduced specially for IoT, which is represented by IoT as a prolonged model of Wireless Sensing Networks (WSNs). Truth to be told is that, it displays IoT as a blend of cloud servers and WSNs, and that offer various administrations to the client.

Second, the design, which has five stages, is a choice which has been proposed for helping to communicate amongst various sectors of a company in order to analyse complicated structure to are reduced functioning comprising of a biological system of more straight-forward and very much characterized parts.

In 2014, CISCO recommended a complete expansion in direction of regular three and five stages designs. The seven stages design of CISCO has the ability of being authorised and to consequently design a broadly obtained allusion design of IoT. The records flow is mostly in two directions in this design. But still the prominent information float relies upon the operation. To illustrate, in a control framework, records and orders travel in the design from the highest point (applications stage) on backside (edge node level), where in a checking purpose, the stream carries from lower to higher point [8, 9].

Giving the details elaborately about each of the allusion design of IoT among the three more than the depth of this article. To discuss briefly the IoT safety assaults and the recovery solutions for them each level in sequence, we have used the CISCO mention design in this article. Now, we quickly discuss every stage of this design [9, 10].

10.2.1 Stage 1—Edge Tool

First stage of the allusion design is usually made up of computing nodes, e.g., controllers, Machines, Intelligent edge node, sensors, RFID readers, etc. Data security and stability must take care into the upward vision from this stage onwards.

10.2.2 Stage 2—Connectivity

This is the conversation stage containing all the factors which allows communication of facts or instruction:

(i) Verbal exchange with and between the stage 1 tools,
(ii) Verbal exchange in between the network stage 2, and
(iii) Transferring the records between the low stage information computations exists at third stages (edge calculating stage).

10.2.3 Stage 3—Fog Computing

This is the third stage of the architecture of the allusion called fog computing. In this stage the network information which is appropriate for the memory and the upper stages computing in stage 4.

In third stage, it is necessary for lowering the calculation pressure in the higher stage to perform fast. Here, calculating powers of servers, computing nodes matters in data evaluation, formatting and decoding is carried out. Thus, the analysing and testing codes are used in 3rd stage [11–29].

10.2.4 Stage 4—Data Collection

Many functions may additionally now did not want on the spot information processing. This stage allows facts to be transformed from action to the facts in relaxed form, i.e., this approves for saving the records for later evaluation and contribute to the advanced computing servers. In stage 4, the primary dutics are to change its structure [11, 12].

From network packets to generate data, lowering statistics via screening and selecting while depot, also to identify even if the information are suitable for greater stages.

10.2.5 Stage 5—Data Abstraction

Stage 5 makes the processing in higher stage easier and more efficient by contributing and storing data. The frequent duties of entities at this degree consist of normalization, denormalization, cross checking, whether the data ready for the next stage and consolidating information in fixed place, collecting different formats of data from different origin and securing data with valid authentication accessing [13, 14].

10.2.6 Stage 6—Applications

The utility stage gives facts interpretation, the place software program collaborate accompanied by data assembling. There are lots of use of IoT in our daily life and can also fluctuate considerably throughout business and requirements of managements.

10.2.7 Stage 7—Cooperation and Processes

The data generated by the IoT system has less importance unless it generates any action. People use the functions according to their specific requirement. Also, the detailed data is being used for different purposes [14, 15].

Within this emerging era of change, IoT is a relatively recent business term which gives it an immense potential for us to succeed. There are various solutions to what IoT means for enterprises, but the core concept is the same; it gathers data, analyzes data, and then creates information into re-engineering techniques and discovers the advantages. Theoretically it seems straightforward, but the implementation of IoT is complicated. In order to execute IoT successfully, various working departments and company divisions must participate, apart from IT departments [15–27].

10.3 Vulnerabilities of IoT

We must prepare for new attacks with the internet of things and design new fundamental defenses. The Internet of Things (IoT) Security Threat Map provides an overlay of the entire set of threat and vulnerability analyses that help customers to shape their strategies. This map of threats sums up all of the top 5 features of increasing study. External threats and the highest internal IoT applications vulnerabilities are the requirements for robust authentication, license & privacy [27–32].

10.3.1 The Properties and Relationships of Various IoT Networks

Combining the utilities market is challenging in leveraging the capacities of various business supporting platforms, implementation and defense integration and the associated root of trust systems of edge devices are growing. There is some an issue amid which efficient implementation of IoT needs to be recognized and tackled [32–39].

This chapter aims to encompass a larger variety of security flaws and IoT frameworks assaults. Compared to other categories, our grouping is special since it separates the attacks into four distinct classes; real, network, device and cryptography attacks. Our category is unique since it divides attacks into four distinct groups, namely physical, network, system and cryptographic attacks, opposed to other types. In numerous current network technologies (WLNs, RFIDs, the internet, etc.), IoT is deployed. There is therefore a need to categorize assaults appropriately to encapsulate and hazard, in order to build and enforce better countermeasures to ensure they are covered [39–45].

Nonetheless, it should be noted that environmental attacks (earthquakes etc.) are overlooked because their reach goes beyond research which focuses on deliberate attacks by an adversary [45–64].

10.3.2 Device Attacks

These assaults rely on the circuitry of the IoT system and the intruder must be physically nearby enough in order to be targeted by the IoT system. In addition, attacks in this group damage hardware life and functionality [63–65].

The next elements are these attacks:

(i) Tampering of Nodes
(ii) Interference of RFIDs
(iii) Jamming of Nodes in WSN
(iv) Malicious injections of nodes
(v) Damage of Physical Items
(vi) Malicious injections of codes

10.3.3 Attacks on Network

Such assaults are based on the network of the IoT device so the intruder does not even have to be near to the network.

(i) Analysis of Traffic attacks
(ii) Spoofing of RFID
(iii) Cloning of RFID
(iv) Unwanted access to RFID
(v) Information and Routing Attacks

10.3.4 Some Other Issues

10.3.4.1 Customer Delivery Value

The research problem is obviously connected significantly to the achievement of IoT results. But IoTs do not like this for other businesses.

They can realize how these approaches will have a long-term effect on the performance, consumer experience and profitability. There is no greater IoT implementation challenger than the gaps in understanding the client problem statement and this whole cycle requires extensive retrospection. Consequently, it is important for IoT consultants to define and develop key success metrics with an IoT solution [65–79].

10.3.4.2 *Compatibility Problems With Equipment*

The processing of data is primarily conducted by various devices, plcs, etc. connecting to IoT gateways for the storage and transfer of cloud data. Based on their priorities and performance, businesses ought to specifically classify facilities, appliances, and obsolete devices. When heritage machines do not have the said PLC and sensors, it is more important to incorporate IoT. It is a fast move to attach external sensors to the old computers, but it is not confirmed, which makes it a really challenging challenge.

It is also strongly recommended that before IoT deployment the physical hardware and the resulting compatibility problems be established.

10.3.4.3 *Compatibility and Maintenance*

While the development market has been well developed over the past 20 years, computer vendors do have to take care of usability problems when designing their networks and fixing IoT concerns. Networks can not only support a wide spectrum of IoT edge devices but also provide innovative features to provide advanced capabilities to their goods. Updating such tools poses protection and usability problems [80, 82].

10.3.4.4 *Connectivity Issues in the Field of Data*

This may be the most underestimated obstacle regardless of the substantial increase in accessibility. However, several places already remain in which IoT deployment is a problem for data accessibility. This includes how IoT devices interact with the Gateway & Cloud and how they produce knowledge. Many IoT gateways are GPRS and Wi-Fi/LAN compliant, but the traditional devices are data generated by PLC, telemetry and RTU systems. Of this purpose, a suitable edge layer must be built to transfer data to the IoT network that converts transport and application format protocols.

It will enable us to identify the correct combination of the protocols before applying an IoT [82–84].

10.3.4.5 *Incorrect Data Collection and Difficulties*

Knowing that the whole configuration has not encountered problems and the program is working, but inaccurate data collection will also occur. Incorrect data is processed because of any kind of unpleasant event or the software's incapacity to handle such faults in time. This contributes to incorrect analysis that does not support correct judgments. This difficulty in IoT implementation will affect both businesses and clients greatly [84, 85].

10.3.4.6 *Security Concern*

Security is by far the main concern in the production of IoT. As each system is linked to a wider network, the cumulative attack area is significantly greater than a conventional network design. To make matters worse, several computers move through various networks, which may enable Internet criminals circumvent certain protection measures by gathering malware on the road. Many IoT-edge systems are also autonomous, so that traditional network security protocols cannot consider risk assessments. Therefore, a variety of IoT protection issues need to be addressed together [85, 86].

This is important to presume that every computer connected to the network is now infected in a manner to defend organizations from potential attacks. This enables them to build protection and authentication protocols that screen devices rigorously and allow them to prevent automatic access to potentially sensitive information [86–90].

10.3.4.7 *Problems in Computer Confidentiality*

Recently, businesses and users fear over computer protection as multiple Ransom-ware attacks that arise [90–93]. There is even an opportunity to benefit proprietary property through corporate espionage. IoT service providers must therefore make sure their data is safe. The use of a robust governance mode, allowing protected access to confidential information and documents, will help with these issues of data protection. For efficient IoT deployment this step of preparation, which determines multiple data-related protection policies is crucial [94, 95].

10.4 Challenges in Technology

The true benefit of an IoT approach [4, 96, 97] is accomplished by actionable observations from the IoT data obtained. This includes a high-performance analysis infrastructure that can accommodate the enormous volume of data that would eventually be applied to the solution. This must be considered by data analytics collaborators in planning the infrastructure for IoT deployment to include data collection, cleaning and view. The absence of sufficient space to add real-time or predictive analytics to a solution for IoT that can therefore help to resolve this critical challenge for IoT.

10.4.1 Skepticism of Consumers

In addition to all of the aforementioned operational issues, businesses will still deal with consumers' cynicism regarding the internet of things. A survey of 90 percent of the user lacked trust in IoT protection, according to Dutch cybersecurity agency Gemalto, while 65 percent were worried that hackers were able to obtain control of their computers. Since many IoT edge devices have been designed for use at home, addressing these issues is crucial to various companies [98, 99].

Transparency is a strong step in increasing customer trust. People want to know what data they collect, how it is used, where it is stored and how it is protected. They would like to know what happens if one of their devices is compromised and what remedies are available if the servers of the company are broken. Clearly and proactively communicating this information can lead to misconceptions about IoT safety being dispelled and consumer confidence gained [4, 5].

While the IoT revolution is already here, the challenges of its implementation should not be taken for granted by organizations. Failure to resolve these areas may contribute to humiliating technology vulnerabilities, service interruptions or faulty goods, which makes it vital that businesses focus greatly on the cutting-edge IoT network machine strategies. Working closely with a data centre allows them to create effective frameworks that allow them to offer the diverse service types that users require from IoT apps [1, 6].

IoT focuses on enhancing the lives and well-being of people, either by encouraging individuals to settle for better decisions and have more beneficial existences (less pressure, less upsetting work, more beneficial prosperity for individuals with handicaps), or by making activities inside the framework that positively affect society, the economy, and condition [11–25].

With the Internet of Things an ever increasing number of things are interconnected and information sharing among themselves.

It can help track force, gas, and water sources in a city; traffic clog, auto collisions, development zones, schools, or upsetting neighbourhoods. Besides, with so much information being gathered, it is essential to sort out and categorize this information into helpful information for choice taking. People or other PC instruments will at that point execute certain choices [26].

10.5 Analysis of IoT Security

Any IoT structure can be divided into five layers of security threats as follows:

(i) sensing layer security threats
(ii) network layer safety issues
(iii) middleware layer safety issues
(iv) application layer gateways safety issues
(v) application layer safety issues.

In one IoT program, each of these layers utilizes an assortment of innovations which bring various issues and dangers to security. At these four

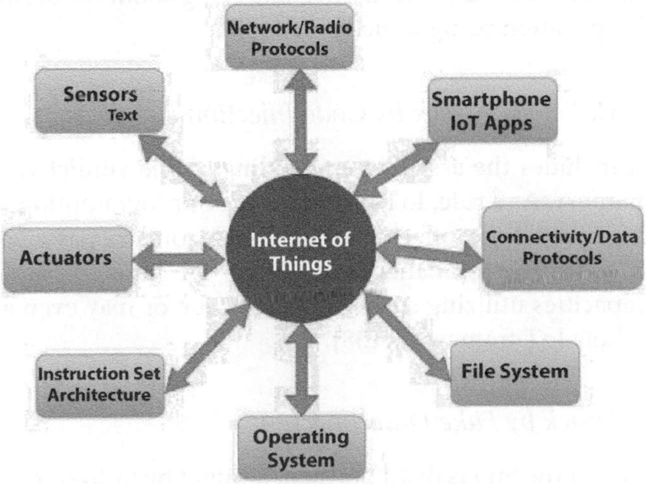

Figure 10.2 Different components of the Internet of Things.

layers, Figure 10.2 showcases different components of IoT. Additionally talked about in this area are the unique security concerns related with the passages that connect those layers.

10.5.1 Sensing Layer Security Threats

The sensing layer discusses genetically actuators and predetermined IoT sensors. Sensors feel the physical incident that is taking place around them. In relation to the sensed information, actuators are involved in the physical environment. There are various types of sensors that can be used to detect details of different kinds such as smoke position sensors, humidity sensors, camera sensors, temperature, ultrasonic sensors, etc. Chemical, electronic, electrical or mechanical sensors can sensor the physical world. Diverse layer detecting innovations are utilized in different IoT applications, for example, WSNs, GPS, RFID, RSNs and so forth [56, 57]. Coming up next are significant security dangers which can be experienced at the detecting layer.

10.5.1.1 Node Capturing

IoT executions require actuators, including sensors and low-power hubs. Those hubs are powerless against the foes different assaults. The aggressors can endeavour to catch or expel a malevolent hub inside the IoT organize. The new hub can give off an impression of being a piece of the system however the aggressor controls it. This may bring about the security of the whole IoT application being undermined [59].

10.5.1.2 Malicious Attack by Code Injection

The assault includes the assailant embeddings some vindictive code into the hub's memory. As a rule, IoT hub firmware or programming is updated broadcasting in real time, offering assailants a secondary passage to embed malevolent code. The assailants may compel the hubs to play out some intended capacities utilizing such vindictive code or may even attempt to get to the whole IoT framework [58].

10.5.1.3 Attack by Fake Data Injection

In the event that the hub is distinguished, it might be utilized by the assailant to embed incorrect information into the IoT system. This may bring about bogus outcomes and the IoT application can glitch. This strategy can likewise be utilized to trigger a DDoS assault by the aggressor [60, 78, 91].

10.5.1.4 Sidelines Assaults

Other than direct assaults on the hubs, different side-channel assaults can prompt touchy information spillage. Processor micro architectures, electromagnetic spread and its capacity utilization open significant data to rivals. Attacks as an afterthought channel can be founded on "laser-based assaults," "timing assaults," "electro-magnetic assault," or power consumption [62, 63]. Present-day chips deal with different counter estimates while actualizing the cryptographic modules to keep away from such side-channel attacks.

10.5.1.5 Attacks During Booting Process

During the boot cycle, the edge gadgets are powerless against numerous assaults. That is on the grounds that the inherent security forms now are not permitted. The assailants can exploit this weakness and endeavour to assault hub gadgets at restart. Since edge gadgets are normally low controlled and frequently experience patterns of rest wake, the boot stage in such gadgets is accordingly significant [61].

10.5.2 Network Layer Safety Issues

The principle highlight of the system layer is the transmission to the preparing unit of the data acquired from the detecting layer. The key security issues looked at the system layer are as per the following.

10.5.2.1 Attack on Phishing Page

Phishing attacks likewise allude to assaults where an insignificant exertion put by the assailant may target numerous IoT gadgets. Probably a portion of the gadgets will turn into an objective of the assault, the aggressors anticipate. There is an opportunity over the span of clients visiting site pages on the Internet to discover phishing destinations.

At the point when client record and secret key have been undermined, the client's whole IoT organize is powerless against digital assaults. The system layer in IoT is entirely helpless against assaults by phishing destinations [62, 63].

10.5.2.2 Attacks on Access

This is a kind of assault where the IoT network is accessed by an unapproved person. The gatecrasher will stay undetected in the system for quite a while to come. The point or objective of this kind of assault is to take significant information or data, rather than causing the system to hurt. IoT frameworks get and transmit significant information constantly, and are in this manner amazingly helpless against these attacks [64, 65].

10.5.2.3 Attacks on Data Transmission

IoT applications do a ton of handling and sharing information. Information is significant and is frequently the object of programmers and different rivals. Information put away on nearby servers or cloud has a security chance. However, information going starting with one area then onto the next or in travel is substantially more powerless to digital assaults. There is a ton of information development in IoT applications between sensors, actuators, cloud, etc. In these information developments, different connection advancements are utilized and in this manner, IoT applications are defenceless against information penetrates [68, 69].

10.5.2.4 Attacks on Routing

In such attacks, malignant hubs in an IoT application that endeavor to divert the steering ways while travelling information. Sinkhole assaults are a particular type of directing assault where an enemy publicizes a fake most brief steering way and brings hubs into it to course traffic. A wormhole assault is another assault that, whenever joined with different assaults, for example, sinkhole assaults, can turn into a genuine security danger. A warm-gap is an out of band association for simple parcel transmission between two hubs. An aggressor may manufacture a problem area on the web between an undermined hub and a PC and endeavour to go around straightforward security conventions in an IoT system [66, 67, 70].

10.5.3 Middleware Layer Safety Issues

The capability of the middleware in IoT constructs a layer of deliberation between the layer of the system and the layer of application. Middleware can likewise offer solid stockpiling and computational capabilities.

This layer gives APIs that satisfy application layer necessities. The middleware layer includes retailers, constant data stores, AIs, fiber frames, etc. [70].

Despite the useful middleware layer for offering a safe and protected IoT structure, different attacks are additionally indefensible. These attacks seize credit for the whole IoT program by infecting the middleware. The knowledge base and cloud protection face other key security issues in the middleware layer. Different potential assaults are talked about as follows inside the middleware layer.

10.5.3.1 Attack by SQL Injection

Even middleware is susceptible to attack by "SQL Injection (SQLi)." In such assaults, assailant can implant pernicious SQL explanations in a program. At that point, the aggressors can acquire private information of any client and may even change fields in the store [71].

10.5.3.2 Attack by Signature Wrapping

XML marks are utilized in the Web administrations utilized in middleware. The aggressor breaks the mark calculation in a mark wrapping assault, and can perform tasks or change spied message by misusing loopholes of "Simple Object Access Protocol (SOAP)" [63].

10.5.3.3 Cloud Attack Injection with Malware

The assailant can deal with cloud malware infusion, embed noxious code or supplement a implicit engine into the cloud. The assailant claims to be authentic assistance by attempting to construct a vindictive help module or a virtual machine case. Along these lines, the aggressor can gain admittance to the casualty's administration demands for administration and catch touchy information that can be changed according to the case [61].

10.5.3.4 Cloud Flooding Attack

This attack works nearly the equivalent in the cloud as a DoS attack and influences administration quality (QoS). The assailants are continually sending various solicitations to a database for exhausting cloud assets. Those assaults can significantly affect cloud frameworks by raising the cloud server load [63].

10.5.4 Gateways Safety Issues

Gateway is a wide layer that assumes a key job in interfacing numerous gadgets, individuals, kinds of stuff, and cloud administrations. Entryways additionally help in the arrangement of IoT PC equipment and programming arrangements. Doors are utilized to decode and encode IoT information, and to decipher correspondence conventions between various layers [76]. IoT organizes today are heterogeneous with numerous passages in the middle of, including "LoraWan," "ZigBee," "Z-Wave," and "TCP/IP" stacks [75]. A few of the security issues of the IoT portal are listed below.

10.5.4.1 On-Boarding Safely

While actualizing another PC or sensor in an IoT association, making sure about the encryption keys is essential. Gateways fill in as go-betweens between the new gadgets and the administration administrations and all keys go through the portals. The doors, especially during the on-boarding process, are vulnerable to man-in-the-centre assaults and listening in to catch the encryption key [78].

10.5.4.2 Additional Interfaces

The decrease of the attack surface is an essential strategy to be held as a primary concern when the IoT gadgets are mounted. The IoT entryway maker must uphold just the necessary interfaces and conventions. So as to dodge secondary passage verification and data gets through administrations and highlights ought to be restricted for end clients [77].

10.5.4.3 Encrypting End-to-End

In order to ensure information classification, a genuine beginning to complete protection of the application layer is necessary. The application does not permit the scrambled messages to be unscrambled by somebody other than the genuine beneficiary. Despite the fact that Zigbee and Zwave conventions bolster encryption, this is not start to finish encryption, since the entryways are relied upon to unscramble and re-scramble the messages so as to change over the data starting with one convention then onto the next. This entryway level unscrambling makes the information helpless against information penetrates [79, 80].

10.5.5 Application Layer Safety Issues

The application layer cooperates legitimately with end clients and offers administrations. In this layer, IoT advances, for example, savvy houses, keen meters, brilliant urban areas, shrewd networks, and so on. This layer has exceptional security challenges, such as information burglaries and privacy issues, which are not present in several layers. For different applications in this layer, security problems are routinely fundamental. A sub-layer between the "device layer" and the "application layer" also includes various IoT constructs, typically referred to as a support or middleware layer [81]. The support layer provides various managements and helps to distribute and prepare knowledgeable assets. The main security concerns are listed below regarding the application layer encounters.

10.5.5.1 Theft of Data

IoT applications handle a ton of basic and private data. Travel information are considerably more powerless against assaults than information very still, and there is a ton of information development in IoT applications. The clients will be hesitant to disclose their private information on IoT applications at a time when these systems are powerless against information robbery assaults. A part of the techniques and shows used to make sure about IoT applications against data theft are data encryption, data separation, device and framework confirmation, insurance affirmation, etc [84, 85].

10.5.5.2 Attacks at Interruption in Service

These attacks are also called unauthorized interruption attacks or DDoS attacks in current literature. Different examples of these attacks on IoT applications occurred. These assaults deny real clients the benefits of using the IoT applications by making the servers or the system too misleadingly occupied to even consider reacting [82, 83].

10.5.5.3 Malicious Code Injection Attack

In the most part, attackers are looking for the briefest or fastest way they can hack into a program or device. In the event that, because of insufficient code tests, the gadget is defenceless against malignant contents and confusions, at that point, this will be the primary section point an aggressor will choose. By and large, assailants use "XSS (cross-web page scripting)"

[80–86] to embed some malignant content into a site that they in any case trust. An effective XSS assault will bring about an IoT account being hacked and can incapacitate the IoT program.

10.6 Improvements and Enhancements Needed for IoT Applications in the Future

PCs and cell phones give a scope of security highlights, for example, firewalls, hostile to infection applications, randomization of the location space, and so forth. By and large, these well-being insurances are missing in various IoT items at present available. There are rising security gives presently confronting the IoT applications. There is yet no very much characterized structure and particular for a start to finish IoT application. The IoT application is not an independent gadget, it is a coordinated framework that requires work from numerous people it enterprises.

A few different items and advancements are utilized at any layer beginning from detecting to application. These include an incredible scope of edge hub sensors and actuators. There are a few degrees of availability, for example, cell arranges, Insteon, Dash7, WiFi, Bluetooth and so on. A handshake framework is required among every one of these essentials.

Likewise, various gadget the executives advancements are utilized at various levels in the proportional IoT structure, for example, Zigbee, 6LOWPAN, ISA100, remote HART, RFID, Z-Wave, Bluetooth, NFC, and so on. The default HTTP convention can't be utilized in the application layer after that. HTTP isn't perfect for asset compelled settings, since it is substantial weight and in this manner requires a noteworthy overhead parsing. Therefore, there are several alternative protocols that have been implemented for IoT environments at the application layer as well. Examples are JavascriptIoT, "SMQTT," "MQTT," "XMPP," CoAP, "AMQP," "M3DA," etc., [49, 86, 87].

The significant trade-offs between cost viability, solidness, dependability, well-being, inclusion, dormancy, and so on are because of the outrageous assortment of conventions, advancements, and gadgets in an IoT application. On the off chance that one measurement is enhanced for development, another measurement can debase. For instance, executing an excessive number of security checks and conventions on all IoT applications information exchanges will step by step increment the application's expense and inactivity, rendering it unsatisfactory for clients. A commonplace IoT application comprises a wide range of associated gadgets, topographies, domains, and innovations.

Regardless of whether one of the gadgets or innovations or their mix stays powerless, that might be the reason for all protection danger of application. The range is viewed as solid as the most fragile connection. As of late, the quantity of feeble connections in IoT applications has expanded significantly [33–35]. As a bad gui to delete customer's WiFi-mystery term in a sharp home IoT programme, for example, even important IoT applications, such as the sharp bulbs and canny portal-locks.

An overwhelming proportion of the customer-related data and the atmosphere are distributed globally to make it sharper. This information can suggest a ton of private data, and this could be another reason for peril to a man and society at large. Thus, the current IoT application structure and engineering require significant changes and moves up to make it productive, steady, and powerful.

- ✓ To gauge the level of hazard associated with sending these gadgets in various applications, powerful infiltration testing for IoT gadgets is required. A need rundown can be drawn up dependent on the hazard in question, and the frameworks can be appropriately conveyed in various applications [30–32].
- ✓ Since a definitive goal of all IoT applications is to manufacture a self-sufficient framework requiring negligible human impedance, it could be helpful to utilize some man-made reasoning (AI)-based procedures or calculations to ensure IoT applications. This will assist with decreasing the heap of IoT investigates and contact [20–27].
- ✓ Any IoT security system that is being actualized ought to be tried and adaptability affirmed. The security conventions don't work for few clients as it were. The genuine dangers just start to come as the program gets open and starts to be generally utilized in the open area. Subsequently, legitimate arranging and methodology are required.
- ✓ Since the IoT gadgets and applications are expanding quickly, a methodology should be intended to adapt to the expense and force limitations expected to be confronted soon. It could take a change in perspective from an incorporated way to deal with some decentralized methodology, where gadgets can speak with one another naturally and securely. It will help decrease the program support costs and diminish limit imperatives [40–44].

- ✓ Aside from the difficulties raised by outside entertainers, there are different circumstances where the sensors in an IoT application start to gather or send wrong information.
- ✓ These blunders might be anything but difficult to oversee on account of a unified design; however, on account of an independent decentralized engineering, they can turn into a bottleneck.
- ✓ Broken perusing or information transmission may prompt bothersome outcomes. Therefore, so as to approve the information, the component should be built up to grow, especially on account of dispersed engineering [65–67].
- ✓ Encryption techniques are utilized at various layers and conventions inside the IoT arrangement. All things considered, the full program incorporates various phases of encryption, decoding, and reencryption cycles. Such circles are making the machine powerless against assault. Start to finish encryption will be a decent method for halting various attacks.
- ✓ At whatever point a framework wishes to speak with another framework, it will authorize a verification technique. Computerized testaments can be a promising alternative for consistent verification of bound characters attached to cryptographic conventions.
- ✓ Since most IoT applications use cloud administrations for information stockpiling and recuperation, it is likewise critical to consider the dangers brought about by the cloud.
- ✓ Cloud is a mutual system that is utilized by numerous clients, and there might be noxious cloud clients that might be the wellspring of IoT related information dangers.
- ✓ The information ought to be put away in the cloud as ciphertext, and no ciphertext ought to be unscrambled to the server. It will additionally help information insurance and spare us from the general dangers related to utilizing cloud administrations [68, 70].
- ✓ To shield client and condition information from being captured, a system dependent on encryption strategies, for example, RSA, SHA256, or hash chains are required. IoT frameworks should be arranged with the end goal that the detected information can be transmitted in a sheltered and confirmed way. This will assist with making trust in IoT applications among people, government organizations, and businesses.

10.7 Upcoming Future Research Challenges with Intrusion Detection Systems (IDS)

There are some design and efficiency issues that are yet to be tended to in the utilization of blockchain and AI for IoT assurance. The security of Blockchain is based on its deployment method and the use of programming and facilities for this use. Since all information portals are available, consumers would be able to uncover personal data. Presently, the size of blockchain regularly continually develops as the quantity of excavators develops. This raises stockpiling costs and decreases the speed of correspondence over the whole system, making issues, for example, versatility and the accessibility of blockchain [54, 55]. A lot of machine learning algorithms exist. The selection of an efficient method suitable for the task is therefore imperative. Selecting a wrong algorithm will generate "garbage" performance and result in loss of energy, productivity and accuracy. Similarly, choosing the wrong set of data would result in input of "garbage" generating the wrong results. The adequacy of an AI approach relies upon specific factors just as the unpredictability of information assortment. At the point when the information are not grouped and arranged the forecast exactness ought to be lower.

The authentic information may likewise contain a few indistinct qualities, exceptions, fragmented qualities, and inconsequential information. IoT frameworks create a lot of information and in this manner cleaning and pre-processing the information accurately is a difficult activity. Various highlights, for example, quality arrangement, direct relapse, numerous relapses, disposal of redundancies and pressure of information are critical to viably utilize AI to ensure the IoT.

A portion of things to come look into headings in this field are:

- The gates between various layers have to be secured in the IoT system. Gateways provide the attackers with an simple entry point into IoT network. Rather than explicit encryption strategies for specific conventions, start to finish encryption will be a plausible way to deal with ensure the information going through the entryways.
- The information for convention interpretation should just be unscrambled at the planned goal and not at the portals.
- The current blockchain foundation is profoundly obliged as far as the number of nodes in affirmed systems and the number of nodes in consent free systems.

- Alongside countless nodes or clients, different agreement calculations are intended to accomplish high throughput.
- Blockchain's manipulative-evidence work winds up in a rundown of a ton of trash information and addresses.
- There is a great deal of out of date information that is rarely expelled, including the addresses of the brilliant agreements that have been lost. This influences the general application execution and better approaches to deal with the trash information in the blockchain proficiently should be made.
- Close to the IoT node, information preparation is basic for the proficient conveyance of IoT applications in close ongoing.
- In order to thwart the data travel for examination, distinctive AI-based computations can be altered to separate the data in the hub itself. It can furthermore improve application security by thwarting the trading of data.

Customary interruption recognition and avoidance procedures, similar to firewalls, get to control components, and encryption, have a few impediments in completely shielding systems and frameworks from progressively advanced assaults like forswearing of administration. Furthermore, most programmes based on these methods have adverse consequences and the lack of ongoing improvements to harmful procedures. During the last ten years, however, many machine learning (ML) and IoT procedures have been implemented in order to identify the disruption with a view to increasing the pace and flexibility of recognition. These tactics are also used to retain forward thinking and detailed the basis for assault knowledge.

Artificial Intelligence (AI) based Intrusion Detection Systems (IDSs) can accomplish agreeable discovery levels when adequate preparing information is accessible, and AI models have adequate generalizability to distinguish assault variations and novel assaults. What's more, AI based IDSs don't depend intensely on area information; in this way, they are anything but difficult to plan and build. Profound learning is a part of AI that can accomplish extraordinary exhibitions. Contrasted and conventional AI strategies, profound learning techniques are better at managing enormous information. In addition, profound learning techniques can consequently take in highlight portrayals from crude information and afterward yield results; they work in a start to finish design and are down to earth.

Huge volumes of data i.e. big data get generated each and every day. Therefore, providing protection and handling such data becomes a very hectic task. Interruption could be described as other types of exercises which do not approve and which damage the data framework. This involves the assault that can present a possible danger to privacy, trust or accessibility of knowledge. For instance, exercises that would make the PC administrations inert to real clients are viewed as an interruption.

An IDS is a product or equipment framework, which recognizes the reticence of PC frameworks so that safety is taken into account. The IDS aims to classify different types of communication and software malicious tools that could not be differentiated from conventional firewalls. It is important to ensure the transparency, respectability or confidentiality of PC systems is achieved by actions that are negotiated. IDS frameworks could be comprehensively categorized into two gatherings: "Signature Based Intrusion Detection System (SIDS)" and "Anomaly Based Intrusion Detection System (AIDS)."

Interruption detection ensures that possibilities within a PC structure or software are slowly checked and disrupted so as to detect possible episodes and even preclude unapproved entry. Usually, data are obtained from a variety of networks and programme sources and then data are exchanged in order to resolve diligent security concerns. Since the Internet is a source of multiple risks of device assaults, various mechanisms are in place to avoid Internet assaults.

In particular, IDSs allow the framework to counter external aggressions. In other words, IDSs aim at providing a mass of security to deal with the attacks on the Internet by PC frameworks. IDS may be used to differentiate between harmful systems exchange and using PC frameworks, although this undertaking cannot be performed by the ordinary firewall. The acknowledgment of an intrusion relies on the presumption that gatecrashers do not exactly want a legitimate customer [67, 69].

Customary ways to deal with Signature based Intrusion Detection System (SIDS) look at organize bundles and have a go at coordinating against a database of marks. Be that as it may, these procedures can't recognize assaults that range a few bundles. As current malware is increasingly refined it might be important to remove signature data over numerous parcels. The above includes the IDS to check previous bundles' substance. There are many methods in which marks are rendered as state machines, structured string designs and semantically conditions as regards having a mark for SIDS in general.

Similarly, Anomaly based Intrusion Detection System (AIDS) has the main advantage of being able to identify zero-days incidents because it is not based on a signature database to recognize the abnormal activity [26]. When the activity studied varies from normal behavior, AIDS causes a danger signal. AIDS also has several advantages. Second, they will discover

Table 10.1 Comparative analysis of techniques for intrusion detection.

	Benefits	**Limitations**
SIDS Techniques	Quite productive for detecting minimal false detection infringements. Identify the intruders immediately. Predominant for identifying the known assaults. The concept is straightforward.	Should be refreshed much of the time with another mark. SIDS is intended to recognize assaults for known marks When a past interruption has been adjusted marginally to another variation, at that point the framework would be not able to distinguish this new deviation of the comparable assault.
AIDS Techniques	Could be utilized to distinguish new assaults. Could be utilized to make interruption signature.	Helps can't deal with encoded bundles, so the assault can remain undetected and can introduce a danger. Difficult to manufacture a typical profile for an extremely powerful PC framework. Initial testing is essential.

malicious internal behaviors. If an attacker starts transacting on a compromised account that is not detected in the user operation, the alarm will be triggered. Second, a cybercriminal individual has very difficulty identifying regular user activity without making an alert as the program is made up of custom profiles [70, 72].

Table 10.1 shows the comparative study of signature based and anomaly based intrusion detection systems.

10.8 Conclusion

In the last decade, the advent of the IoT model resulted (and will continue to lead) in numerous challenges for protection or privacy assaults in case of both IoT and big data. Unfortunately, in the IoT domain, threats to security are not well known. In this report, many IoT protection threats or problems and countermeasures were outlined in a level-by-level way. In the last decade, the advent of the IoT model and big data usage resulted (and will continue to lead) in numerous challenges to protection or privacy assaults.

Unfortunately, in the IoT domain, threats to security are not well known. In this report, many IoT protection threats or problems and countermeasures were outlined in a level-by-level way. This is of most extreme significance to secure the Internet of Things pushing ahead. When appropriately treated, individual information gathered by IoT gadgets presents a Privacy Threat. Application control will likewise require tight validation to maintain a strategic distance from the proliferation of the capturing and botnet. In this manner, new innovations in light of security ought to be worked to ensure the customer and business information created by IoT gadgets.

In this examination, diverse security dangers at various layers of an IoT system are distinguished. In general, a way to deal with protection from top to bottom will be required, with security layers conveyed. On account of the great practice rules given by activities, for example, the IoT, the issues encompassing endpoint security can be bit by bit improved. In any case, how to secure the correspondence conventions that will empower potential IoT usage on a scale. One possible solution would be to create a new data protocol with both user-friendly and robust security features. However, implementing a new protocol is difficult, and many protocols already compete in the same field. Therefore, one of the most widely used protocols will be a safer option. Future research defines another way of dealing with an information convention with inherent security capabilities, taking into account the proposed structure. Research is needed on strategies for making reliable elements, lightweight encryption and decoding of information, and minimal printing of security libraries.

References

1. Bhunia, S., Hsiao, M.S., Banga, M., Narasimhan, S., Hardware trojan attacks: Threat analysis and countermeasures. *Proc. IEEE*, 102, 8, 1229–1247, 2014.
2. Salmani, H. and Tehranipoor, M.M., Vulnerability analysis of a circuit layout to hardware Trojan insertion. *IEEE Trans. Inf. Forensics Secur.*, 11, 6, 1214–1225, 2016.
3. Wehbe, T., Mooney, V.J., Keezer, D.C., Parham, N.B., A novel approach to detect hardware Trojan attacks on primary data inputs, in: *Proc. ACM Workshop Embedded Systems Security*, p. 2, 2015.
4. Bhasin, S. and Regazzoni, F., A survey on hardware Trojan detection techniques, in: *Proc. IEEE Int. Symp. Circuits and Systems*, pp. 2021–2024, 2015.

5. Shila, D.M. and Venugopal, V., Design, implementation and security analysis of hardware Trojan threats in FPGA, in: *Proc. IEEE Int. Conf. Communications*, pp. 719–724, 2014.
6. Priyadarshini, S.B.B. and Panigrahi, S., A distributed scalar controller selection scheme for redundant data elimination in sensor networks. *International Journal of Knowledge Discovery in Bioinformatics (IJKDB)*, 7, 1, 91–104, 2017.
7. Priyadarshini, S.B.B., Panigrahi, S., Bagjadab, A.B., A distributed triangular scalar cluster premier selection scheme for enhanced event coverage and redundant data minimization in wireless multimedia sensor networks. *Indian J. Sci. Res.*, 14, 2, 96–102, 2017.
8. Priyadarshini, S.B.B., Panigrahi, S., Bagjadab, A.B., A distributed approach based on maximal far-flung scalar premier selection for camera actuation. *12th International Conference on Distributed Computing and Internet Technology (ICDCIT 2016)*, KIIT University, Bhubaneswar, Odisha, Published in the series of *Lecture Notes in Computer Science (LNCS)*, Springer, 15th–18th January 2016.
9. Tehranipoor, M. and Koushanfar, F., A survey of hardware Trojan taxonomy and detection. *IEEE Des. Test Comput.*, 27, 1, 10–25, 2010.
10. *NSA TEMPEST Series*, 2016. [Online]. Available: http://cryptome.org/#NSA-TS.
11. Tanaka, H., Information leakage via electromagnetic emanations and evaluation of TEMPEST countermeasures, in: *Information Systems Security*, pp. 167–179, Springer, Berlin, Heidelberg, 2007.
12. Vuagnoux, M. and Pasini, S., Compromising electromagnetic emanations of wired and wireless keyboards, in: *Proc. USENIX Security Symposium*, pp. 1–16, 2009.
13. Nia, A.M., Sur-Kolay, S., Raghunathan, A., Jha, N.K., Physiological information leakage: A new frontier in health information security, accepted for publication in *IEEE Trans. Emerg. Topics Comput.*, 2010.
14. Brandt, A. and Buron, J., Home automation routing requirements in low-power and lossy networks, 2010. [Online]. Available: https://tools.ietf.org/html/rfc5826.
15. Ganz, F., Puschmann, D., Barnaghi, P., Carrez, F., A practical evaluation of information processing and abstraction techniques for the internet of things. *IEEE Internet Things J.*, 2, 4, 340–354, 2015.
16. Anjomshoa, F., Aloqaily, M., Kantarci, B., Erol-Kantarci, M., Schuckers, S., Social behaviometrics for personalized devices in the internet of things era. *IEEE Access*, 5, 12199–12213, 2017.
17. Priyadarshini, S.B.B., Panigrahi, S., Bagjadab, A.B., Mishra, B.K., An investigative prolegomenon on various clustering strategies, their resolution and future direction towards wireless sensor systems. *International Conference on Emerging Technologies in Data Mining and Information Security (IEMIS)*, vol. 2, Kolkata, February 23-25, 2018.

18. Priyadarshini, S.B.B. and Panigrahi, S., A distributed scheme based on minimum camera actuation employing concentric hexagonal scalar premier selection for data redundancy minimization. *15th International Conference on Information Technology*, IEEE, Bhubaneswar, December 22-24, 2016, e-ISBN: 978-1-5090-3584-7.
19. Priyadarshini, S.B.B., Singh, D., Panda, M., A comparative study of redundant data minimization and event coverage in wireless multimedia sensor networks (WMSNs). *International Conference on Applied Machine Learning (ICAML)*, IEEE, Bhubaneswar, September 27-28, 2019.
20. Dey, N., Ashour, A.S., Bhatt, C., Internet of things driven connected healthcare, in: *Internet of Things and Big Data Technologies for Next Generation Healthcare*, pp. 3–12, Springer, Cham, 2017.
21. Frustaci, M., Pace, P., Aloi, G., Fortino, G., Evaluating critical security issues of the IoT world: Present and future challenges. *IEEE Internet Things J.*, 5, 4, 2483–2495, Aug. 2018.
22. Priyadarshini, S.B.B., A hybrid approach based on scalar cluster leader selection for camera activation (HASL-CA) in wireless multimedia sensor networks (WMSNs). *International Conference on Applied Machine Learning (ICAML)*, IEEE, Bhubaneswar, September 27-28, 2019.
23. Priyadarshini, S.B.B. and Panigrahi, S., A quadrigeminal scheme based on event reporting scalar premier selection for camera actuation in wireless multimedia sensor networks. *J. King Saud Univ. Eng. Sci.*, Elsevier, 31, 1, 52–60, 2017.
24. Priyadarshini, S.B.B. and Panigrahi, S., Redundant data minimization using minimal mean distant scalar leader selection for event driven camera actuation. *International Conference on Information Technology (ICIT)*, IEEE, pp. 142–147, 2016.
25. Fernández-Caramés, T.M. and Fraga-Lamas, P., A review on the use of blockchain for the internet of things. *IEEE Access*, 6, 32979–33001, 2018.
26. Nath, M.P., Goyal, K., Prasad, J., Kallur, B., Chat bot—An edge to customer insight. *Int. J. Res. Sci. Innov.*, V, V, 29–32, 2018.
27. Suthaharan, S., Big data classification: Problems and challenges in network intrusion prediction with machine learning. *ACM SIGMETRICS Performance Evaluation Review*, vol. 41, pp. 70–73, 2014.
28. Nath, M.P., Sagnika, S., Das, M., Pandey, M., Object recognition using cat swarm optimization. *Int. J. Res. Sci. Innov.*, IV, VIIS, 47–52, July 2017.
29. Nath, M.P. and Sagnika, S., Capabilities of chatbots and its performance enhancements in machine learning, in: *Machine Learning and Information Processing, Advances in Intelligent Systems and Computing*, 1101, pp. 183–192, 2020.
30. Elhayatmy, G., Dey, N., Ashour, A.S., Internet of things based wireless body area network in healthcare, in: *Internet of Things and Big Data Analytics Toward Next-Generation Intelligence*, pp. 3–20, Springer, Cham, 2018.

31. Bhatt, C., Dey, N., Ashour, A.S. (Eds.), *Internet of Things and Big Data Technologies for Next Generation Healthcare*, 2017.
32. Meidan, Y. *et al.*, ProfilIoT: A machine learning approach for IoT device identification based on network traffic analysis. *SAC2017 32nd ACM Symp. Appl. Comput.*, pp. 506–509, 2017.
33. Nath, M., Muralikrishnan, J., Sundarrajan, K., Varadarajanna, M., Continuous integration, delivery, and deployment: A revolutionary approach in software development. *Int. J. Res. Sci. Innov.*, 5, VII, 185–190, 2018.
34. Mhetre, N.A., Deshpande, A.V., Mahalle, P.N., Trust management model based on fuzzy approach for ubiquitous computing. *Int. J. Ambient Comput. Intell.*, 7, 2, 33–46, 2016.
35. Nath, M.P., Pandey, P., Somu, K., Amalraj, P., Artificial intelligence & machine learning: The emerging milestones in software development. *Int. J. Res. Sci. Innov.*, 5, IX, 36–44, 2018.
36. Lin, J., Yu, W., Zhang, N., Yang, X., Zhang, H., Zhao, W., A survey on internet of things: Architecture, enabling technologies, security and privacy, and applications. *IEEE Internet Things J.*, 4, 5, 1125–1142, Oct. 2017.
37. Chen, L., Thombre, S., Järvinen, K., Lohan, E.S., Alén-Savikko, A., Leppäkoski, H., Bhuiyan, M.Z.H., Bu-Pasha, S., Ferrara, G.N., Honkala, S., Lindqvist, J., Ruotsalainen, L., Korpisaari, P., Kuusniemi, H., Robustness, security and privacy in location-based services for future IoT: A survey. *IEEE Access*, 5, 8956–8977, 2017.
38. Sahani, A., Priyadarshini, S.B.B., Chinara, S., The role of blockchain technology and its usage in various sectors in the modern age: Various roles of blockchain and usecases in different sectors, in: *Blockchain and AI Technology in the Industrial Internet of Things*, pp. 221–245, IGI Global, 2021.
39. Priyadarshini, S.B.B., Bagjadab, A.B., Mishra, B.K., Digital signature and its pivotal role in affording security services, in: *Handbook of E-Business Security*, pp. 365–384, 2018.
40. Priyadarshini, S.B.B., Bagjadab, A.B., Mishra, B.K., Security in distributed operating system: A comprehensive study, in: *Cyber Security in Parallel and Distributed Computing: Concepts, Techniques, Applications and Case Studies*, pp. 221–230, 2019.
41. Farris, I., Taleb, T., Khettab, Y., Song, J., A survey on emerging SDN and NFV security mechanisms for IoT systems. *IEEE Commun. Surv. Tut.*, 21, 1, 812–837, 1st Quart., 2019.
42. Gharaibeh, A., Salahuddin, M.A., Hussini, S.J., Khreishah, A., Khalil, I., Guizani, M., Al-Fuqaha, A., Smart cities: A survey on data management, security, and enabling technologies. *IEEE Commun. Surv. Tut.*, 19, 4, 2456–2501, 4th Quart., 2017.
43. Din, I. U., Guizani, M., Kim, B.-S., Hassan, S., and Khan, M. K., Trust management techniques for the internet of things: A survey. *IEEE Acess*, 7, 29763–29787, 2019.

44. Mosenia, A. and Jha, N.K., A comprehensive study of security of internet-of-things. *IEEE Trans. Emerg. Topics Comput.*, 5, 4, 586–602, Dec. 2017.
45. Nath, M.P., Sridharan, R., Bhargava, A., Mohammed, T., Cloud computing: An overview, benefits, issues & research challenges. *Int. J. Res. Sci. Innov.*, 6, II, 25–35, 2019.
46. Yang, Y., Wu, L., Yin, G., Li, L., Zhao, H., A survey on security and privacy issues in internet-of-things. *IEEE Internet Things J.*, 4, 5, 1250–1258, Oct. 2017.
47. Yu, W., Liang, F., He, X., Hatcher, W.G., Lu, C., Lin, J., Yang, X., A survey on the edge computing for the internet of things. *IEEE Access*, 6, 6900–6919, 2018.
48. Xia, X., Xiao, Y., Liang, W., ABSI: An adaptive binary splitting algorithm for malicious meter inspection in smart grid. *IEEE Trans. Inf. Forensics Secur.*, 14, 2, 445–458, 2019.
49. Jose, A.C. and Malekian, R., Improving smart home security: Integrating logical sensing into smart home. *IEEE Sensors J.*, 17, 13, 4269–4286, Jul. 2017.
50. Zhang, Q. and Wang, X., SQL injections through back-end of RFID system, in: *Proc. Int. Symp. Comput. Netw. Multimedia Technol*, pp. 1–4, Jan. 2009.
51. Kolias, C., Kambourakis, G., Stavrou, A., Voas, J., DDoS in the IoT: Mirai and other botnets. *Computer*, 50, 7, 80–84, 2017.
52. Li, C. and Chen, C., A multi-stage control method application in the -ght against phishing attacks, in: *Proc. 26th Comput. Secur. Acad. Commun. Across Country*, 2011.
53. Eckhoff, D. and Wagner, I., Privacy in the smart city-applications, technologies, challenges, and solutions. *IEEE Commun. Surv. Tut.*, 20, 1, 489–516, 1st Quart., 2018.
54. Dlamini, N.N. and Johnston, K., The use, benefits and challenges of using the Internet of Things (IoT) in retail businesses: A literature review, in: *Proc. Int. Conf. Adv. Comput. Commun. Eng. (ICACCE)*, pp. 430–436, Nov. 2016.
55. Stanciu, A., Balan, T.-C., Gerigan, C., Zam-r, S., Securing the IoT gateway based on the hardware implementation of a multi pattern search algorithm, in: *Proc. Int. Conf. Optim. Elect. Electron. Equip. (OPTIM) Int. Aegean Conf. Elect. Mach. Power Electron. (ACEMP)*, pp. 1001–1006, May 2017.
56. Swamy, S.N., Jadhav, D., Kulkarni, N., Security threats in the application layer in IoT applications, in: *Proc. Int. Conf. IoT Social, Mobile, Analytics Cloud (I-SMAC)*, pp. 477–480, Feb. 2017.
57. Cha, S.-C., Chen, J.-F., Su, C., Yeh, K.-H., A blockchain connected gateway for BLE-based devices in the internet of things. *IEEE Access*, 6, 24639–24649, 2018.
58. Abdul-Ghani, H.A., Konstantas, D., Mahyoub, M., A comprehensive IoT attacks survey based on a building-blocked reference model. *Int. J. Adv. Comput. Sci. Appl.*, 9, 3, 355–373, 2018.

59. Xiao, L., Wan, X., Lu, X., Zhang, Y., Wu, D., IoT security techniques based on machine learning: How do IoT devices use AI to enhance security? *IEEE Signal Process. Mag.*, 35, 5, 41–49, Sep. 2018.
60. Wang, W., Xu, P., Yang, L.T., Secure data collection, storage and access in cloud-assisted IoT. *IEEE Cloud Comput.*, 5, 4, 77–88, Jul. 2018.
61. Bocek, T., Rodrigues, B.B., Strasser, T., Stiller, B., Blockchains everywhere-a use-case of blockchains in the pharma supply-chain, in: *Proc. IFIP/IEEE Symp. Integr. Netw. Service Manage. (IM)*, pp. 772–777, May 2017.
62. Shae, Z. and Tsai, J.J.P., On the design of a blockchain platform for clinical trial and precision medicine, in: *Proc. IEEE 37th Int. Conf. Distrib. Comput. Syst. (ICDCS)*, pp. 1972–1980, Jun. 2017.
63. Blanco-Novoa, Ó., Fernández-Caramés, T., Fraga-Lamas, P., Castedo, L., An electricity price-aware open-source smart socket for the internet of energy. *Sensors*, 17, 3, 643, 2017.
64. Huh, S., Cho, S., Kim, S., Managing IoT devices using blockchain platform, in: *Proc. 19th Int. Conf. Adv. Commun. Technol. (ICACT)*, pp. 464–467, Feb. 2017.
65. Samaniego, M. and Deters, R., Internet of smart things-IoST: Using blockchain and clips to make things autonomous, in: *Proc. IEEE Int. Conf. Cogn. Comput. (ICCC)*, pp. 9–16, Jun. 2017.
66. Muhammed, T., Mehmood, R., Albeshri, A., Katib, I., Ubehealth: A personalized ubiquitous cloud and edge-enabled networked healthcare system for smart cities. *IEEE Access*, 6, 32258–32285, 2018.
67. Barik, R.K., Dubey, H., Mankodiya, K., SOA-FOG: Secure serviceoriented edge computing architecture for smart health big data analytics, in: *Proc. IEEE Global Conf. Signal Inf. Process. (GlobalSIP)*, pp. 477–481, Nov. 2017.
68. Wilson, D. and Ateniese, G., From pretty good to great: Enhancing PGP using bitcoin and the blockchain, in: *Proc. Int. Conf. Netw. Syst. Secur.*, Springer, pp. 368–375, 2015.
69. Lei, A., Cruickshank, H., Cao, Y., Asuquo, P., Ogah, C.P.A., Sun, Z., Blockchain-based dynamic key management for heterogeneous intelligent transportation systems. *IEEE Internet Things J.*, 4, 6, 1832–1843, Dec. 2017.
70. Li, Y. and Wang, S., An energy-aware edge server placement algorithm in mobile edge computing, in: *Proc. IEEE Int. Conf. Edge Comput. (EDGE)*, pp. 66–73, Jul. 2018.
71. Singh, D., Tripathi, G., Alberti, A.M., Jara, A., Semantic edge computing and IoT architecture for military health services in battle-eld, in: *Proc. 14th IEEE Annu. Consum. Commun. Netw. Conf. (CCNC)*, pp. 185–190, Jan. 2017.
72. Pan, C., Xie, M., Hu, J., ENZYME: An energy-efficient transient computing paradigm for ultralow self-powered IoT edge devices. *IEEE Trans. Comput. Aided Des. Integr. Circuits Syst.*, 37, 11, 2440–2450, Nov. 2018.
73. Oyekanlu, E., Nelatury, C., Fatade, A.O., Alaba, O., Abass, O., Edge computing for industrial IoT and the smart grid: Channel capacity for M2M

communication over the power line, in: *Proc. IEEE 3rd Int. Conf. Electro-Technol. Nat. Develop. (NIGERCON)*, pp. 1–11, Nov. 2017.
74. Huang, Y., Lu, Y., Wang, F., Fan, X., Liu, J., Leung, V.C., An edge computing framework for real-time monitoring in smart grid, in: *Proc. IEEE Int. Conf. Ind. Internet (ICII)*, pp. 99–108, Oct. 2018.
75. Markakis, E.K., Karras, K., Zotos, N., Sideris, A., Moysiadis, T., Corsaro, A., Alexiou, G., Skianis, C., Mastorakis, G., Mavromoustakis, C.X., Pallis, E., EXEGESIS: Extreme edge resource harvesting for a virtualized fog environment. *IEEE Commun. Mag.*, 55, 7, 173–179, Jul. 2017.
76. Basudan, S., Lin, X., Sankaranarayanan, K., A privacy-preserving vehicular crowdsensing-based road surface condition monitoring system using fog computing. *IEEE Internet Things J.*, 4, 3, 772–782, Jun. 2017.
77. Dubey, H., Monteiro, A., Constant, N., Abtahi, M., Borthakur, D., Mahler, L., Sun, Y., Yang, Q., Akbar, U., Mankodiya, K., Fog computing in medical internet-of-things: Architecture, implementation, and applications, in: *Handbook of Large-Scale Distributed Computing in Smart Healthcare*, pp. 281–321, Springer, 2017.
78. Gu, L., Cost efficient resource management in fog computing supported medical cyber-physical system. *IEEE Trans. Emerg. Topics Comput.*, 5, 1, 108–119, Dec. 2017.
79. He, S., Cheng, B., Wang, H., Huang, Y., Chen, J., Proactive personalized services through fog-cloud computing in large-scale IoT-based healthcare application. *China Commun.*, 14, 11, 1–16, 2017.
80. Ni, J., Zhang, A., Lin, X., Shen, X.S., Security, privacy, and fairness in fog-based vehicular crowdsensing. *IEEE Commun. Mag.*, 55, 6, 146–152, Jun. 2017.
81. Kraemer, F.A., Braten, A.E., Tamkittikhun, N., Palma, D., Fog computing in healthcare-a review and discussion. *IEEE Access*, 5, 9206–9222, 2017.
82. Sood, S.K. and Mahajan, I., A fog-based healthcare framework for chikungunya. *IEEE Internet Things J.*, 5, 2, 794–801, Oct. 2018.
83. Gao, S., Peng, Z., Xiao, B., Xiao, Q., Song, Y., SCoP: Smartphone energy saving by merging push services in fog computing, in: *Proc. IEEE/ACM 25th Int. Symp. Qual. Service (IWQoS)*, pp. 1–10, Jun. 2017.
84. Kotenko, I., Saenko, I., Branitskiy, A., Framework for mobile internet of things security monitoring based on big data processing and machine learning. *IEEE Access*, 6, 72714–72723, 2018.
85. Merchant, K., Revay, S., Stantchev, G., Nousain, B., Deep learning for RF device fingerprinting in cognitive communication networks. *IEEE J. Sel. Top. Signal Process.*, 12, 1, 160–167, Feb. 2018.
86. Aman, M.N., Taneja, S., Sikdar, B., Chua, K.C., Alioto, M., Token-based security for the internet of things with dynamic energyquality tradeoff. *IEEE Internet Things J.*, 6, 2, 2843–2859, Apr. 2018.
87. Aman, M.N. and , K. C. *Chua, and, "Secure Data provenance Internet Things," Proc. ACM Int. Workshop IoT Privacy, Trust, Secur.*, pp, 11–14, 2017.

88. Aman, M.N., Chua, K.C., Sikdar, B., Mutual authentication in IoT systems using physical unclonable functions. *IEEE Internet Things J.*, 4, 5, 1327–1340, Oct. 2017.
89. Novo, O., Blockchain meets IoT: An architecture for scalable access management in IoT. *IEEE Internet Things J.*, 5, 2, 1184–1195, Apr. 2018.
90. Valtanen, K., Backman, J., Yrjol, S., Blockchain-powered value creation in the 5G and smart grid use cases. *IEEE Access*, 7, 25690–25707, Feb. 2019.
91. Aman, M.N. and Sikdar, B., ATT-Auth: A hybrid protocol for industrial IoT attestation with authentication. *IEEE Internet Things J.*, 5, 6, 5119–5131, Dec. 2018.
92. Ozyilmaz, K.R. and Yurdakul, A., Designing a blockchain-based IoT with ethereum, swarm, and lora: The software solution to create high availability with minimal security risks. *IEEE Consum. Electron. Mag.*, 8, 2, 28–34, Mar. 2019.
93. Javaid, U., Aman, M.N., Sikdar, B., BlockPro: Blockchain based data provenance and integrity for secure IoT environments, in: *Proc. 1st Workshop Blockchain-Enabled Netw. Sensor Syst.*, pp. 13–18, 2018.
94. Yu, Y., Li, Y., Tian, J., Liu, J., Blockchain-based solutions to security and privacy issues in the internet of things. *IEEE Wirel. Commun.*, 25, 6, 12–18, Dec. 2018.
95. Miller, D., Blockchain and the Internet of Things in the industrial sector. *IT Prof.*, 20, 3, 15–18, 2018.
96. He, D., Chan, S., Guizani, M., Security in the Internet of Things supported by mobile edge computing. *IEEE Commun. Mag.*, 56, 8, 56–61, Aug. 2018.
97. Alphand, O., Amoretti, M., Claeys, T., Dall'Asta, S., Duda, A., Ferrari, G., Rousseau, F., Tourancheau, B., Veltri, L., Zanichelli, F., IoTchain: A blockchain security architecture for the internet of things, in: *Proc. IEEE Wireless Commun. Netw. Conf. (WCNC)*, pp. 1–6, Apr. 2018.
98. Muñoz, M.C., Moh, M., Moh, T.-S., Improving smart grid security using Merkle trees, in: *Proc. IEEE Conf. Commun. Netw. Secur.*, pp. 522–523, Oct. 2014.
99. Sehgal, V.K., Patrick, A., Soni, A., Rajput, L., Smart human security framework using internet of things, cloud and fog computing, in: *Intelligent Distributed Computing*, pp. 251–263, Springer, 2015.

11

Potential, Scope, and Challenges of Industry 4.0

Roshan Raman* **and Aayush Kumar**

Department of Mechanical Engineering, The NorthCap University, Gurugram, India

Abstract

Industry 4.0 is a prototypical idea of transforming the current manufacturing modus operandi into a much smarter, efficient, effective, and safer chain with the fusion of artificial intelligence, big data analysis, Internet of Things, and other advanced computing technologies in the human-machine interface. Industry 4.0 provides us with several opportunities to take the manufacturing standards to a higher level. For instance, big data analysis with its three dimensions, velocity, variety, and volume, can help us in forecasting manufacturing problems by the historical data of the manufacturing process, and it even provides appropriate solutions to prevent the problem from occurring and dealing with it if it does. Another example of embeddable technology is the Internet of Things, which involves varied sensors collecting data with three major features, context, omnipresence, and optimization. Context refers to the advancing of object-environment interaction, omnipresence provides us with the information of the environmental state of an object, and optimization refers to the improvements in the connection of operators in the network of human-machine interface. Though these technologies improve the industries a ton, there are still challenges in the execution of these ideas. Challenges, such as cyber threats, investment issues, requirement of complete autonomy exist, thus, these should be addressed. This review article covers all such opportunities in Industry 4.0 and challenges in its implementation.

Keywords: Industry 4.0, optimization, cyber physical systems, artificial intelligence, enabling technologies

**Corresponding author*: roshanmaithil@gmail.com

Jyotir Moy Chatterjee, Harish Garg and R. N. Thakur (eds.) A Roadmap for Enabling Industry 4.0 by Artificial Intelligence, (201–214) © 2023 Scrivener Publishing LLC

11.1 Introduction

A successful production includes delivery of a product with consistently acceptable quality without any failure, be it the safety of the workers, be it the maintained production rate, be it the raw material wastage, or be it the other 99 factors included. Industries saw the first revolution in the 1700s with the mission to mechanize the production processes, achieving eight times the production volume with the inculcation of steam-powered engines. The second upheaval came in the 19th century took the production volumes through the roof with the arrival of assembly lines and electricity. This was mostly credited to Henry Ford (1863–1947) who took the idea of mass production from a slaughterhouse and engrained it in the industry. The third revolution (starting in the 1970s) came with not only increasing the volume and velocity of production but also improving the quality of production together with increasing precision with memory programmable controls and partial automation. This takes us to the fourth industrial revolution [1–3].

11.2 Key Aspects for a Successful Production

Some of the factors that need strict monitoring for a successful and smooth production are:

- Worker safety—worker safety is a topic often neglected, though it is one of the most important ones out there. An injury or a death of a worker in the manufacturing unit does not only damage the worker and his well-wishers' emotional states but also takes a hit at fellow employees' morale and emotional states. And someone who is not able to focus on what he does, may cause damage to himself and the company in many ways. Apart from the emotional side of the damage, there is heavy financial damage also aimed towards a company. An injury to a worker can cause damages in fines to up to $32,000 and death can hit as high as $1,120,000, which is a concern for most businesses. Now, this does not include the Damages caused to the overall name of a company because any such news of injury and death can cause a firm to lose clients and employees. Therefore, worker safety is an important issue to be discussed and to be improved with the proper implementation of technology [5].

- Raw material wastage—every manufacturing firm has one thing in common, they use some form of raw material to make the final good. And when rough handling of such starts, many entities are affected, the business, the market, the environment, and many more. The raw material waste reduction does help many businesses to improve the overall profitability and revenue, whereas a very positive side of managing the raw material is that this protects the environment from any intoxicants. Not even that, raw material wastage increases the lead time and stops the manufacturer from providing a lean and competitive service [6–9].
- Employee workload distribution—healthy environment at the workplace is an essential component of any firm. In any case, where the employees are burdened with workload more than they anticipate, there is certainly a dissatisfaction spread affecting the quality and velocity of the production. Therefore, the workload balance should be kept in check to ensure the production parameters are maintained [4, 6].
- Raw material supply chain—supply chains consist of all the processes involved from procuring raw material to giving out the final product. The supply chain usually starts with the vendors or suppliers. A supply chain plan that is aligned with a company's business strategy is required for the best profitability. Irrespective of how well a firm decides to remain competitive in the market, the supply chain should inevitably support this initiative. The supply chain consists of numerous activities that function together to manufacture a new product; these procedures lay the groundwork for an industry to make a major decision. The supply chain offers an added advantage over rivals for any organization. The greater the value produced, the higher will be the demand for a product and, as a result, the better will be the profit. Hence, effective supply chain management is necessary for a smooth production flow.
- Machine allocation—any raw material procured is a waste until it is processed. For any further steps, particular machines are taken into use. If in any case these machines are not arranged and allocated smartly, there is a certainty that chaos will follow, and the production would be everything but smooth. That is why a good layout, schedule, and allocation are required in manufacturing.

- Equipment maintenance—let us ask a question, what would happen to the production line if in case any one of the machines is under maintenance or is not able to function properly? The answer to this depends on how much data are monitored regularly to be used to predict any breakdowns and plan maintenance accordingly in advance. If not, it is likely that the production line would definitely suffer a great deal of damage. That is why equipment maintenance should be a priority to prevent any manufacturing delays.
- Future product requirements—a forecast of demands and design changes can help firms to have a competitive edge. That is the reason it is important to keep in mind that future design requirements are forecasted and are met when the time comes.
- Hiring the right skilled employees—a machine and raw materials are useless until there is someone who understands the equipment and knows how to process the raw material into a meaningful and good quality product. That is why it is also one of the most important things to keep in mind.

11.3 Opportunities with Industry 4.0

Now, apart from all the challenges that might come with Industry 4.0, we shall discuss all the major opportunities that it presents. Let us take a look at a few of them

- Optimization and automation—tools like deep learning and machine learning are one of the biggest breakthroughs of the 21st century. These allow the engineer to optimize the production lines and even automate them to a great extent [6–10]. Thus, Industry 4.0 components present us with an opportunity to optimize the manufacturing units and automate them on the way.
- Mass data, real-time supply chains management—as discussed above, it is critical to maintain and monitor the supply chains in manufacturing. Industry 4.0 components, such as big data Analysis aid us to manage the supply chains in real time [11–15].
- Incredible maintenance and monitoring—every machine in the universe needs some maintenance or the other to

perform. Even us humans need some time to time. The advanced sensors of the 21st century collect an amazing amount of data and it is very easy now to monitor the equipment in real time to see if they are performing as they should and if any breakdown is expected anytime soon [16–19]. Even, tools like Machine Learning aid in getting to a remedy faster. Many software packs developed by companies allow us to get a remedy even before the machine breaks down and even can schedule maintenance of the equipment at the appropriate time. And thus, Industry 4.0 is a big hand in equipment management [20–24].

- IoT Enabled quality improvements—what is better, cutting-edge accuracy or cloudy human judgment? It is clear with the current industry trends that Manufacturing industries need a critical fusion of quality improvement tools like IoT. With the implementation of IoT-based equipment and systems, it is expected that the production Velocity and Quality will improve drastically since the process would be automated and the machine can do the same task with the same accuracy it is programmed to achieve thousands of times [2–10].
- Superior sustainability and working conditions—imagine, a safe risk-free working environment. Now, implementation of Industry 4.0 takes us to a level where we can automate the production processes significantly that dangerous processes that used to cause injury or death to the workers can be done automatically behind closed walls for instance accidents while metal cutting was one of the biggest danger that workers used to face but now it is done automatically in factories with Industry 4.0 tools implemented and only an operator is required who after configuring the machine may just need to monitor the metal cutting in case sensory systems are not implemented thus making the job safer. And as far as sustainability goes, it is expected to go off the charts when we talk about machines doing machining i.e. when automated machinery goes ahead and does the job [23–27].
- Earn customer loyalty with personalized opportunities—any customer would be glad to return to the original vendor/firm for his needs if he gets the right quality, price, and delivery velocity. And to the very obvious observation, these factors are improved if processes are supplemented

with the Industry 4.0 tools like AI, Data Analytics, and IoT. Moreover, if these are implemented correctly then surely and certainly, the ability of a manufacturer to produce customized products/variety of products from the same set of production lines improves, and thus a customer with personalized opportunities would be someone who returns to the firm.

As time went by, we discovered new manufacturing technologies and thus we progressed from a manual mechanical production line to today's automatic assembly lines. This transition has helped us to be more responsive and adaptive to ever-volatile market demands and challenges like embedding, predictability, adaptability, and robustness to unanticipated circumstances.

11.4 Issues in Implementation of Industry 4.0

- Intelligent judgment and mediation structure: more autonomy and sociality capabilities as major aspects of self-organized systems are required in smart manufacturing systems, however, today's systems have only three capabilities, i.e., a lack of autonomy.
- High-speed IWN protocols: the IWN network used today cannot give out adequate bandwidth for deep communication and exchange of a high amount of useful and quality information, but it is excellent to the weird web in the manufacturing ecosystem.
- Manufacturing specific big data and analytics: the challenge that is encountered when we talk about using big data analytics is collecting high-quality and integral data from manufacturing systems. The footnotes of the data entities are varied, and it is boosting content to incorporate diverse data repositories with different semantics for advanced data analytics [29–32].
- System modeling and analysis: To reduce the fluidic equations and conclude the correct model, systems should be designed as self-organized manufacturing systems. Though simple systems are not a big challenge, however, research is underway for complex manufacturing systems.

- Cyber Security: The need to protect the manufacturing lines and system data from cyber security threats has been increasing dramatically with increased connectivity and inculcation of standard communication protocols of Industry 4.0 [12–30].
- Modularized and Flexible Physical Artifacts: One of the best ways to speed up production processes is distributed decision making and when processing a product or a machine, testing of all parameters should be clubbed together to increase distributed decision making. So, creating a modularized and smart conveying unit that can dynamically reconfigure the production routes is needed.
- Investment Issues: For most new technology-based manufacturing endeavors, the question of investment is a very generic one. For the time being, an SME will be required to make a large investment to execute Industry 4.0. The deployment of all of Industry 4.0's pillars necessitates a significant financial commitment on the part of a corporation.

Now, After all the discussion on how Industry 4.0 can be an angle to the modern industries, we should discuss all the potential tools that area in Industry 4.0 Toolbox.

11.5 Potential Tools Utilized in Industry 4.0

- Big data analytics—big data analysis is part of sophisticated algorithms to some very large, disparate data points. These large datasets might include organized, quasi, and complex databases, and collected from a range of domains and volumes varying from terabytes to zettabytes. A database that may be too massive or complicated to be collected, retained, or subsequently adapted in a traditional data store is referred to as big data. For example, sensors, devices, video/audio, networks, and log files all contribute to big data. Like most other organizations, the manufacturing sector also employs advanced analytics, but with a stronger emphasis. Cloud computing and the IoT platform may be used to acquire massive datasets from intelligent sensors and predict patterns that might significantly enhance supply-chain effectiveness. Big data analysis helps businesses discover previously unknown factors that are causing production bottlenecks. Manufacturers employ customized analysis of the data to effectively understand the underlying cause of the limiting factor, after recognizing the fundamental cause of the problem. This allows businesses to reduce costs, reduce waste, and increase productivity.

- Artificial intelligence—artificial intelligence (AI) refers to a computer's or a computer-controlled robot's capacity to accomplish tasks ordinarily undertaken by intelligent individuals. This term is frequently used to describe a project that aims to develop a platform with human-like cognitive skills. It includes reasoning ability, recognition of meaning, generalization, and learning from experience. When used correctly, artificial intelligence provides several benefits for the industrial business. I have compiled a list of three of the most important benefits for the manufacturing industry today: reduced Errors, lower costs, and increased revenue [28–30].
- Machine learning—the science that makes a computer work without being explicitly programmed is called machine learning. Machine learning over the last decade has enabled self-driving vehicles, realistic speech recognition, successful online searches, and a significantly improved understanding of the human genome. This capacity to convey concerns in real-time not only improves visibility and data but also allows manufacturers to drastically minimize downtime and scrap, which now occur due to occasional human-based monitoring. Machine learning systems may also give predictive insights, helping industries to move away from reactive settings and toward ones that prevent problems before they happen. Machine learning provides for early detection of possible manufacturing process problems in predictive maintenance. Preventative repairs are significantly less expensive than restoring damaged equipment or a process that has already created tens of thousands of dollars in scrap, thus alerting the team to possible difficulties saves money. It also reduces the financial effect of a big disruption.
- Deep learning—deep learning, a subset of machine learning, is also a valuable tool. Deep learning is a machine learning approach that allows computers to learn by example, just like humans. Deep learning is an important element of self-driving cars, capable of recognizing pause signs and

distinguishing between pedestrians and streetlight posts. Given their success at a variety of tasks and the desired outcomes that these approaches provide, the inclination for Deep Learning methods to be used in current production systems is expected. We can solve issues in an area where computers were never thought to be suitable using Graphics Processing Units (GPUs) and innovative algorithms. Computers can now tackle visual tasks, such as picture identification—perhaps with greater accuracy than human's results when he competed against ConvNet on the ImageNet dataset, natural language processing, translation, and other human-centric activities. We are teaching computers not simply things that come naturally to humans, but also how to manage occupations where we fall short.

- Internet of things—IoT is a physical entity having smart sensing elements, processing of data, programming, as well as other capabilities that communicate and transfer data between devices and computers via the internet or even other network infrastructure. Industry 4.0 advances digital media from past decades to a whole nother height, with connectivity through the IoT, access to actual data, and the integration of technologically robust systems. Industry 4.0 takes a much more holistic, integrated, and proactive understanding of the manufacturing system. It increases cooperation and access across departments, partners, vendors, goods, and people by bridging the gap between both the real and the virtual system. Industry 4.0 enables corporate executives to have a deeper understanding of and control over all aspects of their operations, as well as to use actual information to boost productivity, optimize processes, and enhance competitiveness.
- Cyber-physical systems—a CPS is an intelligent computer system that uses computer-based algorithms to operate or monitor a mechanism. A CPS, without a doubt, is placed somewhere at the core of Industry 4.0. It is an internet-connected physical system, such as a pump or compressor, that has been equipped with computing and control techniques like sensing devices. An IP address-assigned entity may self-monitor, generate information on its operation, and communicate with other linked entities or even the outside world. It is a self-contained, self-regulating system. As the Fourth Industrial Revolution progresses, industrial firms will

increasingly rely on the tenets of CPS to help them achieve operational excellence through productivity gains, efficient deployment of all resources (both material and human), customer satisfaction, and increased shareholder value [32–34].

- Cloud computing—companies with collaborative delivery chains advantage from leveraging the cloud in several methods in Industry 4.0. Multiple companions withinside the delivery chain can also additionally see centralized facts in actual time, permitting control to be extra proactive. If occasions extrade or a hassle emerges, groups can also additionally reply fast to make sure and enhance performance whilst proscribing the probability of recurrence. Cloud computing is one of the pinnacles 5 Industry 4.0 technology being deployed with the aid of using manufacturers, with a reputation fee of 85%. According to Intel and Oracle, 60% of 1200 managers of medium to huge international production businesses sense cloud infrastructure is needed to realize the promise of Industry 4.0 technology.

11.6 Conclusion

Thus, Industry 4.0 excels in solving all forms of modern manufacturing problems and even improving the overall quality and rate of production. One of the key features of Industry 4.0 is the removal of repetitive and physically exhausting tasks with the aid of sophisticated technologies of automation. However, it is also to be noted that the tools are very difficult to implement in all firms due to adaptability and specific requirement of the operating systems based on the software applications and skilled labor. In an industrial setup, any technology that is adopted individually will have a reduced impact unless and until it is used in conjunction with various tools of automation. Moreover, it is expected that utilizing Industry 4.0 tools together will open up new avenues for embracing the future to make production systems more adaptable, reliable, and collaborative.

References

1. Oztemel, E. and Gursev, S., Literature review of industry 4.0 and related technologies. *J. Intell. Manuf.* Springer, 31, 1, 127–182, 2020. https://doi.org/10.1007/s10845-018-1433-8.

2. Sartal, A., Bellas, R., Mejías, A.M., García-Collado, A., The sustainable manufacturing concept, evolution and opportunities within industry 4.0: A literature review. *Adv. Mech. Eng.*, 12, 5, 1–17, 2020. https://doi.org/10.1177/1687814020925232.
3. Xu, B., Shen, J., Liu, S., Su, Q., Zhang, J., Research and development of electro-hydraulic control valves oriented to industry 4.0: A review. *Chin. J. Mech. Eng. EN* Springer, 33, 1, 1–20, 2020. https://doi.org/10.1186/s10033-020-00446-2.
4. Fraga-Lamas, P., Fernández-Caramés, T.M., Blanco-Novoa, Ó., Vilar-Montesinos, M.A., A review on industrial augmented reality systems for the industry 4.0 shipyard. *IEEE Access* Institute Electrical Electron. Engineers Inc., 6, 13358–13375, 2018. https://doi.org/10.1109/ACCESS.2018.2808326.
5. Kamble, S.S., Gunasekaran, A., Gawankar, S.A., Sustainable industry 4.0 framework: A systematic literature review identifying the current trends and future perspectives. *Process Saf. Environ. Prot.*, 117, 408–425, 2018. https://doi.org/10.1016/j.psep.2018.05.009.
6. Kerin, M. and Pham, D.T., A review of emerging industry 4.0 technologies in remanufacturing. *J. Clean. Prod.*, Elsevier Ltd., 237, 1–39, 2019. https://doi.org/10.1016/j.jclepro.2019.117805.
7. Mishra, D., Roy, R.B., Dutta, S., Pal, S.K., Chakravarty, D., A review on sensor based monitoring and control of friction stir welding process and a roadmap to Industry 4.0. *J. Manuf. Processes,* Elsevier Ltd., 36, 373–397, 2018. https://doi.org/10.1016/j.jmapro.2018.10.016.
8. da Silva, F.S.T., da Costa, C.A., Crovato, C.D.P., da Rosa Righi, R., Looking at energy through the lens of Industry 4.0: A systematic literature review of concerns and challenges. *Comput. Ind. Eng.*, Elsevier Ltd., 143, 2020. https://doi.org/10.1016/j.cie.2020.106426.
9. Abdirad, M. and Krishnan, K., Industry 4.0 in logistics and supply chain management: A systematic literature review. *Eng. Manag. J.*, 33, 3, 187–201, 2021.
10. Sony, M. and Naik, S., Industry 4.0 integration with socio-technical systems theory: A systematic review and proposed theoretical model. *Technol. Soc.*, 61, 1–47, 2020. https://doi.org/10.1016/j.techsoc.2020.101248.
11. da Silva, V.L., Kovaleski, J.L., Pagani, R.N., Technology transfer in the supply chain oriented to industry 4.0: A literature review. *Technol. Anal. Strateg. Manage.*, Routledge, 31, 5, 546–562, 2019.
12. Zhong, R.Y., Xu, X., Klotz, E., Newman, S.T., Intelligent manufacturing in the context of industry 4.0: A review. *Engineering*, 3, 5, 616–630, 2017. https://doi.org/10.1016/J.ENG.2017.05.015.
13. Sony, M. and Naik, S., Critical factors for the successful implementation of industry 4.0: A review and future research direction. *Prod. Plan. Control*, 31, 10, 799–815, 2020. https://doi.org/10.1080/09537287.2019.1691278.

14. Osterrieder, P., Budde, L., Friedli, T., The smart factory as a key construct of industry 4.0: A systematic literature review. *Int. J. Prod. Econ.*, 221, 1–52, 2020. https://doi.org/10.1016/j.ijpe.2019.08.011.
15. Parente, M., Figueira, G., Amorim, P., Marques, A., Production scheduling in the context of Industry 4.0: review and trends. *Int. J. Prod. Res.*, Taylor Francis Ltd., 58, 17, 5401–5431, 2020. https://doi.org/10.1080/00207543.2020.1718794.
16. Sony, M., Pros and cons of implementing industry 4.0 for the organizations: A review and synthesis of evidence. *Prod. Manuf. Res.*, 8, 1, 244–272, 2020. https://doi.org/10.1080/21693277.2020.1781705.
17. Bányai, T., Introductory chapter: Industry 4.0 and its impact on logistics-a retrospective review, in: *Industry 4.0-Impact on Intelligent Logistics and Manufacturing*, IntechOpen, 2020, https://doi.org/10.5772/intechopen.89387.
18. Liao, Y., Deschamps, F., de Freitas Rocha Loures, E., Ramos, L.F.P., Past, present, and future of Industry 4.0-a systematic literature review and research agenda proposal. *Int. J. Prod. Res.*, Taylor Francis Ltd., 55, 12, 3609–3629, 2017. https://doi.org/10.1080/00207543.2017.1308576.
19. Piccarozzi, M., Aquilani, B., Gatti, C., Industry 4.0 in management studies: A systematic literature review. *Sustainability (Switzerland)*, 10, 10, 1–24, 2018. https://doi.org/10.3390/su10103821.
20. Mariani, M. and Borghi, M., Industry 4.0: A bibliometric review of its managerial intellectual structure and potential evolution in the service industries. *Technol. Forecast. Soc. Change*, 149, 1–24, 2019. https://doi.org/10.1016/j.techfore.2019.119752.
21. Mittal, S., Khan, M.A., Romero, D., Wuest, T., A critical review of smart manufacturing & Industry 4.0 maturity models: Implications for small and medium-sized enterprises (SMEs). *J. Manuf. Syst.*, Elsevier B.V., 49, 194–214, 2018. https://doi.org/10.1016/j.jmsy.2018.10.005.
22. Ibarra, D., Ganzarain, J., Igartua, J., II, Business model innovation through industry 4.0: A review. *Proc. Manuf.*, 22, 4–10, 2018. https://doi.org/10.1016/j.promfg.2018.03.002.
23. Maskuriy, R., Selamat, A., Maresova, P., Krejcar, O., David, O.O., Industry 4.0 for the construction industry: Review of management perspective. *Economies* MDPI Multidiscip. Digital Publishing Institute, 7, 3, 1–14, 2019. https://doi.org/10.3390/economies7030068.
24. Franciosi, C., Iung, B., Miranda, S., Riemma, S., Maintenance for sustainability in the industry 4.0 context: A scoping literature review. 51, 11, 903–908, 2018. https://doi.org/10.1016/j.ifacol.2018.08.459.
25. Newman, C., Edwards, D., Martek, I., Lai, J., Thwala, W.D., Rillie, I., Industry 4.0 deployment in the construction industry: A bibliometric literature review and UK-based case study. *Smart Sustain. Built Environ.*, 10, 4, 557–580, 2021. https://doi.org/10.1108/SASBE-02-2020-0016.

26. Pereira, A.C. and Romero, F., A review of the meanings and the implications of the industry 4.0 concept. *Proc. Manuf.*, 13, 1206–1214, 2017. https://doi.org/10.1016/j.promfg.2017.09.032.
27. Dewangan, B.K., Agarwal, A., Choudhury, T., Pasricha, A., Satapathy, S.C., Extensive review of cloud resource management techniques in industry 4.0: Issue and challenges. *Software Pract. Exp.*, 51, 12, 2373–2392, 2021. https://doi.org/10.1002/spe.2810.
28. Müller, F., Jaeger, D., Hanewinkel, M., Digitization in wood supply–a review on how Industry 4.0 will change the forest value chain. *Comput. Electron. Agric.*, Elsevier B.V., 162, 206–218, 2019. https://doi.org/10.1016/j.compag.2019.04.002.
29. Kamble, S.S., Gunasekaran, A., Ghadge, A., Raut, R., A performance measurement system for industry 4.0 enabled smart manufacturing system in SMMEs-a review and empirical investigation. *Int. J. Prod. Econ.*, 229, 1–39, 2020. https://doi.org/10.1016/j.ijpe.2020.107853.
30. Saucedo-Martínez, J.A., Pérez-Lara, M., Marmolejo-Saucedo, J.A., Salais-Fierro, T.E., Vasant, P., Industry 4.0 framework for management and operations: A review. *J. Ambient Intell. Humaniz. Comput.*, 9, 3, 789–801, 2018. https://doi.org/10.1007/s12652-017-0533-1.
31. Manavalan, E. and Jayakrishna, K., A review of internet of things (IoT) embedded sustainable supply chain for industry 4.0 requirements. *Comput. Ind. Eng.*, 127, 925–953, 2019. https://doi.org/10.1016/j.cie.2018.11.030.
32. Klingenberg, C.O., Borges, M.A.V., Antunes, J.A.V., Industry 4.0 as a data-driven paradigm: A systematic literature review on technologies. *J. Manuf. Technol. Manage.*, 32, 3, 570–592, 2021. https://doi.org/10.1108/JMTM-09-2018-0325.
33. Davies, R., Coole, T., Smith, A., Review of socio-technical considerations to ensure successful implementation of industry 4.0. *Proc. Manuf.*, 11, 1288–1295, 2017. https://doi.org/10.1016/j.promfg.2017.07.256.
34. Sartal, A., Bellas, R., Mejías, A.M., García-Collado, A., The sustainable manufacturing concept, evolution and opportunities within industry 4.0: A literature review. *Adv. Mech. Eng.*, 12, 5, 1–17, 2020. https://doi.org/10.1177/1687814020925232.

12

Industry 4.0 and Manufacturing Techniques: Opportunities and Challenges

Roshan Raman and Aditya Ranjan*

Department of Mechanical Engineering, The NorthCap University, Gurugram, India

Abstract

The needs of the business are evolving at a fast pace, and companies are rolling out and investing in innovative solutions, new products/services, new business models to stay ahead in market competitions. At the consumer level, the demands of the individualism of products are increasing. The new-age customers want to customize their products, make suggestions for product innovation and express interest in taking part in the development processes. The fluctuations in the demands of the volatile market are one of the main drivers of paradigm shifts in manufacturing processes as this requires fast and flexible adaptability. By an estimate, the demands will double by 2050. By this estimate, it makes clear that there is a need for a sustainable and energy-efficient manufacturing system. This is where Industry 4.0 comes into play. In the past decades, there has been steady development in the field of information technology in general. These developments in a way have brought a revolution in the way we live and how the business/industries are performed. This new age Industrial Revolution paves way for intelligent manufacturing systems that are flexible, adaptive, energy-efficient, and innovative. This revolution involves various technologies, such as wireless networks, data analysis, AI, human-machine interaction, and 3D Printing. However, in addition to these opportunities and transformations, there lie challenges, too. Integration of data and analyzing them efficiently, floor level process flexibility, and security of the systems are some of the main challenges to the smart systems. However, fortunately, the pace at which mankind has been able to resolve problems and bring out solutions gives hope that these smart systems are not far from reality.

Keywords: Industry 4.0, efficient manufacturing system, industrial revolution

**Corresponding author*: aditya20meu004@ncuindia.edu

Jyotir Moy Chatterjee, Harish Garg and R. N. Thakur (eds.) A Roadmap for Enabling Industry 4.0 by Artificial Intelligence, (215–226) © 2023 Scrivener Publishing LLC

12.1 Introduction

Businesses in the 21st century are changing rapidly. Various technologies are being used to create new ideas. Therefore, companies are rapidly evolving themselves to be ahead in the race. They are investing heavily in various technologies, which provide better consumer and workplace experiences. Some of the technologies are listed below:

a. CPS: A cyber-physical system (CPS) is a computerized system that controls a mechanism using computer-based algorithms. In CPS physical and software components are intricately intertwined, allowing them to function on different spatial and temporal scales. Moreover, it reflects diversified and unique characteristic modes, and interact with each other in different ways depending on the circumstances. This technology allows for a more efficient manufacturing environment, eventually promoting a smarter production system [1].
b. Internet of Things Technology: IoT has emerged as one of the most important technologies of the 21st century in recent years. The technology can share and collect data with minimal human intervention by employing a less expensive computer, cloud, big data, statistics, and mobile technology. The Internet of Things (IoT) is a network of physical items that are equipped with sensors, software, as well as advent technologies to communicate and share data with other electronic tools.
c. Cloud computing technologies (CCT): The distribution of numerous online services is known as cloud computing. The essential functions of CCT are the storage of data, server and host design, monitoring databases, and computer programming. However, instead of saving data on a hard drive, cloud-based storage allows to save them in a remote place. It can obtain data and software applications to operate it as long as the electronic gadget has access to the internet.
d. Big Data and Advanced Analysis Techniques: In manufacturing, different processor and sensors may be used in different computers and devices. The data from these devices are huge which are beyond conventional analysis. Big Data

Analytics helps in compiling the data and helps in gaining valuable information quickly.

In addition to various advanced technologies being developed, the demands of products at the consumer level are also evolving. Individualism of the product, high customization, speed of delivery, and quality of finished product are in high demand. The new-age customer wants to get involved in the manufacturing process and suggest innovative methods.

By estimate, the population of the world will be almost 10 billion. Therefore, as a result, the demands will also nearly double. Hence, it makes necessary to have infrastructure which is energy-efficient, sustainable, and meets all demands. This is where Industry 4.0 is introduced. Industry 4.0 has been defined as "a name for the current trend of automation and data exchange in manufacturing technologies, incorporating the above-stated technologies to create a smart factory." It has become a hotspot for most global industries. It is a revolution in making which will have a great influence on overall manufacturing techniques and industries. This revolution involves various technologies such as wireless networks, data analysis, AI, human-machine interaction, and 3D Printing. However, in addition to these opportunities and transformations, there lie challenges, too such as [2].

1. Smart product advancement
2. Development of the underlying network
3. Assessment and handling of Big data
4. Digital Manufacturing
5. Training of employees
6. Security of systems
7. Floor level process flexibility

Industries are one of the most crucial pillars of a country's economy. This revolution will be able to confront all the growing demands of sustainability and quality successfully. Fortunately, the pace at which mankind has been able to resolve problems and bring out solutions gives hope that these smart systems are not far from reality [3].

12.2 Changing Market Demands

The manufacturing industry is one of those industries that is experiencing continuous structural changes due to changing world needs and styles.

Stamper (2013) highlights continuous global development that contributes to productivity levels [4].

12.2.1 Individualization

One of the obvious advances is the growing need to customize products. Customers' desire to customize products involving industries such as textiles, furniture, personal computer, automobiles, and machinery is growing exponentially. Businesses also pay close attention to customer preferences and individual needs, which increases the level of customization. Therefore, industries must become accustomed to these developments. The new customer now expresses wishes, makes product innovation proposals, and actively participates in the development and production processes at the same time.

12.2.2 Volatility

Volatility is viewed as the primary driver of production paradigm shifts. From the perspective of large and small economic developments, volatility defines the relative size of price volatility, stock prices, exchange rate, interest rates, and all markets within a given period, although volatility is not a measure of the direction of volatility. The relatively brief impacts of an enterprise, seasonal variations, lifecycles, and other macroeconomic conditions are all important factors that influence the volatility of manufacturing industries, notably in sales. Subsequent firms will have to invest in flexibility and agility since traditional technologies could no longer bear uncertainty.

12.2.3 Efficiency in Terms of Energy Resources

A stable and reliable source of raw form of materials and energy is critical to an industry's competitiveness. Ambitious climate goals, global population expansion, and a global increase in income will all influence the energy sector's future development. By one estimate, demand will double by 2050. Therefore, it becomes clear that the way society is using resources will fundamentally change. Every manufacturing company's strategic goal should include resource productivity and resource efficiency. Any waste in production, such as overproduction, quality difficulties, or unused adaptability capability, has economic and societal ramifications [5].

12.3 Recent Technological Advancements

Some new technical prospects for manufacturing's future are:

a. Data, computational power, and connectivity
b. Knowledge and statistics
c. The interface between humans and machines
d. Conversion from computerized to physical world

The continual development and elaboration of future manufacturing technologies are driving research endeavors in this field. Following are some of the developments in inter-disciplinary fields which are leading to the 4th Industrial Revolution:

1. Cyber-Physical Production System (CPPS)
CPPS are deep interconnections that offer real-time data access and processing. It is one of the most important advancements in the computer and information technology disciplines. Futuristic technologies such as autonomous cars, robotic surgery, smart electric grids, smart manufacturing, and implanted medical devices are some of the applications of CPS [6]. It is a development that combines the development of computer science, information technology, and manufacturing science and technology. It consists of various sub-systems that are interconnected at all production levels. The new industrial revolution uses this advancement to link virtual space and the physical world which in turn makes a factory smarter and wiser leading to a better production environment. Some of the requirements for CPS and CPPS includes:

a. Self-repair and Self-organization
b. Safety
c. Remote Diagnosis
d. Autonomous navigation
e. Efficiency increase
f. Real-time control
g. Flexible to customization at all levels

The expectations from these advancements are enormous which include applications of various other technologies, too such as multi-agent systems, sensor networks, data mining, etc. Some R&D challenges which the researchers find related to CPPS:

a. To build an autonomous system having the capability of self-awareness at all times and can devise its action plan.
b. Development of new and tested algorithms for cooperative learning and distributed detection.
c. Autonomous scheduling for better time management and results.
d. d. Developments of new integrated systems which fuse the virtual and real worlds.

Cyber-Physical Production System (CPPS) is considered as one of the major milestone steps in the development of advanced manufacturing systems. It would be a vital contributor to the new Industrial Revolutions.

2. Internet of Things Technology
Kevin Ashton of Procter & Gamble, later MIT's Auto-ID Centre, created the term "Internet of Things" on his own in 1999. Internet of things simply means that more than one thing is connected to the internet rather than its functioning.

There are growing consumer applications of IoT such as:

a. Smart Home: Home automation for lighting, heating and cooling, media and security systems, and video surveillance systems.
b. Eldercare: assistance for those with disabilities and elderly individuals with safety and emergency alert features.
c. Medical and healthcare: remote health monitoring, electronic wristbands, specialized biomedical sensors.
d. Transportation: smart traffic control, smart parking, electronic toll collections.

The Industrial applications include:

a. Manufacturing: Various production devices with sensing, identification, processing, communication, actuation, and networking capabilities are connected [7].
b. Agriculture: Data collection on temperatures, rainfall, moisture, wind direction, insect attack, and soil composition

assist in making intelligent decisions to increase type and effectiveness.

c. Maritime: Alerts for boat flooding, fire, and deep discharge of batteries.

3. Cloud Computing Technologies

Cloud Computing technologies are one of the most popular technologies in the market right now as it increases productivity, save money, increase speed and efficiency, performance and security [8].

It is a shift from previous conventional storage means to more advanced remote-based storage. There are various Cloud Computing Technologies such as:

a. Virtualization: The process of building a virtual environment on a server to execute different programs and operating systems. A virtual machine is a software computer or software program that may not only work as a physical computer but also behave as one, doing duties such as launching applications or programs on the user's demand.
b. Service-Oriented Architecture: Allows businesses to access on-demand cloud-based computing solutions as their business needs change. SOA has the advantages of being simple to maintain, platform-agnostic, and highly scalable.
c. Grid Computing: Distributed computing is another name for grid computing. It is a processor design that brings together many computing resources from diverse places to achieve a single purpose.

4. Big Data and Advanced Analysis

The rigorous process of analyzing big data to detect information including patterns and insights, relationships, market dynamics, and client preferences that may allow the industry in making better decisions frequently.

It entails complicated applications that include predictive models, statistical algorithms, and what-if analyses, all of which are powered by analytics systems.

12.4 Industrial Revolution 4.0

The main characteristics involved in any industrial revolution in the manufacturing sector are technological, socioeconomic, and cultural.

1. Utilization of alternative energy sources
2. New devices are developed to enhance efficiency
3. A new factory system and organization of labour
4. Increasing application of science and technology in the industry

During the first industrial era, water and steam power were harnessed to operate the industry. Man's status as a machine's engine came to an end with this revolution. The second stage of the revolution utilized electric power to enable mass production. The change in this revolution made it impossible for man to work as a slave for machines. Electronics and information technologies were employed to automate the manufacturing sector in the third phase of the revolution. This drastic change helped the man to stop working at machines manually. The fourth industrial revolution, which is a digital revolution, is characterized by the fusion of technologies outlined earlier in this chapter. The fourth Industrial Revolution stands apart from the third one in velocity, scope, and systems impact. This makes this phase of industry a distinct one. The pace at which technological breakthroughs are being invented is disrupting almost every aspect of the manufacturing sector. It is an exponential rather than a linear transformation. Hermann outlines a very well explanation of Industry 4.0 as follows: "Industry 4.0 is a collective term for technologies and concepts of value chain organization. Within the modular structured Smart Factories of Industry 4.0, Cyber-Physical Systems (CPS) monitor physical processes, create a virtual copy of the physical world, and make decentralized decisions. Over the IoT (Internet of Things), CPS communicate and cooperate with each other and humans in real-time. Via the Internet of Services (IoS), both internal and cross-organizational services are offered and utilized by participants of the value chain" [9].

According to the definition presented, four mean elements or fundamental technologies in Industry 4.0 are recognized:

1) Smart Factories
2) Cyber-physical systems
3) Internet of Things
4) Internet of Services

The following points illustrate how Industry 4.0 has huge economic potential [10]:

a. Customer-specific objectives are fulfilled

b. Agility
c. Decision making is more effective
d. Increased productivity of resources
e. Creating value opportunities through new services
f. Work-life balance
g. A high-wage and competitive economy

These changes will bring enormous cost reductions in the manufacturing industry.

To shift from Industry 3.0 to Industry 4.0, a perfect objectives-oriented plan should be chalked out. The eight planning objectives to achieve Industry 4.0 are as follows [11]:

1. System standardization involves the development of a reference architecture. There is a need to develop a set of uniform standards so that a network can be linked and integrated to several manufacturers and businesses enterprises.
2. Efficient management—future factories will feature huge and complicated systems that must be efficiently handled. To maximize management, appropriate plans and an explanatory model must be developed.
3. Construction of robust and sustainable communication infrastructure. Industry 4.0 places rigorous requirements on network applications, which must satisfy these requirements and should be consistent, robust, and of excellent quality.
4. Safety and security are crucial. It is vital to guarantee that manufacturing facilities and products do not pose a threat to people or the environment, as well as to prevent product abuse and unauthorized access to industrial facilities.
5. Workplace layout and design—material, process, and environmental changes create high expectations on production management to achieve humane, automated, and ecologically friendly products and control
6. Training and professional development for employees- Employers have the responsibility and obligation to train their employees. To help workers in adapting and evolving themselves in terms of skill requirements. However, it is necessary to build lifelong learning and continual career development programs.
7. Focusing on implementing a regulatory environment. It is evident that new technologies bring with them new

difficulties including commercial data, accountability, personal information, and import tariffs. Standardization, model agreements, contracts, auditing, and other types of effective control are essential.

8. Optimizing productivity and sustainability. Advanced materials, processes, technologies, and other strategies can help to boost energy efficiency while reducing and mitigating the environmental impact due to pollution and waste.

12.5 Challenges to Industry 4.0

In this section, the top challenges to Industry 4.0 are discussed. Industry 4.0 as discussed above is an inter-disciplinary change in the system, the challenges are also diverse:

a. Data Integration
In our data-driven culture, data is produced in several ways. In the manufacturing environment, data is collected and acquired from a variety of sources, including machine sensors, process data, product data, quality data, plant data, logistics data, data from partners, and infrastructure data. Such data presents several issues and necessitates the development of novel storage, processing, and management strategies. New algorithms, models, tools, and visualization approaches are necessary to harness the data and obtain substantial advantages. Data engineers must analyze this data, discover links across data streams, and derive previously undiscovered insights from it.

The above-mentioned issues can be removed, and hardware, software, and operational expenses can be lowered, if the systems are well-integrated. However, such integration is quite difficult to perform as it requires changes in data structure and understanding of different source data models.

b. Process Flexibility
Changing markets demand the personalization of highly customizable products. Such personalization and customization necessitate cost-effective flexibility at the manufacturing level. The production environment must be adaptive at the process level to give such flexibility. The current technology on the work floor is insufficient and does not allow for process flexibility.

Flexibility at different levels in production requires a variability management mechanism as it is needed in other areas. Change management at the production level is quite challenging. Since processes are spread across different departments, clear process ownership in terms of adaptation or change is also missing. A change structure is also essential since it is often impossible to maintain required modifications in a specific region, which would have an impact on the entire scenario due to dependencies. In the event of a change, the appropriate adjustments are conveyed via printout or email communication. These modifications are frequently handled independently within every sector with no specific standards in place, which further adds to the complexity and cost of handling them. To ensure effective flexibility, process standardization and synchronization among multiple firm departments are required.

c. Security
Security is a major concern for any organization right now, and this will continue to be in the future. Industries strive to keep their employees, goods, and the surroundings of their manufacturing facilities safe from potential threats. There is an increasing trend to use smart devices in production. By the end of this decade, there will be roughly 50 billion IoT devices. These gadgets will be used in homes, factories, and other public places. On the one hand, the gadgets' connectivity offers a variety of advantages that make our lives easier. On the other side, it poses a greater danger in terms of security. Monitoring such manufacturing equipment is a difficulty from both a software and hardware standpoint, which is often disregarded. To avoid risks or due to configuration changes installed in this equipment dispersed throughout a geographic location or inside a plant, all equipment, whether industrial machines, laptops, tablets, or smartphones, must be updated regularly. It is also time-consuming to keep track of upgrades and manage such gadgets.

12.6 Conclusion

Through analyzing current literature survey, this study has conducted a complete assessment of Industry 4.0 and gives an overview of Industry 4.0, scope, and potential challenges. This article contains an up-to-date overview of current Industry 4.0 research. The evolution of the industry is a complicated and agile process involving both humans and machines. With CPS, Industry 4.0 accelerates the digitalization of production, enabling interconnected networks of humans and robots to communicate and collaborate while sharing and analyzing data, aided by big data and cloud computing across the whole manufacturing production chain. Industry 4.0, in collaboration with advanced techniques, processes, and tools, enhances time and financial productivity by maintaining a high-quality product. Consequently, Industry 4.0 will help the industry accomplish a completely substantial level of functional growth and productivity. There will arise a new horizon of smart manufacturing and processing industries focused on machine-to-human interaction and the manifestation of synergistic products. However, there is indeed a significant way to go in terms of improving manufacturing to the point where it can meet all principal parameters.

References

1. Tesch da Silva, F.S., da Costa, C.A., Paredes Crovato, C.D., da Rosa Righi, R., Looking at energy through the lens of Industry 4.0: A systematic literature review of concerns and challenges, in: *Computer and Industrial Engineering*, vol. 143, Elsevier Ltd., Brazil, 2020. https://doi.org/10.1016/j.cie.2020.106426.
2. Bartodziej, C.J., *The Concept Industry 4.0*, November 18, Springer, Germany, 2016.
3. Osterrieder, P., Budde, L., Friedli, T., The smart factory as a key construct of industry 4.0: A systematic literature review. *Int. J. Prod. Econ.*, 3, 221, 2020. https://doi.org/10.1016/j.ijpe.2019.08.011.
4. Bartodziej, C.J., *The Concept Industry 4.0*, November 18, Springer, Germany, 2016.
5. Parente, M., Figueira, G., Amorim, P., Marques, A., Production scheduling in the context of Industry 4.0: Review and trends. *Int. J. Prod. Res.* Taylor Francis Ltd., 58, 17, 5401–5431, 2020. https://doi.org/10.1080/00207543.2020.1718794.
6. Bányai, T., Introductory chapter: Industry 4.0 and its impact on logistics-A retrospective review, in: *Industry 4.0-Impact on Intelligent Logistics and Manufacturing*, IntechOpen, Hungary, 2020, https://doi.org/10.5772/intechopen.89387.
7. Klingenberg, C.O., Borges, M.A.V., Antunes, J.A.V., Industry 4.0 as a data-driven paradigm: A systematic literature review on technologies. *J. Manuf. Technol. Manage.*, 32, 3, 570–592, 2021. https://doi.org/10.1108/JMTM-09-2018-0325.
8. Dewangan, B.K., Agarwal, A., Choudhury, T., Pasricha, A., Chandra Satapathy, S., Extensive review of cloud resource management techniques in industry 4.0: Issue and challenges. *Software Pract. Exp.*, 51, 12, 2373–2392, 2021.
9. Mohamed, M., Challenges and benefits of industry 4.0: An overview, 5, 5, 2018.
10. Osterrieder, P., Budde, L., Friedli, T., The smart factory as a key construct of industry 4.0: A systematic literature review. *Int. J. Prod. Econ.*, 6, 221, 2020. https://doi.org/10.1016/j.ijpe.2019.08.011.
11. Zhou, K., Liu, T., Zhou, L., Industry 4.0: Towards future industrial opportunities and challenges. *12th International Conference on Fuzzy Systems and Knowledge Discovery (FSKD)*, 2015.

13

The Role of Multiagent System in Industry 4.0

Jagjit Singh Dhatterwal[1], Kuldeep Singh Kaswan[2]* and Rudra Pratap Ojha[3]

[1]*Department of Artificial Intelligence & Data Science, Koneru Lakshmaiah Education Foundation, Vaddeswaram, AP, India*
[2]*School of Computing Science and Engineering, Galgotias University, Greater Noida, India*
[3]*G L Bajaj Institute of Technology and Management, Greater Noida, UP, India*

Abstract

Recent trends, such as low production costs, even though more sophisticated and distinctive product lines, are needed for customers—provide a great number of difficulties to the production process. A paradigm change is taking place in the industrial sector. The number of integrated will replace the conventional centrally managed production processes, based on the self-regulatory capacity of intelligent equipment, commodities, and mechanical components, which interact constantly. The new Industry 4.0 framework, this idea is the deployment of intelligent digital network systems, where machinery and goods talk to one another to build intelligent industries for self-regulatory manufacturing. This article describes, in the first instance, the essence, primary objectives and basic features of Industry 4.0. After this, automated vehicles based on multiagent systems are developed. These systems incorporate the working robots through machine learning, a key component of Industry 4.0.

Keywords: Multiagent system, artificial intelligence, intelligent robot, 3D printing, cryptography

**Corresponding author*: kaswankuldeep@gmail.com

Jyotir Moy Chatterjee, Harish Garg and R. N. Thakur (eds.) A Roadmap for Enabling Industry 4.0 by Artificial Intelligence, (227–246) © 2023 Scrivener Publishing LLC

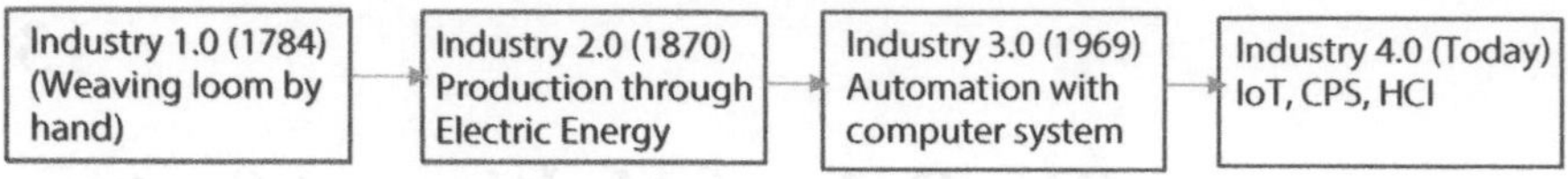

Figure 13.1 Stages of industrial development.

13.1 Introduction

The pace of innovation is the next notion of Industry 4.0. The theory of the design shows that industrialization was defined by a steam engine's introduction during the 1st industrial revolution. Mass manufacturing using electrical automated machines was the 2nd disruptive innovation. Automated production through deployment of industrial robots [1] was the 3rd disruptive innovation. The development of technology is the period in which intelligent robots are used. The commodities in this idea regulate their own manufacturing since such goods and components interact throughout their manufacture with machines and equipment through innovative product identifiers. Smart plants will self-regulate and operate themselves optimally. It, therefore, indicates that, throughout manufacturing, virtual and actual realities fuse [2]. The features, primary objectives, and pillars of the notion of industry 4.0 are presented in the first line of the series in Figure 13.1.

13.2 Characteristics and Goals of Industry 4.0 Conception

The foundation of the design of Industry 4.0 is to introduce network-based smart systems, which produce their own self-regulation: people, machinery, devices, and goods are constantly in communication [3, 4]. Products manage their own manufacture, and communicative products regulate the production planning.

Everything works in intelligent factories in the conversations of products and machines, which are connected in a channel itself, connected by digital chain, using the highest quality equipment for transforming industry into a network settings system [5], based on information communication technologies, sensors, and software applications. There is new technology, such as the digitalization of machinery, systems, and goods to enable constant connectivity. The design aims to make factories smarter and build a digital platform, bringing together the key tools: sensors, Internet of Things, big data, and cognitive hosting. Industry 4.0 is the genesis of the German Government's strategic plan to promote the global industry's digital transformation, which was launched at the Hanover Exhibition in 2011 [6]. This idea has been widely adopted recently, not just in Europe, but worldwide. According to the design, the five main parts of digital networking may be described by:

- smart machines;
- vertical networking;
- horizontal, smart workpieces;
- digital workpieces;
- intelligent machines.

The main objectives of the design of Industry 4.0 are:

- production optimization, which will enhance productivity;
- efficiency in manufacturing which will be more efficient, more adaptable, or customized;
- process automation improvement efficiency;
- maximizing the use of human and mechanical resources;
- to adapt more effectively to shifting market needs,
- to provide new business models and possibilities [7].

Conceptual results will be:

- digitalization of physical systems;
- satisfaction of the customers who necessitate more complex and nuanced products in small quantities;
- traditional manufacturing technology required procedures and watched closely, replaced by distributed systems;
- self-regulation of factories that optimize the way they are operated; Industry 4.0, a digitalized world of economical and manufacturing operations that is globally interconnected [8].

In nine technology pillars, the Boston Consulting Group defined the foundations of Industry 4.0 [9]:

- Robots independent. More autonomously and cooperating automated machines are already becoming. Humanoid machines can interact to increase efficiency and the quality of their products. These robots can accomplish more difficult jobs and handle unforeseen problems [10].

- Integration of the horizontally system with the quality of the system. The objective is to maximize the functioning of the supply chain by joining each member of the value chains in the related diversification of systems elements (e.g. suppliers, manufacturers, service providers, customers). Vertical integration aims to optimize manufacturing process reconfiguration through the connection of pervasive computing (sensors, actuators etc.) [11].
- The Internet of Things for Industry (IoT). Industrial IoT enables equipment to connect and interact. It is a network link and data interchange for things, such as goods, machineries, machinery, cars, or other built-in devices, so that gadgets are more cost effective and more efficient. System gathers and exchanges enormous quantities of data inside the digitized networks supply chain, ensuring information flow in among system parts [12].
- Simement. Process modeling is critical for designing the product, planning the manufacturing and when flowing materials, or when simulating unanticipated unpredictable occurrences. Simulations will more frequently also be utilized in production plant in the future. Simulated is a technology to deliver real-time data in a virtual environment that can contain machines, equipment, goods, and individuals to observant the physical universe. It is an efficient instrument for maximizing output and resource use [13].
- Manufacture of additives. Manufacturing technology is a language for the description of technologies, which construct 3D things by layer after layer (3D printing). This method gives the opportunity to manufacture more complicated components that other approaches cannot attain. It offers greater versatility and productivity in the manufacture of smaller quantities and bespoke finished items [14].
- Computer cloud. The cloud provides infinite processing capacity for the reception, storage and analysis of big data necessary for optimum system operations. Stored information and services may be accessed through the Internet at any location and device [15]. It enables all system parts to coordinate their work and concurrently work in real time on sharing data and information.

- Reality increased. Enhanced reality gives the opportunity to view the actual environment by changing it into a virtualized environment [16]. In the use of applications, the information pertaining to the user's real environment becomes participatory and technologically open to manipulation.
- Big information. Smart networking systems demand enormous amounts of information that are virtually uncontrollable. This collection of data is known as big data. The gathering and assessment of this information will become crucial to determining in real time, as per the IoT principals. This large quantity of information is analyzed to enhance the functioning of production systems.
- Security of cybers. It is important to secure the enormous volume of data transmitted on the networks. Cryptography encompasses technology and methods meant to safeguard computer network, organizations, and data [17].

13.3 Artificial Intelligence

This chapter will describe the system's knowledge and offer several factory control techniques, e.g., public knowledge innovations, system supervising, agents as one-size-fits-all approach, and multiagent systems as a number of cooperative stakeholders [18].

The manufacturing system must remain robust and adaptable to handle challenging surroundings throughout operation. Intellectual control methods should really be calculated to automatically consider the changes that occur, eliminating continual human assistance and expenses. How to supply the flexible monitoring system with intellectual content. The control techniques machine learning is an artificial intelligence (AI), supervision and specialist understanding are employed in such systems to give versatility. Because they are viewed as producing systems whose diverse control layers are upgraded with cognitive technology and architecture from the shop floors to the business level, the benefits analysis show that intelligent systems will be ready to organize production practices for future problems [19].

Figure 13.2 shows and collects several forms of intelligent machines, which are used and linked to the numerous domains throughout use, based on literature study. For instance, self-adaptation of logic controller during manufacturing and lean can be carried out with the use of the

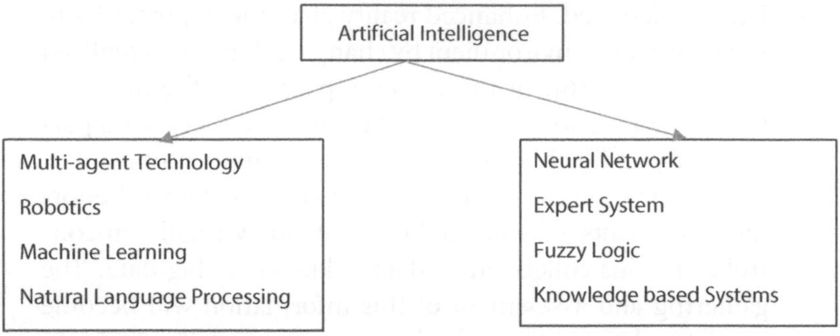

Figure 13.2 Parts of artificial intelligence.

evolutionary algorithm to learn flouted logic or even flouted logic with diagnostics agents.

The text states that McCulloch and Pits performed the first work regarding AI in 1943, and recommended that an artificial neuron prototype be produced. New area "artificial intelligence" was introduced in 1956 by McCarty.

For instance, the research objectives and techniques have pushed examples of flexible production technologies using expertise to assist such automated judgments. The first is to discuss the knowledge-oriented systems [20].

13.3.1 Knowledge-Based Systems

Facts, theories, rules, and processes are information in knowledge-based systems. The "Information Based System" (KBS) according to Tasso et al. is a software system that is able in certain specific areas of expertise to enable thorough description of information and to use it via suitable reasoning processes to give a high degree of solving a problem effectiveness. Since the KBSs symbolize machine intelligence and are competent to carry out the functions that are historically regarded as distinctive that are exclusive to people's knowledge, the KBSs are independently competent to solve difficulties. In conventional control methods, advanced information technology may be viewed as a conventional extension of the physical equation. Comprehensive engineering, sophisticated technology and production processes control, adaptable robotic and manipulative manufactured computer architecture, diagnostics, interpreting of the collected data, budgeting, reporting, and scheduling, and more are utilized in experience and understanding systems [21].

An expert system representation of KBS performs cognitively hard tasks at the extremely high level and emphasizes the subject. They give interpretations for the results obtained issue solving approaches above general computer science algorithms. In addition to engineering—also in medical and commerce, they are commonly employed in many areas. Expert system is a system based on fugitive logic and may be combined to achieve greater effectiveness with other machine intelligence approaches (for example, neural networks, genetic algorithms) [22].

The literature discusses the benefits and inconveniences of such systems:

- Innovations based on knowledge (KB) provide advantages to identify disruptions since these activities rely on a large quantity of information and are compensated for them.
- They enforce the uniform representations of expertise, allow the gradual increase of information to be made possible by adding rules, and allow for unexpected but meaningful connections (also the operator of the knowing base's proactivity may lose control) [23].
- As indicated, design may be improved by reduction of work and the creation of sufficient, theoretical approaches of understanding for hardware and software that address future problems to the productive system.

As the disadvantages suggest:

- Due to the quantity of information, the knowledge-based systems are complex to develop.
- Explicitly list the control alternatives and practically no system generalization capability.

The essential concept of answering inquiry queries is that control techniques generate control selections depending on the descriptions of expertise and certain external sources, such as plant establishment and the goal of decision-making. Knowledge typically collaborates with a conventional platform that comprises specific plant understanding. The system makes use of two types of expertise: plant knowledge and experience (explanatory methodology) and managerial understanding (a prescriptive character). Academic success of the KBS is seen as an adaptability in traditional control algorithms. In the heater, for example, the transition is defined by multiple stages, each with its own temperature controller. Based on expert knowledge, the management system may be programmed to work in a variety of conditions with increased productivity (a prescriptive nature of the information). They are not replacing specialists, but rather increasing their expertise [24].

13.4 Multiagent Systems

Because agents are one of the tools of intelligent machines to build flexible intelligent infrastructure and can also be utilized, the following advantage of agents will be discussed.

An agent is an autonomous computer entity with a real concern and goal-oriented capacity to be successful, even proactively, in flexible and transparent surroundings in the respect that it monitors and acts on it to achieve its goals. In other words, agents constitute a software-embedded modeling method [25].

Agents are usually classified into contemplative and responsive agencies. Consensus building agents are quite versatile but performing responses can become excessively complicated and sluggish. The architectural Belief Desire-Intention (BDI) of Rao and Georgieff's differentiated itself for the deliberation agency implementations.

Because reactionary agents do not have to cope with complicated, symbolic global models or react fast to relevant environmental inputs. Only situation-action connections create the outcome based on the inputs. In many situations, the solvent can be replaced without loss of performance by various responsive compounds. Because reactive agents are simple to create, enough for the suggested control model, the flexibility architectural may be employed.

A multiagent system is called a grouping of interacting agents (MAS). The interacting cooperating agents can work together in a complicated actual world. They achieve their own goals by combining semiautonomous critical thinkers, communications, cooperation, negotiations, and responsibilities [26].

Many investigations on application of agents have shown and are discussed in the next sentence of several existing approaches and various manufacturing agents.

13.4.1 Agent Architectures

Several techniques, such as holonic and multiagent applications, have developed in recent decades. Rockwell Automation Inc. has developed a Directorate for Agent Research to spend heavily in investigating different mitigation systems based on holonic and multiagent systems.

Holonic and agent-focused systems vary in parallel processing calculation with the benefit of reaction rate to disruptions from conventional networks [27].

• Holonic manufacture ("holo" from Greece) is described, claiming that from the early 1990s, it was created to tackle rising sophistication, product adaptation, fluctuating demand and costs. This design comprises of independent units operating in a flexible structure. He argues that holonic production has a much wider viewpoint than heterarchical architecture in compared to heterarchical construction and not only controls the entire manufacturing operations. But holonic HMS systems provide loose, flexible communications in contrast to hierarchy's process control which never oblige a holon to execute a certain duty [28].
• Agent-based administration is a behavioral software system that operates independently and cooperatively. It may be done hierarchically or here. It may also allow for the realization of holonic building. Several architectures in science holonic and multiagency have already been proposed:

- Holonic manufacturing and engineering reference architecture The PROSA (Product-ResourceOrders-Staff-Architecture) is comprised of fundamental holons, holons of business, resources, orders and linguistic activity, and employs holons to represent goods, resources, instructions and logical operations. PROSA cover methods to hierarchy and heterarchy of control.
- The ADACOR holonic architecture emphasizes the quick response to developments and changes, enhancing the flexibility and adaptability of production control networks in tense situations. The frequent incidence of disruption was characterized.
- GRACE multiagent system—distributing the PROCE and quality control in assembly plants that produce white goods. GRACE is an interagent multiagent system.
- PABADIS—the idea of cooperation production plants is used as agents in the manufacturing method of the controlling the operation, encapsulation of residences, goods, and shop floor management. This method comprises of the use of mobile-agent technology for centralized (for connections with ERP) and decentralized elements. HMS basic principles are primarily agents that are in the central unit and work with the basic building block of the processing

unit from afar. Unlike HMS, PABADIS moves order key components, migrates via the system and carries out duties for various controller entities based on the basic foundation of the main processor [29].

Hundreds of additional designs exist, and various industrial-domain implementations or techniques are detailed in surveys. In production control systems, dynamical hybrid control topologies are contrasted.

MAS is no longer only a scholarly idea. There are several techniques in the industry in the orientation of the MAS application, e.g., appropriate for selected applications. A multiagent control system for a Kraft Recovering Boiler is provided for the heater applications, inference evaluation of boilers pollutants using multiagent simulation. Agents are used in connected grid intelligent energy technology. Conveyor's MAS implementations include the control of holonic chain convey, a production facility that employs agents as interconnectors between legacy systems and the cloud I4.0, a shop/floor management software, and a collaborative effort. In the chapter, it is demonstrated that it is valid to create an agent-based infrastructure based on consumer uses.

The accompanying actual operational new factories are known (mostly in Germany): The Mercedes Chrysler P2000+ cylinders head fabricating system for internal combustion engines in Birmingham, Holofoils, is intended to enhance material flow and profitability in the manufacturing companies.

The agent monitors and manages the bodies, paint and assembling shops of the Bremen automobile facility of DaimlerChrysler, Rockwell Management Agent-based chilled water system in the United States Navy, etc. You may find further material about submissions here. All the studies are always in favor of agents, since, according to Amro M. Farid, MAS plays a critical role in maintaining the overall resilience of the interconnected cyber-physical integral approach as intelligent and decentralized regulatory techniques. Furthermore, agent-based implementations offer several advantages before agent: resilience, scalability, adaptability, and productivity. Although agent technology continues to demonstrate its advantages over traditional techniques, there is no major use in industry. Technology and human element are the reasons: operator and developers are not, at first, competent to use new technology; second, there are several industry barriers, such as investment, compatibility, real-time limitations, etc. Nevertheless, agent technology holds the possibility of overcoming increased production difficulties because it offers conceptual models and execution architecture that are important elements of future control systems for deliberate decision taking, negotiation, and coordination [30].

In the survey, Paulo Leitão gives the term of the time issue of addressing contemporary manufacturing control systems compared with conventional MAS and production control systems, historically used bureaucratic and hierarchical methods of control They are responsible for the following tasks: scheduling, planning, and execution (dispatching, monitoring, etc.). Algorithms with many functions proposed are complex. When complete up-to-date processes data is required, organizing and budgeting may not have the same time schedule for execution, which generates time issues. This calls for an actual operating condition that works continuously and adjusts to changing order needs. In his investigation, he believes that the traditionally centralized techniques demand sophisticated and dispersed systems and networks in Figure 13.3.

MAS control mechanisms handle smart and decentralized control and classify them according to by the following characteristics:

- A complicated issue is split into a number of small problems mapped into an intelligent control unit in the decentralized approach;
- Every control panel is independently operated, with its own goals, information, and intelligence capabilities;
- Global hegemony decisions (e.g., programming, monitoring, and troubleshooting) are made by many control modules [31].
- Some control devices, for example robots and Computer - aided manufacturing, are coupled to physical robotic systems;

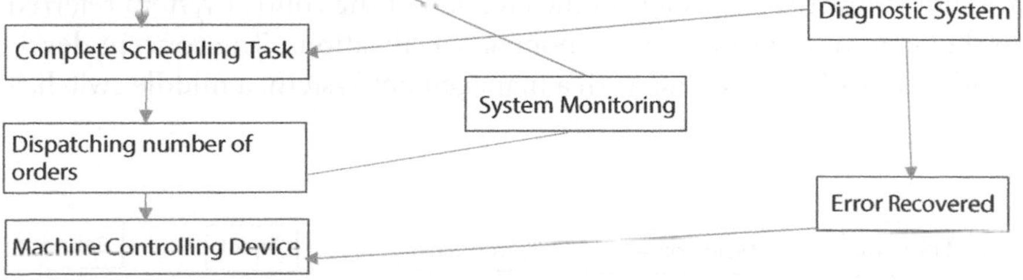

Figure 13.3 Traditional control of manufacturing systems.

- Control devices should have numerous key properties, such as reconfigurability, robotics, and learning.

In it, also, a comparative of the standard control methods and the smart solution disseminated is offered.

It is worth noting that the principles of Industry 4.0, by employing Internet technology that would allow new techniques of data incorporation and data analysis, need the simpler implementation of data processors and the connectivity of all automated pyramid stages. All the computer resources required to generate customized goods for the intended usage are essential to be conscious of. Agent-based systems are, therefore, the simplest and not inexpensive approach to implement I4.0 and to migrate from old systems to the I4.0 [32].

13.4.2 JADE

The group FIPA has created a set of specifications for the administration of agents, for contact with agents and for the transmission of knowledge. Java Agent Development Framework (JADE), a Java-based toolset that conforms to FIPA, is among the most prominent open-sourced frames in this sector. JADE software is a powerful agent system that supports the development and operation of agents in Figure 13.4. The FIPA standardizing efforts focused at software agents, as self-government creatures that communicate with and operate on a greater decision-making degree or elevated degree of control via a specialized agent vocabulary.

JADE gives filed methods for communications among agents. They are all recorded in the agent platforms containers allows the user to access additional behaviors. The agent's behavior is accomplished using procedures in line with Figure 13.4, which illustrates the behavior functions in the class diagram in SYSML. The notion is derived from introducing dependencies between agents' behaviors.

The next chapter will discuss the deployment of adaptable JADE MAS and now show the next stage in the creation of the control system referred to the setup of the software component specifications. The concept developed is comprised of a PLC with a management system, a middle switch, a

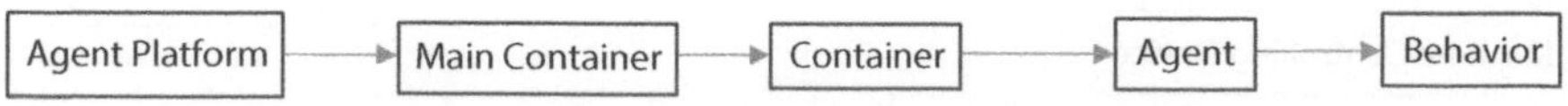

Figure 13.4 Relationship between the main architectural elements.

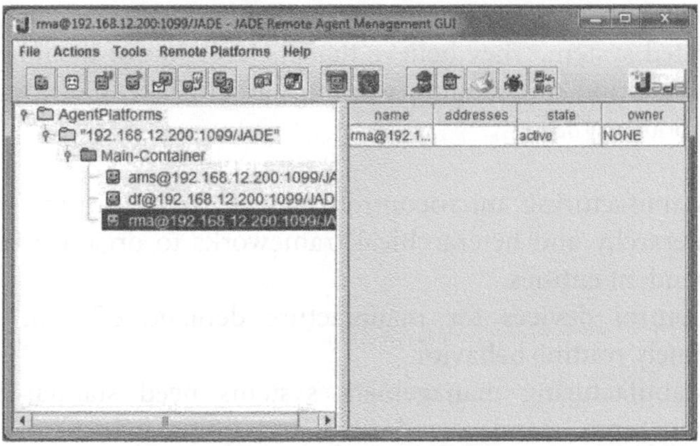

Figure 13.5 Agent container AMS.

bus adapter, a PC, and a server-service container connecting all parts. The containers offer all authorized agents with communications.

Container implementation in Jade is shown in Figure 13.5.

13.4.3 System Requirements Definition

Many experts say that machine intelligence is the thing that will interact, share intelligence, bargain and decide, and hence control oneself, in the future industry. In order to create an intelligence-flexible control system, the production system will also be more flexible and responsive to the "smart factory" paradigm, the system level needs and system attributes will be established. The MAS architecture previously defined utilized in the construction of a flexible management system should also satisfy the system criteria specified in this paragraph. Many writers set the standards for contemporary companies and production systems to handle the automating problems. In order to manage the system, the first prerequisites arose from the entire department: the monitoring system must have a short schematic design, lower operational costs and also protected claim to decent rate and manufacturer control conversations to meet the challenges of organizations today and automated production mechanisms. The criteria should satisfy production volume and apparatus changing flexibility; human interaction and attractiveness; current systems and standards compliance; incorporation into existing control technology and runtime environments; extended and reconfigurable; security, web integration, etc.

Giret and Trentesaux are successfully assessed as far as flexibility, agility, and polyvalence are concerned. It is achieved by means of distributed, smart production systems, employing smaller handling systems instead of a complicated system. They believe that the creation of flexible behavior and the adaptation to changing working circumstances need autonomy and collaboration [33].

- Manufacturing microcontrollers need to be arranged in hierarchy and heterarchical frameworks to organize independent entities.
- Control devices for manufacture demand efficient and timely routine behavior.
- Manufacturing management systems need standardized structures, standardized tibia and fibula, which can be coupled through standardized interfaces and modulation schemes with different levels of the system.

Production systems need to be produced in a responsible way.

13.4.4 HMI Development

More than one physical connection is available in the management system. The operation can add the tables in the columns list using this little GUI (there are three columns in the example here), and send the systems "STOP," "START" messages. In addition, the operator will get feedback on each Fischer Technik model sensor and engine output bytes for an overwhelming number of backup agencies.

Any feedback about the operation of agents will be displayed. GUI displays, as well as the date and place of this action, that the agent has been restarted (to demonstrate GUI work).

13.5 Developing Software of Controllers Multiagent Environment Behavior Patterns

13.5.1 Agent Supervision

In taking crucial choices, the supervisor agent was installed with an edge. There is no band speed restriction in the supplied Fischer Technik model; hence, no consideration has been paid to optimize the speed and PID settings. However, it might be feasible in the future with different models.

SA features a GUI to give the operator with the critical plant operating data.

The communication among people and agents from Jade is represented by the Supervisory Agent and its graphical user interface (GUI). Using cyclic queries from the PLC, EA signal is communicated and presented on a GUI. The tables of each of the three entry fields are labeled "true" (table is inaccessible) or "false." By pressing the "add" button, the information provided to the dispatcher agent will display the information, for example, the first character is supplied in "101," "1" denotes Table 1, and "0" denotes that Table 2 is inaccessible. The starter instruction is then transmitted to EA by clicking the "start" button (communication contents: "1") and to the EA by clicking the "stop" button ("0"). Moreover, if an unexpected failure is made by the elevated agent (HA), it will be resumed by SA. The primary operations relate to the GUI, which uses messages from and to agents. In addition, class and engagement diagrams must depict behaviors and actions of SA.

In the connections, a table with the relevant metadata and an activity diagram are provided to better characterize each executed behavior, an effectiveness graph depicting the supervising agent's productive volume in JADE.

13.5.2 Documents Dispatching Agents

Due to the obvious blocks structure, the DA's primary role in the system is to identify the destination routes for the blocks. The architecture of the EA blocks is compared to previously reported tendencies. "00" represents "table 1" or "01" represents "table 2"; "10" represents "table 3" or "11" represents "no free table." If the template previously exists, EA sends it to the structured table.

If no block was saved, a novel feature entry is generated with that pattern. In another example, the reschedule agent determines the target table. For this DA sends the RA a communication with a block sequence and three table statements ("1010 | 101," for example). The DA will send an EA message with a target table when the target table has been established by the RA (e.g., "10"= goal is "Tisch3"). After the DA receives a SA message, you have hit the "add" button on the GUI. This is a three-figure message (for example, "101"), where the input tables are represented. You must choose the target table, because it is also impossible for tables to be designated as targets to be launched as "occupied."

The introduction to a class graph in papyrus technology by the supervisor agent is depicted.

In the auxiliary, a table containing pertinent details and an activity diagram are supplied to better define each done behavior for each activity.

Diagram of the activities showing the dispatcher agent's overall job carried out in JADE is shown.

13.5.3 Agent Rescheduling

As previously indicated, it is the rescheduler agent's responsibility to establish the different target path for the additional kind of temporary ferromagnetic specified on the blocks and, if requested, to provide that position to the DA.

The rescheduler agent validates the assignment of the target table to the structure of the DA block. For the new element arrangement, the RA will get a message from the DA containing the block sequence and the three table statements (e.g., "1010 101"). After the RA has established the target table, the message will be returned to the DA with the block sequence and the targeting table (e.g., "1010 S 10"). The last two protagonists match the destination table but the first four patterns' components. The two strings are "S" separately.

The representation of the rescheduler agents in the perspective of a sequence diagram in parchment application.In addition, a table with relevant information and activity diagram in the attachment is given to further describe each completed behavior.

A diagram of activities which shows the general work of a JADE-based rescheduler agent.

13.5.4 Agent of Executive

The amount of managing the voltages and bus connection connections is indicated by the Administrative Representative. On the Pi control, which represents the existing system and keeps all the directions for blocks within, the management agent may be put (destinations). Another option is to keep the outdated technologies on the pi controller and give commands to the control system, which is primarily responsible for managing the mobility models.

The Management Agency monitoring and supervision of the conveyor system. The PLC is forwarded with a Modbus TCP/IP communication to see the presently operating inputs (sensors) and outcomes (motors). These queries are run cyclically in the milliseconds interval in order to provide real-time access to the text comprehension of PLC data. EA demonstrates therefore if the Supervisor Agency got the orders "start" or "stop" in a ticker behavior (SA). A character is included in this message ("1" = "start," "0" = "stop"). The "management"—behaviors starts with a "start" signal. The blocks are transferred from the storehouse and the induced electromagnetic sensors are inserted electronically. This is how the blocks are found.

After the message has been identified, a block size structure and the condition of the three columns will be transmitted to the dispatcher agent (DA). The following message is: "1010 | 110," for instance. The first four letters are the block patterns ("1010") while the final three are the formulas. A table with enough information and activity diagram will be displayed in the attachments for a clearer description of each accomplished behavior.

A diagram of activities showing the general work of JADE executive agent.

13.5.5 Primary Roles of High-Availability Agent

Two primary roles were incorporated: one, the greater agent (HAA) monitors the IP of the agencies who registered in the system so that any attacks are contained and secondly, agents are backed up if they have been terminate or failed.

By HAA, the system's dependability is enhanced. If one of these agencies (SA, DA, EA or RA) happens, HAA begins again after a while. The HA also verifies each agent's Internet protocol address and ends each agent's Internet protocol address at a foreign location.

Of course, the qualities may always be adjusted to the customer's wishes. Subsequently, the Agent's key actions are provided and illustrated on papyrus software activity diagrams.

The rescheduler agent's description in the sequence diagram in the papyrus technology is illustrated.

A schematic showing the overall functioning of the JADE-implemented high-availability agent is shown. In the attachments, the modeling of all behaviors is provided.

It shows the general perspective of the link between agents with a brief overview. The graph shows that only one duplicate of the agent may be linked to each other in the systems.

All the stated conducts were supplied in the summary in this chapter for the entire execution of each agent. No problems were identified during the tests. The cross of the control scheme and accessibility of demonstrated functions provides a range of capabilities, such as flexibility change of tracks, flexible hardware requirements, and adaptable operations.

13.6 Conclusion

The chapter contents were split into two sections. First, the principle of the automation trend of industry 4.0 was introduced by having to introduce its main targets and expected outcome measures, then the modules of this industrialization, which can be characterized as a cyber world that manages every aspect from consumption to designing products, were evaluated. The first element was Industry 4.0 smart accurate detection and assimilation of communications technology like 3D printing, cloud-based services, increased reality, the Internet of Things, etc. is part of that evolution. Second, autonomously, systems, which are a useful determinant of the success digitalization of the production and for the creation of a smart manufacturing known as multiagent systems. In the industrial application, these agents may be weapon opportunists, sensors, machine intelligence controllers. A table containing all the essential aspects explained the function of AI in the ecosystem of collaborative robots.

References

1. Ahuett-Garza, H. and Kurfess, T., A brief discussion on the trends of habilitating technologies for industry 4.0 and smart manufacturing. *Manuf. Lett.*, 15, 60–63, 2018.
2. Agostini, L. and Filippini, R., Industry 4.0 and industrial IoT in manufacturing: A sneak peek. *Eur. J. Innov. Manag., 22*, 406–421, 2019.
3. Jay, L., Behrad, B., Hung-An, K., A cyber physical systems architecture for industry 4.0–based manufacturing systems. *Manuf. Lett.*, 3, 18–23, 2015.
4. Stock, T. and Seliger, G., Opportunities of sustainable manufacturing in industry 4.0. *Proc. CIRP*, 40, 536–541, 2016.
5. Robla-Gomez, S., Becerra, V.M., Llata, J.R., Gonzalez-Sarabia, E., Torre-Ferrero, C., PerezOria, J., Working together. A review on safe human-robot collaboration in industrial environments. *IEEE Access*, 5, 26, 754–773, 2017.
6. Zhong, R.Y., Klotz, X., Xu, E., Newman, S.T., Intelligent manufacturing in the context of industry 4.0. A review. *Engineering*, 3, 5, 616–630, 2017.
7. Sung, T.K., Industry 4.0: A Korea perspective. *Technol. Forecast. Soc. Change*, 132, 40–45, 2017.

8. Vaidya, S., Ambad, P., Bhosle, S., Industry 4.0–a glimpse. *Proc. Manuf.*, 20, 233–238, 2018.
9. Burke, R., Mussomeli, A., Laaper, S., Hartigan, M., Sniderman, B., The smart factory–responsive, adaptive, connected manufacturing, *Int. J. Oper. Prod. Manag.*, 33, 1408–1434, 2013.
10. Kostal, P., Kiss, I., Kerak, P., The intelligent fixture at flexible manufacturing. *Ann. Faculty Eng. Hunedoara–Int. J. Eng.*, 9, 1, 197–200, 2011.
11. Industry 4.0–the next revolution is here!, *Int. J. Retail Distrib. Manag.*, 46, 466–486, 2018.
12. Avornicului, M., Cloud computing: Challenges and opportunities for small and medium sized business. *World Forum Economic*, 16, 111, 32–45, 2013.
13. Gubán, M., Non-linear programming model and solution method of ordering controlled virtual assembly plants. *Proceedings of Logistics–The Eurasian Bridge: Materials of V International Scientifically-Practical Conference*, Krasnoyarsk, pp. 49–58, 2011.
14. Bonarini, A., Matteucci, M., Restelli, M., Concepts for anchoring in robotics, in: *AI*IA 2001: Advances in Artificial Intelligence. AI*IA 2001. Lecture Notes in Computer Science*, vol. 2175, Springer, Berlin, Heidelberg, 2001. https://doi.org/10.1007/3-540-45411-X_34
15. Matthias, B. and Reisinger, T., Example application of ISO/TS 15066 to a collaborative assembly scenario. *47th International Symposium on Robotics*, Munich, 2016, Retrieved from https://www.researchgate.net/publication/310951754_Example_Application_of_ISOTS_15066_to_a_Collaborative_Assembly_Scenario.
16. Stone, P., Ave, P., Park, F., Multiagent systems: A survey from a machine learning perspective. *Robotics*, 8, 345–353, 1995.
17. Yan, Z., Jouandeau, N., Cherif, A., A survey and analysis of multi-robot coordination. *Int. J. Adv. Robot. Syst.*, 10, 399–412, 2013.
18. El Zoghby, N., Loscri, V., Natalizio, E., Cherfaoui, V., Robot cooperation and swarm intelligence. *Wireless Sensor and Robot Networks: From Topology Control to Communication Aspects*, pp.168–201, World Scientific Publishing Company, 2014. ffhal-00917542f
19. Kaswan, K.S. and Dhatterwal, J.S., Machine learning and deep learning algorithm IoD, in: *The Internet of Drones: AI Application for Smart Solutions*, CRC Press, 2021.
20. Lima, P.U. and Custodio, M., Artificial intelligence and systems theory: Applied to cooperative robots. *Int. J. Adv. Robot. Syst.*, 1, 141–148, 2004.
21. Wei, X., Artificial intelligence in robot control systems. *IOP Conf. Ser. Mater. Sci. Eng.*, 363, 12–19, 2018.
22. Fox, D., Burgard, W., Kruppa, H., Thrun, S., A probabilistic approach to collaborative multi-robot localization. Special issue, *Autonomous Robots Heterogeneous Multi-Robot Syst.*, 8, 3, 325–344, 2000.

23. Prorok, A., Bahr, A., Martinoli, A., Low-cost collaborative localization for large scale multi-robot systems. *Proceedings–IEEE International Conference on Robotics and Automation*, pp. 4236–4241, 2012.
24. Wawerla, J. and Vaughan, R., A fast and frugal method for team-task allocation in a multi-robot transportation system. *Proceedings–IEEE International Conference on Robotics and Automation*, pp. 1432–1437, 2018.
25. Srinivsan, S., Singh, J., Kumar, V., Multi-agent-based decision support system using data mining and case based reasoning. *IJCSI*, 8, 4, 2, 1694–0814, July 2011.
26. Blum, C. and Li, X., Swarm intelligence in optimization, in: *Swarm Intelligence. Natural Computing Series*. Blum, C. and Merkle, D. (eds), Springer, Berlin, Heidelberg, 2008. https://doi.org/10.1007/978-3-540-74089-6_2.
27. Daugherty, P.R. and Wilson, H.J., Human + Machine: Reimagining work in the age of AI, Harvard Business Review Press, Audible Studios on Brilliance Audio, 2018.
28. Sun, S. and Chen, J., Knowledge representation and reasoning methodology based on CBR algorithm for modular fixture design. *J. Chin. Soc. Mech. Eng.*, 28, 6, 593–604, 2014.
29. Earl, C., The fuzzy systems handbook: A practitioner's guide to building, using, and maintaining fuzzy systems, *SIAM Rev.*, 37, 281–282, 1995.
30. Benyoucef, L. and Grabot, B., *Artificial Intelligence Techniques for Networked Manufacturing Enterprises Management*. Springer Series in Advanced Manufacturing, India, 2010.
31. Haupt, R. and Wiley, A., Algorithms practical genetic algorithms, John Wiley & Sons, Inc., Hoboken, New Jersey, 1998.
32. Bayindir, L. and Sah, E., A review of studies in swarm robotics. *Turk. J. Electr. Eng. Comput. Sci.*, 15, 115–147, 2007.
33. Baheci, I. and Sahin, E., Evolving aggregation behaviours for swarm robotic systems: A systematic case study. *Proceedings of IEEE Swarm Intelligence Symposium*, Pasadena, pp. 333–340, 2005.

14

An Overview of Enhancing Encryption Standards for Multimedia in Explainable Artificial Intelligence Using Residue Number Systems for Security

Akeem Femi Kadri[1], Micheal Olaolu Arowolo[2*], Ayisat Wuraola Yusuf-Asaju[3], Kafayat Odunayo Tajudeen[1] and Kazeem Alagbe Gbolagade[1]

[1]Department of Computer Science, Kwara State University, Malete, Nigeria
[2]Department of Computer Science, Landmark University, Omu-Aran, Nigeria
[3]Department of Information and Communication Science, University of Ilorin, Ilorin, Nigeria

Abstract

In spite of the increasing use of machine learning models in the applications of cyber-security, such as intrusion detection system (IDS), the vast majority of developed models are still considered black boxes. In order to improve conviction organization by permitting human specialists to grasp the basic data indication and fundamental perceptive, the use of eXplainable artificial intelligence (XAI) to interpret machine learning models has become increasingly important. Because of advancements in Internet technology and the development of efficient compression techniques, the security of digital video storage and transmission has recently gotten a lot of attention. The improvement has permitted the widespread use of video in a variety of strategies, as well as the communication of complex information, such as medical, military, and political secrets. These multimedia data are constantly subject to interception by hostile and unauthorized people all over the world when transmitted over an open network (Internet). Encryption, whether entire or selective encryption, is a frequently used and appropriate solution for tackling these security challenges. The entire video encryption strategy (also known as the Nave Approach) has been proven and demonstrated to provide a higher level of video security. However, because of its slowness in processing

**Corresponding author*: Arowolo.olaolu@gmail.com

Jyotir Moy Chatterjee, Harish Garg and R. N. Thakur (eds.) A Roadmap for Enabling Industry 4.0 by Artificial Intelligence, (247–274) © 2023 Scrivener Publishing LLC

huge amounts of video data, it is computationally expensive and so has limited applicability in video encryption. This research proposes methods for improving multimedia encryption standards in explainable artificial intelligence using residue number systems for security.

Keywords: Encryption, multimedia, RNS, security, decryption

14.1 Introduction

In current age, the fast development of wireless communication systems, individual communication systems, and smart card information makes suggestion more susceptible to misuse. The communication substance might be intercepted, or system services could be leveraged to deceive. Before these information systems are widely deployed in society, it is critical that they be made secure [62].

The growing problem of data and information security breaches has prompted major measures to ensure data and information security in electronic system communications. The effectiveness of security solutions is critical to the usage of modern automated e-commerce systems, net funding, e-government services, mobile business, Public Key Infrastructure, and other applications. When resource-constrained situations and real-time performance needs must be considered in IT systems, these security risks are amplified. As a result, substantial investigations in the computing aspects, networking, and steganography has been conducted on these IT security challenges [13].

Video data security for online and real-time multicasting multimedia commerce is critical. Traditional data encryption models, such as AES, DES among others, on the other hand, may not be suited for multimedia applications due to their incapability to meet the real-time limitations executed by applications of multimedia. Lightweight encryption methods are appropriate for video applications [17]. As more enterprises and transactions take place over less secure networks, communicating securely is becoming more important. In the early days of the internet, everyone knew who they were on the internet, and everyone was assumed to be trustworthy. However, times have changed, and it is now vital to encrypt and validate connections [47]. Fortunately, protocols have evolved to allow for the safe and secure sharing of information. Since the dawn of written communication, efforts have been focused on the advancement of secret communication techniques, a science known as cryptography [37, 38].

A public-key pair with a public-private keys are frequently utilized for detecting cryptologic procedures by employing asymmetric pair keys with a public-private key. For encoding and decoding, public-key uses that key couple. The public key is completely dispersed extensively and easily accessible by the public. The private key is not to be shared but kept private at all times [24].

Data encrypted with public keys may be deciphered individually through private-key when prearranged. Data encrypted with the private key, on the other hand, can only be decoded with the public key. Encryption and digital signatures are accomplished with this functionality. Protected communications, strong authentication, and message integrity are all possible with public-key cryptography [34].

Artificial intelligence (AI) is the future's most technological innovations. It is seeing increasing use in important smart city applications, such as transportation, education, healthcare, public governance, and power systems for data-driven decisions. Simultaneously, it is gaining prominence as a means of defending vital security infrastructure from threats, attacks, damage, or unwanted access. Numerous artificial intelligence (AI) applications can be beneficial, but may not be completely comprehended by human and engaged with the output in the manner essential by their framework [49]. Enabling AI to justify its decision could help to alleviate this problem. Understanding what humans need to make decisions and what knowledge the AI has can make obtainable in order to design operative understandable AI approaches. Explainable artificial intelligence's (XAI) purpose is to provide a way to explain the reason for the produced result. Using XAI, a new generation of AI techniques may be emerging. XAI provides a basic link between model features and outcome [29].

Residue number system (RNS), on the other hand, is a nonweighted numeral approach, that differs from other weighted number systems, including binary and fraction. Carry-free arithmetic processes, such as adding, deduction, and multiplication, are inherent in residue arithmetic. Each output digit is a role of one digit from respective operands, making it self-determining of all supplementary numbers. This characteristic contributes to a significant increase in processing speed, which is a key factor in cryptography applications [12].

For smaller and larger messages in multimedia, this study gives an overview study for encryption and decryption with some intrinsic qualities from the residue number system (RNS).

14.2 Reviews of Related Works

AI methods based on machine learning are opaque. Giving a perspective of AI's explainability challenge in this article, emphasizing its ethical importance, the permissible execution of a robust explainability prerequisite: officialdoms that choose to systematize decision making ought to be validly required to validate the ability to clarify and rationalize algorithmic choices affecting the security, truths, and openings of affected decisions. The demands of Rawlsian public reason can be used to deduce this legal obligation [29].

By analyzing public key cryptosystems and applying the residue number approach, it was suggested that an overview of public key cryptosystems be provided [18]. This public key cryptosystem can be utilized in an extensive variety of microelectronic gadgets, including personal computers, wireless mobile devices, smartcards, computer hardware security units, network applications, like gateways, routers, firewalls, and web server storages, as well as network appliances like routers, gateways, and firewalls. This paper delves into the details of public key cryptography and residue number systems, as well as their applications in data and information security.

For a secure TFTP protocol, symmetric encryption with preshared public parameters is proposed [32]. Advances in embedded system communication technologies have resulted in a scenario where practically all systems must now integrate security for data protection. Because of its speed and simplicity, the Trivial File Transfer Protocol (TFTP) is ideal for usage in fixed systems; but without security safeguards, it is vulnerable to a variety of assaults. For example, attackers can gain access to information and modify it during the upgrade of wireless access points (WAPs), then install malicious programs to disrupt the system. This paper offers a secure Diffie Hellman Key Exchange implementation in TFTP that uses preshared public constraints to allow revelries to obtain unique secret keys lacking possibility of man-in-the-middle (MITM) attacks. To drastically minimize computing requirements in TFTP communication, the implementation is coupled with compression and encryption technologies.

It was suggested that efficient fully homomorphic encryption from (Standard) be used, with encryption based on a new relinearization algorithm [9]. All earlier systems, on the other hand, were based on intricacy conventions about principles in several rings. They depart after every previous work's "squashing paradigm." They offer a new dimension-modulus reduction strategy that decreases the decryption intricacy of system lacking presenting extra conventions and shortens the ciphertexts. They employ our approach to build asymptotical effective LWE-based-single-server-private information retrieval (PIR) procedure because its ciphertexts are relatively short. Achieving security contrary to temporal opponents, their protocol's communication complexity is bits per single-bit query.

An accounting data encryption with data encryption standard algorithm was proposed [14], The DES procedure is a block encryption procedure for encrypting and decrypting 64-bit packet information. The real key length is 56 bits since apiece eighth bit key is utilized as an equivalence bit. The algorithm structure for encryption and decryption is similar, the sequence where subkeys are utilized is inverted. Keying 64-bit plain text can yield 64-bit ciphertext yield in the controller of subkeys; alternatively, entering 64-bit ciphertext can yield 64-bit plaintext. The DES algorithm's privacy is determined, and a small percentage of secrets are deemed weak, which are readily evaded in applied implementations. The 3DES algorithm is a torrent of DES procedure, it uses the same encryption mechanism as the DES method. This article describes the DES algorithm's encryption process and introduces the 3DES algorithm's components. The results of the experiments reveal 3DES encryption has an improved encryption outcome. Furthermore, the 3DES encryption efficacy is yet to be significantly impacted. To some extent, the 3DES encryption method realizes an encryption operation per time, it resists in-depth exploration outbreaks, by improving DES algorithm's safekeeping.

Analyzing the basic notions of FHE, actual implementation, state-of-the-art strategies, drawbacks, merits, problems, application areas, and application frameworks concentrating on neural networks proposed [40]. FHE development has made significant strides in recent years. However, practitioners looking for suitable implementations nearly entirely address existing research in homomorphic neural networks. It still lacks in-depth and detailed evaluations. They concentrate on privacy-preserving homomorphic encoding cryptosystems for neural networks, recognizing present keys, unresolved concerns, encounters, openings, and investigate prospects.

The use of the genetic algorithm with residual numbers is presented as a new text encryption and decryption scheme. As a consequence of the rise of digital computers and communication, data security is a key problem that are involved in communication, particularly in cyberspace [38]. The genetic algorithm (GA) among intrinsic qualities from RNS are used to create a revolutionary three-incrusted text encryption and decryption technique proficient for encoding and decoding a little character or representation. The suggested system's simulation findings show that it is chaotic to the eye, a huge key interplanetary collected at various phases of the organization, with a high data rate while encrypting both tiny and large communications.

Reviews on key(s), as well as keyless image encryption procedures, was suggested [45]. The use of digital data and images has grown in recent years, maintaining secure picture transmission has become increasingly important. Picture encryption is used to make image applications more secure. This study presents a survey of several picture encryption approaches that are currently in use. The focus of the study is on two categories of image encryption: image encryption with keys and lacking keys. It similarly goes over some of the characteristics of an effective picture encryption scheme. The document provides an overview of the most widely used algorithms and research papers in the field of picture encryption.

A look at video encryption algorithms used at different stages of compression video data safety is perilous for online multimedia commerce and immediate video multicasting [44]. Traditional data encryption algorithms like the DES, AES, on the other hand, may not be suited for multimedia applications owing to their failure to meet the present limitations executed by multimedia claims. Lightweight encryption methods are appropriate for video applications. This research investigates the use of encryption algorithms at various levels of compression. This real-time video compression and encryption provides security for applications such as video conferencing, investigation TV camera information shield, and so on. The examination of adding numerous encryption algorithms in the compression phases, such as transformation and coding stages, was provided using the generic structure of a video encoder.

Safe health information broadcast in IoT-based dispersed schemes using memetic optimization and cryptographic encryption. The IoT dispersed technologies in the healthcare sector is a critical character in exchanging health-associated documents and information between enterprises to diminish medical test imitation [44]. Because this information is sensitive, it is imperative that the exciting contents be transformed in a secure manner. The memetic algorithm, an evolutionary algorithm, is utilized to encrypt the text communications in this paper. Discrete wavelet transform 1 then 2 levels are then used to inject the encrypted data into the medical images. When retrieving a hidden message from an encoded letter, the memetic algorithm's reverse technique is used. Five RGB photos and grayscale pictures are utilized to evaluate the suggested method to illustrate its precision. The proposed algorithm's findings were assessed using numerical procedures, and demonstrated the relevance of information transmission in a stable environment in healthcare systems. It can be enhanced with blockchain technology in the impending to include the privacy-preserving of health data.

Insider threat detection in the workplace has long been a prominent topic of study. Human emotional states are discovered using a variety of physiological signs such as the galvanic membrane retort, electro-cardiogram, and electro-encephalogram to aid distinguish probable insider coercions (EEG). This research describes an insider risk assessment system that uses EEG brain-wave indications and explicable deep and machine learning procedures to recognize anomalous EEG indicators suggesting a probable insider danger besides assess capability for burden. With an emotive perception EEG equipment through five probes, to be cost-operative. Data were collected from 17 persons in various emotional states for this investigation. The various emotional levels were recorded and grouped into: small, regular, average, and high. The information was gathered although the participants showed several pictures from the methodical worldwide emotional image system. Removing noise from corporal activities and alternating, the EEG signals were preprocessed. The data was then utilized to train using two and one-dimensional CNN, as well as other algorithms, with classification accuracies of 96% [5].

Current breakthroughs in machine and deep learning, this study gives a short-term investigative evaluation of existing works in respect to explainability of AI. A transitory antique outline and classification is proposed with frames of fundamental issues in relations of explainability, based on the four principles of explainability recently proposed by the National Institute of Standards. Methods pertaining to the topic that have recently been published are then disparagingly assessed and investigated. In conclusion, new research orders are recommended [7].

Understanding humans need for decision making and AI knowledge make accessible in order to design operative explainable AI approaches to meet this necessity. This paper shows how to capture such needs using an example. We look at how a cyber defense team's operational planner (senior human analyst) can utilize a junior expert cybernetic mediator to scan, investigate, and provide information on susceptibilities and occurrences on the goal and similar systems. They investigated the relations essential to comprehend yields and participate extra human knowledge. This is an example of how XAI can be integrated into a real-world bi-directional workflow: to construct an idea and transitory it up the knowledge cable, the senior expert wants to be intelligent to grasp the advanced analyst's outcomes, mostly the traditions and suggestions. The app is a partnership involving junior analyzer machines and expert sentient researchers to develop awareness of risks, exposures, occurrences, probable outcome intrusions, and solutions on the expedition cyberspace domain to which their group has been committed [21].

The most of machine learning methods are considered as data recorder, view of the increasing use of certain algorithms in computer security solutions (for instance, an intrusion detection system (IDS)). Through use of eXplainable Artificial Intelligence (XAI) to comprehend machine-learning algorithm is becoming more essential in order to increase authentication schemes by permitting expert systems to understand the data structure verification and scientific analysis. Rendering to IDS, trust management's important duty is to comprehend the impact of harmful data in order to detect any system intrusion. The accurateness of the several categorization methods for confidence in IDS was the focus of prior investigations. They rarely disclose information about their actions and reasoning that is provided by the advanced algorithm. As a result, we explored the decision tree model in the extent of IDS in this study to address the XAI idea to enhance trust management. For IDS, we employ basic decision tree algorithms that are easy to understand and uniform approximate a social method to decision making by breaking the optimal down to numerous slight subchoices. Their method was tested by mining rules from a well-known KDD target dataset. They associated the decision tree method's accuracy to other state-of-the-art procedures [30].

Image security and digital video watermarking using a residual chaotic system in the ever-evolving field of multimedia technology, data security has emerged as a significant issue [60]. When creating chaotic systems, traditional chaotic systems typically demand greater bit-width reiterative controls to alter the cohort degree of chaotic systems. To carry out this work, they suggested a ubiquitous residual chaotic system (RCS) for picture encryption in various multimodal machine vision domains. They can use residue number system (RNS), which again is widely used for VLSI, to build huge synthetic data by initializing an operands linear combination it over in Galois Field (GF). Further, they were using the Box-Muller algorithm to produce RCS that drastically accelerates the R/B reverse transition process. Experiments revealed that indeed the secret susceptibility and textual susceptibility of the recommended encryption key can both be acceptable, and so the technique could cipher pictures quickly and successfully. After that, we recommended a hologram steganographic methodology utilizing blocking selecting. Regarding the key unique evaluation parameters, the 4×4 illumination blocks are classified into five groups, and the corresponding sorts of frames are selected. When studying the performance characteristics of encrypted cipher pictures, combining quantitative and intensity evaluations, many of the findings suggest that their approach has acceptable uniqueness and reliability. The video encoder rate of growth within a specified tolerance, the transparency is strong, and the steganography potential have indeed been substantially increased. The mark is secure and robust, which include reencoding interference, outage probability, and Probabilistic minimal filtration. Conventional techniques are significantly slower, inefficient, and insecure than the algorithms they suggest. As a consequence, it is a reasonable alternative technique for a wide range of communication situations.

In the residue number system, it was recommended to use floating-point arithmetic for coding process [23]. The RNS is recognized because of its concurrent computing, which has been used in such a broad variety of important purposes in previous decades, notably wavelet transform, neural network, decryption, and increased computations. But, in the other end, comparability, sign recognition, overflowing prevention, and split are indeed challenging to manage in RNS. Several solutions for this kind of approaches existing in the literature primarily help local dynamic ranges (down to a few scores of bits), rendering it mainly useful in reduced workloads. Subsequently, a method is introduced which enables for the implementation of unbounded moduli collections having encryption keys extended dynamic variations of approximately to so many thousands of bits. This approach distinguishes through others in how it requires quite on high-speed typical floating-point procedures, making it ideal for implementations and inexpensive to develop on a diverse range of fundamental solutions that require IEEE 754 computation. In this research, they generalize this strategy and show how it is used to develop successful RNS information blocks, which including computing the maximal value of an aggregate of RNS values on gpu hardware. Thus, according their analytical outcomes on either an NVIDIA RTX 2080 GPU. the proposed method improves execution runtime by 39 % and storage utilization by 13 percent compared toward a mixed-radix converter technique for arbitrary residues as well as a 128-moduli set with a 2048-bit pixel density.

FPGA-based effective binary-to-residue-number transformation topology. The most fascinating hypothetical examination field (RNS) has become the residue number system [59]. Its prominence is due to inadequate of carry propagation in between the conceptual pieces. A crucial stage in the implementation of any modules procedure is conversion from RNS to binary. RNS is extensively used for existing data transmission and interactive applications key improvements, notably low energy consumption, fast response, and consistency. Throughout many contexts, the transformation of the results from residue to binaries is critical to developing information architectures based on residual computation. This paper introduces a new framework for concurrent forward transformation of signed numbers (residue to binary numbers). The mapping of this predicted design on FPGA was also addressed in this paper, demonstrating that it is quite effective on FPGA technology.

In ternary valued logic, a novel moduli set aimed at residue number system was proposed, because it offer parallel, high-speed, carry-free, and low-power arithmetic, designed for digital signal processing (DSP) [22]. The moduli set is one of the most significant factors to consider while constructing RNS systems. Due to dynamic range, system's speed, and hardware complexity are all influenced by the moduli's shapes and numbers. Novel moduli set, 3^n-2, 3^n-1, 3^n, was proposed. These moduli set with pairwise prime moduli, allowing for the widest dynamic series conceivable. Ternary valued logic (TVL) is a probable real replacement for traditional binary logic for creating logic and arithmetic circuitry (BL). Using TVL, the microchip length and cumulative latency can reduce. For all these moduli sets, the connected connections are calculated basically in ternary estimated logic, also arithmetic within those moduli sets benefits from exceptionally fast procedures, as well as simple reverse-forward alteration (RNS to TVL *vis-à-vis*). Lexical cohesion that may be made important progress such as range and temporal complexities.

Filtering with a digital FIR system and a residue number system [36] RNS is a modular arithmetic system where there are no interdigit carries when adding or multiplying two numbers. Incorporating RNS arithmetic into digital filter implementations can result in significant speed gains. In this investigation, they use RNS computing to create variable amplitude (FIR) computational filtration on microcontrollers. Four 8-bit broad sense microcontrollers were used to produce a three-moduli microprocessor. The consequences of a linear system FIR filter were included on this processing unit.

RNS-based parallel transmission system employing rotationally symmetric signal transduction provides software's characterization and backdrop of the RNS arithmetic, and even the summative assessment of the RNS arithmetic, by means of non-redundant and redundant moduli orthogonal transmission-based approaches throughout an additive noise (AWGN) medium [28]. Redundant RNS codes have been used to protect sensitive information that is conveyed. This novel program's analyzing components are not exclusive to those found in standard trackers. Even before residue numbers are transformed back to binary codes, a specific adjudication method named as a ratio statistic test is established, and comprises eliminating several of the lowered analog circuitry outcomes. This improves the efficiency of the process.

This strategy varies from standard "errors and reversals" deciphering, which requires the computation and filling of the obliterated signals (or bits) during the decryption process. They suggest that its analog waveform content can be regained by interpreting the saved or undiscarded codes, based on the principles of RNS arithmetic. The numerical findings demonstrate that the technique suggested is a high-efficiency equivalent broadcast approach for high-bit-rate message, with a coding advance of 2-dB over AWGN channels and a bit error rate of 10X6.

Detecting and Correcting Recurrent Errors By using Chinese Remainder Theorem and a Redundant Residue Number System (CRT) [2]. The Redundant-Residue Number System (R-RNS) is being used to illustrate a record low technique for detecting and correcting numerous errors. RRNS is made by merging many redundant residues, giving it the ability to identify and rectify errors. The Chinese Remainder Theorem (CRT) and a novel approach are used in the proposed multiple error correction strategy to considerably streamline the integer error-correcting procedure. The result is bit better from the recent advancements, whereby the error signal is predicted to use an iterative algorithm such as mixed integer, as well as the suggested multi error-correcting approaches do not really involve extensive loops to fix the problems.

RNS novel approach to data-path advancement for low-power, as well as high-performance DSP applications, was proposed. The inflexibility of instruction planning sets an upmarket leading processors and microprocessors, which became a main impediment to developing RNS-based models [12]. Technological advancements in semiconductor technology have reignited interest in RNS for application-specific computing in recent years. RNS computations are appealing and also relevant in recent applications of digital signal processing, due to at least two distinct causes. To begin with, RNS's modular and distributive qualities are employed to boost performance, particularly in evolving circulated and pervasive computing stands like wireless ad hoc networks, cloud, as well as applications that demand soft error tolerance. Second, given the ongoing compression of corresponding metal oxide semiconductor (CMOS) digital cohesive circuits, energy efficiency becomes a crucial driver. The grade of computing correspondence in RNS provides choice for optimizing energy performance, especially for length of long word arithmetic, like cryptographic algorithms used for implementation of hardware. The goal of this presentation is to demonstrate this revolution by highlighting recent RNS developments and encouraging the creative usage of RNS for new applications. Various RNS applications are studied in order to show unusual number system might be used to profit implementation.

The antiquity residue number system has reawakened scholarly attention recently, and it has evolved as an intriguing competitor in the realm of safe embedded applications [52]. Furthermore, throughout this review, we look at certain recent and unusual RNS applications in postquantum encryption, cyber architecture, and asymmetric cryptography. We look at how to include residue arithmetic into these approaches, including how to automate secure and stable RNS cloud platforms. This assessment should function as a practical guide to residue arithmetic, as well as providing directions for future research and outstanding issues that RNS could effectively solve.

Over the years, a significant amount of study on RNS and efficient cryptosystems for multimedia has been recommended employing RNS arithmetic for Cryptography, although RNS has been widely used in RSA coding. Recently, studies on RNS's underlying image security have looked in the literature, considerably contributive to the growth of RNS-based cryptosystems as a practicable design alternative. New RNS applications have recently been proposed in the disciplines of networking, SDN, and cloud computing. This old mathematical method provides a wealth of fresh study possibilities. This paper examines the classic design issues of RNS arithmetic in cryptography and expands on the discussion to incorporate novel RNS applications in cryptography and multimedia.

14.3 Materials and Methods

A moving picture is created by a sequence of images from a visual multimedia source. Frames are another name for these graphics. The resolutions and frames per second of a multimedia can vary (FPS). Multimedia resolution refers to the number of pixels each frame, whereas FPS refers to the number of frames per second that change. The intricacy of the procedure, data transmission interruption, node energy consumption, and added features all have a role in data transmission dependability. It is critical to have a dependable RNS that can increase information transmission reliability, reduce the complexity of decoding with correctness, and perform well using a large number of simulations [10].

14.3.1 Multimedia

The term "multimedia content encryption" refers to the use of either classic or new encryption techniques to safeguard multimedia content. Until now, several data encryption algorithms, for example RSA, AES, or IDEA, have been suggested and widely used, with the majority of them being utilized in binary as well as text data. It is tough to directly use with multimedia data because they frequently have a lot of redundancy, is huge, and requires real-time activities like presenting, copying, cutting, bit rate conversion, among other things. Unique multimedia content are typically turned into encoded multimedia contents with the use of encryption method controlled by an encryption key [15]. The encrypted information can be disseminated over the network as well as the terminus; encrypted multimedia material is decoded using the decryption algorithm through decryption key to reveal the original multimedia content. Multimedia encryption knowledge was originally described 1980s to 1990s, it became a popular study area. There are three stages to its development: compressed data encryption, raw data encryption, and partial encryption. There were insufficient multimedia encrypting solutions for raw data proposed before the 1990s [15]. Multimedia encryption has traditionally relied on picture element scrambling or variation, in which the image or audiovisual is transposed to produce unreadable data. To permute picture or video data, early encryption algorithms, such as space filling curves and Euro-crypto are utilized, which confound the relationship between adjacent image pixels or video pixels. These approaches have a low computational complexity and are inexpensive. Furthermore, the permutation process alters the relationship between adjacent pixels, making future compression techniques ineffective [15].

Wireless multimedia sensor networks will play a key part in the Internet of Things, offering rich content for an endless variety of monitoring and control situations. As more applications rely on multimedia data, security problems have grown, and novel techniques to securing such networks have emerged. However, the regular processor, memory, and energy limits of multimedia-based sensors have created new hurdles for data encryption, leading to the development of new security techniques [15].

Network security has typically relied on encryption schemes. Encryption analysis techniques like the Data Encryption (DES), the Advanced Encryption (AES), the Rivest, Shamir, and Adelman (RSA), the Triple DES (3DES), the International Data Encryption Algorithms (IDEA), and Scalable Encryption Algorithm (SEA) all perform on digital signals of input information. In many other circumstances, if whether additional data is audio, video, texts, or images, the encryption situation repeats. When metadata are not in actual time, these can be treated as a standard binary stream, and the methods described can be applied. When a number of constraints are involved, achieving multidimensional information integrity can be difficult [15].

Because of current advancements in computing network technology, the distribution of digital interactive program content via the cyberspace is huge. However, the increased number of digital documents, processing equipment, and the global accessibility of Internet entree has formed an ideal intermediate for restricted rights scheme and rebellious multimedia content dissemination. Protecting academic possessions of multimedia content on compact disk networks is become a crucial requirement. Multimedia data types encompass a large number of different data kinds. There are several types of information classified as cooperative media information. These are frequently used in the construction of mineral-summarized mixed media scenarios, stages, or coordinating apparatuses [56]. The fundamental classifications are as follows: texts; The assembly where contents are deposited can transform dramatically. Aside from ASCII credentials, contents are frequently stored in processor accounts, databases, records, and annotations on larger media items. With the approachability and proliferation of graphical user interfaces (GUIs), as well as content textual styles. The job of storing content is becoming more complex, allowing for improvements (shades, shading ...).

For still photographs, there is a huge difference in quality and storage capacity. Digitalized images are a series of pixels that correspond to a certain location in the client's graphical display. JPEG, PNG, BMP, and tiff are the most common image formats. Audio is an undoubtedly well-known information type that is coordinated in the majority of usage. It is a true space condenser. A single second of sound might require up to 2-3 megabytes of storage space. To pack it in the right order, a few ways are used.

From a user's perspective, media equipment provides a number of essential benefits, including increased completion time, reduced calculation and expense, well-organized data storage capacity. Cost: Media compute provides cost effective armed to its service providers by efficiently multiplexing media inside such as video, picture, and audio using a common infrastructure, server utilization, optimization, virtualization, mobility, and routine processing. In our local system, there is no requirement for actually acquiring a communications or reserve, which reduces the cost. Compatibility: Media enables the media to be accessed from anywhere using any smart device. Storage: Media knowledge has a variety of options for storing media content that generates revenue. It is also safer because the store's media material will be duplicated without the need for manual intervention.

Multimedia's drawbacks include the following: expensive, difficult to configure, and not only compatible.

14.3.2 Artificial Intelligence and Explainable Artificial Intelligence

When compared to traditional model-based optimization, one major difficulty with AI is a lack of knowledge and trust. Deep reinforcement learning, for example, is unable to describe the basic characteristics that influence actions. This flaw is the most serious, and it has an impact on cyber-security trust management (e.g., malicious vehicle identification). Furthermore, recent research has demonstrated that Bayesian inference is extremely vulnerable to insufficient data. As a result, the need for statistical AI algorithms to measure uncertainty is rising, particularly when it comes to connecting huge data inputs and procedure design to predicted wireless key performance metrics (KPIs). Rather than attempting to develop computational AI algorithms intrinsically explainable, a recent surge of interest in "explainable AI," in which computational AI algorithms are developed to elucidate the AI black-box paradigm. As a result, dependable AI describes its conclusions such that a human expert can comprehend the fundamental data indication and connecting cognitive [3].

Recently, AI has shown to be a significant achievement by exceeding expectations in a variety of applications. The grouping of effective learning procedures and their large parametric space accounts for the experimental accomplishment of machine learning (ML) models. Because the parametric learning space is made up of hundreds of layers and millions of parameters, ML and DL models are termed complicated black-box models. Due to the models' black-box nature, AI professionals (e.g., engineers and developers) must seek a direct grasp of the method by which they work. Transparency, is the polar reverse of model black-box, is increasingly expected to reduce the risk of making unjustifiable decisions that does not permit for full descriptions of their performance. Binary forecasts are examples of insufficiency in precision medicine because of the sensitivity of pharmaceutical drugs to patients. In terms of cyber-security, false predictions might expose systems to attacks leading to zero-trust security for important systems [51].

As a result, the focus of contemporary AI research has shifted to the topic of explainable AI, which is critical for increasing the applied distribution of AI-based solutions. Consideration of interpretability during the creation of AI-based solutions can help them be more implementable because interpretability aids independence in decision making, detecting and correcting predisposition in the training dataset (imbalanced dataset); interpretability improves resilience of AI-based results by exposing latent argumentative agitations that can cause predictions to shift; by giving eloquent variable interpretation and connection of model cognitive; interpretability increases the faith in AI-based solutions. The following characteristics can be used to classify description methods and methodologies for AI and ML interpretability: in-model, premodel, and postmodel; inherent and post hoc; model-precise and model-uncertainty; and so on [19]. Feature engineering and a rule-based model investigates the decision tree technique for recognizing the features of malicious attacks in order to improve IDS conviction.

14.3.3 Cryptography

Cryptography is used to secure multimedia. In reality, several cryptographic fundamentals are employed as building blocks (primitives) for multimedia security applications. Cryptography is the study of techniques (referred to as cryptosystems) that are used to achieve the following objectives: nonrepudation, confidentiality, data integrity, authentication cryptanalysis is the study of ways for breaking existing cryptosystems. Because cryptography and cryptanalysis are so intertwined, cryptology is often referred to as a combined study of cryptography and cryptanalysis [4].

There are a variety of cryptography algorithms available for various reasons, and some of them are in use on the Internet to provide secure communications. As sensor nodes get more capable, and security concerns become more widespread in WSN situations, several of those techniques are being directly used or adapted for wireless sensor networks [4].

Cryptography, which literally translates to "undisclosed script," is the art of changing messages for secure and impenetrable to unlicensed users. Cipher text refers to the original data/message before it is modified. Encoding is the procedure of altering plaintext to encryption text, and decipherment is the process of converting cipher text back to plaintext. The sender employs an encryption algorithm, whereas the recipient employs a decryption algorithm. As a result, encryption and decryption assist in the secure transmission of messages as well as the protection of messages from unauthorized users. Symmetric key, asymmetric key, and hash cryptography algorithms are the three types of cryptography algorithms [55].

Cryptography using Symmetric (Secret) Keys This cryptographic approach employs two separate methods for encryption and decryption, with the transmitter and receiver both using the same key. The transmitter encrypts data with this key and an encryption method, and the receiver decrypts the data with the same key and the associated decryption algorithm [27]. The following are some examples of commonly used Symmetric key cryptography algorithms.

Advanced encryption standard (AES): a symmetric block encryption standard established by the National Institute of Standards and Technology (NIST) that is used to secure data. Encryption and decryption are done with the same key. It features a changeable key length of 128, 192, or 256 bits, with 256 being the default. It encrypts 128-bit data blocks in 10, 12, or 14 rounds, depending on the key size [57].

Data encryption standard (DES) is a symmetric block encryption standard endorsed by the National Institute of Standards and Technology (NIST). The DES encryption algorithm is the most widely used encryption technique on the planet. With slight modifications, the same algorithm and key are utilized for encryption and decryption. DES takes a 64-bit long plain-text, a 56-bit (8 bits of parity) as input and produces a 64-bit block as output [35].

The 3DES Triple Data Encryption Algorithm (TDEA or Triple DEA) is a symmetric-key block cipher standard that is identical to DES but triples the encryption level. As a result, this approach is slower than other block ciphers. 3DES uses a 64-bit block size and a 192-bit key size [42].

BLOWFISH: Blowfish is a symmetric key cryptographic technique that encodes 64-bit blocks with keys ranging from 128 to 448 bits in length. In terms of throughput and power consumption, Blowfish outperforms other algorithms [64].

RC4: The RC4 (Rivest Cipher 4) is a public key stream cipher technique that requires the secure exchange of a shared key. Standards such as IEEE 802.11 use the RC4 encryption method with 40 and 128-bit keys in WEP (Wireless Encryption Protocol). The cipher uses a secret internal state that is divided into two sections to generate the key stream: Two 8-bit index-pointers and a variation of all 256 imaginable bytes (signified "i" and "j"). The key-scheduling algorithm is used to initialize the permutation using a variable length key, characteristically amid 40 and 256 bits (KSA) [58].

Asymmetric (public) Key Cryptography (Asymmetric) Key Cryptography (Asymmetric) Key Cryptography (Asymmetric). This cryptographic approach employs two separate encryption and decryption methods, as well as a public key for encryption and a private key for decryption. The message is encrypted by the sender using his or her public key. With the use of a private key, the recipient decrypts the cipher text [16]. The following are some of the most extensively used Asymmetric key cryptography algorithms:

Rivest-Shamir-Adleman (RSA) is a widely used asymmetric encryption/decryption method that uses a public key and a private key. Every person has entree to the public key, used to encrypt messages. Messages that have been encrypted with the public key can only be decrypted using the private key. It protected user data by encrypting it before storing it, requiring user authentication before storing or retrieving it, and establishing secure data transport channels. The RSA algorithm is run using a 4096-bit key size. The RSA algorithm entails three steps: key generation, encryption, and decryption [1].

DIFFIE-HELLMAN: Whitfield Diffie and Martin Hellman initially announced the scheme in 1976. Diffie–Hellman key exchange is a specific type of cryptographic key exchange. It allows two people with no prior knowledge of one another to create a shared secret key together across an unsecure communication channel. A symmetric key cipher can then be used to encode subsequent communications using this key [26].

PAILLIER: An asymmetric algorithm, the Paillier cryptosystem. Its homomorphic possessions permits this system to perform regular addition operations on numerous encrypted values to produce the encrypted sum, which can then be decrypted without knowing the values that made up the sum [53].

Cryptography based on hashing Hash functions are a key building block in the field of cryptography, and they are utilized in a wide range of applications such as message integrity and authentication, digital signatures, secure time stamping, and a slew of others. A hash function H is a computationally efficient technique that takes an arbitrary-length message M and possibly a fixed-length key K (in the case of a keyed hash function) as inputs and produces a fixed-length output D known as the message digest. $D = H(K, M)$ D stands for Message Output, K is for Fixed Key Length, and M stands for Input Message Length. The following is a list of some of the most often used Hashing cryptographic algorithms [50].

MD5: MD5 (Message Digest5) is a cryptographic hash function with a 128-bit hash value that is widely used. It converts a variable-size message into a 128-bit output with a fixed length. The input message is broken into 512-b block chunks, and then the message is padded to make it divisible by 512. In this case, the sender encrypts the message with the recipient's public key, and the receiver decrypts it with its private key [48].

MD6 is a cryptographic hash function that uses the MD6 Message-Digest Algorithm. MD6 employs a significantly different tree-based manner of operation that allows for increased parallelism. MD6 can be thought of as a tree-like structure, with a 4-to-1 compression algorithm reducing the message's overall length at each level [11].

Secure Hashing Algorithm (SHA): SHA (Secure Hashing Algorithm) is a hashing algorithm. The SHA-1 hash function is the most widely used SHA hash function, although it will be gradually supplanted by the newer and stronger SHA-2 hash function. TLS, SSL, SSH, and PGP are just a few of the apps that use it now. SHA1 generates a 160-bit digest of any file or input of any size. The SHA-256 technique generates a 256-bit (32-byte) hash that is nearly unique. This makes it ideal for password verification, challenge hash authentication, anti-tampering, and digital signatures. SHA-256 is one of the most powerful hash functions known, and it is one of the successor hashes functions to SHA-1. 32-bit words were used to compute SHA-256 hash functions [41].

14.3.4 Encryption and Decryption

Encryption is the process of converting information, such as a file or a mail message, into cipher text, which is unreadable without a decoding key, so that only the intended receiver can read it [25].

Decryption is the process of turning encoded data back to its original unencrypted form. In cryptography, a key is a long string of bits that encryption and decryption techniques use [54]. A hypothetical 40-bit key is represented by the following example: 10101001 10011110 00011100 01010101.

Information can be shown as a variety of numbers, letters, or symbols, depending on the type of encryption used. Cryptography professionals make it their mission to encrypt data or break codes in order to get encrypted data. The usage of encryption software is required for manual encryption. These are computer programs that digitally encrypt various bits of data. Manual encryption necessitates the user's full engagement. The files to encrypt are selected, and then an encryption type is selected from a list provided by the security system [63].

Transparent Encryption: Another sort of computer software encryption is transparent encryption. It may be downloaded into a computer and used to automatically encrypt everything. Because it does not leave anything that might be forgotten when employing manual encryption, it is one of the most critical secure methods of encryption available. Every executable program and file created on the computer has an encrypted copy that can resist power surges and safeguards data in the event that the computer is stolen [46].

Symmetric Encryption: The entire encryption process is carried out by a computer software application. You may simply encrypt data on your own. Symmetric encryption is one of the simplest ways to accomplish this. In this case, a letter or number in the encryption code corresponds to another letter or number. You may encrypt any written text by substituting letters and numbers for their corresponding coded counterparts [6].

Asymmetric Encryption: Asymmetric encryption is a safe and simple method of encrypting data that you will receive. It is usually done on a computer. A public key can be provided to anyone or put anywhere for everyone to view. They can use the key to encrypt information and send it to you. When drafting emails, this is a common practice. This means that after encrypting the data with the public key, it can only be read by those who have access to the private key [24].

Symmetric Decryption: In symmetric encryption, the material is encrypted and decrypted using the same mathematical equation. A simple letter substitution cipher, such as A=B, B=C, and so on, is symmetrical because the procedure is simply reversed to decrypt the message. If you use symmetric encryption to send a message, the recipients must also have the key to decrypt it [43].

Asymmetric Decryption: Asymmetric decryption, often known as public-key decryption, employs a scheme based on two connected keys. In this system, anything encoded with one key must be decrypted with the other key, and so forth. When you encrypt a message with someone's public key, you know that it can only be read by someone who has the associated private key [61].

Hashing: Hashing is an encryption method that employs a one-way encryption key. If you hash a certain amount of data, you will have a unique output string, but it will be hard to reconstruct the data from the string. You can validate the data by re-encoding it and comparing it to the returned string. This can be used as a sort of encoding error correction. When you hash a message and provide that value to your correspondents, you assure that they can hash the message and compare the values for themselves. Recipients know the message is complete and unaltered if the two output strings match [39].

14.3.5 Residue Number System

RNS is a collection of integer illustrations ("residue numbers" or "residue codes") and rules for addition, deducting, and multiplying them. An RNS enables hardware implementations in which an integer is represented in parallel by multiple independent tiny arithmetic units. Each arithmetic unit does addition, subtraction, and multiplication simultaneously and independently, without the use of carries, borrows, or partial products. These operations can be completed quickly, in a timeframe that is largely independent of the operation and operands. The congruence relation, which is defined as follows, is the foundation of residue number systems [33].

The residue number system (RNS) is an unweighted, carry-free number system that allows for extremely fast, parallel, and fault-tolerant operations. As a result, it is a tough contender for digital signal processing (DSP) applications that require high performance, low power, and fault tolerance. Digital filters, digital communications, discrete Fourier transform (DFT), image processing, and video coding are all examples of applications where addition, subtraction, and multiplication are important. The RNS, on the other hand, could not be widely implemented in general-purpose processors because activities like division, sign detection, magnitude comparison, and overflow detection are difficult to implement and can have a negative impact on the design's overall performance. Many solutions for these difficult operations have been proposed [31].

The residue-to-binary converter (reverse converter (RC)) is used by the majority of them. This component represents the majority of the RNS's overhead. Choosing the right moduli set, on the other hand, is another crucial aspect of creating an effective RNS with enough dynamic range (DR) If m divides exactly the difference of x and y, two integers a and b are said to be congruent modulo m; it is customary, especially in mathematics tests, to write x ≡ y (mod n) to represent this. For example, 10≡7 (mod 3); 10≡4 (mod 3); 10≡1 (mod 3), and 10≡2 (mod 3). We will suppose that the number n is a modulus or base, and that its values exclude unity, which creates only trivial congruences. If a and b are the quotient and remainder, respectively, of the integer division of a by n|, x = a.n+ b, then we get x≡ b by definition (mod n). The number r is known as the residual of a with regard to n, and it is commonly written as b = xn. The set of least positive residues modulo m refers to the set of n minimum values that the residue can take, such as {0, 1, 2, . . . n} and so on. Assume we have a collection of N positive and pairwise approximately prime moduli, {n1, n2,....., nM}. Let N be the moduli's product. Then, in the residue number system, every number A < N has a unique representation, which is the set of residues {inA : 1≤ i ≤ M} [20].

In the modeling of a residue number system, the moduli must be capable of efficient representation and balance. Consider the following scenario to better understand the efficient representation. Let us say the moduli are 13 and 17. This set has a dynamic range of 221 and requires 4 and 5 bits to represent the relevant residues, respectively. The representational efficiency for this choice of moduli is low, as the two moduli are 13/16 and 17/32, respectively. The conversion of residue to decimal has some speed constraints. The Chinese remainder theorem (CRT) and mixed radix conversion are two unique methods for residue to decimal conversion (MRC) [8].

14.4 Discussion and Conclusion

Various options for safeguarding information with residue arithmetic in security applications with artificial intelligence were described in this paper. We showed how RNS has become a feasible implementation option for the most widely used public-key systems, such as encryption and decryption. Although RNS makes it simple to do basic arithmetic operations like addition and multiplication. However, other operations are more difficult to implement. Division, magnitude comparison, sign determination, scaling, and overflow detection are some of the unimplementable or difficult-to-implement functions. Although there is work being done in this area to have these processes done using the residue number system, so that the system emerges as a better option for data processing in the rising technology. Without a doubt, the success of machine learning techniques is critical to the growth of AI. It will open the way for smart city applications to manage high-frequency, real-time data. However, it is difficult to see how such strategies function in the context of highlighting. To battle any cyber security issues, this is a must. If any AI-based cyber security component lacks forensic value and remains a black box, it loses credibility faster than the rest. As a result, XAI plays a critical role in assuring the security, privacy, and trustworthiness of smart city deployments.

References

1. Abid, R., Iwendi, C., Javed, A.R., Rizwan, M., Jalil, Z., Anajemba, J.H., Biamba, C., An optimised homomorphic CRT-RSA algorithm for secure and efficient communication. *Pers. Ubiquit. Comput.*, 1, 1–14, 2021. https://doi.org/10.1007/s00779-021-01607-3.
2. Aremu, I.A. and Gbolagade, K.A., Redundant residue number system based multiple error detection and correction using chinese remainder theorem

(CRT). *Software Eng.* (Science Publishing Group), 5, 5, 72, 2017. https://doi.org/10.11648/j.se.20170505.12.

3. Abiodun, O., II, Jantan, A., Omolara, A.E., Dada, K.V., Mohamed, N.A., Arshad, H., State-of-the-art in artificial neural network applications: A survey. *Heliyon*, 4, 11, e00938, 2018. https://doi.org/10.1016/j.heliyon.2018.e00938.
4. Abomhara, M., Khalifa, O.O., Zakaria, O., Zaidan, A.A., Zaidan, B.B., O. Alanazi, H., Suitability of using symmetric key to secure multimedia data: An overview. *J. Appl. Sci.*, 10, 15, 1656–1661, 2010. https://doi.org/10.3923/jas.2010.1656.1661.
5. Al Hammadi, A.Y., Yeun, C.Y., Damiani, E., Yoo, P.D., Hu, J., Yeun, H.K., Yim, M.-S., Explainable artificial intelligence to evaluate industrial internal security using EEG signals in IoT framework. *Ad Hoc Netw.*, 123, 102641, 2021. https://doi.org/10.1016/j.adhoc.2021.102641.
6. Andress, J. Chapter 5–Cryptography. The basics of information security (Second Edition). pp. 69–88, Boston, Syngress, 2014.
7. Angelov, P.P., Soares, E.A., Jiang, R., Arnold, N.I., Atkinson, P.M. Explainable artificial intelligence: An analytical review. Wiley Interdisciplinary Reviews: Data mining and knowledge discovery, 11, 5, e1424, 2021.
8. Babenko, M., Deryabin, M., Piestrak, S.J., Patronik, P., Chervyakov, N., Tchernykh, A., Avetisyan, A., RNS number comparator based on a modified diagonal function. *Electronics*, 9, 11, 1784, 2020. https://doi.org/10.3390/electronics9111784.
9. Brakerski, Z. and Vaikuntanathan, V., Efficient fully homomorphic encryp. tion from (standard) {LWE}. *SIAM J. Comput.*, 43, 2, 831–871, 2014. https://doi.org/10.1137/120868669.
10. Caputo, A.C., Introduction to digital video security. *Digital Video Surveillance and Security*, 1–21, 2014. https://doi.org/10.1016/b978-0-12-420042-5.00001-0
11. Chander, B., The state-of-the-art cryptography techniques for secure data transmission, in: *Handbook of Research on Intrusion Detection Systems*, pp. 284–305, 2020. IGI Global.
12. Chang, C.-H., Molahosseini, A.S., Zarandi, A.A.E., Tay, T.F., Residue number systems: A new paradigm to datapath optimization for low-power and high-performance digital signal processing applications. *IEEE Circuits Syst. Mag.*, 15, 4, 26–44, 2015. https://doi.org/10.1109/MCAS.2015.2484118.
13. Chebotareva, A. A., Chebotarev, V. E., Rozanov, A. S., Communication society and security: Current threats and legal maintenance. *Digital Communication Management*, 2018. https://doi.org/10.5772/intechopen.75756
14. Chen, M., Accounting data encryption processing based on data encryption standard algorithm. *Complexity*, 2021, 1–12, 2021. https://doi.org/10.1155/2021/7212688.

15. Cheng, S., Wang, L., Ao, N., Han, Q., A selective video encryption scheme based on coding characteristics. *Symmetry*, 12, 3, 332, 2020. https://doi.org/10.3390/sym12030332.
16. Conrad, E., Misenar, S., Feldman, J., Domain 3: Security engineering (Engineering and management of security). CISSP Study Guide, 103–217, 2016. https://doi.org/10.1016/b978-0-12-802437-9.00004-7
17. Dumbere, D.M. and Janwe, N.J., Video encryption using AES algorithm. *Second International Conference on Current Trends In Engineering and Technology-ICCTET 2014*, pp. 332–337, 2014, https://doi.org/10.1109/ICCTET.2014.6966311.
18. Eseyin, J. and Gbolagade, K., An overview of public key cryptosysems and application of residue number system. *Kampala Int. Univ. J. Humanit.*, 4, 2, 37–44, 2019.
19. Gade, K., Geyik, S.C., Kenthapadi, K., Mithal, V., Taly, A., Explainable AI in industry. *Proceedings of the 25th ACM SIGKDD International Conference on Knowledge Discovery & Data Mining*, pp. 3203–3204, 2019, https://doi.org/10.1145/3292500.3332281.
20. Gbolagade, K.A., New adder-based RNS-to-binary converters for the moduli set. *ISRN Signal Process.*, 2011, 1–7, 2011. https://doi.org/10.5402/2011/272768.
21. Holder, E. and Wang, N., Explainable artificial intelligence (XAI) interactively working with humans as a junior cyber analyst. *Hum. Intell. Syst. Integr.*, 3, 2, 139–153, 2021. https://doi.org/10.1007/s42454-020-00021-z.
22. Hosseinzad, M. and Navi, K., A new moduli set for residue number system in ternary vlued logic. *J. Appl. Sci.*, 7, 23, 3729–3735, 2007. https://doi.org/10.3923/jas.2007.3729.3735.
23. Isupov, K., High-performance computation in residue number system using floating-point arithmetic. *Computation*, 9, 2, 9, 2021. https://doi.org/10.3390/computation9020009.
24. Johnson, L., Chapter 11—Security component fundamentals for assessment. Security Controls Evaluation, Testing, and Assessment Handbook, 2nd ed.; p. 536, Academic Press, Cambridge, MA, USA, 2020.
25. Khairullah, M., A novel steganography method using transliteration of bengali text. *J. King Saud Univ. Comput. Inf. Sci.*, 31, 3, 348–366, 2019. https://doi.org/10.1016/j.jksuci.2018.01.008.
26. Lancrenon, J., Khader, D., Ryan, P. Y., Hao, F., Password-based authenticated key establishment protocols, in: *Computer and Information Security Handbook*, Morgan Kaufmann, pp. 705–720, 2013.
27. Li, S., IoT node authentication. *Securing the Internet of Things*, 69–95, 2017. https://doi.org/10.1016/b978-0-12-804458-2.00004-4.
28. Yang, L.-L. and Hanzo, L., A residue number system based parallel communication scheme using orthogonal signaling. I. System outline. *IEEE Trans. Veh. Technol.*, 51, 6, 1534–1546, 2002. https://doi.org/10.1109/TVT.2002.804850.

29. Maclure, J., AI, explainability and public reason: The argument from the limitations of the human mind. *Mind. Mach.*, 31, 3, 421–438, 2021. https://doi.org/10.1007/s11023-021-09570-x.
30. Mahbooba, B., Timilsina, M., Sahal, R., Serrano, M., Explainable artificial intelligence (XAI) to enhance trust management in intrusion detection systems using decision tree model. *Complexity*, 2021, 1–11, 2021. https://doi.org/10.1155/2021/6634811.
31. Miguens Matutino, P., Chaves, R., Sousa, L., Arithmetic-Based Binary-to-RNS Converter Modulo $\{2^n \pm k\}$ for -bit dynamic range. *IEEE Trans. Very Large Scale Integr. (VLSI) Syst.*, 23, 3, 603–607, 2015. https://doi.org/10.1109/TVLSI.2014.2314174.
32. Mohamed, N., Yussoff, Y.M., Isa, M., Hashimah, H., Symmetric encryption using pre-shared public parameters for a secure TFTP protocol. *J. Eng. Sci. Technol.*, 12, 98–112, 2017.
33. Molahosseini, A.S., de Sousa, L.S., Chang, C.-H. (Eds.), Embedded systems design with special arithmetic and number systems. Springer International Publishing, Cham, Switzerland, 2017.
34. Obaid, T.S., Study a public key in RSA algorithm. *Eur. J. Eng. Res. Sci.*, 5, 4, 395–398, 2020. https://doi.org/10.24018/ejers.2020.5.4.1843.
35. Paar, C. and Pelzl, J., The data encryption standard (DES) and alternatives, in: *Understanding Cryptography*, pp. 55–86, Springer, Berlin Heidelberg, 2010, https://doi.org/10.1007/978-3-642-04101-3_3.
36. Pardikar, V.P., Tummala, M., Rao, B.V., Digital FIR filtering with residue number system. *Int. J. Electron.*, 63, 3, 307–315, 1987. https://doi.org/10.1080/00207218708939132.
37. Peacock, T., Ryan, P.Y., Schneider, S., Xia, Z., Verifiable voting systems. in: *Computer and information security handbook*, Morgan Kaufmann, pp. e293-e315, 2013.
38. Agbedemnab, P.A.N., Baagyere, E.Y., Daabo, M., II, A novel text encryption and decryption scheme using the genetic algorithm and residual numbers. *Kalpa Publications Computing*, 12, 20–31, 2019.
39. Pramanik, P.K.D., Pareek, G., Nayyar, A., Security and privacy in remote healthcare: Issues, solutions, and standards, in: *Telemedicine technologies*, pp. 201–225, Academic Press, 2019.
40. Pulido-Gaytan, B., Tchernykh, A., Cortés-Mendoza, J.M., Babenko, M., Radchenko, G., Avetisyan, A., Drozdov, A.Y., Privacy-preserving neural networks with homomorphic encryption: Challenges and opportunities. *Peer Peer Netw. Appl.*, 14, 3, 1666–1691, 2021. https://doi.org/10.1007/s12083-021-01076-8.
41. Quilala, R.L., Sison, A.M., Medina, R.P., Modified SHA-1 algorithm. *Indones. J. Electr. Eng. Comput. Sci.*, 11, 3, 1027, 2018. https://doi.org/10.11591/ijeecs.v11.i3.pp1027-1034.
42. Rabah, K., Theory and implementation of data encryption standard: A review. *Inf. Technol. J.*, 4, 4, 307–325, 2005. https://doi.org/10.3923/itj.2005.307.325.

43. Radwan, A.G., AbdElHaleem, S.H., Abd-El-Hafiz, S.K., Symmetric encryption algorithms using chaotic and non-chaotic generators: A review. *J. Adv. Res.*, 7, 2, 193–208, 2016. https://doi.org/10.1016/j.jare.2015.07.002.
44. Rajagopal, S. and Shenbagavalli, A., A survey of video encryption algorithms implemented in various stages of compression. *Int. J. Eng. Res. Technol.*, 2, 2, 1–12, 2013.
45. Ranjan, K.H.S., Fathimath, S.S.P., Aithal, G., Shetty, S., A survey on key(s) and keyless image encryption techniques. *Cybern. Inf. Technol.*, 17, 4, 134–164, 2017. https://doi.org/10.1515/cait-2017-0046.
46. Regueiro, C., Seco, I., de Diego, S., Lage, O., Etxebarria, L., Privacy-enhancing distributed protocol for data aggregation based on blockchain and homomorphic encryption. *Inf. Process. Manage.*, 58, 6, 102745, 2021. https://doi.org/10.1016/j.ipm.2021.102745.
47. Reyna, A., Martín, C., Chen, J., Soler, E., Díaz, M., On blockchain and its integration with IoT. Challenges and opportunities. *Future Gener. Comp. Sy.*, 88, 173–190, 2018. https://doi.org/10.1016/j.future.2018.05.046.
48. Rountree, D., Security for Microsoft Windows system administrators: Introduction to key information security concepts. Elsevier, 2011.
49. Sairete, A., Balfagih, Z., Brahimi, T., Amin Mousa, M., Lytras, M., Visvizi, A., Editorial-artificial intelligence: Towards digital transformation of life, work, and education. *Proc. Comput. Sci.*, 194, 1–8, 2021. https://doi.org/10.1016/j.procs.2021.11.001.
50. Salem, I.E., Salman, A.M., Mijwil, M.M., A survey: Cryptographic hash functions for digital stamping. *J. Southwest Jiaotong Univ.*, 54, 6, 2019.
51. Sarker, I.H., Machine learning: Algorithms, real-world applications and research directions. *SN Comput. Sci.*, 2, 3, 160, 2021. https://doi.org/10.1007/s42979-021-00592-x.
52. Schoinianakis, D., Residue arithmetic systems in cryptography: A survey on modern security applications. *J. Cryptogr. Eng.*, 10, 3, 249–267, 2020. https://doi.org/10.1007/s13389-020-00231-w.
53. Sen, J., Homomorphic encryption-theory and application. Theory and practice of cryptography and network security protocols and technologies, InTech, 31, 2013.
54. Shareef, F.R., A novel crypto technique based ciphertext shifting. *Egypt. Inform. J.*, 21, 2, 83–90, 2020. https://doi.org/10.1016/j.eij.2019.11.002.
55. Shparlinski, I., Computational diffie-hellman problem, in: *Encyclopedia of Cryptography and Security*, pp. 240–244, Springer, US, 2011, https://doi.org/10.1007/978-1-4419-5906-5_882.
56. Singh, G. and Supriya, S., A study of encryption algorithms (RSA, DES, 3DES and AES) for information security. *Int. J. Comput. Appl.*, 67, 19, 33–38, 2013. https://doi.org/10.5120/11507-7224.
57. St Denis, T. and Johnson, S., Advanced encryption standard. *Cryptography for Developers*, 139–202, 2007. https://doi.org/10.1016/b978-159749104-4/50007-8

58. Stošić, L., and Bogdanović, M. RC4 stream cipher and possible attacks on WEP. Editorial Preface, 3, 3, 2012.
59. Thakur, U.N., Mallick, S., Moitra, R.M., Kotal, M., Zakaria, S., Chakraborty, A., Pramanik, S., Mukherjee, D., Mukherjee, C., FPGA based effecient architecture for conversion of binay to residue number system. *2017 8th IEEE Annual Information Technology, Electronics and Mobile Communication Conference (IEMCON)*, pp. 700–704, 2017, https://doi.org/10.1109/IEMCON.2017.8117238.
60. Tong, G., Liang, Z., Xiao, F., Xiong, N., A residual chaotic system for image security and digital video watermarking. *IEEE Access*, 9, 121154–121166, 2021. https://doi.org/10.1109/ACCESS.2021.3108196.
61. Virtue, T. and Rainey, J. Privacy and security in healthcare. HCISPP Study Guide, 61–89, 2015. https://doi.org/10.1016/b978-0-12-802043-2.00004-5
62 Yaacoub, J.-P.A., Salman, O., Noura, H.N., Kaaniche, N., Chehab, A., Malli, M., Cyber-physical systems security: Limitations, issues and future trends. *Microprocess. Microsyst.*, 77, 103201, 2020. https://doi.org/10.1016/j.micpro.2020.103201.
63. Yaacoub, J.-P., Noura, H., Salman, O., Chehab, A., Security analysis of drones systems: Attacks, limitations, and recommendations. *Internet Things*, 11, 100218, 2020. https://doi.org/10.1016/j.iot.2020.100218.
64. Yahia, A., Mohamed, M.A., Saleh, A., Research on various cryptography techniques. *Int. J. Recent Technol. Eng.*, 8, 2S3, 395–405, 2019. https://doi.org/10.35940/ijrte.B1069.0782S319.

15

Market Trends with Cryptocurrency Trading in Industry 4.0

Varun Khemka, Sagar Bafna, Ayush Gupta, Somya Goyal* **and Vivek Kumar Verma**

Manipal University Jaipur, Jaipur, Rajasthan, India

Abstract

The world sees something in crypto beyond just being a fictitious money system. There is more to digital assets, like Bitcoin, Ethereum, and Ripple, than only being able to send people money for pizza. I think this is the most misunderstood part about crypto in general—what lies behind the digital assets, not just what they can currently do. It is easy for people to look at something and say, that is not useful. Think about the internet back in the day. All it was back then was message boards and awkward websites, but no one knew what it really could do. No one knew that one day we would use it for just about everything. There is impact of cryptocurrency in today's world and market is still adjusting, in the works. Most businesses do not allow cryptocurrency as a form of payment because of the recent problems. its price is also not stable. Once the price stabilizes, it will be easier for businesses to accept payment methods through cryptocurrency battle.

Bitcoin has a lot of beneficial consequences for investment inflows, allowing for more price and conversion rate possibilities. Our world is divinely focused on making a better, more innovative future. Automation, cryptocurrency, blockchain, and artificial intelligence are all instances of how new technology will continue to develop and eventually take over our industry. We have conducted extensive case studies on market, trading, fee structure and carbon footprint due to blockchain technology. The chapter is organized as follows: section 15.1 of this paper gives a layout of history of cryptocurrency and bitcoin. Section 15.2 gives detail analysis of blockchain technology, mining and how cryptocurrency uses blockchain technology. It also gives details about meaning of crypto in market and how crypto exchanges between each another. Section 15.3 gives information about trading

**Corresponding author*: somyagoyal1988@gmail.com

Jyotir Moy Chatterjee, Harish Garg and R. N. Thakur (eds.) A Roadmap for Enabling Industry 4.0 by Artificial Intelligence, (275–294) © 2023 Scrivener Publishing LLC

in crypto and its advantages and disadvantages. Section 15.4 gives the in-depth analysis of fee structures and carbon footprint in blockchain.

Due to the increased flexibility, cyber security, absence of middleman, which decrease its cost and many more advantages, it can be concluded that cryptocurrency and blockchain is the future of all industry.

Keywords: Cryptocurrency, blockchain, consensus, mining, decentralized, exchange, carbon-neutrality, ethereum virtual machine (EVM), nonfungible tokens (NFT)

15.1 Introduction

Over the course, the cryptocurrency market has grown at an astonishing rate. More than 10,000 cryptocurrencies have been created since the public release of the first cryptocurrency [1], Bitcoin, in January 2009, the majority with barely a sliver of success. This is still a topic of industrial research [2]. Very few research was made on this topic. The bulk of it is only focused on Bitcoin rather than a wider range of cryptocurrencies, and it is being constantly outpaced by fluid industry developments and increasing government regulation of the markets. Thus, there exists a necessity for thorough research on this industry. This chapter aims to give a succinct but thorough examination of the cryptocurrency sector, with a focus on Bitcoin, the first decentralized cryptocurrency. Examining theoretical economic disparities between existent coins will receive special focus.

Since the crypto assets are yet to be completely deciphered, generalizing prior work, trading methods, market management, risk management, and so on, is beneficial. While concentrating on cryptocurrency trading and various application of blockchains, we are also putting light on issues, such as environmental effects of blockchain, carbon neutrality and the fundamental structure of block chain [3]. We also highlight the issue of high transaction fees and how we can deal with it.

15.2 Industry Overview

15.2.1 History (From Barter to Cryptocurrency)

Discrete incidents have impacted the path of human history through discontinuously accelerating progress. Without a doubt, one of these milestones is the introduction of money in the form of uniform coins, which occurred approximately 600 BC in Lydia [4].

This initial generation of currency influenced Mediterranean culture in a variety of ways, and it was responsible for a steady expansion in commercial transactions. Merchants did not have to rely on bartering, good for good, or service for service any longer [5]. Paper money, which first appeared during the Renaissance, was the second generation.

It was first presented by Italian banks and then adopted by well-known national banks. The invention of electronic transactions in the 20th century expedited the circulation of currency throughout the economy, increasing growth. Central banks may easily raise the supply of currency without physically producing it now. Following the financial crisis of 2008, all major central banks used quantitative easing initiatives (QE) to dramatically expand their monetary base, as seen in Figure 15.1. Coincidentally, a whole new financial asset appeared around the same period [6]. The Bitcoin was the first cryptocurrency.

Similarly, to a traditional currency, the online currency coined as cryptocurrency makes it possible to facilitate the interaction between two parties regarding any goods or services without relying on a single institute. They use mathematical functions to correlate data between a network and validate that the transactions are unique and different. Bitcoin being the first successful decentralized cryptocurrency was launched in 2008 by Satoshi Nakamoto, an anonymous developer.

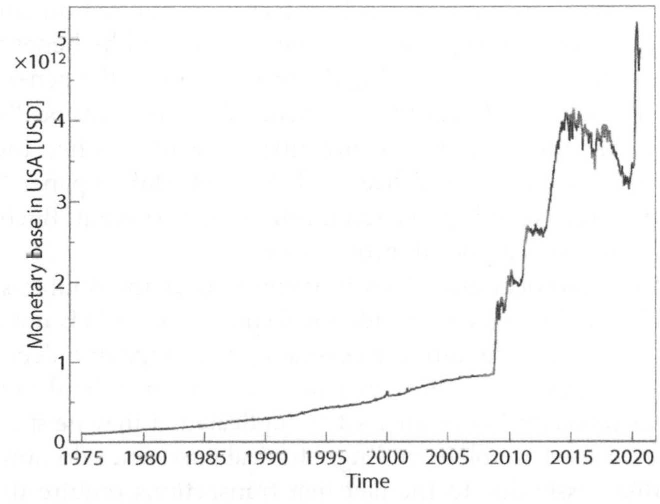

Figure 15.1 Monetary base in USD [1].

By decentralizing the whole network, the whole financial system is aimed to be revolutionized by removing controlling entities. Bitcoin has been successful to dominate the virtual currency market. Its users instead transact with the coin over a peer-to-peer network. It gained a lot of attention when it first came out in 2011, and a plethora of substitute coins popped up as a result.

In 1983, Chaum invented eCash, an anonymous electronic money system. The primary distinction between cryptocurrencies and eCash is that eCash was a centralized system (by the help of banks) [19]. Money was stored digitally on the user's local computer using software that was cryptographically signed by a bank [19].

15.2.2 In the Beginning Was Bitcoin

Bitcoin is a peer-to-peer virtual foreign money that become first released with the aid of using Satoshi Nakamoto in a 2008. "Commerce at the Internet has come to depend nearly totally on economic establishments serving as relied on 1/3 events to manner digital payments," Nakamoto writes with inside the first paragraph of his paper. While the gadget is good enough for maximum transactions, its miles however susceptible to the trust-primarily based totally model's intrinsic flaws." Furthermore, the presence of a relied-on middleman increases transaction prices, effectively "reducing off the opportunity of small, informal transactions."

Nakamoto aimed to construct a coin that might take away the want for a relied on important authority and as an alternative rely upon cryptographic verification. Low transaction fees, low transaction time (time among transactions), and pseudo-anonymity could all be benefits of this system. Only through documenting the transaction on the general public ledger, regularly referred to as the "blockchain," can bitcoins be dispatched or received. Bitcoins do not have any intrinsic worth; rather, their fee is decided completely through deliver and demand. Unlike paper "fiat currency," that is created and sponsored through a government, Bitcoin is not always generated or supported through one.

The Bitcoin protocol ambitions to triumph over the double-spending hassle (basically, the usage of the identical coin twice), this is not un usual place in cashless fee structures, necessitating the usage of a depended on 1/3 party (along with a credit score card corporation or bank) to test the transaction's integrity. When an asset is duplicated, it may be spent severe times, that is called double-spending. Physical currencies do now no longer have this hassle due to the fact that transactions require the switch of belongings possession. A virtual file, on the alternative hand, may be copied. Cryptocurrency's security and its potential to shield in opposition to virtual copying, is constructed inside its blockchain or public ledger structures. These structures preserve possession and transaction time-stamp records, stopping virtual copying and, as a result, double spending.

Bitcoin was first made public on January 3, 2009; however, it did not start trading for more than a dollar until February 2011. On December 4, 2013, Bitcoin hit an all-time high of $1151 per coin, after which it has slowly dropped. Despite this drop, daily trading volume appears to have remained stable over the past year [7]. Blockchain is a virtual ledger of financial transactions that may be used to document something with intrinsic value, now no longer simply economic transactions. A blockchain, in its maximum easy form, is a set of constant information entries with timestamps, which might be controlled through a collection of machines that are not associated with any unmarried institution. Each of those information blocks is encrypted cryptographically and joined in a chain.

15.3 Cryptocurrency Market

15.3.1 Blockchain

15.3.1.1 Introduction to Blockchain Technology

Blockchain is a digital registry of interactions between users that can be used to record anything with intrinsic value, not just financial transactions [8]. In simple, a blockchain is a network containing data of all previously occurred transactions between its users with crucial information controlled by all its network validators. The blocks are bound together and are cryptographically encrypted (Figure 15.2 for workflow).

A Bitcoin Block has five fields:

- Magic number • Block size • Block Header • Transaction counter • Transactions

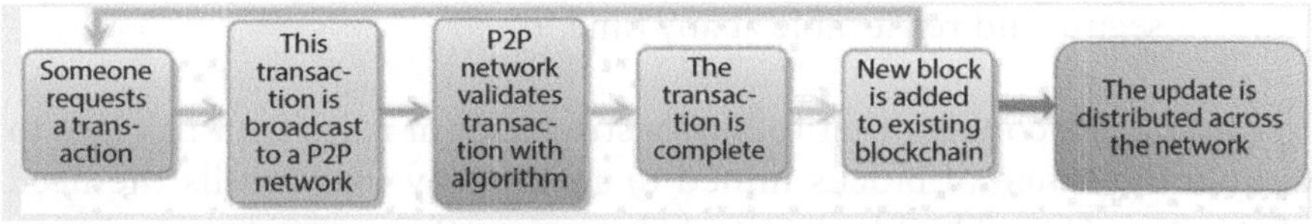

Figure 15.2 Workflow of blockchain technology.

In the era of technology, any machine whether it is a car, a motor, a generator, a transformer, needs some kind of fuel to run on (for example petrol, diesel or electricity). Just like that, the blockchain technology uses Fees as a fuel to power its functions. The way bitcoin blockchain is designed, the history of transactions is stored in a ledger consisting of blocks connected to each other and in order to add a new block to the existing blocks, a mathematical equation needs to be solved using a lot of computational power. The miners use their computational power and in return get bitcoin as reward. The bitcoin comes from two sources – one is the new bitcoin released into the blockchain through the miner, and the other is the transaction fees that bitcoin users add to their transactions as an incentive to get their transaction priority over others [9].

15.3.1.2 Mining

Every cryptocurrency system we have looked at has a blockchain, which is a network made up of public validators. When a payer sends money to a payee, a transaction is generated. Mining is the process of validating and confirming the authenticity of new users interacting with the network and piling them into the existing network [10]. Every time a new interaction with the network occurs, the blockchain records the ownership of the token. A malevolent user could set up numerous nodes and try to validate a transaction that isn't valid. To avoid this, miners must complete a resource-intensive task. Miners are rational profit applicants, so the Bitcoin protocol offers rewards as either fees used in transactions or an entirely new coin promoting the individual intention to mine.

The commission of material exhaustive can be any of the following:

- **Proof of Work** used to authenticate outcome of an exhaustive task that validate that authenticates the commission has been done [24].
- **Proof of Stake** that keeps the system transparent exposing the tokens held by miners [24].
- **Proof of Retrievability** that is essential to expose miner that the information he is tasked with accumulating remains secure and retrievable at any time.

Mining is a concept that follows a strong set of rules kept in place to uphold the range of blocks mined in such a way that fulfills the need of its users [11]. The block is tested via way of means of the primary miner who computes the proof, and the praise is a tiny a part of the circulating tokens. The validation produced via way of means of the miner desires to be tested and it is heavily required that this process is quick and simple.

15.3.1.3 From Blockchain to Cryptocurrency

Verification and authentication is a vital system in cryptocurrencies; most effective miners may also validate statistics. Miners create new blocks with inside the blockchain via way of means of acquiring statistics from preceding blocks, becoming a member of them with the preceding block's hash to get the latest block's hash, after which storing the derived hash within side the cutting-edge block [12]. Blockchain miners take delivery of and validate statistics earlier than broadcasting them to the relaxation of the network. When the miner approves the record, every node has to upload it to the network. In other terms, it is now part of the blockchain network, and miners utilize it to earn Bitcoin and different cryptocurrency tokens. Unlike blockchain, cryptocurrency is associated with using tokens primarily based totally on dispensed ledger era [12]. Any transaction regarding buy, sale, investment, and so forth makes use of a blockchain product as in tokens. Blockchain is an era that serves as a network's dispensed ledger and is used to energy bitcoin.

Are cryptocurrency and blockchain the same?

No, cryptocurrencies is an application based on blockchain technology. The tokens that are used to send cost and pay for records on these networks are known as cryptocurrencies. They can be thought of as blockchain tools, but in particular cases, they can also be used as resources or utilities.

15.3.2 Introduction to Cryptocurrency Market

15.3.2.1 What is a Cryptocurrency?

First let us start with the definition. The new type of currency known as cryptocurrency is a decentralized mode of transfer of goods between two parties that uses cryptographic mechanisms to execute financial records. Decentralization, transparency, and immutability are all benefits of cryptocurrency [13]. As we have already observed how this technology is used for cryptocurrencies, the fundamental basis for it is the lack of financial institution intermediaries. Traders gain from the absence of a "middleman" since transaction rates are lowered.

In case a financial institution's database is compromised, for example, the financial institution will simply repair any misplaced or compromised records the usage of its backup. Albeit a part of the cryptocurrency community is compromised, the opposite a part of the community may be capable of efficiently validate records (transaction). Cryptocurrencies additionally enjoy the reality that they may be now no longer ruled with the aid of using a crucial authority. The blockchain's decentralized nature means that cryptocurrencies are theoretically impervious to authorities manage and intervention.

Table 15.1 Nomics website.

Exchanges	Category	Supported currencies	Fiat Currency	Registration country	Regulatory authority
CME	Derivatives	BTC and Ethereum (CME 2020)	USD	USA (CME 2020)	CFT (CME 2020)
CBOE	Derivatives	BTC (CBOE 2020)	USD	USA (CBOE 2020)	CFTC (CBOE 2020)
BAKKT (NYSE)	Derivatives	BTC (BAKKT 2020)	USD	USA (BAKKT 2020)	CFTC (BAKKT 2020)
BitMex	Derivatives	12 cryptocurrencies (Bitmex 2020)	USD	Seychelles (Bitmex 2020)	–
Binance	Spot	98 cryptocurrencies (Binance 2020)	EUR, NGN, RUB, TRY	Malta (Maltatoday 2020)	FATF (Binance 2020)
Coinbase	Spot	28 cryptocurrencies (Coinbase 2020)	EUR, GBP, USD	USA (Bloomberg 2020)	SEC (Coinbase 2020)
Bitfinex	Spot	> 100 cryptocurrencies (Bitfinex 2020)	EUR, GBP, JPY, USD	British Virgin Island (Bitfinex 2020)	NYAG (Bitfinex 2020)
Bitstamp	Spot	5 cryptocurrencies (Bitstamp 2020)	EUR, USD	Luxembourg (Bitstamp 2020)	CSSF (Bitstamp 2020)
Poloniex	Spot	23 cryptocurrencies (Poloniex 2020)	USD	USA (Poloniex 2020)	–

15.3.2.2 *Cryptocurrency Exchanges*

Digital currency exchange (DCE), often known as a cryptocurrency exchange, is a business that expedites the trading of cryptocurrencies. These exchanges can play a crucial role as marketplace makers, amassing a fee primarily based totally at the users bid, or as an identical platform, clearly imposing a fees for the experience. Customers can trade cryptocurrencies at these DCEs.

Table 15.1 presents the top or traditional cryptocurrency exchanges according to the position list, compiled on "nomics" website (Nomics, 2020).

15.4 Cryptocurrency Trading

15.4.1 Definition

Cryptocurrency trading is defined as exchange of cryptos between two parties in purpose of making a profit. The three elements that make up the definition of cryptocurrency trading are the currency being traded in, the mode of operation, and the trading strategy used. The item being exchanged, "a particular cryptocurrency," is the object of cryptocurrency trading. The operation mode of trading is determined by the type of transaction in the cryptocurrency market, which can be divided into "trading of crypto Contract for Differences (CFD)" (a contract between two parties, often referred to as "buyer" and "seller") and "exchange of cryptocurrencies via a crypto exchange." An investor-formulated trading strategy in cryptocurrency trading is an algorithm that defines a set of accepted rules for exchanging on cryptocurrency marketplaces.

15.4.2 Advantages

- **Unprecedented changes**—Cryptocurrencies are susceptible to drawing hypothetical interest and investors because to their extreme volatility. Intraday price movements can offer enormous profit opportunities, but they also come with a greater risk.
- **Market being open 24 hours a day**—Unlike the stock and commodities markets, the cryptocurrency market is not materially transacted from any particular place. The bitcoin market is open the whole day, the whole week because it is

a decentralized market. Cryptocurrency transactions can be carried out in a variety of locations throughout the world with minimum restrictions.
- **Near anonymity of traders**—Cryptocurrency purchases are made on-line and do not want the revelation of non-public information. Cryptocurrencies are also able to provide some privacy advantages to consumers with considerations regarding fraud and privacy mounting.
- **Peer-to-peer transactions** (transactions between individuals)—The nonobligation of financial organization as a middleman, is one of the foremost attractive options of cryptocurrencies. As antecedently indicated, this has the potential to cut back group action costs. This practicality may additionally attractiveness to users who are cautious of ancient systems.
- **"Smart" capabilities that can be programmed**—Other benefits to cryptocurrency owners include limited ownership and voting rights by using governance tokens. Cryptocurrency may also conceivably incorporate a fragmentary possession hobby in bodily belongings along with art work or actual estate.

15.4.3 Disadvantages

- **Scalability issue.** The hassle of era infrastructure limits the quantity of transactions and the velocity with which they may be finished and aren't at par with conventional forex buying and selling. In March 2020, scalability issues induced a multi-day buying and selling halt, hurting buyers who desired to switch cryptocurrencies from their non-public cash to exchanges.
- **Problems with cyber security.** Cryptocurrencies are prone to cybersecurity loopholes and can fall for hackers because they are a digital technology. Any unchecked vulnerability can result in the loss of millions of dollars. Constant maintenance of the security infrastructure is necessary, in addition to the use of advanced IT security measures in addition to those used in orthodox banks.
- **Regulations.** It has become a major issue for the Authorities throughout the world about the nature and regulation of cryptocurrencies, owing to the fact that some characteristics

of the system and the perils correlated with it, are mostly concealed. We are yet to see a world-wide accepted governing system for cryptocurrencies. In order to govern digital currencies, three types of regulatory systems are used: locked system in China, open and tolerant system in Switzerland, and the firm system in the United States (UKTN 2021). Simultaneously, we see that other nations, such as India, are lagging behind in terms of bitcoin adoption. "It doesn't make sense," Buffett stated.

15.5 In-Depth Analysis of Fee Structures and Carbon Footprint in Blockchain

15.5.1 Need for a Fee-Driven System

First, let us look at the issues that occur when attempting to put up a truly decentralized system. A code including the information about the currency, its present owner, the digital signatures of the parties involved, as well as the time and date of the transaction, is used in a transaction. This code is transmitted over the network made up of several nodes (computational powers running the network software) [14]. It is required that all the nodes come to an agreement of the previous transactions that have occurred, and whether the newer transaction is valid or not, to prevent attacks, such as Denial-of-Service (DoS) attack or double spending (having multiple records of the same transaction). To bring all of the nodes to a consensus a fee-based method was developed, which would validate the authenticity of a transaction while simultaneously making it prohibitively expensive to compromise the system's integrity.

This consensus is known as Proof-of-Work (PoW) consensus. Under this consensus, users submit their transactions which then awaits confirmation from miners. When a miner solves the cryptographic mathematical challenge, a new block is added to the longest chain of existing blocks and the block includes pre-defined number of transactions, which then gets validated. The miners are essentially vying for the chance to have their block approved by the network. This technique increases the cost and processing power required to break into and alter data stored on the network, making it prohibitively expensive for any hacker to penetrate and manipulate the data [15]. The fees for the miner to be rewarded on successful block addition determine the priority of one transaction over another [15].

A transaction with incredibly low fees (negligible amount) has the probability of never getting added to the blockchain even in infinite time. The fundamental problem of PoW is it necessitates a massive amount of processing capability to solve the cryptographical problem resulting in considerable consumption of electricity to run the GPU's.

A newer consensus was proposed known as Proof-of-Stake (PoS) algorithm utilized by blockchain networks to achieve distributed consensus. Here the algorithm decides who becomes a validator of the network according to a minimum requirement of coins they hold [16]. The likelihood of validating a new block is dependent on the validator's stake in the network, not on their processing capacity. But in this case, the validator is not eligible for any block reward, just network fees. PoS systems are much more cost and energy efficient than the PoW systems and additionally provide stronger immunity to centralization by adding a greater number of nodes in the network as shown in Figure 15.3. However, since the only reward for the validators are the transaction fees, it results into higher conflict between its users to prioritize their transaction eventually leading to higher transaction fees.

15.5.2 Ethereum Structure

With the recent explosion of smart contracts in blockchain, newer implementations, such as decentralized finance (DeFi), decentralized apps (dApps), and nonfungible tokens (NFTs) have skyrocketed into the mainstream media and they all started on the ethereum blockchain. The Ethereum blockchain apps are true, immutable, and always interoperate

Figure 15.3 PoW Vs PoS.

as they are written. From this point of view, the terminology of smart contracts is justified in that they are the ultimate in contracts that always follow the terms set at their establishment [15].

An effective World Computer is made feasible by the ethereum virtual machine (EVM), which enables operations for computing and data storage [16]. A transaction is its unit of engagement, whereas gas is its metering unit. Using more computation and storage in ethereum means that more gas is used and it is implemented to provide the miners an incentive to operate the EVM. To cover the usage of EVM's computation and storage facilities, a transaction must provide enough Gas.

15.5.3 How is the Gas Fee Calculated?

As the transaction fees are nominal compared to 1 ETH (ethereum's personal token ether), it is calculated in terms of gwei, a small amount of 1 ether unit. 1 gwei is equivalent to 0.000000001 ETH. According to the latest London upgrade in the network, the total fee you pay for transactions is calculated with the given formulae [17].

And the Total fee for a transaction = Gas limit*(base fee + priority fees)

15.5.3.1 Why are Ethereum Gas Prices so High?

As the ethereum blockchain hosts more than three thousand decentralized applications as well as other tokens and NFT's, all are looking to have their transactions included alongside the ethereum network users. Since the number of miners are limited, they are put in a situation where they must choose selected number of transactions to validate [18]. So, the miners prioritize which transactions to include from the mempool based on priority fees they offer, resulting in high fluctuations of Gas fees. NFT that are minted on this blockchain will generally cost anywhere from $60 and $250, depending on the stress on the network. Users are fighting for the preference of their transaction over the other users leading to even higher fees.

15.5.3.2 Carbon Neutrality

Carbon Neutrality is a term you must have come across social media or in industries. So first, let's find out what is carbon neutrality and how is it applicable in blockchain technology [19].

15.5.3.2.1 What is Carbon Neutrality?

Carbon Neutral or Net Zero Carbon is a state achieved by a company, a service or a product, when they balance out the carbon emissions caused by them and compensate for what they have produced by funding an equivalent amount of carbon savings elsewhere in the world.

So, how is carbon footprint and carbon neutrality applicable in blockchain? Well, the increasing popularity of cryptocurrency and its sky rocketing prices have brough the attention to mining resulting in higher competition creating a necessity for higher computational capability and cheap electricity [20]. Miners need this cheap electricity to run their hardware twenty-four by seven, but also to power large air-conditioning systems that prevent everything from overheating [21]. We have witnessed the birth of a worldwide computer arms race, with operators racing to develop larger and more powerful systems in order to secure this in-demand digital gold.

When a transaction is completed (which takes around ten minutes), it is updated on the blockchain and transferred to the hard disc of every Bitcoin user on the planet. As more individuals join the network, the amount of data generated increases, as does the amount of power required to maintain it. According to statista.com, a single Bitcoin transaction consumes 741 kilowatt-hours (kWh) of energy, which, in the real world, is enough electricity to power an ordinary home for 50 days. It has been estimated that almost half of the Bitcoin's total CO2 emissions come from China, while 13.1% from US and 17.2% from Europe (Figure 15.4).

Many of China's Major Bitcoin operations had been previously setup in areas of cheap excess electricity such as near hydroelectric stations or

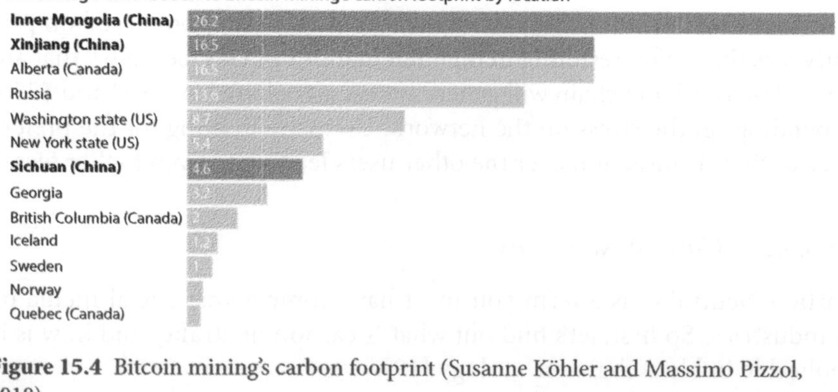

Figure 15.4 Bitcoin mining's carbon footprint (Susanne Köhler and Massimo Pizzol, 2018).

around coal mines (in Inner Mongolia) [22]. Even though China is world's largest source of renewable energy, it is also the largest carbon emitter and generates two-third of its electricity from coal. In an attempt to lower this carbon emission and energy usage, China has shut down most of its major mining operations and imposed several restrictions.

Another crucial flaw of bitcoin is that there is a limited supply available and over time as the supply becomes shorter the complex cryptographic problems become tougher demanding more and more processing capability. Charles Hoskinson, co-founder of Ethereum said that bitcoin's success leads to higher price, leading to more competition and thus more energy exhausted in mining it.

But carbon footprint is not only limited to bitcoin, but to other blockchains too such as Ethereum. The carbon footprint of a single Ethereum transaction was estimated to be 103 kg of CO2 and enough electrical energy to power an average home for 30 days (see Figure 15.5). The rise of

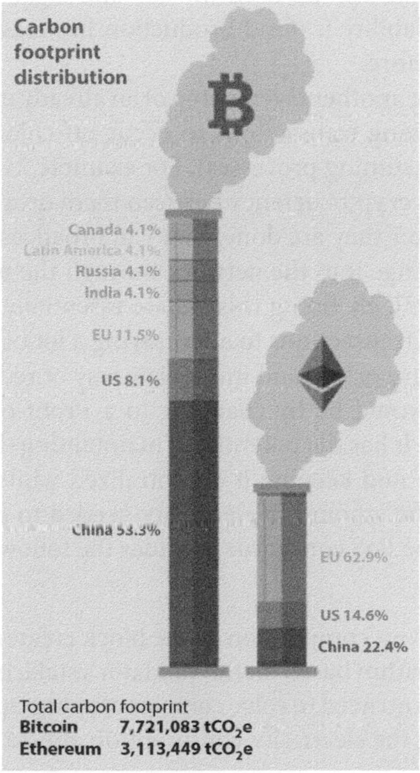

Figure 15.5 Comparison between bitcoin and Ethereum carbon footprint (2019).

NFT's has raised the question of whether digital ownership of a product is better than physical ownership and whether the energy required to run this system is harmful for the environment in the long run. We are essentially trying to power 21st century technology with 19th century power sources.

15.5.3.2.2 How do we Reduce Carbon Footprint?

As the popularity of bitcoin and blockchain technology keeps rising, we need to take action against the CO_2 emissions before it gets out of hand. Below are a few steps:

- By changing the source of electricity consumed from non-renewable source of energy to renewable source. Cleaner energy's like solar energy, wind energy, if replace the current coal consumption, the CO_2 emissions will drastically reduce.
- Using the excess heat generated by data centres to grow fruits and vegetables by pairing it to a greenhouse project. The heat can also be used for fish and algae farming providing scalability in food production in areas that was not possible before.
- By building another layer on top of an already existing blockchain allowing transactions to occur off-chain (away from energy consuming processes). For example, two parties can exchange a cryptocurrency between them on a second channel, and after they are done, they can broadcast the result of their exchange into the network through the proof-of-work method [23]. By doing this we are essentially reducing the number of transactions to a few saving a lot of energy.
- The most important and immediate way of reducing carbon footprint would be by changing to a Proof-of-Stake (PoS) consensus. It has the potential of maintaining the integrity of blockchain and keeping it decentralized while significantly reducing the amount of electricity needed to process transactions. The PoS consensus provides the following pros over PoW.

    1. There is no competition as the block creator is chosen by an algorithm based on the validator's stake in the network
    2. There is no need to solve complex cryptographic problems making the electricity consumption almost negligible

3. There is no competition between the miners and no reward for creating a block, so the block creators take the transaction fee as reward
4. In order to commit a 51% attack, you would need to control 51% of the staked coin, which will result in depreciation of the currency you own a major share of. Hence, there are stronger incentives to keep the network secure and healthy

   Ethereum developers have been proposing to switch to proof-of-stake for many years and they finally did in the London fork minimizing the carbon footprint and taking one more step towards carbon neutrality.

- Using the high finances involved in the crypto markets to contribute toward greener future by donating to amazon forests and building multiple sources of renewable energy sources. There are a great number of projects working toward offsetting the carbon footprint and by helping them, we can truly work toward a carbon neutral future.

15.6 Conclusion

This industry has evolved at unprecedented pace. Even when cybercrimes are at an all time high, the industry has remained tough and resistant to these external factors! Faced with large-scale extortion, such as Bitstamp, Gox, and Coincheck, it has endured and risen above such invasions. The never-ending cycle of new currencies that keep on promising new features but fail to deliver on them demonstrate the point that bitcoin is here to stay. The major flows in the financial system have the potential to be rectify them and lead to an even stronger system. Bitcoin might not be the industry's long-term leader, but it is the industry's survival that Bitcoin owes to the pioneering anarchic coin.

The techniques of mining of various cryptocurrencies, as well as other qualities and features of the systems, were compared, contrasted, and examined in this chapter. Major cryptocurrencies now employ proof of work (PoW), proof of stake (PoS), or a fusion of both for their ecosystem. While proof of work (PoW) requires a lot of resources, Proof of Stake cannot operate on its own. It has been discovered that a combination of the two is most effective. Cryptocurrencies employ a variety of hash algorithms for proof of work. The bulk of them use a lot of CPU power, while the others use a lot of memory. Use of severe memory-intense hash functions mining techniques have demonstrated to be quicker. The newer projects are evaluating with their mining protocols and algorithms in hope of improving their performance, and some are even attempting to find mining substitutes aiming toward a more eco-friendly and sustainable industry.

References

1. Crypto-currency market capitalizations. [Online]. http://coinmarketcap.com/. Accessed on March 01, 2022.
2. Bitcoin: A peer-to-peer electronic cash system, 2008. [Online]. https://bitcoin.org/bitcoin.pdf. Accessed on March 01, 2022.
3. Schwartz, D., Youngs, N., Britto, A., *The Ripple Protocol Consensus Algorithm*, Ripple Labs Inc., https://doi.org/10.48550/arXiv.1802.07242. (https://arxiv.org/abs/1802.07242)
4. King, S. and Nadal, S., PPCoin: Peer-to-Peer Crypto-Currency with Proof-of-Stake, 2022. from https://www.researchgate.net/publication/265116876_PPCoin_Peer-to-Peer_Crypto-Currency_with_Proof-of-Stake
5. https://nubits.com/sites/default/files/assets/nu-whitepaper-23_sept_2014-en.pdf. online resource
6. http://www.npr.org/blogs/thetwo-way/2013/11/27/247577278/man-laments-lossof-thousands-of-bitcoins-as-value-hits-1-000.
7. http://www.coindesk.com/mt-gox-loses-340-million-bitcoin-rumouredin-solvent/. Accessed on March 01, 2022
8. http://dealbook.nytimes.com/2014/01/21/why-bitcoinmatters/. Accessed on March 01, 2022.
9. https://blockchain.info/. Accessed on March 01, 2022.
10. Ren, L., *Proof of Stake Velocity: Building the Social Currency of the Digital Age*, Self Published-White Paper, 2014.
11. Dwork, C., Naor, M., Pricing via processing or combatting junk mail, in: *Advances in Cryptology — CRYPTO*' 92. CRYPTO 1992. Lecture Notes in Computer Science, Brickell, E.F. (eds), vol. 740, Springer, Berlin, Heidelberg, 1993, https://doi.org/10.1007/3-540-48071-4_10
12. Arvind N. and Jeremy C., Bitcoin's Academic Pedigree: The concept of cryptocurrencies is built from forgotten ideas in research literature. Queue 15, 4 (July-August 2017), 20–49, 2017. https://doi.org/10.1145/3134434.3136559
13. [Online]. https://www.stellar.org/papers/stellar-consensus-protocol.pdf. Accessed on March 01, 2022.
14. Lamport, L., Shostak, R., Pease, M., The byzantine generals problem. *ACM Trans. Program. Lang. Systs.*, https://fred.stlouisfed.org. Accessed on March 01, 2022.

15. https://ethereum.org/en/developers/docs. Accessed on March 01, 2022.
16. https://docs.solana.com/transaction_fees. Accessed on March 01, 2022.
17. https://github.com/bitcoin/bitcoin. Accessed on March 01, 2022
18. Rogaway, P. and Shrimpton, T., Cryptographic hash-function basics: Definitions, implications, and separations for preimage resistance, second-preimage resistance, and collision resistance, in: *International Workshop on Fast Software Encryption*, Springer, pp. 371–388, 2004.
19. Ahamad, S.S., Nair, M., Varghese, B., A survey on crypto currencies, in: *4th International Conference on Advances in Computer Science, AETACS*, Citeseer, pp. 42–48, 2013.
20. Chaum, D., David chaum on electronic commerce how much do you trust big brother? *IEEE Internet Comput.*, 1, 6, 8–16, 1997.
21. Eisenmann, T.R. and Barley, L., Paypal merchant services, 2006. Available at hbs.edu.
22. Kohler, S. and Pizzol, M., via The new scientist: Cointelegraph news, 2019.
23. Mankiw, N.G., *Principles of Macroeconomics*, Cengage Learning, 2014.
24. Mukhopadhyay, U., Skjellum, A., Hambolu, O., Oakley, J., Yu, L., Brooks, R., A brief survey of cryptocurrency systems. *2016 14th Annual Conference on Privacy, Security and Trust (PST)*, 2016.

16

Blockchain and Its Applications in Industry 4.0

Ajay Sudhir Bale[1]*, Tarun Praveen Purohit[2], Muhammed Furqaan Hashim[2] and Suyog Navale[2]

[1]*Department of Electronics and Communication Engineering, New Horizon College of Engineering, Bengaluru, India*

[2]*School of Engineering and Technology, CMR University, Bengaluru, India*

Abstract

Blockchain is one among the many advancements in emerging technologies brought to Industry 4.0. Blockchain can be used for both small-scale and large-scale industries to increase data transparency, security, and privacy. Industry 4.0, or the fourth industrial revolution, is a collection of cutting-edge manufacturing procedures that enable businesses to reach their goals and objectives more quickly. Several studies on Industry 4.0 technologies, such as the artificial intelligence (AI), Internet of Things (IoT), and blockchain have been done in recent years. These innovations open the doors to plenty of possibilities across the supply chain and production factories. Blockchain has grown in popularity and is now a widely recognized technology with the ability to transform industrial and supply chain settings. Various fields now offer intriguing insights on blockchain and its benefits. This chapter examines Blockchain's background, its huge potential for Industry 4.0, as well as the various drivers, challenges, and capabilities of blockchain enhancing the experience of Industry 4.0.

Keywords: Blockchain, cryptocurrency, digital currency, Industry 4.0, future technologies, technology

**Corresponding author*: ajaysudhirbale@gmail.com

Jyotir Moy Chatterjee, Harish Garg and R. N. Thakur (eds.) A Roadmap for Enabling Industry 4.0 by Artificial Intelligence, (295–314) © 2023 Scrivener Publishing LLC

16.1 Introduction

After extensive evolution of technology over the previous phases of industrial revolutions, Industry 4.0 utilizes the latest form of scientific advancements in computation, electronics, and telecommunication technology to build sophisticated interconnected systems that communicate with one another over the entire manufacturing processes. Industry 4.0 is transforming our lives and changing the landscape of the world's economy. Automating the industrial systems is one the most important factors of industry 4.0. As a result, a large amount of real time data is required to be processed to ensure that all the interconnected systems remain in sync with each other. In order to deal with issues relating to the authenticity and transparency of data involved in the implementation of industry 4.0, it is important to look at systems that are capable of ensuring trust for data transactions.

Blockchain is the culmination of technological developments over the years and a combination of various cryptographic systems. It is a digitally distributed and decentralized network that powers smart contracts and enables transparency, traceability, and authenticity in managing data records [1]. Blockchain was initially designed with a focus to revolutionize the financial system with cryptocurrency as a means to replace fiat currency. But due to the underlying technology of blockchain, its potential in changing the traditional methodologies of several other sectors of the industry, such as healthcare, education, agriculture, supply chain and so on, are being explored [2].

Industry 4.0 involves many different systems that need the technology of blockchain and are also capable of utilizing its potential to fuel their processes, improving security, transparency, and time. The upcoming chapters explain about cryptocurrencies, history of blockchain and cryptocurrency, the different industrial revolutions, and the different applications of blockchain in Industry 4.0.

16.2 About Cryptocurrency

Cryptocurrencies are digital currencies that rely on decentralized networks called Blockchain's to verify transactions and keep track of records. A blockchain could be distributed information that's shared across nodes in every electronic network. Rather than a centralized exchange where transactions are created by banks, they use secret writing or a third-free peer-to-peer electronic system [3]. It stores data in a very digital format and they are essential for keeping a secure and localized record of transactions in cryptocurrency systems. Cryptocurrency transactions are mobile, nontaxable, and do not need the employment of a bank. Cryptocurrencies are divided into two types: coins and tokens. Tokens are created on the prime of another blockchain, whereas crypto-coins are native to their own blockchain. All transactions are clear due to the localized structure of cryptocurrencies blockchain, which can be accessed by making use of either blockchain explorers or a private node that allows anybody to witness transactions in the time period. As new blocks are added and validated, every node stores a copy of the chain that is updated. As a result, crypto-coins could also be followed where they travel [4].

There are numerous secret writing ways and cryptological approaches, like public-private key pairs, elliptical curve secret writing, and hashing functions, known as "crypto". Bitcoin, the primary cryptocurrency, was created in 2009 and remains the foremost well-known nowadays [5]. Satoshi Nakamoto—for the most part, assumed to be a name for a personal or cluster of people whose true identity is unknown—created the currency. However, Nakamoto's involvement with bitcoin came to an end in 2010. In an email to another crypto developer, the last correspondence anybody had with Nakamoto claimed that they had "moved on to other things" [6]. The inability to put a face to the name has sparked a lot of conjecture about Nakamoto's identity, especially as the quantity, popularity, and prominence of cryptocurrencies grew. There are several cryptocurrencies out there on the market right now. Each cryptocurrency claims to possess a singular purpose and specification. Litecoin, Peercoin, Ripple, Alphacoin, and Aircoin are a number of the opposite common cryptocurrencies that have grown their popularity since 2011 [7]. In 2021, there will be 6000 cryptocurrencies, with roughly 2000 of them inactive. Several investors are postponed by the high incidence of cryptocurrency mortality. As a result, cryptocurrencies are not backed by any government or business organization creating a case for their legal standing in numerous monetary jurisdictions throughout the globe has proved troublesome. Cryptocurrencies' legal position has ramifications for their use in regular transactions and trade. The chance of various cryptocurrencies failing has prompted many countries to ban such digital monetary exchanges, claiming that cryptocurrency commercialism may change unlawful transactions and disrupt government operations [8]. The Republic of El Salvador, on the opposite hand, became the primary country to recognize Bitcoin as legal money on September 7, 2021 [9].

Several other national governments are working closely with experts to ensure Bitcoin's long-term viability.

Crypto mining, the phrase relates to a crucial part of the Bitcoin ecosystem: the verification and generation of money. The process of "mining" is carried out using high-tech equipment that solves a tough computational arithmetic problem. The process is restarted when the first machine solves the puzzle and obtains the next block of bitcoins [10]. The competitive process for cryptocurrency mining employs the proof-of-work (PoW) mechanism to verify and add new transactions to the blockchain. Mining cryptocurrency is time-consuming, costly, and seldom rewarding. Individual miners, mining pools and Cloud mining are some of the methods of crypto mining that can be practiced.

Individual miners—anyone with access to the Internet may buy specialized miner gear. In the early 2010s, this was more practical than it is now. New currencies emerge all the time, and if they use the proof-of-work (PoW) approach rather than proof-of-stake (PoS), normal PCs or machines with high-end GPUs may be enough to mine them [11].

Mining pools—a mining pool is a group of miners that pool their resources and share their processing power across a network in order to split the reward equitably based on how much effort they put in to increase the chance of finding a block.

Cloud mining—cloud mining applies the same notion of outsourcing computational labor to cryptocurrency mining, allowing users to rent the processing power of a specialized miner from a cloud mining firm located anywhere in the globe instead of purchasing expensive machines [12].

In the United States and most other nations, bitcoin mining is legal. According to a research conducted by the Law Library of Congress in November 2021, Algeria, China, Bangladesh, Iraq, Egypt, Nepal, Morocco, Tunisia, and Qatar are among the nations where bitcoin mining is prohibited. Due to energy concerns, Russia has recommended a ban, while Sweden is pressing for a ban inside the EU [13].

16.3 History of Blockchain and Cryptocurrency

Stuart Haber and Scott Stornetta [14], two cryptographers, came up with the basic concept for blockchain technology. Their study focused on how to connect a series of transactions in a chronological manner. Bitcoin transactions are recorded on the blockchain, which is a distributed ledger [15].

The recent boom in the crypto industry calls for a detailed study of its history to understand what it is and how it can be expected to grow. Despite the fact that Bitcoin, also known as BTC, was the first cryptocurrency, attempts to build online currencies with encrypted ledgers had previously been made. Two examples of these notions that were created but never fully implemented are B-Money and Bit Gold [16].

In the years 2008 to 2009, Satoshi Nakamoto, whose true identity is unknown, created Bitcoin by combining numerous ideas from game theory and information science [14] and published a white paper that introduced the core concept behind bitcoin and blockchain. The white paper was published in 2008 and bitcoin became a reality in 2009. With a payout of 50 Bitcoins, Nakamoto mined the first block of Bitcoins. The "genesis block" [17] is the name given to this block. Hal Finney got the first 10 Bitcoins [18] from Satoshi Nakamoto after downloading the Bitcoin client. This was the first Bitcoin transaction in history. Bitcoin, which was practically worthless in 2009 has grown exponentially over the years and is continuing its upward rise. Figure 16.1 represents the different processes involved in the blockchain technology.

Hundreds of other decentralized cryptocurrencies have been created by various parties after Nakamoto's remarkable creation. Bitcoin, Ethereum, Bitcoin Cash, Ripple, Litecoin, Dash, NEO, NEM, Monero, and a number of other cryptocurrencies are now among the most popular and valuable cryptocurrencies. It is undeniably an interesting and exciting period in history.

Now that cryptocurrencies like Bitcoin have shown their worth, capacity to operate in the real world, and purchasing power [19], an increasing number of banks, financial institutions, trade organizations, and retailers are accepting them as legal forms of cash and payment.

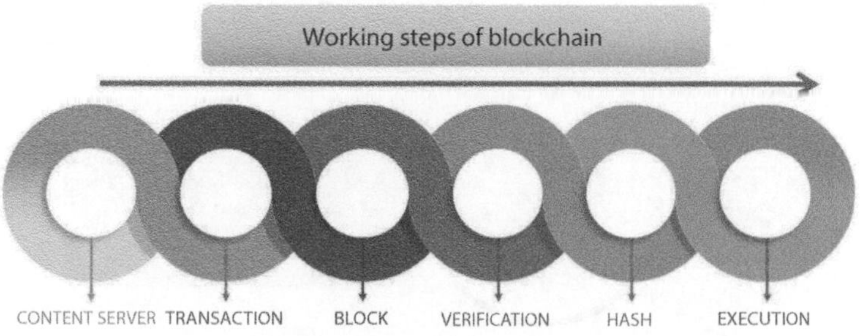

Figure 16.1 Working steps of Blockchain [53]. This depicts the different processes involved in a blockchain network for one piece of data. As a result of this, any data that passes through a blockchain network is believed to be safe as it undergoes a series of steps to verify it.

16.4 Background of Industrial Revolution

The word "industrialization" describes a set of economic and social processes that have changed as a result of the emergence of more efficient ways to generate value [1]. In a broader sense, industrialization is associated with the process of converting an economy that is predominantly agrarian to one that is based on the production of products in industries and machine manufacturing. Inventions and advances in science and technology have revolutionized industrial processes century after century throughout history. These changes have ultimately resulted in mass production of high quality products, leading to enormous economic growth

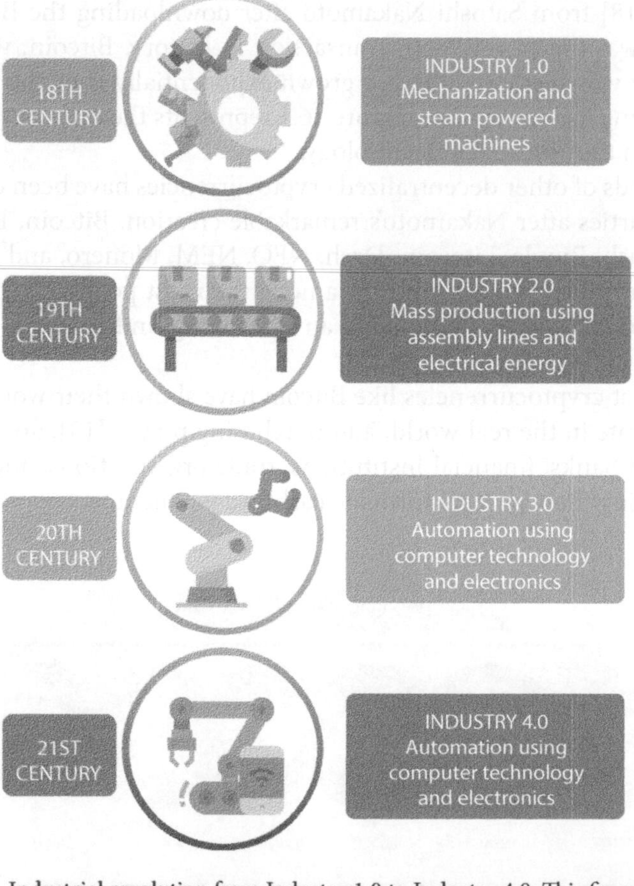

Figure 16.2 Industrial revolution from Industry 1.0 to Industry 4.0. This figure presents all the major advancements that took place during each industrial revolution that transformed the landscape of that period.

around the world. As seen in Figure 16.2, the different phases of technological revolutions throughout history came to be known as the different industrial revolutions.

16.4.1 The First Industrial Revolution

Britain was the birthplace of the first industrial revolution and the first industrial revolution can be traced back to the late eighteenth century [21]. It was a significant point in history because it advanced social, cultural, political, and geopolitical processes around the globe, and was also a driving force behind the transition from an agrarian to an industrial economy. During this time, steel and steam power were widely used in manufacturing, resulting in widespread adoption of mechanization in industries [20, 22].

The victory of the steam engine was another significant driver of the first industrial revolution. Since the engine was largely driven by coal, it demonstrated how coal could be successfully employed as a source of energy to power machines [23]. Mechanization lowered the number of workers needed in factories to produce items, while also improving product quality and increasing production rates enormously. This sparked a period of rapid economic expansion and increased wages, allowing workers to buy more products and services, such as better food and housing, and therefore improving their standard of living [24].

16.4.2 The Second Industrial Revolution

The second industrial revolution, sometimes known as the Technological Revolution, lasted from 1870 to 1914, but some of its significant events may be dated back to the 1850s [25]. It is commonly referred to as the "age of scientific advancement" because of the tremendous increase in scientific advancements and discoveries during this time period. As a result, numerous new inventions for standardization and mass manufacturing of items were introduced into the industries.

Industries were predominantly powered by coal and steam power prior to the second industrial revolution. With further breakthroughs in science and technology, an English scientist, *Michael Faraday* [26, 27], invented the electric motor that was capable of converting electrical energy to mechanical energy [28]. The assembly line [22, 29, 30], which was established by Henry Ford, an American businessman, father of mass production, and creator of the Ford Motor Company, was another notable innovation from this time period. This was a game-changer that changed the way manufacturing and industries worked.

16.4.3 The Third Industrial Revolution

As a result of its contribution to information and technology, the third industrial technology is also commonly referred to as the *Digital Revolution*. Since its birth in the late 1900s, it was marked by a large adoption of computers and electronics for automation and digitization, in addition to the rise of the Internet and the discovery of nuclear energy [31].

One of the initial catalysts of the third industrial revolution was the creation of the Advanced Research Projects Agency Network (ARPANET) [32]. It laid down the fundamental foundations of the Internet and sparked the age of information technology. This period of time observed a massive use of electronics for the automation of manufacturing processes. Additionally, advances in telecommunications laid the fundamental foundation for widespread globalization, enabling businesses to move their manufacturing facilities to cheaper nations and revolutionize business structures all over the world [31, 33].

16.4.4 The Fourth Industrial Revolution

The fourth industrial revolution is the most recent revolution in the world of industries, and it is defined by digitization, personal linked devices, digital transformations, AI technologies, data analytics, automation, and Industrial IoT [31]. It further develops on the advancements of its previous revolution. It advances manufacturing systems that have already implemented and installed computer technology for their operations by expanding them through a network connection and allowing every other unit in an industrial facility to communicate and be enabled for smart processing.

In order to create enhanced and better communication among the different players and linked elements in a manufacturing line, industries utilize technologies, such as big data analytics, Cloud, and IoT, which have recently emerged in full force. This might be the start of an industrial revolution that eradicates the use of traditional nonrenewable resources in production lines. The fourth industrial revolution replaces these environmentally harmful resources with wind, solar, and geothermal energy. Large-scale digitization, the development of IoT networks and IIoT, artificial intelligence, machine learning, cloud computing technologies and big data are all examples of the developments in the Industrial 4.0.

16.5 Trends of Blockchain

One of the ways of evaluating the trends of a topic is by visualizing the amount of research done on that particular topic over the years. In order to do so for blockchain, the mentions of the term "blockchain" have been taken from Google Scholar.

The trend of mentions of the term "blockchain" in Google Scholar is depicted in Table 16.1.

Table 16.1 The trend of mentions of the term "blockchain" over the years, from 2015 to 2021 [34].

Years	Number of mentions
2015–2016	7,250
2016–2017	22,300
2017–2018	40,900
2018–2019	1,44,000
2019–2020	58,200
2020–2021	1,42,000

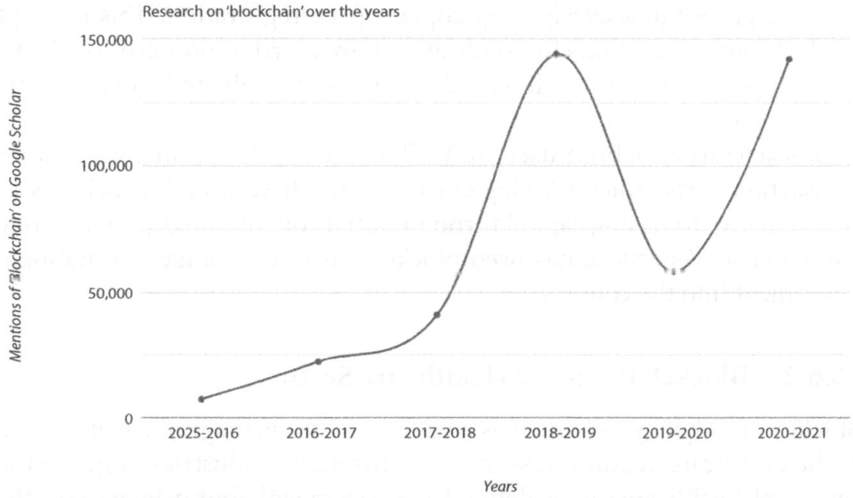

Figure 16.3 Visualization of the trend of mentions of the term "blockchain" over the years, from 2015 to 2021.

In Figure 16.3, the number of mentions is plotted against the vertical axis and the years are plotted against the horizontal axis.

16.6 Applications of Blockchain in Industry 4.0

Blockchain's entire value and impact on the developments of Industry 4.0 have yet to be properly established. However, the prospects of blockchain's potential in different industrial sectors are plenty. Owing to its security and verification standards, it is widely used for financial transactions all over the world today. Furthermore, using cryptocurrencies for financial transactions over the blockchain network eliminates the problems associated with the conversion and usage of foreign currencies and fiat money [35].

Blockchain is a fantastic tool to keep track of safe transactions. In addition, blockchain has the ability to contribute value in a variety of other sectors in Industry 4.0.

16.6.1 Blockchain and the Government

Transparency is a key feature of blockchain-based systems, as decentralization allows all users to see and verify data. Some citizen services might benefit from blockchain technology, which enables independent government claim verification [36]. For example, Sweden, Estonia, and Georgia are experimenting with blockchain-based land registers [36], which allow multiple parties to securely keep copies of the registration. This concept might be effective in quickly settling or fully averting property conflicts. The danger of distrust is lessened when individuals and governments exchange records.

Blockchains have been used by Wall Street investment firms to reduce transaction costs, Silicon Valley entrepreneurs have used blockchains as an alternative to raising capital through initial coin offerings [37], and one government, Venezuela, has used blockchains to encourage international investment into the country.

16.6.2 Blockchain in the Healthcare Sector

Blockchain is being acclaimed as a useful tool for managing sensitive data in the healthcare, medical research, and insurance industries [38]. On the base level, healthcare can be defined as a system with four primary constituents as can be seen in Figure 16.4: (a) fundamental providers of healthcare services, such as doctors, nursing staff, and hospital administration

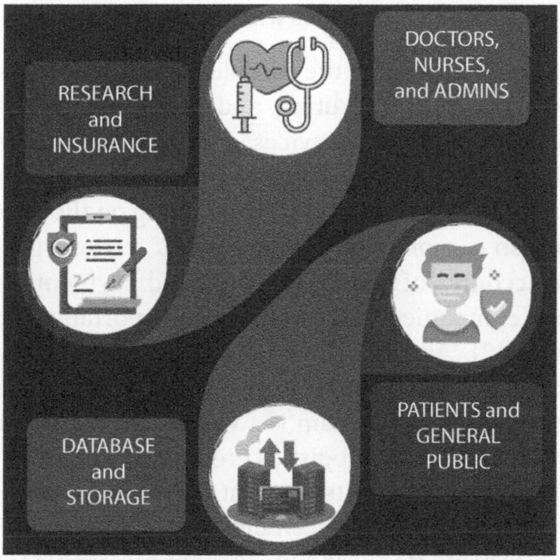

Figure 16.4 Four elements or constituents of the healthcare industries.

employees; (b) essential elements involved in healthcare services, like research in medical and insurance; (c) beneficiaries of healthcare and health-related services, such as patients or the general public; and (d) back-end databases or storage facilities for health and healthcare records.

A significant volume of patient information and health data is produced in the healthcare system before and during various stages of clinical research. Blood tests, quality assessments, calculations, and wellness surveys from several persons must be preserved carefully. The system has often resorted to storing this information in papers as a measure of safety, but the data dissolves over time due to several factors. Additionally, verifying a patient's data from one healthcare center to another has always been full of uncertainty as any wrong diagnosis could have a catastrophic effect on the patient [1, 39, 40].

Blockchain is built with a combination of current cryptographic techniques and includes a framework for exchanging cryptographic data. With the help of this technology, the patient's name and their basic details in addition to date of birth, treatments, diagnosis, and other healthcare-related history are documented in an Electronic Health Record (EHR) by the healthcare practitioner and stored in the cloud [1]. Similarly all details including birth records, death records, insurance details, and many more can be safely stored on cloud and accessed from any part of the world with the help of blockchain technology.

16.6.3 Blockchain in Logistics and Supply Chain

The supply chain gets tied up in the complex processes of product creation and distribution. Planning, executing, and controlling the effective movement and storage of products, services, and all related information from point of origin to point of destination to meet consumer demands are all part of the supply chain activities [41]. Depending on the product, the supply chain may also comprise numerous phases, various geographic locations, multiple accounts of players involved and payments, in addition to multiple people, companies, and modes of transportation involved in the logistics process [42]. As a result, supplies are delayed, often for months. Due to the complexity and lack of transparency of traditional supply chains and logistics operations, blockchain is a viable solution that may be introduced to improve supply chain logistics processes through its sophisticated technology. The different benefits brought in by blockchain in the process of logistics and supply chain has been depicted in Figure 16.5.

With its high security standards, blockchain can enable transparency of data and its access among the supply chain stakeholders and improve trust within the system. Using smart contracts [43], a product of blockchain technology, a more cost saving mechanism can be achieved by powering leaner, more automated, and error-free processes. The product received by the recipient can also be safely checked and verified for authenticity by the use of blockchain.

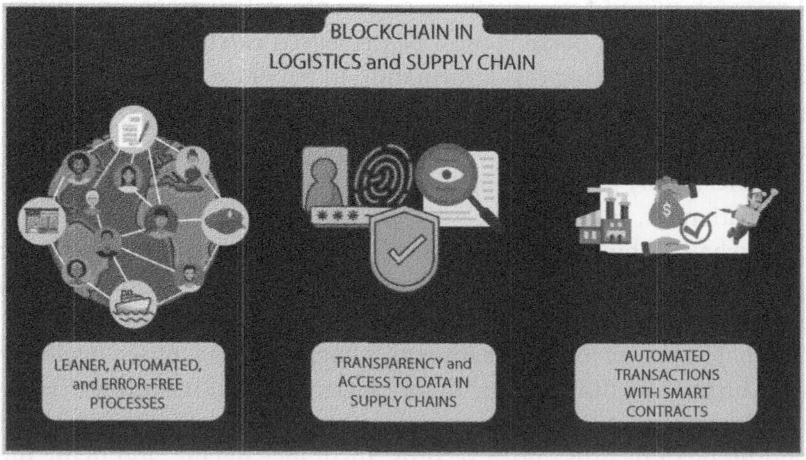

Figure 16.5 Blockchain in logistics. This illustration depicts how blockchain improves supply chain and logistics processes.

16.6.4 Blockchain in the Automotive Sector

In the automobile industry, blockchain may be employed by a variety of projects and partners. With the further growth of Industry 4.0, its value for manufacturing is promising. Blockchain technology may be effectively deployed to manage payments across the automobile sector, including for car manufacturers and vehicle sales, ridesharing and carsharing services, and integration with other technologies, due to its promising potential as a financial instrument [44]. Using a blockchain distributed ledgers, automakers can achieve a high level of transparency throughout even the most congested supply chains, allowing them to decrease costs and improve efficiency, It Aids in the prevention of counterfeiting and vehicle hacking, When cars are tokenized, they can be transferred safely and easily, similar to how bitcoin works, making vehicle ownership transfer easier [45]. Fleet owners can track the location of all of their cars and employees using RFID tags and data stored in the blockchain, making vehicle ownership transfer easier. With a simple QR code scan, a car's service history may be stored on the blockchain, and the technology can be used to ensure that only genuine OEM-supplied components are used for repairs or replacements. In order for self-driving cars to be safe, massive amounts of data must be processed, evaluated, and supplied safely and quickly. Blockchain offers a dependable and secure means of doing so, with the potential to hasten the delivery of Levels 4 and 5 vehicles. Cryptocurrency is quickly becoming the preferred method of payment for hundreds of the UK's top car dealers, including Redline Specialist Cars, Saxton 4x4 and Benz Bavarian [46], many of the industry's most well-known companies have recognized the potential of incorporating crypto financing into their operations. Whether it is preserving financial data or boosting the integrity of common ownership, blockchain has the potential to transform the way information is maintained in future autos [47]. For example, to ensure ethical cobalt sourcing, Ford has begun a blockchain trial on IBM's platform. By monitoring the cobalt supply chain on the blockchain, Ford hopes to prevent companies from utilizing child-mined cobalt in lithium-ion batteries [48]. According to Ledger Insights, Tesla released its 2020 Impact Report, which indicates the business is employing two blockchain systems to track raw materials used in electric car batteries. The business seeks to purchase them from environmentally friendly sources, which is in accordance with Tesla's purpose.

16.6.5 Blockchain in the Education Sector

The majority of people link blockchain technology with cryptocurrencies such as Bitcoin. Data is organized into blocks on a blockchain, which is chronologically linked together, making it relatively straightforward to track the data's origins and validate its legitimacy. One field where blockchain is just getting started is education. Only 2% of higher education institutions have used blockchain technology, according to a 2019 poll by research company Gartner, with another 18% aiming to do so in the next two years [49]. It allows students to have more influence over their education. The student owns the data associated with his or her identification, not a central authority such as a university. Students have the choice of storing, fully owning, and managing who has access to their data throughout their lives. Learners may then double-check the qualifications listed on their resumes and have more control over what prospective employers can view. Student records, which are one of the most labor-intensive activities of any institute or university, might benefit from the usage of blockchain to update grades and issue transcripts, as well as let students securely access their data. Using the smart contract concept on the blockchain, instructors create exam papers, as well as the answer key and scoring system. The test may be completed online, and the responses can be scored using blockchain technology. When a student transfers from one institute to another, the new institute may quickly access the student's data by granting access to the blockchain. Students' data may be safeguarded via blockchain, which ensures their identification, privacy, and security. Students, for example, are unable to update earlier educational qualifications stored on the blockchain, but they may do so with paper records. Furthermore, because blockchain stores just a hash of data, anonymity is guaranteed. Before being stored on the blockchain, the data might be encrypted if desired [50]. India has set a high bar for itself through the National Education Policy 2020 (NEP-2020). The goal is to achieve a 100% Gross Enrolment Ratio (GER) in school by 2030, and to increase it to 50% in higher education by 2035 [51].

The application of blockchain technology in education faces significant technological challenges. The proof-of-work, or consensus process for the verification of new blocks, is the first and arguably most difficult (see the Introduction section). The larger a blockchain grows, the larger and more expensive its proof-of-work (mining) becomes. A second important reason for blockchain's limited real-world use in education, in my opinion, is its lack of congruence with an authentic philosophy of education's long-term growth. This is a comprehensive and complicated problem. Another disadvantage of blockchain is latency, which occurs when a transaction takes too long. Furthermore, various papers, such as [54], show a critical security flaw in the blockchain-based system, the so-called 51% attack [52].

The implementation of blockchain in education might help to improve the efficiency of the school environment and maximize the use of people and physical resources. A significant component is gaining access to essential student or graduate-related data, which is typically stored in a university database with restricted access or in the form of physical documents. This challenge is addressed by blockchain technology, which also allows for alignment with the growing "open data" movement.

16.7 Conclusion

The growth of blockchain has been enormous since the very introduction of its core concepts. Industry 4.0 on the other hand, is fuelled with the technological advancements of digitization and has automation as one among its core principle values. The convergence of these two elements—blockchain and industry 4.0—builds the next generation of systems for all the different industrial sectors across the globe. Blockchain fits perfectly in the frame of the fourth industrial revolution which calls for transparency, digitization, automation, and security. With the dynamic infusion of blockchain, all the industrial processes and systems can be transformed to meet the needs and requirements of Industry 4.0.

Although digitization and automation brings about a great deal of sustainability in the industry, there is a need to create an eco-friendly blockchain network environment. At the present date, the different nodes that are connected to the network may not utilize a sustainable source of energy for powering their system. It is important to bring about a green revolution for blockchain in order to successfully establish complete sustainability in Industry 4.0. Nonetheless, in the previous chapters, we have seen how blockchain is an important factor in different industrial sectors and holds the potential of being one among the pillars of Industry 4.0. With more and more research underway, blockchain too shall be designed and developed with the goal of making it sustainable to protect our planet.

References

1. Javaid, M., Haleem, A., Singh, R.P., Khan, S., Suman, R., Blockchain technology applications for Industry 4.0: A literature-based review. *Blockchain: Res. Appl.*, 2, 4, 100027, 2021. https://doi.org/10.1016/j.bcra.2021.100027.
2. Capgemini.Com, Blockchain and Industry 4.0, Retrieved March 26, 2022 from https://www.capgemini.com/au-en/wp-content/uploads/sites/9/2018/10/Blockchain-and-Industry-4.0.pdf.
3. Gatabazi, P., Kabera, G., Mba, J.C., Pindza, E., Melesse, S.F., Cryptocurrencies and tokens lifetime analysis from 2009 to 2021. *Economies*, 10, 3, 60, 2022. https://doi.org/10.3390/economies10030060.
4. Hayes, A., Blockchain explained, in: *Investopedia*, March 5, 2022. https://www.investopedia.com/terms/b/blockchain.asp.
5. Frankenfield, J., Cryptocurrency, in: *Investopedia*, March 2, 2022. https://www.investopedia.com/terms/c/cryptocurrency.asp.
6. Nasim, S., The mystery of bitcoin founder "Satoshi Nakamoto", Linkedin.Com, https://www.linkedin.com/pulse/mystery-bitcoin-founder-satoshi-nakamoto-solutions/. Accessed February 16, 2022. founder-satoshi-nakamoto-solutions/.
7. Gandal, Neil and Halaburda, Hanna, Competition in the Cryptocurrency Market (September 29, 2014). CESifo Working Paper Series No. 4980, http://doi.org/10.2139/ssrn.2506577
8. The Tribune India, Banning cryptocurrencies could lead to more unlawful usage: BACC. *Tribune India*, November 25, 2021. https://www.tribuneindia.com/news/business/banning-cryptocurrencies-could-lead-to-more-unlawful-usage-bacc-342682.
9. Alvaro Trigueros-Argüello and Marjorie Chorro de Trigueros. Bitcoin as legal tender in El Salvador: The first fifty days. *Georget. J. Int. Aff.*, November 30, 2021. https://gjia.georgetown.edu/2021/11/30/bitcoin-as-legal-tender-in-el-salvador-the-first-fifty-days/.
10. Hong, E., How does bitcoin mining work?. *Investopedia*, March 14, 2022. https://www.investopedia.com/tech/how-does-bitcoin-mining-work/.
11. Crypto mining. (n.d.), in: *PCMAG*, Retrieved March 24, 2022, from https://www.pcmag.com/encyclopedia/term/crypto-mining.
12. Stevens, R., What is cloud mining? *CoinDesk*, December 9, 2021. https://www.coindesk.com/learn/what-is-cloud-mining/.
13. Haegele, B., A complete guide on how bitcoin mining works. *GOBankingRates*, November 30, 2021. https://www.gobankingrates.com/investing/crypto/how-to-mine-bitcoins/.
14. Hays, Demelza. Blockchain: An overview. *LSE Business Review* (22 Feb 2018), London School of Economics and Political Science. Available https://blogs.lse.ac.uk/businessreview/2018/02/22/blockchain-an-overview/
15. Sheldon, R., A timeline and history of blockchain technology. *TechTarget*, August 9, 2021. WhatIs.Com, https://whatis.techtarget.com/feature/A-timeline-and-history-of-blockchain-technology.

16. Marr, B., A short history of Bitcoin and crypto currency everyone should read. *Forbes*, December 6, 2017. https://www.forbes.com/sites/bernardmarr/2017/12/06/a-short-history-of-bitcoin-and-crypto-currency-everyone-should-read/?sh=680ce4f03f27.
17. Chaturvedi, A., The history of cryptocurrency. *Coin Crunch India*, February 8, 2022. https://coincrunch.in/2022/02/08/the-history-of-cryptocurrency/.
18. Chohan, U.W., A history of bitcoin. *SSRN Electron. J.*, 2017. https://doi.org/10.2139/ssrn.3047875.
19. Thakur, K.K. and Banik, G.G., Cryptocurrency: Its risks and gains and the way ahead. *IOSR Journal of Economics and Finance,* 9, 2, 38–42, 2018.
20. Simandan, D., Industrialization, in: *International Encyclopedia of Human Geography*, Edition 1, pp. 419–425, 2009. https://doi.org/10.1016/B978-008044910-4.00178-4.
21. Britannica, Industrial revolution, in: *Encyclopedia Britannica*, Mar. 13, 2022, [Online], Available: https://www.britannica.com/event/Industrial-Revolution, Accessed: 18 March 2022.
22. Mohajan, H.K., The first industrial revolution: Creation of a new global human era. *J. Soc. Sci. Humanit.*, 5, 4, 377–387, Oct. 2019.
23. Clark, G., A farewell to alms: A brief economic history of the world, in: *The Princeton Economic History of the Western World*, Jan. 2009.
24. Khan, A., The industrial revolution and the democratic transition. *Business Review Q1*, 2008, Federal Reserve Bank of Philadelphia. Available https://www.philadelphiafed.org/-/media/frbp/assets/economy/articles/business-review/2008/q1/khan_demographic-transition.pdf
25. Chew, K.W. and Ling, T.C., *The Prospect of Industry 5.0 in Biomanufacturing*, 1st ed, P.L. Show (Ed.), CRC Press, Boca Raton, Florida, Jul. 2021. https://doi.org/10.1201/9781003080671.
26. Pearce Williams, L., Michael Faraday, in: *Encyclopedia Britannica*, Sep. 18 2021, [Online], Available: https://www.britannica.com/biography/Michael-Faraday. Accessed: 20 March 2022.
27. Al-Khalili, J., The birth of the electric machines: A commentary on Faraday (1832). Experimental researches in electricity. *Philos. Trans. R. Soc. A*, 373, 2039, 1–12, Apr. 2015. https://doi.org/10.1098/rsta.2014.0208.
28. Round and round it goes. *Nat. Phys.*, 17, 977, 2021. https://doi.org/10.1038/s41567-021-01361-6.
29. Tomac, N., Radonja, R., Bonato, J., Analysis of Henry Ford's contribution to production and management. *Pomorstvo*, 33, 1, 33–45, 2019. https://doi.org/10.31217/p.33.1.4.
30. Torrero, E.A., Automating the production line: Henry Ford began it all when he designed the first car assembly line in 1914. *IEEE Spectr.*, 14, 11, 71–72, Nov. 1977. https://doi.org/10.1109/MSPEC.1977.6501657.
31. Ward, K., Timeline of revolutions. *Manufacturing Data Summit*, February 18, 2019. https://manufacturingdata.io/newsroom/timeline-of-revolutions.

32. Roberts, L., The arpanet and computer networks, in: *A History of Personal Workstations*, pp. 141–172, Association for Computing Machinery, New York, NY, USA, 1988. https://doi.org/10.1145/61975.66916.
33. Roberts, B., The third industrial revolution: Implications for planning cities and regions. *Working Paper Urban Front. 1*, Academia, 2015. Available https://www.academia.edu/13065352/The_Third_Industrial_Revolution_Implications_for_Planning_Cities_and_Regions.
34. Google Scholar Google.Com. Retrieved March 24, 2022, from https://scholar.google.com/schhp?hl=en&as_sdt=0,5.
35. Supply Chain Game Changer™, How industry 4.0 is changing and how blockchain fits! Supply Chain Game Changer™, 17 Apr. 2022. https://supplychaingamechanger.com/how-industry-4-0-is-changing-and-how-blockchain-fits/.
36. Boeding, K., and Richard M., 3 potential benefits of blockchain for government. Boozallen.Com. https://www.boozallen.com/s/insight/blog/3-potential-benefits-of-government-blockchain.html.
37. Clavin, J., Duan, S., Zhang, H., Janeja, V.P., Joshi, K.P., Yesha, Y., Erickson, L.C., Li, J.D., Blockchains for government: Use cases and challenges. *Digital Gov. Res. Pract.*, 1, 3, 1–21, 2020. https://doi.org/10.1145/3427097.
38. Meinert, E., Alturkistani, A., Foley, K.A., Osama, T., Car, J., Majeed, A., Van Velthoven, M., Wells, G., Brindley, D., Blockchain implementation in health care: Protocol for a systematic review. *JMIR Res. Protoc.*, 8, 2, e10994, 2019. doi: 10.2196/10994.
39. Aggarwal, S., Kumar, N., Alhussein, M., Muhammad, G., Blockchain-based UAV path planning for healthcare 4.0: Current challenges and the way ahead. *IEEE Netw.*, 35, 1, 20–29, January/February 2021. http://doi.org/10.1109/MNET.011.2000069.
40. Ejaz, M., Kumar, T., Kovacevic, I., Ylianttila, M., Harjula, E., Health-blockedge: Blockchain-edge framework for reliable low-latency digital healthcare applications. *Sensors*, 21, 7, 2502, 2021. https://doi.org/10.3390/s21072502.
41. Rejeb, A., Rejeb, K., Simske, S., Treiblmaier, H., Blockchain technologies in logistics and supply chain management: A bibliometric review. *Logistics*, 5, 4, 72, 2021. https://doi.org/10.3390/logistics5040072.
42. Tijan, E., Aksentijević, S., Ivanić, K., Jardas, M., Blockchain technology implementation in logistics. *Sustainability*, 11, 4, 1185, 2019. https://doi.org/10.3390/su11041185.
43. De Filippi, P., Wray, C., Sileno, G., Smart contracts. *Internet Policy Rev.*, 10, 2, 1–9, 2021. https://doi.org/10.14763/2021.2.1549.
44. Turpitka, D., Blockchain in the automotive sector: Three use cases and three challenges. *Forbes*. December 22, 2021. https://www.forbes.com/sites/forbestechcouncil/2021/12/22/blockchain-in-the-automotive-sector-three-use-cases-and-three-challenges/?sh=78b2c3d2508e.

45. Admin User, Blockchain technology and the automotive industry. *Capital Lease Group*, October 15, 2020. https://www.capitalleasegroup.com/news-and-updates/blockchain-in-the-automotive-industry-how-this-cryptocurrency-darling-is-changing-the-game/.
46. Irishtechnews.Ie. Retrieved March 23, 2022, from https://irishtechnews.ie/cryptocurrency-and-future-of-automotive-industry/.
47. Chowdhury, M., How will blockchain change the automotive industry in the future?. *Analyticsinsight.Net*. https://www.analyticsinsight.net/how-will-blockchain-change-the-automotive-industry-in-the-future/. Accessed September 28, 2021
48. Zigurat Global Institute of Technology. *Blockchain Technologies in the Automotive Industry*. ZIGURAT Innovation and Technology Business School, 18 Apr. 2019. https://www.e-zigurat.com/innovation-school/blog/blockchain-automotive-industry/.
49. How blockchain is used in education, May 13, 2021. Maryville Online. https://online.maryville.edu/blog/blockchain-in-education/.
50. Steiu, M.-F., Blockchain in education: Opportunities, applications, and challenges. *First Monday*, 25, 9, 2020. https://doi.org/10.5210/fm.v25i9.10654.
51. Rustagi, N., Blockchain in schools and colleges. *Indian Express*, December 30, 2021. https://indianexpress.com/article/opinion/blockchain-technology-education-nep-7696791/.
52. Turcu, C., Turcu, C., Chiuchisan, I., Blockchain and its potential in education. *Arxiv [cs.CY]*, 2019. http://arxiv.org/abs/1903.09300.
53. Abid H., Mohd J., Ravi P.S., Rajiv S., Shanay R., Blockchain technology applications in healthcare: An overview, *International Journal of Intelligent Networks*, 2, pp. 130–139, 2021, ISSN 2666-6030. https://doi.org/10.1016/j.ijin.2021.09.005.
54. Lin, I-C., and Tzu-Chun L., A survey of blockchain security issues and challenges. *Int. J. Netw. Secur.*, 19.5, 653–659, 2017. https://doi.org/10.6633/IJNS.201709.19(5).01.

Index

Printed and bound by CPI Group (UK) Ltd, Croydon, CR0 4YY
27/10/2024
14580128-0002